A Suspicious Science

The Uses of Psychology

RAMI GABRIEL

Oxford University Press is a department of the University of Oxford. It furthers
the University's objective of excellence in research, scholarship, and education
by publishing worldwide. Oxford is a registered trade mark of Oxford University
Press in the UK and certain other countries.

Published in the United States of America by Oxford University Press
198 Madison Avenue, New York, NY 10016, United States of America.

© Oxford University Press 2023

All rights reserved. No part of this publication may be reproduced, stored in
a retrieval system, or transmitted, in any form or by any means, without the
prior permission in writing of Oxford University Press, or as expressly permitted
by law, by license, or under terms agreed with the appropriate reproduction
rights organization. Inquiries concerning reproduction outside the scope of the
above should be sent to the Rights Department, Oxford University Press, at the
address above.

You must not circulate this work in any other form
and you must impose this same condition on any acquirer.

Library of Congress Cataloging-in-Publication Data
Names: Gabriel, Rami, author.
Title: A suspicious science : the uses of psychology / Rami Gabriel.
Description: New York, NY : Oxford University Press, [2023] |
Includes bibliographical references and index.
Identifiers: LCCN 2022053528 (print) | LCCN 2022053529 (ebook) |
ISBN 9780197513583 (hardback) | ISBN 9780197513606 (epub) |
ISBN 9780197513613
Subjects: LCSH: Psychology—History.
Classification: LCC BF81 .G33 2023 (print) | LCC BF81 (ebook) |
DDC 150.9—dc23/eng/20221212
LC record available at https://lccn.loc.gov/2022053528
LC ebook record available at https://lccn.loc.gov/2022053529

DOI: 10.1093/oso/9780197513583.001.0001

Printed by Sheridan Books, Inc., United States of America

A Suspicious Science

Contents

Preface	vii
Introduction	1

PART ONE

1 Empirical Psychology: Mind in a Lab	5
2 Metaphor in Empirical Psychology	28
3 Contemporary Empirical Psychology	50
Interlude Mythology, Belief, and Superstition	82

PART TWO

4 Popular Psychology	90
5 The Discursive Uses of Psychology	104
6 Drugs and the Technology of Agency	125
7 Art and Reflexivity: Creative Uses of Psychology	141
Conclusion	157
Acknowledgments	163
Notes	165
References	221
Index	257

Preface

In psychology, our passionate attempts to understand the mind are framed through analogies and causality. The purpose of this book is to provide a systematic exploration of psychology as (a) an empirical science, (b) a language for normativity, pathology, and aspiration, (c) a discursive set of therapeutic practices, (d) a basis for psychopharmacology, and (e) a platform for imaginative culture.

My goal is to refine our understanding of the extent and limits of the field as a science and therefore as a set of discourses about science, truth, biology, mind, and meaning. In addition to conceptual analysis, history and anthropology are employed toward articulating a more interdisciplinary, multilevel, global, humanistic form of psychology that may serve to orient the field. My method includes a critical assessment of the nature of explanations provided through psychology in the various stages of investigation (including discovery, practice, methodology, and presentation to the public). This makes for a tall order, and thus in order to offer a coherent epistemic analysis, not every aspect of the field is investigated with the same attention or detail. I make clear particular editorial decisions in this respect and direct those readers most interested in examples to Chapters 5 and 6.

First, some words about terminology. *Use* refers to the ways in which psychology and its accumulated vocabulary is enlisted to solve and motivate our actions, activities, norms, epistemological bedrock, ethical approaches, and institutional domains. This approach draws from Wittgenstein's late formulation of language games in which the meaning of a word is its use in the language and forms of life (§43 and §340); to understand a language means to be master of a technique (§199). Therefore, the meaning of psychology lies in its uses (§197). I focus on *uses* because I am particularly concerned with how epistemological and ontological distinctions from science and philosophy come to exist as practices.

The subject of psychology, the mind, has taken on the metaphysical stature held by soul and self as a crucial stage for identity, aspiration, and

viii   PREFACE

discourse on value and meaning.[1] In the modern era, the mind is conceived of as the seat of thought, of consciousness. Psychology is then the study and practices by which we conceive of subjectivity and the brain. This territory spans biology as we have gained insight into the evolution and anatomy of the brain, phenomenology insofar as we have developed qualitative measures of introspection, and ethics as clinical psychology and neuropharmacology play a role in how individuals manage their being in society. And yet many psychologists, being as they are immersed in a particular set of practices, may balk at the breadth of uses that I am putting forward as of a piece. To them, I say that rather than delimit the phenomena to the approach in which we were trained, we must follow how techniques and concepts are being used and implemented in the world. Proposing and testing theoretical models in the laboratory is only one aspect of how psychology proliferates in terminology and societal practices. The success reflected in the ubiquity of psychology should not stop us from critically engaging the lacuna sprinkled throughout the domain. Like its early 20th century founders William James and Wilhelm Wundt, we should remain open to its continuing development.

Suspicious Uses

Claims made by psychologists about the nature of the mind from Freud to cognitive neuroscience have generated several schools of skeptics. First, the *ontologically suspicious* are dubious that psychological terms refer to anything—natural or real—at all. This position has been espoused, for example, by philosophers such as Daniel Dennett, Patricia Churchland, and Paul Churchland. In accord with the work of Gilbert Ryle (1949), Dennett successfully alerts us to the metaphysical canards inherited from Cartesianism. He directs us to be suspicious of mental content. Rather, we should focus on quantitative data generated through the study of dynamic brain activity.[2] According to him, we are virtual machines that self-stimulate consciousness through cultural memes and language. While I agree with his critique of the Cartesian theater, I part ways with Dennett's later work, which follows up these insights into an arid landscape of computationalism and conceptual logical analysis. Rather, I take mental content seriously by implementing a neutral monist approach in which consciousness has the functional purpose of interoceptive allostatic emotional sentience.

Also in the ontologically suspicious wing, the Churchlands seek to replace the vagaries present in discourse about the mind, especially those terms codified in folk psychology, with specific neuroscientific components and their functional descriptions. Basically, psychology is too immature a science and the terms it is currently using, such as "will," "remember," and "self," do not mean what psychologists think they mean.[3] In fact, we do not know what they refer to outside of our own discourse about them. Because of this inaccuracy, conceptual analysis is doomed. Instead, these skeptics recommend experimental, theoretical, and synthetic work as more productive.[4] Indeed, analysis of the mindbrain as in Robert Cummins (1983) and more recently in the work of Carl Craver and William Bechtel follows through on this ontological suspicion of the terminology inherited from preneuroscientific discourses. As will become evident, I have sympathies with this latter mechanistic approach, albeit as supplemented by an evolutionary framework which emphasizes the role of affect.[5]

On the other hand, *epistemological suspicion* based on investigation of the historical record is articulated in the work of a different breed of philosophers exemplified by Michel Foucault. These thinkers, such as Bruno Latour, Roger Smith, Thomas Szasz, and Frantz Fanon, each in their own way conceive of psychology as enmeshed in a sociology of knowledge and power, and the development of modern institutions of state authority and control. Their critiques are largely based on historical evidence— for example, Foucault's work on the genesis of psychoanalysis as a medical science which strips the subject of power and knowledge in the work of Jean Charcot.[6] While this approach is ultimately not where I land, it is clear that history clarifies the context of knowledge production in psychology and that power in the form of institutions, gatekeeping, and intellectual lineages shapes the possibilities of exploration. This position is in line with the work of Hans-Georg Gadamer, who orients us through a hermeneutics of meaning which questions the ultimate capacities of reason within their historical and technological/methodological limits. Similarly, Ludwig Wittgenstein in Philosophical Investigations locates our epistemic convolutions in misunderstandings endemic to how language obfuscates custom, rules, and other practices that come to constitute knowledge. To address these important epistemological suspicions, I draw from the writings of psychologists Kurt Danziger and Jerome Kagan, who expertly describe the role of context in the behavioral sciences.

X PREFACE

Good Uses

Some psychologists are happy to ignore this lineage of critical inquiry as a nonscientific ambush by humanities scholars. My project, launched as it were from within the field of psychology, remains faithful to the hope of securing a systematic interdisciplinary multilevel project for understanding the mind while also taking into account humanistic critiques about the context of psychology as a science. Accordingly, in the final part of the book, I reflect specifically upon psychology's relation to the human sciences and the arts.

My sympathies with these epistemological and ontological suspicions ultimately led to my adopted focus on the *uses* of psychology. *Use* refers to both explicit reference to mental concepts, including those couched in neuroscientific networks, as well as implicit cultural frames such as medical, juridical, and practical institutions which mediate knowledge about the mind. This includes therapeutic endeavors, medication, and popular notions of psychic well-being, which may be highly undertheorized but that enact forms of power, authority, and aspiration. These uses demonstrate that our science of the mind is codetermined by cultural context, methodology, intellectual trends, and power as manifested in institutions, capital, and received wisdom.

In addition to synthesizing internal debates in psychology and philosophy with debates about its context as a set of practices, the other unique quality of this book is a formulation of the affective motivations of belief itself. My focus on *emotions* is meant to encapsulate this confluence of forces in the subject by excavating the functional nature of belief. Meaning is thus constructed for individuals through their practices and their allegiances.[7]

The purpose of this book is not to deny that psychologists have delivered knowledge and techniques that are useful. Indeed, an empirical approach to the mind based on evolution, philosophy of mind, and materialist techniques can deliver clarity. The field of affective neuroscience—for example, in the work of Jaak Panksepp, Antonio Damasio, and Frans de Waal—has convincingly demonstrated that our motivations are mediated by subjective experience of the body. My own research as an empirical psychologist has been concerned with the nature of dialectical relations between allostatic motivation, direct perception, and culturally enriched representations.[8] There are certainly questions for which an interdisciplinary psychology is more helpful than other social scientific or simply biological approaches. As I argue in the latter half of the book, developing a model of sensible affective forms of knowledge illuminates such phenomena as the emotional mind of non-linguistic animals and the nature of the imaginary orders that humans construct together.[9]

Discursive practices such as therapy, as well as psychopharmacology, are methods through which we clarify our emotions and thoughts by narrativizing them. Similarly, I will describe how the psychological phenomenon of memory is better understood by the concatenation of philosophy, phenomenology, anthropology, history, and neuroscience. My goal in developing a critical anthropology of the uses of psychology is to articulate an interdisciplinary multilevel psychology.

The frame I employ of historicizing, that is, contextualizing, our current state of the art is concerned with the conditions of belief during modernity.[10] The prevalence of doubt during our episteme is part of the reason why a book about the uses of psychology is more perspicacious than a book about any single form of psychological enterprise. Our uses of psychology reveal more about us than results compiled by any one subfield. I encapsulate this insight by adopting the terminology of *mythology* to portray the explanatory/worldview/truth-telling demands upon the systems of beliefs, rituals, and practices which constitute the uses of psychology. My wedge through this exploration is the insight that beliefs about the mind are mired in our affective need for control. I will be arguing that psychology is a tangle of belief, practice, and institutionalization that by dint of its theoretical aegis has come to serve as a privileged path to secure knowledge about who we are. Psychology is thus contemporary society's preeminent discourse about value, the self, and materialist ontology. Accordingly, it is a suspicious science which enacts our doubts, hopes, and beliefs.

Introduction

It's the best possible time to be alive,
when almost everything you thought you knew is wrong.
— Tom Stoppard, *Arcadia* (1993), scene 4

Psychology is the stage for our drama of self-knowledge. A confused field of inquiry in which neuroscientists and computer scientists keep company with chakra healers and hypnotists, psychology is the space in which we understand the mysteries of who we are. It is the science and set of practices to cure what, in a deep sense, ails us: a lack of control.

For the ancient Greeks, the human mind was the subject of rational philosophy and the target of ritual and tragedy. The intervening centuries have been witness to the substitution of abundance for certitude and have accreted a sediment composed of British empiricism, phrenology, Romanticism, and New Age spiritualisms. Splintered between parlor games and ethical systems, science and medicine, the arts and the humanities, the study of the psychē continues to career between objective rigor and wish fulfillment.

Psychology is part of a rich set of local knowledge practices constituted of cultural symbols from which we draw to make meaning in our lives. At present, it exists within an epistemic niche dominated by scientific ways of knowing. Much of psychology draws from this source of certitude, and yet the confidence we place in the study of mind is misplaced. This is because much about who we are remains unknowable. This leads to a situation in which the knowledge that psychology provides tells us as much about our culture and emotions as it does about the mind itself. Often, it reveals more about what we would prefer the answer to be rather than what we can justifiably claim based on the available evidence. Accordingly, one major theme of this book is the affectively charged relation between doubt and explanation. I argue that the uses of psychology are knowledge practices wherein belief

A Suspicious Science. Rami Gabriel, Oxford University Press. © Oxford University Press 2023.
DOI: 10.1093/oso/9780197513583.003.0001

2 A SUSPICIOUS SCIENCE

and emotional needs are interwoven to compose the mantle that constitutes our understanding of human nature itself.

By describing the goals and methods of diverse forms of psychology, I seek to explain how the emotional need for belief is nested in a set of practices we call psychology. There are myriad ways in which knowledge about the mind is embedded in our cultural practices of explaining ourselves and others. Some are formalized into institutions, such as consultation of medical professionals and the pharmaceutical industry. Some are informal, such as the ways we speak about our motives, and the ways we try to understand ourselves and others by relying upon the explanatory power of mental concepts like forgetting, stress, trauma, and so on. There are also practices which lean on the diffusion of psychological concepts, such as reading about neurotransmitters on the internet or discourse about feelings and identity that take place on social media. While psychology has a substantial empirical wing, the way this information is disseminated, interpreted, and infused into other ways that we relate to each other and conceptualize ourselves is not strictly in line with the scientific worldview; rather it is continuous with prevailing cultural practices. That is why the explanations provided within the field carry implications for our fundamental understanding of what is knowable and thus play a part in how we come to frame our values, institutions, and aspirations.[1] The questions we ask about the mind are shaped by the boundaries of our metaphysical technology, namely, of what we want to know and how we want it to be known. As a set of ideological frames, our metaphysical technology is perpetuated through cultural practices—to name a few, personality tests, Adderall, psychological thrillers, visual illusions, and PET scans. Belief and superstition are intertwined at the heart of our uses of psychology which then serve as reflexive visions of human nature.

Thus, a book about the uses of psychology must also interrogate the conditions of belief by taking into account how myth and ritual ground meaning in our lives. Above all, my focus is upon the ways in which psychology provides us a fundamental constellation for the application of ontological, epistemic, and ethical belief. In the and conclusion of the book, I allude to the survival and syntheses of mythology and superstition in psychology.

My formal purpose is an analysis of sources of knowledge and cultural practices of belief in the contemporary study of the mind. Briefly, psychology serves as a platform for the construction of meaning in our lives because it

INTRODUCTION 3

resides at the locus of what we take ourselves to be at the level of ontology and ethics. The interior crises of existence: the fear, apprehension, anxiety, excitement, effervescence, and addictions we live through are made sense of through the apodictic stories of the mind sciences. By dint of psychology's position between naturalism and superstition, these stories explain where we came from (our origins), where we are going, and how we ought to comport ourselves.[2] My thesis is that explanations are intrinsically embedded within the desires and beliefs from which they spring. Psychology enacts the knowledge practices of a materialist origin story in empirical psychology, and the cosmology of humanism and individualism in the liberal subjectivities of discursive psychology.

I hope to illuminate our uses of psychology by aligning their cultural, emotional, and philosophical motivations. The explanations psychology provides concern what it means to be a human actor and are thus inherently ethical and contextual. Accordingly, analyses presented in the first part of the book which suggest lacunae in empirical psychology motivate a proposal articulated in the second part of the book for an interdisciplinary multilevel psychology that can integrate contextual, historical, and methodological factors.

Overview

A Suspicious Science is divided into two parts with an intervening interlude. Part One describes the history and present practice of empirical psychology. I take stock of the extent and limits of the mind sciences. Chapter 1 features a description of the history and cultural context of the institutionalization of the field. This allows for an exploration of psychology's epistemological and sociological commitments relative to philosophy, religion, and the human and natural sciences. Chapter 2 explores the crucial explanatory role of analogical reasoning exemplified by metaphors of mind. I describe how contemporary psychology draws upon concepts from biology and engineering. A contrast between the discursive and descriptive functions of metaphor use serves as a deliberation upon the pragmatic consequences of analogical reasoning. In Chapter 3, the history of empirical psychology is taken up to the present through discussion of the development of neuroscience and statistics. I take the opportunity to review major critiques of the methodologies employed in empirical psychology vis-à-vis foundational issues in the philosophy of science.

A polemical interlude follows in which I argue that since psychology resides between science and superstition it has come to serve as a modern mythology. I develop the idea that belief is a commitment to a way of experiencing and navigating the human epistemic niche of cultural symbols. I argue that aspects of psychology can be conceived of as superstitious rituals which draw their authority from the epistemic preeminence of science. During the modern era, belief can adhere to descriptive explanation, as it does in the empirical sciences, or it can take an ethical or discursive form as it does in religion, clinical, and popular psychology. I explore the uses of psychology within this epistemic landscape.

In Part Two of the book, I turn to more popular forms of psychology. The focus in Chapter 4 is on self-help literature and its reliance on magical thinking. Popular psychology is the spiritual self-medication of our times; as a wisdom tradition, it provides rituals to enact our beliefs and aspirations. The focus of Chapter 5 is upon discursive uses of psychology. I suggest individualism is the foundational myth of psychodynamic uses of psychology. Technologies of the mind evolve: In the early 20th century, clinical psychology conceived of people as discursive subjects to be treated in therapy through conversation. In Chapter 6, I discuss how the biomedical model has eclipsed the discursive model, thus giving rise to tension in the differing notions of the scope of agency. I contrast discursive and biomedical models through an interdisciplinary multilevel analysis of alcohol addiction. In Chapter 7, I explore the creative uses of psychology; in particular, how mimetic and transcendent forms of art allow for reflexive articulation of norms, values, and meaning. In the Conclusion, I summarize my positive project of drawing together empirical, discursive, and reflexive uses of psychology, as well as my critical project of comparing psychology to superstition.

1

Empirical Psychology

Mind in a Lab

Psychology, merciful God, you still hold with that? It is but a poor bourgeois nineteenth century thing. This epoch is wretchedly sick of it, 'twill soon be a red flag to it, and he who would disrupt life with psychology will simply earn a thwack on the head. We are entering an age, dear boy, that will not wish to be married to psychology.
—Thomas Mann, *Doctor Faustus* (1947), chapter XXV

In this chapter, I describe the origins of psychology's predominant use as an empirical science to understand its epistemological position relative to philosophy, religion, and the human and natural sciences. This includes an evaluation of the early stages of the institutionalization of the field in the German, American, and Russian contexts in which they developed. This chapter prepares the way for a consideration of the pragmatic use of metaphors employed in empirical psychology (Chapter 2), and the current state of the field (Chapter 3).

Introduction

From Myth to Math

One way to approach the hazy origins of the study of the mind is to survey mythical narratives from the ancient world, as narrative tales contain implicit claims about the mind. For instance, Gilgamesh's dream of a meteorite, the intransigent poses of Achilles and Agamemnon, pathos in the *Oresteia* of Aeschylus, fury and ecstasy in *The Bacchae* of Euripides, and the joys and sorrows playfully expressed in the Book of Odes. These

A Suspicious Science. Rami Gabriel, Oxford University Press. © Oxford University Press 2023.
DOI: 10.1093/oso/9780197513583.003.0002

compendiums of the human soul deserve more attention as part of the enterprise of psychology because they are in effect mimetic depictions of humans. Philology and linguistics similarly trace the mind in motion through describing the structure of our communication. By investigating the objects, abodes, and modes of living of our ancestors, paleoarchaeology is also a study of the mind.[1] As we develop a holistic understanding of how our acts and how our bodies manifest the mind, the breadth of psychology grows immense, maybe fatally so.[2]

Explicit study of mind, or at least the deliberate reductionism that implies explicit study in empirical psychology, begins in earnest with medicine, philosophy, and religion. All three branches of philosophy—metaphysics, epistemology, and ethics—are essentially about the mind and the precise nature of its relation to sensation, truth, and reality. Empirical psychology fulfills some epistemic functions that were previously the province of philosophy by employing a materialist ontology enacted through an epistemological adherence to the scientific method as adapted through positivism and pragmatism to deliver a model of the human as a sophisticated learning machine that is born with particular cognitive systems, like language and sensation, to interact with its environment. In this chapter, I describe how these epistemic commitments were developed between the mid 19th and the early 20th century. Religion and theology were similarly dominant before this period; they offered ritual practices to ground metaphysical frames. Belief in in the empirical and therapeutic practices of psychology fulfills some functions that were previously the province of religion. Part of the story I unfold concerns the faith placed in the scientific apparatus during the modern era. The other part of the story is how psychology developed affectively satisfactory explanations and practices.

One major aspect of the use of psychology as a science is that it relies on the reduction of mental phenomena to structures, functions, processes, and anatomical circuits. In 1931, Grace Adams intuited that positivist psychology is essentially pursuing Thomas Huxley's notion that we are nothing but "conscious automata."[3] In pursuing reductionism, psychology adopts a positivist trajectory, wresting the proverbial soul from above nature down to the rag-and-bone shop of the body as part of nature. As we well see, there are more and less graceful ways to implement this post-Darwinian mandate of incorporating the human mind into the natural and human sciences. In this chapter, we trace various positivist and pragmatist attempts to construct a behavioral science of the mind in the last 150 years.

A Particular History

Because its roots lie in disparate practices, presenting a history of psychology is no simple matter. Before the 1850s, study of the mind was natural philosophy of reality and nature. As a way to talk about the self and soul, it was religion. According to philosopher R. G. Collingwood, during the modern era the field developed a strict methodological template that self-consciously modeled itself upon the physical sciences. This partisanship forced study of the mind into the dubious business of seeking presumably unchanging laws of mental life. The most important casualty of this redirection was a rejection of the use of historical methods to study the contingent conditions of human life and the organization of local knowledge practices.[4] Accordingly, the larger question which I work into and around in this particular history concerns the epistemic limits that are a consequence of adopting scientific methods and neglecting historical and anthropological methods.

The formal model of scientific explanation (the Hempelian model) consists of covering laws, or a nomological-deductive model, from which universal laws (i.e., explanans) explain particular events (i.e., explanandum).[5] For example, long-term potentiation, the neural correlate of long-term memory, is said to be the nomological and causal process by which the brain registers and retains neural connections that contain the stuff of memory.[6] Despite the success of such findings, a major issue with formal scientific explanation is that while empirical psychologists attempt to specify principles on the model of the physical sciences by which neural matter functions, "laws" about humans in the behavioral and social sciences are generally not universal, because people behave differently across situations and according to varying contingent cultural norms. This issue of the bifurcation between the study of natural phenomena and human beings is at the core of the debate about the legitimacy of the human sciences.[7] Furthermore, the explananda, thought, is devilishly difficult to isolate as an empirical data point because each event consists of a diverse set of quantitative and nonreducible qualitative elements.

For these reasons, the method adopted by a researcher inordinately determines the results. Thus, it is best to think of the dominant explanations at any given time in terms of a privileging of historical moments of empirically adequate practices.[8] That is to say, in any given experiment the mind is explained or portrayed simply as what the methods we bring to bear reveal, and therefore it is the structure of the methodology/experimental apparatus

8 A SUSPICIOUS SCIENCE

that determines the explanations which are delivered. Sometimes this is useful and seemingly accurate, or accurate enough. Other times we arrive at an impoverished and inaccurate depiction of the explananda. As we will see in the history of empirical psychology, the equipment and assumptions of researchers often determine the manner in which the mind is portrayed.

In response to this deep ontological issue that the method determines the results, the field of psychology has sought increasingly precise and presumably more "objective" methods for observation and description. There have also developed models that take into account uncertainty and probability, most famously the Bayesian approach, through which researchers use Bayes's theorem to indicate the likelihood of particular behaviors and outcomes given the "priors," or context of the situation. After the advent of the neurosciences, there is also a shift from covering law explanations to mechanistic exhibition.[9] These strategies are necessary because observation is ultimately selective and limited, and therefore the results of observation often reveal more about the context of the observation than about the explanandum, human nature, itself.[10] Theories in psychology are overwhelmingly dependent on the authority invested in the methods by which they were discovered, to the point that the implications of the results of experiments are constricted to the methods by which they arose. This methodologism is the reductio ad absurdum of empirical psychology's adoption of the expectations of the physical sciences in which it is necessary to neglect or downplay extra-logical factors such as sociopolitical, economic, and religious cultural environment.[11] As we will see, it is clear that the mind is highly permeable to such contextual factors.[12] Hence, my account of empirical psychology will put an emphasis on how culture, history, and context consistently disrupt the nomological-deductive thrust of the field.

Origins of Empirical Psychology

Empirical psychology began as a branch of natural philosophy before coalescing into a set of positivistic laboratory methods in the 19th century, then a social science in the early 20th century and a behavioral interdisciplinary practice in the late 20th century.[13] These shifts in status reflect the organization of the academy, and the national character of intellectual institutions, as well as trends in methodological practices and interpretative approaches. A broader notion of the history of psychology would not overlook the epistemic "looping" that occurs between belief and explanation as a reflexive process whereby a human creates what it is to be human through the very practice of investigating oneself.[14] Psychology could thus easily be integrated into a larger picture of our political and practical historical activities, our knowledge practices.[15]

The origins of the use of psychology as an empirical science can be traced in part to the trajectory of rationalism introduced during the European Enlightenment (17th and 18th centuries). This includes the seminal work of French philosopher René Descartes (1596–1650), German philosopher Immanuel Kant (1724–1804), and the British empiricists John Locke (1632–1704) and David Hume (1711–1776).[16] Of course, in the Western tradition, the Greeks (Socrates, Plato, and Aristotle) conveyed subtle foundational frameworks by which to understand the relation among thought, behavior, and ethical comportment.[17] Also to be considered are the contributions of the Stoics, the Buddhists, the Patricians, the Scholastics, the Renaissance humanists, and more.[18] Medieval Muslim thinkers, such as Avicenna (980–1037) wrote about psyche (or *nafs*, the breath), and many Buddhist sutras offer incisive proto-psychological analysis of phenomenology and habits of the mind.[19] Throughout these streams one may observe a seesaw between materialist theories and idealistic philosophies; the former prosper in periods of empire, while the latter are prevalent in the wake of destruction.[20]

The respective contexts of these ideas—the European Enlightenment, dynastic Islam, and early Buddhism—determine disparate lineaments of the study of the mind. While we think of science as objective, a consideration of the history of psychology makes clear that the study of the mind is always aligned with its social and cultural context. These determine its uses. Cartesianism, for example, is part of the story of secularization and political liberalism insofar as it treats the individual and one's rationality as the core of epistemological and political considerations of citizenship. Kant's use of nativism enabled a naturalization of rationalist structuralism which paved the way for the codification of human nature essential for the nascent human sciences and colonial notions of difference.

Since the 16th century, quantitative analysis in the natural sciences has proven so successful that it transformed what we expect from any rigorous investigation of the world.[21] The arrogance that proceeds from subsequent scientism is the context for many of the shortcomings demonstrated by psychologists in the 20th century, as discussed in Chapter 3. Below I describe

10 A SUSPICIOUS SCIENCE

how the epistemological position held by psychology on the coattails of the natural sciences obfuscated the extent of its doxastic reach and the reliability of its methodologies. Nevertheless, the field has—sometimes in spite of itself—revealed heretofore unknown facets of the mind as a part of nature. In the following account, I trace the positivist and pragmatist beginnings of psychology in Germany and America before providing a contrastive history of empirical psychology in Russia. This strategy of comparison, which will also be employed in regards to discursive uses of psychology in Chapter 5 allows for an understanding of the epistemic cultural constraints on the study of mind.

Positivism and Methodology in Early Empirical Psychology

Buoyed by the success of the natural sciences, the technological fruits of modernity, and the systematic potential of logic, circles of intellectuals in Vienna and Berlin in the late 1920s devised programs to explain the mind in the terms of a hypothetico-deductive science. These philosophers and logicians disdained the thick descriptions employed in anthropology and German phenomenology and sought rather to quantify mental life in the form of a method that verifies mental phenomena by direct observation and logical proof. The methods and theory whereby psychology is used as a natural science originate in logical positivism.[22] Observation and theory in empirical psychology rely on a methodology whereby operational definitions are generated for mental terms. Mental concepts are thus equated with the manner in which the researcher comes to observe them. As a means of aspiring to the epistemological status of the natural sciences, the accompanying strategy of verificationism in empirical psychology consists of collecting data and then parsing it with the use of complex statistical tools. The legacy of positivism as an adaptation of the physical sciences is apparent in (a) behaviorism and its operationalism of mental terms, (b) methods employed in animal neuroscience, (c) statistical modeling, and (d) connectionist computational models of mind.

Experimental psychology's roots in the human sciences, on the other hand, are most clearly evident in its pragmatism.[23] The American philosophers William James (1842–1910) and John Dewey (1859–1952) were keenly aware of the limitations of an objective science of subjective phenomena. They thus emphasized the vicissitudes of thought, the influence of extra-logical factors, and the import of culture, education, and action. James saw the task of psychology to be providing accurate description of mental phenomena and the causal conditions that give rise to these phenomena. "Psychology. . . assumes as its data (1) thoughts and feelings, and (2) a physical world in time and space with which they coexist and which (3) they know."[24] The sign of mentality for James is the "pursuance of future ends and the choice of means for their attainment."[25] The legacy of pragmatism in empirical psychology is apparent in (a) functionalism and its metaphysical agnosticism, (b) structuralism, and (c) methodological reliance on introspection.

Positivism, pragmatism, and their interwoven legacies are attempts to solve the same problems: how to study a postulated entity in the absence of direct access, and how to quantify an object of study toward generalizing findings into predictive models.

The first problem is inherited from the human sciences and is nearly fatal for objective analysis due to the infinite amount of contextual factors that determine the postulated entity and its range of experience and behavior. Notably, the German founder of experimental laboratory psychology, Wilhelm Wundt (1832–1920), acknowledged these limits of experimentation. While he considered it adequate to study lower psychological functions, higher psychological functions were better served according to him through the rich descriptive methods of anthropology. In addition to his prolific writings on introspectionism, Wundt's other major work was devoted to *Völkerpsychologie*, a kind of social psychology about the historical, ethnographic, and comparative nature of cultural products, including language, myth, and customs.[26] From the beginning, it was apparent to the founders of the field of empirical psychology that methods derived from positivism and the natural sciences were not sufficient to characterize the full range of thoughts and behaviors.

Also formed in the 19th century, the discipline of anthropology provided a descriptive and discursive human science of the mind. In this field, a similar range of approaches were apparent: British anthropologists tended toward a data-driven empirical functionalism, whereas French and continental anthropologists made generalizations and sociological speculations from the armchair.[27] Frenchman Claude Lévi-Strauss (1908–2009) developed a structuralist approach whereby the form of the mind was said to mirror social institutions and artifacts in the world. He accomplished this through

12 A SUSPICIOUS SCIENCE

painstakingly developing a system of basic mental categories. Structuralism has served many masters in the empirical study of humans and nature, as it enables the ordered simplification of vast amounts of information. By creating structural categories, a researcher may study a postulated entity in the absence of direct access by fitting observations into their system. From functionalism to modularity of mind, structuralism has been employed by psychologists to construct models. As we will see in Chapter 2, the use of metaphors is one such structural principle of analogical thinking central to the empirical use of psychology.

The second problem of how to quantify aspects of mind arises directly from psychology's emulation of the natural sciences. At the turn of the 20th century, Germans Ernest Mach (1838–1916) and Wilhelm Wundt (1832–1920) stressed introspective methodologies, whereas American psychologists focused on the observation of animal behavior in controlled settings. Both approaches to quantifying mental behavior relied on operationalism of intentional terms and methodologies developed therein. The assumption, of course, is that empirical psychology experiments on humans are in principle no different from experiments in the natural sciences. And yet, as the pragmatists and Wundt were already aware, from the artifacts of the laboratory to the social roles played by experimental subjects and the researcher's intervention, the derivation of knowledge about the mind unique because it takes place in a social arena. Scientific activity requires consensus between vested interests, for example the researcher who is testing her theory, the intellectual lineage the student is serving, and the trends and momentum of ideas at any given time. These factors bake unexamined biases into the experimental situation. In fact, every research report is the result of actions within an experimental situation couched in a research community further couched within a professional environment, which itself is but a historically defined sector of the knowledge practices of a given society. For example, the development of the concept of trauma through the study of memory in Jean Charcot and Sigmund Freud is part of the story of the development of insurance law and the politicization of victimhood.[28] In general, these social considerations are systematically excluded from discussion and interpretation of experiments and their methodology in order to focus on positivistic and pragmatic goals toward attaining reliable simplifications of the human mind which can be delivered in the language of the natural sciences.

The Negative Evolution of Knowledge Practices

Empirical psychology consists of attempts to explain the mental aspect of organisms. Consider the range in just these few examples: anxiety, spatial navigation, birdsong, and training dogs to do tricks.[29] This awesome scope has the consequence that the field will face an immense burden of theoretical integration to deliver a unified explanation. It also suggests a lack of humility in the face of the complexities of its subject matter. We can understand its ambitions if we view psychology as heir to the optimism inherent in industrialization and modernity that inspired logical positivism; psychology is "a footnote to the nineteenth century," as it were.[30] Auguste Comte's (1798–1857) codification of secular Enlightenment hopes in a positivist program stimulated a zeitgeist of laboratory empiricism.[31] As George Santayana wrote, "A system may contain an account of many things which, in detail, are true enough; but as a system, covering infinite possibilities that neither our experience nor our logic can prejudge, it must be a work of imagination, and a piece of human soliloquy. It may be expressive of human experience, it may be poetical; but how should anyone who really coveted truth suppose that it was true."[32]

From tachistoscopes to PET scans and ever more sophisticated imaging technologies, the methodological tools and interpretative strategies used in empirical psychology are constantly shifting. The history of psychology can thus be conceived of as a negative evolution of knowledge practices: "(T)he hard knowledge that accrues in one generation typically disenfranchises the theoretical fictions of the previous one."[33] In this section, I argue that an emphasis on method, a methodologism, that is the result of positivism and pragmatism traps empirical psychology in a tautological project where method and results point to each other rather than the phenomena under study. This is due partly to the fact that the uses of psychology shift in accord with cultural context, and partly to the field's ambivalence about the nature of its own scope.[34] The issue is that if the methods keep changing, say from psychophysiology to introspectionism to nonsense syllables to associationism and behaviorism, by which principles can we collate data collected from different methods? How do the stages in the evolution of knowledge practices in empirical psychology relate to each other if each one is committed to their own operationalization of mental terms into specific methodologies of generating and collecting data?

14   A SUSPICIOUS SCIENCE

While the early 19th century was characterized by British gentlemen scientists and library philosophers, the latter half is exemplified by the institutionalization of the human sciences in the universities of Germany and the United States.[35] The success of early German psychophysiologists—Ernst Weber, Hermann von Helmholtz, Gustav Feodor Fechner, and Ernst Mach—inspired Wilhelm Wundt to attempt a structural analysis of the human form in the laboratory. Since the psychophysiologists discovered reliable relations between phenomenology and bodily mechanics, like Weber's Law and Fechner's Law, why not pursue further systematic connections between sensations and stimuli? The hopes of the psychophysiological movement inspired not only German experimentalists like Wilhelm Wundt but also early American practitioners like William James and Stanley T. Hall. Their work along with that of German anatomists like Ernst Brücke (1819–1892) coalesced in the careers of latent *naturphilosophers* like Franz Brentano and Sigmund Freud. Unlike German structuralists, both James and Freud maintained space in their theoretical apparatus for the unknown/unknowable in humans; the former called it the spiritual or consciousness, the latter, the unconscious or the "It." Their emphasis on the incompleteness of positivism and the existence of irrational forces aligned with other artistic projects that exemplified modernity, such as Viennese fin-de-siècle arts, and may go some way toward explaining their lasting popularity.

The structural approach employed in Wundt's lab sought the codification of the elements of thought. This was a direct response to Immanuel Kant's (1724–1804) claim that psychology could not submit to the sine qua non of scientific enterprise: quantification.[36] Empiricism required measurement, and it aspired to practicality, objectivity, ethical neutrality and an anti-metaphysical stance.[37] In fact, psychology came to be largely defined by experimental methods, above any theoretical considerations. Early laboratories had to develop their own nomenclature and methods to fulfill their research programs. For example, another German, Max Ebbinghaus (1850–1909) developed a whole system of nonsense syllables and a method by which to memorize and test his memory of them. Embedded in his method were assumptions about what memory is, the affective nature of engrams, the function and nature of retention, the privacy of memory, and other idiosyncratic notions of mechanization and pedagogy.[38] Such methodologism redounded to the way in which subjects in experiments gave verbal expression to their sensations in a kind of ambiguous, metaphorical language. The assumption was that these reports could make introspection public in a way

EMPIRICAL PSYCHOLOGY 15

that expressed the lived whole of experience rather than simply a demand of the artificial laboratory setting.[39] Thus researchers developed tools, like the Likert scale or Alfred Binet's intelligence measures, which were conceived of as standardized measures that would instill validity upon the measures employed.[40] In these tools, analogy was an irreducible element of description: psychologists developed analogies between rating systems and introspective measures in pursuit of reliability. It was the rating system of the Likert scale, for example, which drew together data from different experimental participants. But compare, for example, the evidence that a Likert scale solicits to what an electron microscope allows us to visualize. While the former may be reliable, its validity depends upon tendentious analogies and assumptions. Enforced standardization of experimental tools like the Likert scale is dangerous because each method can be effaced and rendered moot by another method, in a form of negative evolution of methodology. Similarly, when psychologists theoretically justify the validity of postulated mental concepts through operational routines, the concepts are equally susceptible to being replaced as anachronistic due to their reliance on a particular analogical model. It could be said that all scientific inquiry must contend with this problem of the commensurability of its practices, but there is reason to worry that psychology is uniquely unsuited to overcome its methodologism.

Validity, Reliability, and Individual Differences

Early German psychology was mired in philosophical speculation about whether the human sciences could be a natural science at all since their subject matter, the mind, is itself the expression of cultural values.[41] For instance, though he engaged in a prodigious amount of empirical work and writing, Wundt was dedicated to a philosophical vision of the human that may be achieved through the nomothetic generalization of observations of individual responses to a limited set of stimuli. Wundt's work was foundational because it carved out a space for mental action not as a branch of physiology, but as an independent science. He sought the laws of "psychic causality" and linked his structural descriptions to an evolutionary story about the hierarchy of action.[42] He was inspired by a Hegelian zeitgeist in which feelings are central to psychological life.[43] This radical phenomenology, which was only a preliminary stage of Wundt's plan to describe mental content, was expected to lead to intrinsic truths about the eternal form of the human mind.[44]

16   A SUSPICIOUS SCIENCE

Yet the source of evidence which would lead to laws of psychic causality must be derived from the laboratory, whose social context is esoteric and unique: One person is considered a source of data, while the other is the experimental manipulator. This dyad resembles the acts of confession, dissection, examination, and revelation. Further, embedded in the validity and reliability of experimental methodology is the assumption that a stimulus such as a ticking metronome will produce identical or near-identical perceptions. Indeed, there was always conflict between individualism, or the recording of individual differences on the one hand, and the concatenation of a generalized human nature, or supra-individual order on the other.[45] Positivist psychologists sought to derive an ahistorical and universal form of the mind by studying specific historically situated humans. This was to be accomplished by practices of aggregating responses across groups of experimental subjects by using statistics and open-ended methods, such as the questionnaire. Englishman Francis Galton and the early applied psychologists, for instance, were explicitly trying to capture statistical norms of the human mind as a way of fulfilling Darwinian notions of form and structure.[46] It is no surprise that in the industrial landscape of the late 19th and early 20th century in Britain and the United States, applied psychology became a commodifiable discipline linked to business interests and industrial organization. Intelligence testing, for example provided a rationale for the managerial organization of labor.[47]

During this period, personality testing led to a substantial industry for mental hygiene that came to be interwoven with social and ethical norms. The development of expertise and utilitarian categorization of labor through the language of psychology continues in a myriad of forms today with the proliferation of industrial/organizational psychology. Not only are the concepts of productivity tied up with concepts of mental action, but administrative institutions consistently use terms derived from empirical psychology to manage or teach people to manage themselves everywhere from schools to prisons, asylums, corporate environments, church groups, factories, and even within families.[48] The determination of individual differences is a cornerstorne of applied psychology.[49] It allows for the development of an industry devoted to the treatment and assessment of psychopathology.[50] It also creates a psychological language to explain, or rather explain away, the political and economic circumstances that are linked to differences between classes and genders.[51] There is plenty of arbitrariness in creating norms for "character," and personality tests have been duly exploited not only for the subjugation of individuals through the determination of difference but also to buttress esoteric theories such as astrology.[52] The legacy of these early uses of psychology can be equally pernicious, for instance, invasive demographic marketing techniques, the unlawful tracking of online behavior, relentless consumer research, psychological operations, and a wide range of methods to determine and punish and exploit psychopathology in the carceral state. The concepts used in applied psychology are also subject to negative evolution; one of the most famous cases is that of hysteria, which was used to pathologize women who had been sexually and emotionally abused. The term was subsequently revoked from clinical psychology as hopelessly vague.[53]

Essentially, empirical psychology portrays the mind through a set of experimental methods, which are subject to change. In the later 19th and early 20th century, psychological subjects entered the artificial situation of the laboratory, were exposed to artificial stimuli, such as pure tones that are very seldom heard in ecologically valid situations, and limited to responding only on the scales rendered by the given laboratory. It is not hard to see that in such a scenario, a person is cut off from their social identity in the world and becomes simply the producer of a set of responses in a constricted experimental situation.[54] Experimentalism as positivism relies upon interpreting aggregated data and the practice of statistically contrasting control versus experimental intervention groups. These methods dominated much of empirical psychology in Germany and had repercussions in a range of domains, from medical testing to psychopathology, business practices, and how mass society categorizes and sets expectations for its citizens. The other major branch of early psychology takes place in America, so let us turn now to the Western theater, which exemplifies the pragmatic aspect of the empirical use of psychology.

Pragmatism: William James and the American Century

William James is a key figure; he taught the first class on psychology, had a laboratory space by 1875, and wrote a seminal textbook. Throughout his career, James propounded such a wide set of thoughtful views that all who followed could not help but walk in his footsteps. In its excitement and ambivalence, James's approach embodies the American ethos. James's views were born of Calvinism and transcendentalism; they eluded the genteel tradition through adopting radical romanticism and radical empiricism.[55] In his youth, James drifted from the study of nature to physiology and philosophy before becoming excited by the prospects of German experimentalism. He developed a unique form for psychology which maintained roots in metaphysics while also taking into account physiology and experimental methods. The work of early pragmatists like James made a place for psychology as a mental and a social science.[56]

While William James's ideas developed substantially across his long career, they can be characterized by a radical reliance on introspective evidence, a functionalist view of mental processes refined by a pragmatic balance between the possibilities of a structural analysis of the mind through positivistic methods, and an openness to a pluralistic universe.[57] As a radical empiricist, a romantic, and phenomenologist, James maintained that psychology must be true to our experiences, and, correlatively, that knowledge by acquaintance is ultimately the preferred form of evidence. As a pragmatist, he considered a belief to be true only insofar as it had predictive accuracy.[58] James conceived of human knowledge as composed of three concentric rings: a nucleus of immediacy, surrounded by an area of theoretical judgments where belief is supported by reasons, and, finally, a third ring of faith in which beliefs transcend immediacy and are justified on moral grounds.[59] The pragmatism that he, John Dewey, and Charles Sanders Pierce (1839-1914) developed is efficacious at the second ring of knowledge; it aids us in fitting reasons to judgments within a given context. Indeed, James was consistent in claiming we rightfully seek relief from doubt according to a trial of ideas. But while "we are justified in believing what is proved . . . we are also justified in believing what is desirable or right to believe [though] these two justifications do not always coincide."[60] This allowance for fideism demonstrates again his perspicacity about phenomenal experience, emotions, and the way the mind actually works. The third ring is notable because in it we observe that belief is an affective act that does not necessarily coincide with reason; rather, it quells doubt and answers its own questions. Of course, due to its positivist aspirations to be a physical science, psychology must seek answers and objective methods that render beliefs about the mind apodictic. Yet, even early in the development of empirical psychology, James's work suggests that the snakes of truth and belief are hopelessly intertwined in our knowledge practices. I adopt James's assessment of the circles of knowledge to explore how in our era of doubt, when emotional factors concerning the nature and format of explanation determine our allegiances, belief in psychology and its findings reside in the third ring. I pursue this line of thought in the interlude.

EMPIRICAL PSYCHOLOGY   19

While James grounds psychology in physical elements, he is consistently drawn toward metaphysics and a rejection of positivistic or automaton theories of the human form.[61] His ideas about consciousness and experience were of a vague metaphysical hue, sticking closer to the unique post-Darwinian philosophy of Henri Bergson (1859–1941) than to the tenets of positivism.[62] He admits, for example, in *The Principles of Psychology* that he is sympathetic with spiritualism, and he earnestly recounts instances of communication with spirits.[63] This element of his thought—the spooky, wishful resistance, this setting aside of space in a pluralistic universe for wishes, hopes, and the efficacy of will—continues in the popular uses of psychology discussed in Chapter 4.

Reading through James's textbook, *The Principles of Psychology*, it is clear that at the time the field was very much an empirical working out of the theoretical conjectures of the British associationists—with the addition of a better understanding of the brain and nerve physiology. By 1890, the principal fields of experimentation were the connection of conscious states to physical conditions, analysis of the perception of space and time, and the accuracy and laws of retention, influence, and capacity in memory.[64] The main methods of psychology were introspection, experimentation, and comparison.[65] James's analyses of the stream of thought, the self, and emotions have become classic, if controversial, touchstones in the field. William James synthesized his metaphysical principles and devotion to the reality of personal experience with the physicalist doctrines of positivism (more prevalent in the work of his compatriot Stanley T. Hall [1846–1924]), to found an American school of psychology. This amalgam underlies the major uses of psychology in the 20th century when the United States became the largest producer of laboratory psychology studies and related institutions.

Behaviorism

In response to Wundt and James's introspectionist methodology, positivist ambitions in the guise of American behaviorism came to the fore in the early 20th century. One legacy of early experimentalism in Germany and America was that psychology laboratories pursued a methodologism which found its apotheosis in the assumption that there is nothing more to the mind than what can be discovered through experimental observation. The mind is thus rendered as a black box that mediates between stimulus and response.

20 A SUSPICIOUS SCIENCE

Americans John B. Watson (1878–1958) and Burrhus Frederic Skinner's (1904–1990) took on the task of working out the laws of mental association (cf. psychic causality) through the observation and manipulation of two species of rat and one species of pigeon.[66] This approach was heavy on methodology yet metaphysically austere. The rejection of Franz Brentano's thesis of the intentionality or the directedness of mental states enabled the pursuit of an explanation of behavior as exact as the explanation of elementary phenomena in the natural sciences.[67] Psychology was to be a science of behavior which delivered natural laws of psychic causality. The key to this enterprise was the strategy of operationalism, wherein a concept is defined by its verifiable set of physical operations. A concept like learning is treated as synonymous with a set of operations, specifically of reinforcement schedules. For example, a behaviorist would posit that a lab animal "learned" how to do a task once its behavior was sufficiently positively and negatively reinforced. The insight of the behaviorists is that the methods of natural sciences could be brought to bear upon the mind if behavior was treated as the dependent variable and if the independent variable, namely the stimulus, was wholly under the control of the researcher.[68] It was thus possible to quantify associationist notions of learning in the elementary particles of classically conditioned behaviors (i.e., conditioned response and conditioned stimulus paired with unconditioned response and unconditioned stimulus). Behaviorism dominated empirical psychology in the first half of the 20th century, especially in the United States.[69]

B. F. Skinner traced the behaviorist paradigm to 18th-century French philosopher Julien Offray de La Mettrie's (1709–1751) conception of human as machine, and Charles Darwin's (1809–1882) insight that a continuity exists between animal and human mind. Rather than being a space for the unknown as it had been for Sigmund Freud or the spiritual as it had been for William James, the unconscious was the repository of learned associations.[70] Behaviorists are satisfied with an epistemological conservatism that avoids the complexities that accrued to the notion of mind in the centuries since Descartes's postulation of mind-body dualism. In pursuit of a positivistic explanation of mind, the behaviorist paradigm argues that our inferences about the mediating factor between environmental events and overt behavioral changes are largely underdetermined and thus it is more pragmatic to ignore these factors.[71] They argue that using intentional concepts to explain the relation between the two is not as useful as study of behavior itself if one's goal were to derive predictions of behavior. Further, Skinner claims

EMPIRICAL PSYCHOLOGY 21

the private world is either entirely unknowable or unlikely to be known well since the privacy inside the skin imposes more serious limitation than the accessibility of the external world to the scientist.[72] Intriguingly, what behaviorism and materialism have in common is a rejection of the autonomy of the human, that is to say, a rejection of the ethical nature of mind that was crucial for J. S. Mill (1806–1873) and for considering the contextual nature of the psyche.[73]

Within the larger story of the development of empirical psychology, behaviorism can be linked to a post-17th-century version of science more interested in deriving prediction and achieving control than attaining explanation and understanding per se.[74] Final causes of purpose and teleology are thus removed and we are left with a science of crafting experiments and compiling observations.[75] Questions concerning basic motivations became more pressing in the 19th-century investigation of "drives," or intrinsic motivations. This was a way to draw in biological notions like instinct from neo-Darwinian paradigms. In particular, Clark Hull (1884–1952) developed a complex system to integrate findings from behaviorism with theories of motivation.[76] The legacy of this methodology is apparent in subsequent empirical uses of psychology wherein behavioral variables, like reaction time and verbal response, are considered the primary legible sources of information from which to deduce underlying structure.[77]

Indeed, the methods employed in behaviorism over many decades, ranging from scheduled reinforcement to learned helplessness, maze navigation, and much more, while impressive were found wanting in providing answers to certain crucial questions. Behaviorism could not account for serial behaviors like language and skilled motor routines due to the speed of feedback in a reactive model and since the black box model of mind does not have a way to explain hierarchical plans of action. Operationalism, again, was found to be more tautological than explanatory. Many cogent critiques spelled out the difficulties of relying on the study of rats to explain the behaviors of human beings.[78] Though they remained central to animal neuroscience, notions of control through mechanics in a laboratory setting became less popular for the study of human beings. Finally, Noam Chomsky's (b. 1928) argument for inborn syntax which enables language acquisition in humans sounded the death knell of behaviorism and the field swung back to structural explanations of mind, this time neural and modular.[79] Whereas behaviorism focused on learning paradigms, it was cognition, that is, higher psychological functions, which became the focus of study starting in the

22   A SUSPICIOUS SCIENCE

early 1950s. Another negative evolution of knowledge practices occurred in this methodological shift.

Early Cognitive Science

As the reader has observed by now, the way we study the mind also dictates what elements of mind can be studied; that is to say, when the methodology shifts, the subject of study must shift as well. Abilities such as complex perception and language were amenable to structural explanation, so they came to define what we thought of as mind in the mid-20th century. The study of cognition allowed for a complication of the story of learning, which was considered a matter of conditioning during the behaviorist period. Cognitivists posited that intelligence is more than the sum of conditioning trials or the memorization of nonsense syllables (à la Ebbinghaus). Gestalt psychology, an early to mid-20th-century German school that emphasized emergent elements of organization in perception, stressed the importance of form and thus recognized more complex elements of sensation and perception.[80] From the soil of empiricism, elementism, associationism, materialism, and the seeds of Russian reflexology and early American functionalism came a new generation primarily in America that rejected universal laws of learning and opened the subject of psychology up to include such topics as consciousness and imagery.[81] Notions of value, as embodied in drives, also developed in the mid-20th century, providing space for a post-Darwinian sense of why creatures act as they do.[82]

The topic of thinking itself was released from the paradigm of principles of learning that was at the heart of behaviorism. After the 1950s, a burgeoning approach argued that the mind was an evolved machine for the processing of information. This shift allowed the study of thought to be under the same umbrella as linguistics and artificial intelligence as sets of problem-solving functions.[83] During the latter half of the 20th century, psychologists studied the formal constraints of the mind and used the digital computer as a model for a universal machine of problem solving.[84] Other notable formats for empirical psychology are the study of development, personality and social psychology.[85] As discussed in the next two chapters, the availability of new metaphors of mind, like the computer, enabled psychologists to develop unique interpretations of empirical evidence and spin new

EMPIRICAL PSYCHOLOGY 23

methodologies from the basic insights of cognitivism toward the creation of neuropsychology.

To briefly recapitulate: during the 19th and early 20th century, Wilhelm Wundt's laboratory at Leipzig invested first-person introspection with an authority and clarity (à la Cartesian insightfulness) that it probably does not have. William James at Harvard sought to maintain agency and dignity for humans by founding his theory on radical empiricism and pragmatism.[86] In the early 20th century, American behaviorists operationalized behavior as a dependent variable. And, finally, the structuralists of the cognitive sciences modeled the mind on the computer. Through this history we observe how the field of empirical psychology navigated between nomothetic (general, law-like study) and idiographic (particular, individual study) goals. This distinction will prove important as I develop a case for an interdisciplinary multilevel psychology.

While we have been focusing on German and American versions of empirical study of the mind, at this point, considering the development of psychology in other countries during the early 20th century will offer a clarifying contrast. This comparison further buttresses the claim that psychology is not simply the study of human nature, but rather a set of knowledge practices embedded in particular epistemic niches.

Soviet Psychology

In Moscow, Lev Vygotsky (1896–1934) and Alexander Luria (1902–1977) pursued an instrumental, historical, and cultural psychology which sought a balance between nomothetic (law-like) and idiographic (individual cases) approaches.[87] Their "new psychology" of the 1880s paired associationism with a Wundtian introspectionist methodology in the cultural context of Marxist materialism. Luria and Vygotsky plotted a course that admitted hidden psychodynamic causes, physiology derived from the work of Ivan Pavlov (1849–1936), and German Gestalt notions of form and function. In contrast to Western empirical psychology (detailed earlier), which pursued a nomothetic objective model of the mind, Russian psychologists maintained that their subject matter was the irreducible relation of the organism to its environment. In the 1920s, they created a unique synthesis in which Pavlov's theory of higher nervous activity (i.e., conditioned learning) was the material foundation of gestalt properties of higher psychological function that

24   A SUSPICIOUS SCIENCE

were in turn shaped by social relations in the external world.[88] This mediated nature of psychological function they term "instrumental." The relational cultural context of the mind for Russian psychologists was the mediating role of language, which they saw as all-important in the structuring of thought, especially as part of the developmental process.[89] Similarly, they subordinated mental structure to the historical background conditions of the individual.[90] In particular, they investigated the role of culture and language by spending substantial amounts of time studying illiterate communities in the Uzbek and Kazhak lands of central Asia.[91]

What stands out particularly in this contrast is how Soviet psychologists used the same structural elements of conditioned reflex and Wundtian experimentalism to promote an idiographic method which resulted in a model of the mind that eschewed much of the positivist, structuralist tradition. This Soviet synthesis of descriptive and explanatory goals emphasized the adaptable relational nature of the mind. Unlike the early cognitivists who posit an innate structure of the mind, the Soviet synthesis emphasizes practical reason and the regulatory function of language as the central structural elements. This is in line with the background ontological commitments to the materialist tenets of Marxist-Leninist theory which emphasize how material conditions shape consciousness. This is in contrast to the political orientation embodied by the liberal subject in the West. The stress that Soviet psychologists placed on gestalt (i.e., the emergence of form) processes and theorizing the horizontal organization of the brain belie their romantic goal of preserving the wealth of idiographic lived reality against the reductionism of nomothetic structural explanations of mind. For Alfred Luria, truly scientific observation necessitates viewing an event from as many perspectives as possible in order to understand how the thing relates to other things. This dialectical analysis, which assumes that the mind is socially constructed through language, history, and social relations, contrasts with the thrust of American behaviorism and the phenomenology of German introspectionism, and Jamesian pragmatism.

While the tools of measurement and basic knowledge practices (psychophysiology, introspectionism, and pragmatism) of the period between 1860 and 1930 were known throughout Europe, America, and Russia, their respective theoretical syntheses do not cohere. As we can see from the contrast between Russian and Western psychology, the pieces can be put together in at least two very different ways. Except in very basic ways pertaining to sensation and basic cognitive function, it is not simple to bring together the findings of Western and Russian practices, and this is not simply a matter of negative evolution of methodology. Furthermore, the realization of the shortcomings of reflexology in Russia or behaviorism in America, or introspection in Germany did not immediately get communicated outside their respective communities. Thus, vestiges of intellectual traditions experience unique syntheses outside of their original context which lead to unique and irreplicable syncretisms. I argue this is because each national use of empirical psychology assembled particular understandings of its purpose and, more importantly, considered their empirical investigations to be in service of different visions of human nature. Local knowledge practices concerning the mind are intrinsically embedded in their cultural context. That is to say, the extra-logical factors of context, metaphysical commitments, ethics, ideology, power, and influence play a substantial role in the uses of psychology.

In the United States, we observe a kind of pragmatism tinged with Judeo-Christian mysticism, whereas in Soviet Russia, we find the maintenance of Marxist-Leninist notions of humans through a synthesis of material bases and individual agency in sociohistorical context. The need to synthesize empirical visions of mind with cultural factors reveals how psychology— no matter the amount of scientific iconography employed—is always engaged in making presumptions of philosophical cast about human nature.[92] Furthermore, these presumptions, or beliefs, come to be embedded in the methodological paradigms and interpretations thereof that comprise the empirical study of the mind.

Conclusion: Psychology as Local Knowledge Practices

Despite the purported objectivity of its methods and tools, psychology is a continuation, a corollary, of the society from which it arises. Whether labeling degeneracy or creating notions of liberation, psychology is always in use as an adjunct to prevailing cultural projects. There is thus a fundamental link between psychology, on the one hand, and anthropology and history, on the other. The study of the mind in a given location and time period is also necessarily a study of the cultural and historical conditions of that locale.[93] Despite its pretensions to objectivity and aspirations to be modeled on the physical sciences, empirical psychology is necessarily a historical science.[94]

If psychology refers to the ways we conceptualize thought and consciousness, then each culture uses the term "psychology" to define their particular fashion of tending to the unknown using the available symbols and practices that minister to prevailing needs concerning the mind. Psychology may be best conceived of as the practice of tending to the unknown embedded in each of us.[95] Psychology has thus come to accompany religion, metaphysics, and philosophy as a language to articulate our need for sense and purpose. The symbols it uses to this end are drawn from the given culture's metaphysical well and broader social, political, and cultural projects. These considerations outline the cultural epistemic constraints upon the use of psychology as a natural science.

This foray into the uses of psychology in diverse temporal and national contexts, which is continued in Chapter 5, illustrates that psychology may not be the kind of science that can accrue cumulative facts. Instead, it might be best to think of the discipline as a set of local knowledge practices formulated according to the exigencies and values of the given community. Observation is determined by the ways we measure, by our interests and purposes.[96] Launched at the same time as empirical psychology, the project of anthropology provides an informative contrast as it seeks to understand the practices of the Other, the unknown. In the West, the background metaphysical assumptions entail a particular Judeo-Christian post-Enlightenment individualism wherein the scientific method is the most reliable path to truth. The intellectual setting for the central role science plays in contemporary Western thought is derived from an atomistic conception of nature, rationalism, *laïcité*, and individualism.[97] This then forms the basis for considering other local knowledge practices. An interdisciplinary multilevel psychology which includes anthropological and historical methods may be capable of helping psychologists take into account how metaphysical background informs methodology.

The rate of change of metaphysical ontologies about the mind seems to entail psychology is not a cumulative discipline. In this way, psychology would utterly fail one basic qualification of being a science. And yet the modes of reflection; the form of the social rituals; the eagerness, enthusiasm, and effort; the striving; and the finally the efficacy of relief and data generation all remain pragmatically useful. No matter the country or era, we think, believe, and act upon beliefs codified in our local knowledge practices of psychology in similar ways. Understanding that psychological practices are value-laden may confer clarify on their scope and uses.[98] Admitting our intellectual finitude as such can set us free from the burdens of understanding.[99]

After the first 150 years of *positivist* and *pragmatist* empirical psychology, nomothetic generalizations are few and far between. Thus, in the latter part of the 20th and early 21st century, a new generation adopted complex interdisciplinary methods which included sophisticated statistical tools and brain imaging technologies to seek insight into the mind as a multilevel set of *mechanisms*. This current state of empirical psychology will be presented in Chapter 3. In the next chapter, I explore the analogical tools of explanation in psychology.

2

Metaphor in Empirical Psychology

What sort of a science is it whose principal discovery is that the subject of which it treats does not exist?
—Émile Durkheim, *The Elementary Forms of the Religious Life, a Study in Religious Sociology* (1915), p. 88

Introduction

In its early years, empirical psychology relied mainly on hypothetico-deductive explanation and methodology for the justification of its claims. Yet other tools such as imagination and analysis are also required to integrate and understand empirical data, especially in the context of discovery. In this chapter, I explore how analogical modes of explanation loop between experimental results and descriptive explanation. Metaphor, in particular, has been used to transcend the limitations of methodologism because it is capable of framing the purpose, constraints, and goals of experimentation.

The connections that successful metaphor use draws among analogical domains engender discovery, hypothesis formation, and novel interpretation of data. Choosing among theories can often be a matter of selecting the more or less fruitful metaphor.[1] Practically speaking, root metaphors generate research by serving as a starting point, limiting factor, anchor, and conduit for creative intellectual exploration. One of the generative functions of metaphor is providing a connection between a hunch, or preanalytic detection of similarity, a feeling of immanent connection, and a new theory.[2] "It is pictures rather than propositions, metaphors rather than statements that determine most of our philosophical convictions."[3] Of course, metaphors are also the heuristic frameworks that ease communication between scientists and the public.[4] Their use in contemporary psychology enables interactive coupling among model, theory, and observation toward data interpretation and communication.

A Suspicious Science. Rami Gabriel, Oxford University Press. © Oxford University Press 2023.
DOI: 10.1093/oso/9780197513583.003.0003

METAPHOR IN EMPIRICAL PSYCHOLOGY   29

By serving as a bridge between the abstract and the concrete, metaphors provide a sense of scope and emphasis.[5] Since models posit partial and imperfect fit to natural phenomena, the adoption of a given model for a particular field of data is determined by pragmatic benefits.[6] Those benefits include enabling explanation through broadening the associational field, engendering creative abduction, and providing direction for empirical study. One pragmatic element of successful metaphor use is the opportunity to spin off a theoretical model which allows the scientist to refer to phenomena not fully determined by empirical conditions.[7] The abstract nature of analogy is thus a reliable epistemic strategy to handle hidden or unknown entities, as discussed later.

The pursuit of hypothetico-deductive principles and mechanistic explanation in empirical psychology requires analogical thinking to creatively, analytically conceive of the nature of the mind. Metaphors are the pragmatic theoretical unifiers of data as well as conceptual laboratories for developing schemes by which researchers design (i.e., discover) and interpret (i.e., justify) their research. Analogical thought creates order and necessity (or immanent connection) through two principles of association: resemblance and contiguity. There is a sense of satisfaction that arises from the familiarity of building results into a pre-existing structure. Analogical frames are an intrinsic aspect of the metaphysical background into which we are acculturated. The satisfying feeling inspired by achieving order or understanding is thus mediated by salience generated by the sense of control and comfort of enacting a familiar imaginary order.

This chapter provides an assessment of contemporary metaphors of mind as pragmatic paradigms for empirical exploration. The various metaphors currently in use draw from biology and engineering and thus have diverging epistemological consequences for the nature of explanation in psychology.

What Is and What Is Not a Metaphor

Metaphor entails a structural correspondence whereby a comparison of terms that have their own associational fields enriches the semantic field of the phenomenon in question.[8,9] For example, the topic of memory has often been portrayed in the vehicle of a container. The associational semantic field of container allows for the entailments of space and storage in folk notions; that is, "I can't remember, but it is somewhere in there," "I had

30 A SUSPICIOUS SCIENCE

it, but now it's lost." A successful metaphor reverberates through the network of entailments, thus serving as a stimulating guide to disambiguate new discoveries.[10]

When a metaphor is molded into a framework or a model to provide structure for analytical descriptions and entailments, conceptual change in theory construction becomes possible.[11] The elaboration of the generative impetus of metaphor use leads to theory-constitutive practices such as the proposal of models.[12] For example, creating a structural correspondence between memory and space/container coincides with the cognitive science notion of memory banks for short-term memory, working memory, long-term memory, and procedural memories.[13] Through creative abduction, metaphor as model fits the phenomena under investigation into a pattern that generates ampliative inferences. For example, one can ask about localization of the different memory banks in the brain, or about how they relate to each other; researchers have studied how a memory "moves" from short-term loops to long-term "storage," or how during the process of learning a skill becomes stored in procedural memory.[14] Conceptual change enabled thereby includes the collapse of a part of a kind-hierarchy; branch jumping leads to broad recategorization and hierarchical tree redefinition.[15] For example, when memory theorists distinguish between declarative and nondeclarative memories, the latter serve as a way to recategorize learning motor routines as forms of memory under a new hierarchical tree of "procedural memory".[16]

As a model, metaphor enables the identification of relationships among interconnected elements in a system.[17] A model consists of the coupling of one organization of data with another mode of organization.[18] In empirical psychology, these systems usually create equivalences between functional networks of the brain and some schematic model or content, as in descriptions of "remembering" as activations of the associational cortex, or the hippocampus as the site of memory consolidation.[19] Metaphors as models provide a simple frame by which one may ask and interpret how and why a system behaves across a range of settings; thus, it offers predictive accounts for behavior through an exposition of structural elements.[20]

To change metaphors entails, then, a shift in templates, such as looking at the phenomena differently, reordering relationships, comparing events, and discarding or imagining further epistemic manipulations.[21] Sometimes the metaphor provides a new set of theoretical terms and images that is not present in the data itself; in this case of catechresis, it fills a lexical gap and serves an epistemic role in reframing and even creating a way to view the phenomena.[22] In contrast, new terms are often coined to denote heretofore unknown phenomena in physics. The general practice there is to employ nonsense terms that do not have other connotations so as to avoid analogical interpretation.

Some theories are inaccurately described as metaphors; for instance, this occurs when dualistic language is used to describe the mind.[23] While analogical reasoning and figurative description are widespread in the sciences, it is important to grasp what is not metaphor, namely literal description. One example is nonreductionist mechanistic explanation in which we delineate parts and their functioning, for example in manuals of operation or blueprints of human-made machines.[24] Another is the theoretical entities used in behaviorism.[25] With the rise of empirical tools such as neuroimaging and microscopy, it is worth considering whether a literal description of the brain and body is possible and how that would affect the pragmatic use of metaphor in empirical psychology.

In the first section, I explore how philosophical pragmatism motivates theory-constitutive metaphor use. In the second section, I offer a brief illustrative history of metaphors of mind, followed by an exploration of prevalent metaphors in contemporary theory. Section III focuses on metaphors in contemporary psychology, and the concluding sections contrast modes of explanation toward asserting an interdisciplinary psychology.

Metaphors as Useful Fictions

Analogical explanation in scientific thought is continuous with the role that metaphor plays in everyday practical thought wherein we create "as if" scenarios to navigate the world.[26] Metaphors of mind are similarly fictions in search of practical corroboration; we justify an assumption by seeing what comes of it.[27] Kwame Anthony Appiah summarizes Hans Vaihinger: "very often we can reasonably proceed as if what we know to be false is true because it is useful for some purpose to do so."[28] Vaihinger's "as if" philosophy is of a piece with C. S. Pierce's notion that belief in a useful fiction is a habit that enables action; that is, beliefs about the world provide a frame for our actions.[29]

In line with this pragmatic relation between belief and useful fiction, we can state that the broad practical purpose of metaphor is to aid us in moving appropriately through practical or theoretical navigation of the world. In this context, truth simply refers to efficacy: the quality of ideas that allows them to be assimilated, validated, corroborated, and verified.[30] If it leads to successful wayfinding, a description is an effective explanation. Pragmatism is an epistemology of wayfinding; the construction of models based on metaphors is a self-conscious extension of the cognitive capacity to map our environment.[31] Indeed, metaphors do not need to be veridical to lead to interesting or empirically fruitful findings; their usefulness is in creating space for rational and empirical exploration.

The pragmatic function of metaphor in empirical psychology, then, may be to help settle intransigent empirical or rational disputes through tracing practical consequences. A metaphor that is pragmatically true will lead to a model that points researchers in an empirically worthwhile direction. For William James, what a scientist seeks in philosophy is intellectual abstraction that maintains a positive connection to the world. Accordingly, one purpose of empirical psychology is to achieve an understanding of human behavior that enables, among other things, predictions about future behavior and reliable frameworks to understand intentional thought.[32] Metaphor use in empiricism is a process of showing similarities and dissimilarities in phenomena, and bringing into relief the theorist's assumptions therein.[33]

Metaphor can determine ontology insofar as it offers a fundamental redescription that frames our dispositions toward a hidden entity. Indeed, metaphor partially creates what it purports to reveal because it structures how we see what we don't know.[34] Analogy is a practical strategy of disambiguation to conceive of unknown domains. We use analogy in situations when we are confused; for example, when learning a new language, we make analogies with languages and gestures or sounds that we understand. Thus, metaphors of mind occupy a unique position between evidence and trust; we collect enough evidence through an analogical structure that we grow to trust it as a guide for prediction and frame the collection of further evidence.[35] A given metaphor is not necessarily present in the observed phenomenon; it is rather a tool of analysis trusted insofar as it generates insight. Subsequently, some metaphors acquire the trust of the scientific and lay community. It enables direction and structure, while at the same time not necessarily being empirically demonstrable. For example, portrayal of the connectivity of the brain in a connectome is a way of understanding its complexity through the analogy of binding.[36]

Metaphors that reify unreal properties or that focus on artifactual phenomena or relations are not pragmatic; they do not aid empirical wayfinding. For example, to say that the mind is like a radio, that consciousness is being beamed in our heads, while falsifiable, has so far not proven a useful avenue of research. Adopting metaphors in inappropriate circumstances runs the risk of occluding of elements of the phenomena and disregarding properties that are inconsistent with the metaphor.[37] The computer metaphor adopted in cognitive science, for example, occluded the importance of the body.[38]

Presently, no single metaphor of mind can serve a theory-constitutive function; the last 150 years of empirical psychology presents us with a diffusion of data generated by competing laboratories each seeking their own reliable metaphors to interpret evidence.[39]

A Brief History of Metaphors of Mind

The essential function of metaphor in a pragmatic approach to theory construction in empirical psychology is to help us say what we mean in a way in which the partiality of our understanding becomes illuminated.[40] We conceptualize what is unclear in terms of what is more clearly structured.[41] The function of metaphor is thus not only reorganizing our conceptions but also expressing commonly held but imperfectly articulated feelings so as to encourage reflection upon substitution, comparison, and interaction among associational fields.[42] This familiarity comes to feels salient and thus affords curiousity and exploration.[43]

In some cases, metaphor may serve to convey a sense of complexity without specifying precise mappings or relations between the topic and vehicle domain.[44] Cashing out complexity is an important function of the explanatory metaphor; it should clarify the phenomenon without necessarily reducing it. This complexity must then be worked out through empirical research framed by the questions suggested by imposing the model upon the phenomenon.

Psychological theory in the 18th century devolved on metaphors of mind-as-entity characterized by the qualities of tangibility and passivity, with a simplicity of structure.[45] For example, John Locke's simple, tangible, and passive tabula rasa had the quality of being impressible.[46] The frame of mind-as-entity enabled thinkers to activate the entailments of associated ideas from physics, biology, and geology. During the early 19th century, intellectuals

34 A SUSPICIOUS SCIENCE

added a concern to preserve spirituality and the power of the will through moral psychology, for example with the metaphor of "mental hygiene" popularized in Isaac Ray's book from 1863.[47]

In the late 19th century, there was a shift to an emphasis on mind-as-living being wherein "mindscapes," "sentient webs," and other generative metaphors for mind-as-substance predominated. For example, John Stuart Mill made the analogy of mental chemistry and mental mechanics so as to disambiguate how simple principles like reflex arc and laws of association could lead to complex mental phenomena.[48] Victorian physiologists sought to avoid the mind-body problem by naturalizing the mind while not losing the spiritual thread, portraying mind as an entity that "receive(s) nerve-force and generates mind-force."[49] Nerve ganglia at this time are interpreted as an analogy for "sentient webs" which exert immaterial principles.[50] The metaphor of the "mindscape" can be seen here as a way to spatialize mind while still allowing for the dynamics of Descartes's *res cogitans*. For thinkers like Alexander Bain, this allowed one to reject the passive receptacle theory of the British empiricists and appropriate nascent physiological accounts of biological activity.[51]

In the early part of the 20th century, animate and spatial metaphors dominated, while in the latter half of the century systems metaphors were in ascendance.[52] Other dominant metaphors of mind include the "sensorium" or "presence room," and the aforementioned blank slate of the British empiricists which forms the basis for later behaviorist and associationist traditions, as well as the universal Turing machine of the artificial intelligence and cognitive science communities.[53]

In the 20th century, the dominant paradigms in empirical psychology were behaviorism and cognitive science. Each approach describes a different domain of mental function.[54] Behaviorism sought a literal language that eschewed intentionality and metaphor to describe the mind, and it remains at the core of animal neurosciences as a flexible and reliable system for training and manipulating stimuli and responses.[55] Cognitive science and its computational metaphor, on the other hand, systematized mind into units such as "modules" as information processing units, especially in the parallel distributed processing models of connectionism.[56] And yet these metaphors failed to sufficiently address global elements of mind such as affect and subjectivity.[57]

A crucial question is whether shifts in metaphors reflect cultural context or advances in scientific naturalism. Psychologist Kurt Danziger (b. 1926) claims the reciprocal confirmation of symbolic structures at different levels of discourse implies a type of hall of mirrors wherein the root metaphor of an era is formed from a taken-for-granted collective representation.[58] The sociocultural embeddedness of psychological theory is apparent, for example, in shifts in our portrayals of memory.[59] Such shifts among passive, platonic, and cognitive dynamics in the representation of memory dramatize how theories reflect culture and objects encountered when searching for images to conceive of hidden processes of the mind.[60] Consider that the spatialization of the mind in the 18th and early 19th centuries into the brain indicated a step away from Cartesian dualism such that mental life was secularized for the purposes of scientific investigation so as to localize cause and effect in a physical unit. Systems metaphors, like "switchboards" or "sentient webs," then arose as a way of creating sets of spatialized mental units that enabled the imputation of relations therein, and thus more elaborate landscapes of cause-and-effect networks. This approach was amenable to a computational metaphor that instantiated relations of cause and effect units into distributed networks of digital logic gates. These units could be investigated through modeling, as well as serve to explain cognitive dissociations reported in the burgeoning neurosciences. The computer metaphor has been particularly powerful because it links meaningful aspects of mind to meaningless physical processes.[61] One interpretation of why metaphors wax and wane in popularity is that the field at a given time may simply be designating the most complex objects known as the metaphor of mind, adopting, for example, in the early 20th century the "photograph" for our spatial imagistic metaphors and the "switchboard" as a metaphor for neural function.[62]

Metaphors currently used in empirical psychology are demonstrable hybrids built upon the negative evolution of the metaphors highlighted above. We turn now to metaphors of mind that integrate elements of associationist, behaviorist, and computational models.

Contemporary Metaphors Drawn From Biology and Engineering

Metaphors condition scientists' decisions to explore, verify, and corroborate; essentially, they frame the manner in which individuals collate data drawn from disparate research laboratories.[63] In the last two decades, an international community of empirical psychologists has focused on a particular

36 A SUSPICIOUS SCIENCE

set of fruitful models; I discuss this period in the next chapter.[64] In this section I focus on the major metaphors in contemporary experimental psychology and the models which employ them. With an eye to their pragmatic consequences, I describe the interaction between associational fields that each metaphor allows, and the novel discoveries made possible by these forms of selective conceptual perception.

The tenor of mind in contemporary experimental psychology draws upon two major vehicles, biology and engineering. Both are modes of scientific naturalism, and it is largely through them that contemporary psychology employs epistemology adapted from the natural sciences. By employing them, the following associational fields are thus brought to bear on the study of mind: evolution, developmental processes, emergence, the body, and machine learning. Through structural correspondence, concepts from these vehicles render the tenor of mind more tractable to mechanistic exhibition.

The unifying theories of biology are cell theory, evolution theory, genes, and homeostasis.[65] Placing psychology in correspondence with biology allows the entailment of principles like probability, ecology, and a broader range of spatial and temporal scales. This naturalist ontology allows for more sophisticated consideration of the transformations between genotype and phenotype, or innate systems and their developmental trajectory, for example the epigenetics of how environment modifies gene expression.[66] Furthermore, the relation between environment and DNA serves as an associational field for how developmental pathways emerge from an organism's interactive lifeway.[67] Such formulations open up further questions concerning the evolution of development and consideration of the functional telos of mind in an evolutionary context.[68]

The key principles of engineering are testability, maintenance, integrity, external integration, ethics, and management.[69] Taking such a design stance allows psychologists to consider the adaptive functions of mind, creative solutions to problems faced by the organism, and the modes in which these solutions can be implemented. For example, evolutionary psychology employs the method of "reverse-engineering" our behaviors to discover their function in the environment of evolutionary adaptednesss.[70] Other integral ideas include assessment of structure, strength, and cost which take into account stress and strain upon materials. Compression of lability as an effect of environmental feedback demonstrated in the limits of materials has come to serve as a crucial associative principle for neural dynamics.[71] For example, some researchers emphasize how attention is a limited resource that depends upon an organism's motivation and the cognitive load it is under.[72]

Contemporary models illustrate how these metaphors serve pragmatic ends in theoretical and empirical work. The affective sciences characterize mind as evolutionarily nested rational and passional functional neural layers—for example, the hot/cold cognition model, affective neuroscience, and basic emotions theories. By using the vehicle of evolution, affective sciences enlist the epistemological context of biology rather than the formalisms of computationalism.[73] These models trade on the complex relationship between categories of faculty psychology, namely, emotional versus cognitive forces, to argue that the mind is best understood as an integral part of an organism engaged in navigating the world through both innate and learned motivational urges. The affective sciences employ the associational fields of neurochemistry and evolution. Through these interactions it postulates a language of drives, competition, feedback loops, inhibition, and homeostasis. Like other fields that employ the developmental metaphor of evolution, an emphasis is placed on fitting the human mind into the same category as other natural phenomena, including animal minds. All the tools of evolutionary biology, such as identifying homologies, thus become available. Sophisticated concepts from neuroscience concerning areas largely ignored by cognitive neuroscience since they cannot be imaged (e.g., the brain stem), including the volumetric nature of neurotransmission, serve to enrich our understanding of the mind.[74] Bringing evolution to bear on the mind—as in the model of evolutionary psychology and the affective sciences—makes available the associational fields of developmental processes and findings from ethology and evolutionary biology.[75] It also provides a language with which researchers may construe the mind as a part of nature.[76]

While early cognitive neuroscience conducted a quasi-phrenological search for centers (i.e., the memory center, the language center, etc.), contemporary neuroscience emphasizes the distributed nature of networks for storage and action.[77] These metaphors of connectedness and complexity dovetail with engineering metaphors being brought to bear on systems neuroscience.[78]

Embodied, embedded, extended, and enactive (or, 4E) models emerged as a critique of passive, mentalist, representational models and sought to portray mind as emerging through a relationship between body and world. This approach, which includes ecological psychology and some forms of locomotive machine learning, characterizes mind as a spatialized physical system and thus emphasizes real-time active integration of perceptual and motor processes.[79] 4E models reconceptualize mind rhetorically and functionally as a brain-body unit moving through an environment composed of artifacts of mind.[80] This approach emphasizes a biological metaphor of systems that includes the holistic integration between the organism and its environment.[81] These approaches to cognition offer a biologically situated return to the spatialized, physical metaphors of the 19th century. The emphasis on the body as a system relating to its ecological niche seeks to put flesh back on the bones of the rarefied computer metaphors of the cognitive sciences. It also purports to avoid dualism by adopting a neutral monist language to describe the organism in its environment. This anti-representationalism draws from the vehicle of images rather than that of propositions. For example, ecological psychologists describe how we adjudge moving objects based on optic flow on the retina rather than resorting to internal representations of movement in the brain.[82]

Models that emphasize dynamic mechanics in neural systems hearken back to the metaphor of mind as machine, portraying the brain as a sophisticated set of mechanisms that produce determinate regularities.[83] Contemporary dynamic and heuristic models of mind, through associational fields in engineering, emphasize constraints upon computation. Some theorists emphasize the role of temporal and nonlinear factors, while others dwell upon the active, autonomous, and adaptive qualities of biological mind, or the limited resource capacities of neural systems as energy resources.[84] Likewise, bounded rationality is founded on the notion that mind is a logical machine under time and resource constraints that requires adaptive heuristic shortcuts, including predictive and Bayesian processing.[85] Refinements of these models continue: Recently the coding metaphor of neural communication and storage has been criticized as not taking into account the causal structure of the brain and the informational requirements of cognition.[86]

Dynamic mechanics and bounded rationality models locate weaknesses in previous computational metaphors and instead offer concepts drawn from engineering and information theory. In bounded rationality, the optimal logic of computers is contrasted with human rationality to reveal that heuristic mechanisms such as imitation, tallying, and tit-for-tat are necessary to account for human capacities.[87] These models seek the qualifications of ecological validity and parsimony as a reaction against the overly theoretical nature of strong artificial intelligence. Bounded rationality seeks to avoid the Panglossian adaptationism of evolutionary psychology and optimal observer models used in psychophysics by taking into account the limitations of biological minds relative to computer models. This anchors analysis of mind in the design project of engineering. Dynamic mechanics similarly adds the variables of time and energetics as a reaction to the insufficient formulation of temporal dynamics in cognitive modeling. The notion of limits and constraints in materials is drawn from the associational fields of engineering and machine learning. For example, toward broader explanations of the organization of learning, dead reckoning in insects can be described through the variables of time, gravity, and basic sensation.[88]

The metaphors and the respective models discussed above have been fruitful in generating empirical programs, and they are each plausible in a naturalist ontology that seeks a systematic understanding of mind. Many of the models which draw from these predominant metaphors can be related to each other. For example, by virtue of rejecting a disembodied and passive notion of mind, 4E may be melded to a dynamic or affective approach.[89] Eventually, models that employ biological metaphors (e.g., affective sciences, enactivism) could converge. The mechanistic nature of the dynamic model is easily applied to biological entities.[90] These examples illustrate that metaphor use is essential for promoting interdisciplinarity in empirical psychology. Metaphors which draw together disparate domains are thus pragmatic testing grounds for further interdisciplinary collaboration and implementation.

A Pragmatic Assessment of Contemporary Metaphors

A pragmatic approach must suggest empirically limited phenomena, propose a set of verifiable causal units, and make possible new, useful knowledge. When the metaphor is suitable to the explanatory task, meaningful empirical work is generated. Inappropriate metaphors endanger the feasibility of studying the mind by reifying illusory concepts or limiting the horizons of explanation.[91]

A researcher's decision between models and their metaphors will depend upon whether the metaphor achieves precision, plausibility, and a set of interesting and powerful consequences for a systematic understanding of the explanandum.[92] When alternative theories are equally compatible, humans tend to choose a theory based on temperament, or extra-logical considerations like elegance, or economy.[93]

The method by which the precision of each metaphor will be tested empirically varies.[94] Dynamic neural models employ the methodological tool of decomposition into structural and functional aspects, as well as complex computational modeling, whereas 4E models complicate the constitution of mind by emphasizing body-world loops that are constitutive of knowledge and information transfer.[95] We must choose the appropriate metaphor for the phenomena at hand by explicitly weighing the experimental and pragmatic consequences of our choice. When it no longer generates insight, a metaphor has expired as a pragmatic tool.

The rise of biology and engineering metaphors is a consequence of great theoretical advances in the 20th and early 21st centuries in genetics, cell theory, evolution, and material sciences. This knowledge was almost instantly applied to the technology that shapes the sociocultural landscape we inhabit. The modern pipeline between public and private research laboratories in the natural sciences and applied fabrication in the private sector has been effective. In response, psychologists who were previously considered natural philosophers have in the 20th century gone to great lengths to be considered as behavioral scientists engaged in perceptual sciences.[96] Adopting metaphors and methods from biology and engineering is a perpetuation of these efforts. Engineering continues the mechanistic metaphor of matter to which psychology adhered in its behaviorist and cognitive science paradigms.[97] Contemporary empirical psychology has developed sophisticated tools beyond reaction time and rudimentary psychophysics to image the brain, while reverse-engineering the brain demystifies some of our behaviors and allows for effective therapeutic measures in cognitive-behavioral therapy.

We may also enquire into the drawbacks of employing these descriptive and functional metaphors. Whereas discursive approaches to the mind like humanism and psychoanalysis allowed for agentic discourse, descriptive metaphors like biology and engineering tend to emphasize the mechanistic aspects of the mind and reduce experience to physical causes.[98] When a metaphor is discursive, the actor maintains agency; he can exercise control or self-regulation—even if it is only rhetorical—over the mind. However, a mechanistic metaphor as a description of mental processes generally does not leave space for the agentic control of the phenomenological subject.[99] Discursive models allow for the efficacy of introspection; this is because the conscious act of introspection is a linguistic dialogical process which, as in symbolic interactionism, contributes to the process of self-making.[100] By way of illustration, Sigmund Freud's hydraulic metaphor of unconscious energy served as a way to engage in discursive analysis regarding the power of repressed memories upon our behaviors, whereas his later topographic model was a descriptive mechanical spatial metaphor of how memories interact with each other vis-à-vis their position in a mental space.[101]

We can expect that descriptive explanation will tend to reductionism, most likely as formal mechanistic models. Discursive explanation of the human mind, on the other hand, situates it in the broader context of history and culture. 4E models seek an integrative ecologically valid description of perceptual and motor processes that is ultimately to be couched in biological terms of the organism in its environmental niche. Dynamic systems models are descriptive levels of function and structure supporting emergent formal causes modeled as control variables ultimately couched in mechanistic engineering metaphors.[102] There may be ways to locate agency or human values in this frame, since mechanistic explanation leaves room for higher-level theories.[103]

We can expect bounded rationality models to describe the building blocks of practical reason as satisficing information-processing algorithms, as seen in the implementation of "nudge" infrastructures in economic situations.[104] The descriptive, computational metaphor of bounded rationality suggests we are endowed with an adaptive toolbox that frames the world in domain-specific heuristics that guide searches, stop searches, and make decisions.[105] These nonoptimal heuristics are matched to particular environments; they demonstrate the boundedness of rationality to its environmental niche and capacity limitations, including time, and computationally cheap, fast, frugal resources.[106] This metaphor leans on a notion of mind as imperfect adaptive mechanism, which allows us to draw from the language of process, optimality, and other terms from engineering.[107] While there is room for a consideration of social heuristics in moral behavior, the framing of behavior in the field as evolutionarily adapted traits conflicts with our agentic notions of self-mastery and the possibility of self-betterment and efficiency through willful transformation of character.[108]

Models derived from biological metaphors always connect the mind to other phenomenon in nature. From such models we can expect a naturalist epistemology wherein the mind is understood as a material phenomenon, similar to the mind-as-entity metaphor of the Victorian physiologists but with far more detail and less emphasis on spiritual aspects. As an example of a biological metaphor, neo-Darwinism and evolutionary psychology use the model of adaptation to theorize the function and structural origin of cognition. Early versions of this approach, like Freud's drive theory and the selfish gene theory, had the consequence of denying the dignity of the human insofar as agency was portrayed as being in the service of impersonal biological drives.[109]

Adopting a discursive or descriptive approach to the mind has pragmatic consequences for an individual's sense of meaning and for ethical considerations.[110] Indeed, the way we experience and act in the world can be structured by the metaphors we adopt; for example, one's conception of social hierarchy, of top-down or bottom-up economic forces, has immediate social and political utility.[111] Cognitive science has been critiqued as being too individualistic, as focusing all its explanations on the mental processes of the individual; in doing so, it fails to take into account discursive cultural factors that convey the complexity of lived experience and social symbols.[112] Taking these macroscopic cultural factors into account requires the discursive exercise, common in the human sciences, history, and humanities, of considering how ideas, institutions, and social encounters sculpt the mind. Metaphors drawn from anthropology concerning the dialectical loop between the social and the individual are available and may come to be employed more in a future interdisciplinary multilevel psychology.

While it is primarily the responsibility of psychology to cultivate its discursive practices, already thriving in clinical practice as well as in sectors of social and personality psychology, the humanities must maintain their ability to protect difference by continuing to communicate through a diverse international pool of topics and scholars. To maintain discursive and agentic situatedness, the reflexivity of the human sciences must be brought to bear on an interdisciplinary multilevel psychology. Even though the neuro-disciplines will lose some veneer of being wholly "scientific," it is worthwhile for psychology to cultivate knowledge of other disciplines toward generating more common ground for discussion, mutual learning, and possibilities for investigation. As it stands, neuro-disciplinarians hold a coveted position; they take the biological and engineering metaphors to mean that they are tracing the biology of human nature, and that with the help of computer scientists/engineers they are able to develop technologies for the sake of efficiency and eventually to create intelligent life. In fact, their adherence to such hopes indicates a lack of contextual understanding of the history of human sciences and moreover an impoverished notion of the "human."[113]

The role of humanist discursive models of mind in relation to biology and engineering metaphors in psychology is thus to enable consideration of broader contextual stories. To take one example, Barbara Maria Stafford's work suggests that a path to understanding consciousness is available to us in the concept of analogy, specifically that the entire history of art is a way of "taking us back up the Darwinian ladder of evolution to the associative origins of human thought, analogy offers a nonalgorithmic technique for building our perception system to our cognitive system."[114] Understanding how analogy is used in the visual arts is thus a way of grasping how "analogical thinking about thinking yields a more complex psychological picture."[115] Such an approach examines, for example, how comprehension is an active, imaginative form of grasping sense data via making connections, just like in the shadow boxes of Joseph Cornell, or cabinets of curiosities that allow our associative faculties to generate bonds between the inside world of thought and the outside world of objects. This nonreductionist approach creates space for phenomenology and the creative labor of perceiving and thinking about the world in symbols. This metaphorical frame of thought as analogical process is pragmatic as a generator of discourse concerning the relation among the arts, imagination, and analogical thinking; it provides a lens through which the history of art objects is simultaneously a discourse on visual thought.[116] This model could easily inform empirical work on visual pattern recognition and the nature of the imagination. Stafford's work cannot be used to make predictions, but it does offer an example of a rich interpretative context in the humanities through which researchers can identify relationships between abstract principles of analogy and concrete examples of historical art objects.

In considering further how we portray knowledge, whether in a set of formulas, or schematics, a flowchart of mechanical models, or a well-illustrated academic monograph, we can see that the communication of findings is aided by metaphors that are legible and easily displayed. In addition to the traditional purpose of models to enable balance, symmetry, and order, the syntax of a new language of visual models allows insight into interconnectedness, multiplicity, and the decentered nature of contemporary scientific inquiry.[117]

During the early period of empirical psychology, researchers sought positivist (i.e., nomological) and pragmatist models of explanation. In this chapter, I have argued that these models have been collected into or shaped around metaphors that structure inquiry and unite findings from disparate

44 A SUSPICIOUS SCIENCE

research programs. At this point, I consider the kind of explanation that metaphor delivers. Pragmatic assessment of metaphors of mind determines whether these useful fictions adhere to the broader goals of the human sciences.

Descriptive Versus Discursive Explanation

Consideration of the role of metaphor in scientific practice requires engagement with ontological and epistemological issues that are at the marrow of our desire to capture the world in thought. At base, metaphor provides a communicable order of things. Metaphors can be descriptive or explanatory, illustrative or constitutive, informative or evaluative, revealing or masking, and enriching or deforming.[118] Along with mythology and language, metaphor is a type of analogical thinking.[119] If empirical psychology requires the use of metaphor to schematize reality, then as a system of knowledge, psychology may bear deep similarities with mythology. I discuss this further in the interlude.

In this section, metaphors of mind are assessed in regards to their metaphysical consequences. The transcendental realist position is that metaphors explain regularities and dispositional attributes at various levels of macroscopic and microscopic order that are beyond empirical experience.[120] The revelation of hidden structural elements in nature then allows an extension of the reach of scientific understanding. In the service of grasping aspects of the natural world that exist but are beyond our empirical ken, metaphor reorders the semantic field by generating new intensional contents.[121]

This is generally a boon for gaining a theoretical understanding of nature, but it could blinker our view of the phenomenon by focusing our attention on one aspect rather than another. For example, classifying phenomena via a tree metaphor orders evidence very differently than the family resemblance model, thus obscuring the subtleties of the latter frame.[122] Metaphors can be abused when this tool for tentative description becomes a tool of presumptuous prescription.[123] By shifting how we individuate the elements of nature that we believe we are studying, metaphor use can lead to unwarranted reification and confusion about the structure and delineation of natural kinds.[124] For example, the rise of brain imaging technologies transformed our notions of causation, reifying the esoteric techniques and the interpretative palette of localization.[125]

METAPHOR IN EMPIRICAL PSYCHOLOGY   45

Our choice of models is thus important pragmatically, epistemologically, and ontologically for the experimental programs we pursue. Thus, it is notable that the negative evolution of knowledge practices demonstrates how we pivot between models and paradigms relative to social and cultural context.[126] The paradigm shift to the cognitive sciences in the late 20th century, for example, reflected changes in the accepted foundations of mind from associationist network to computer, areas of interest from reward learning to linguistics and visual search, and modes of investigation from reinforcement schedules to modeling thought as an algorithm. At each step, we are in danger of reifying theoretical or methodological entities by overextending the metaphor because paradigms based on metaphors function as "theory plus" additional methodology, instruments, and metaphysical suppositions.[127] For example, the cognitive revolution was a theory that the mind functions like a computer plus the methodology of modeling, instruments for tracking reaction time, eye gaze, and so on, and the metaphysical assumption of scientific naturalism.

Alternatively, a paradigm may just be an exemplary solution to an earlier problem faced in the field, in which case the truth of a paradigm is its pragmatic success as a verificationist, or empirically adequate, process for investigating an earlier problematic.[128] This approach reflects a strong pragmatism wherein we are no longer connecting scientific endeavor toward the philosophical notion of truth as correspondence with reality, but rather binding experimentation to our tools, models, and metaphorical frames.[129] In which case, methodologism may continue to plague the loftier aspirations of empirical psychology.

The method by which we investigate a given phenomenon, be it via recording eye movement or measuring estrogen levels, is motivated by the ontological frame of the underlying causal story of the behavior. A given scientific theory is a family of models ranging from small-scale to macroscopic causal stories. Shifts in scientific terminology indicate increasing specificity while also reflecting a greater sense of authority for certain schools within the intellectual community. The metaphor in ascent at any given time devours the research resources in the field.[130] Each generation of scientists receives an education within a given set of metaphorical frames that have a buzz in that era, and to a large extent this determines what these individuals find worth studying. The success of a generation of scientists depends upon securing useful, illustrative, informative, revealing verifiable metaphorical frames for empirical work, and then demonstrating how the adopted metaphor enables

46 A SUSPICIOUS SCIENCE

progress in picking out ontologically real and verifiable elements of the mind. In this way, methodology is the practical instantiation of the link between pragmatism and metaphor.

While scientific knowledge is relevant to our medical and biological investigations of the natural world, as a human science, psychology additionally bears upon ethical and existential questions and thus must take into account notions of responsibility and meaning. If psychology is the study of human nature, then what kind of explanatory model of ourselves do we need? What makes a particular metaphor more apt is how aesthetic, moral, practical, and intellectual rationality is brought to bear on the truthfulness of a metaphor.[131] To bring in a Nietzschean consideration: we tend to conceive of the nature of mind and reality according to what we want the truth to be. Beliefs, like which metaphorical frame seems the most reasonable to adopt are dictated by affective needs and reactions because there is a human weakness to letting belief ride on "lively conception" and "instinctive liking."[132] Ultimately, the most pragmatic approach to metaphors as forms of explanation is that we need an understanding of the world sufficient to our needs.[133] To understand this motivation to explain, I discuss of metaphors of mind in popular culture and the ethical function of explanation.

In its pragmatic aspect, scientific explanation refers to evidence unto facts in the form of cause-and-effect processes, classification systems, laws, data, observations of empirical tests, and so on. That is, a model explains by pointing to concatenated evidence in the service of systematic understanding. This accumulated image of the phenomena can thereafter be harnessed toward technological innovation or simply more veridical ways of perceiving the world. The purpose of explanation in the sciences is thus discovering facts and subsequently elaborating upon this evidence through technology like machines, and pharmaceutical drugs, toward making life easier or more pleasurable through alleviating or simplifying tasks and problems. The explanatory metaphor in the psychological sciences is thus ultimately a tool to appraise the mind and our position in the world.[134] In this way, analogical explanation supplements and guides nomothetical-deductive explanation.

Turning to the models summarized above, we can enlist perspectival realism to contextualize how a scientist must do their best to explain phenomena, given (a) the limitations of their perspective and (b) how much of a theory is underdetermined by the evidence.[135] Whereas a reductionist functional approach has more esoteric, technological applications, a holistic, discursive approach lends itself more readily to ethical use. If we were to attempt to satisfice our practical needs with a model, we ought to turn to discursive metaphors like those of the humanities and their interdisciplinary models, the affective sciences, bounded rationality, and in a nonscientific frame, faith. On the other hand, if our goal is satisficing the need for a totalizing explanatory model, the mechanistic frames of dynamic mechanics plus some evolutionary theory offer useful metaphors and models. But there is a trap lying in wait for scientists who achieve success with a particular methodology: They begin to only pose problems that are likely to be solved with the metaphor at hand, thus obscuring both the phenomena and the explanatory efficacy of science.[136]

The public is increasingly informed about the brain as the assumed epicenter of thought, though many of the details are liable to distortion. We live in a culture where discourse about the causal supremacy of the brain abounds.[137] General findings from experimental psychology filter into the broader intellectual world at a steady rate, though no hegemonic metaphor of mind spans popular and technical uses of psychology. It seems most likely that an explanatory and causal pluralism will be our best bet in the long run.[138]

Conclusion: Toward an Interdisciplinary Psychology

How we unpack the role of cultural frames in our endeavors to study the nature of the mind seems to require not only successful experiments and contextualized brain imaging but also scholarly interaction with systems of knowledge both within (i.e., anthropology, sociology, humanities, etc.) and outside of (i.e., biology, genetics, engineering, etc.) the human sciences. Psychology would benefit from dialogue about the nature and scope of the field itself.[139] Ideally, the metaphors of mind with which we move forward will neither obfuscate elements of human dignity nor reify our technological achievements. It is the responsibility of the psychological sciences to seek out and eventually deliver the metaphor(s) that encapsulate the function, context, and purpose of mind. In this context, a discursive, biological model with space for descriptive localized mechanistic exhibition may be the most pragmatic metaphor.

Ideally, an interdisciplinary multilevel psychology that followed this path of mixed metaphors for descriptive and discursive needs would allow for the phenomenological reality of immanence and mimesis in imaginative culture, and the contextual setting provided by historical sciences. Additionally, it would maintain roots in the impulses and methods of anthropology to secure a story of sources—for example, What use does psychology play in a given locale? How do the methods employed speak to other elements of the culture and its unique historical approach to reality? I explore these questions in the second part of the book.

The task of the history of human sciences vis-à-vis an interdisciplinary multilevel psychology is to develop relations between different purposes and forms of understanding, and to encompass the reflexive links between knowledge and practice.[140] A given age's ways of conceiving of the mind through metaphor is a palimpsest of the desires and cosmologies now entombed. Tradition is that self-encounter of the human mind, and horizon is the vantage point of knowing the relative significance of your finite position. We understand the horizon of the questions we are asking by regaining concepts from the past in a way that includes our own comprehension of them, that is, the "fusion of horizons" necessary for empirical psychology to attain a respectable position in the human sciences.[141]

Through this study of the pragmatic uses of metaphor, we can consider psychology not as a cumulative positivist project, but rather as a negative evolution of paradigms plus the syncretic methodologies and pathologies of the present.[142] Recent work in psychology, for example, problematizes accepted metaphors and models through the use of cross-cultural data.[143] The biggest challenge to transforming what we expect from psychology is that practitioners are unlikely to give up the fruitful high ground of technological and epistemological eminence. Nevertheless, psychologists and philosophers would benefit greatly from adding reflexive human sciences and anthropological methods to their knowledge practices, not only because they would be more capacious interlocutors and collaborators, but because the lack of context for the uses of psychology obscures the significance and meaning of its findings. Empirical psychology ought to include historical context and anthropology so that in addition to descriptive principles of mechanism, psychologists can discursively approach the phenomena as part of our broader cultural projects. This chapter gets at these issues in at least one way because it demonstrates that metaphors of mind are drawn from local knowledge practices.

The deployment of psychology in concordance with a historical anthropology embodies a type of psychoanalytic discourse with the Other which would enrich our understanding of the symbolic sphere we inhabit.

It is time empirical psychology adds historical and anthropological methodology so that in addition to descriptive principles of mechanism and verificationism, a new generation of psychologists will approach the phenomena with a view to more discursive, contextualized, and empathetic explanation.

3

Contemporary Empirical Psychology

Thales: We haven't gained a thing by this maneuver
since Proteus, when he's found, will promptly melt away
and even if he answers, What he says only leaves you astonished and
perplexed.
Still, his kind of advice is what you need, so let's go and have a try
with him!

—Johann Wolfgang von Goethe, *Faust II* (1832), Act II (Stuart
Atkins, Trans.)

In this chapter, we recapture the thread of the history of psychology from the
mid-20th century to the present. I conclude the first part of the book on empirical psychology with a discussion of the philosophy of science.

Cognitive Science

Biology and engineering, the two main sources of metaphors of mind, are
united in the cognitive sciences. The "cognitive revolution" consisted of
development of models of internal information states to explain how the
mind functions.[1] Its methodology eschewed introspection and behaviorist
paradigms prevalent during the first part of the 20th century, focusing rather
on modeling higher level thought. The architecture of the mind was assumed
to be inferable from behavioral measures such as reaction times, as well as
verbal and written responses.[2]

Taking over the domain of the term "mental," "cognitive" was derived from
20th-century theories about ethics and then, via logical positivism, made its
way into the terminology of philosophical psychology starting in the 1950s.
Cognitivism entails conceptualizing mental phenomena by their function;
this allows psychologists to avoid behaviorist agnosticism concerning the

A Suspicious Science. Rami Gabriel, Oxford University Press. © Oxford University Press 2023.
DOI: 10.1093/oso/9780197513583.003.0004

existence of mental entities. While debate continues about the "mark of the cognitive," the notion that mental actions are information states has achieved a position of epistemic dominance.[3]

As detailed in the last chapter, study of the mind enlists analogical thinking for the pragmatic purposes of model construction and interpretation of empirical findings. Accordingly, the British associationist notion that an idea is the copy of a sense impression provides the analogical basis for the cognitive model that mental states are informational states in the format of *representations*. In internally restaging sensory input, mental representations are said to mediate between perception and action. The theory of representations has been critiqued as a reversion to the homuncular metaphor of the Cartesian theater. In response, cognitivists drew from logical positivism and Anglo-American analytical philosophy to position representations as informational states that function like truth-evaluable propositions.[4] Representations in the form of sentence-like propositions are treated as analogues for neuronal communication. This digital language of code undergoes operations in the form of algorithms. In this way the computational metaphor of neural firing as a representational code replaced the Cartesian theater metaphor of consciousness.[5] Notably, the ultimate format of these representations in the brain, sometimes called the language of thought debate, has not yet been resolved.[6]

Likening the mind to an information-processing machine made possible the modeling of mental states into the language of logic and digital code. Claude Shannon's (1916–2001) notion of information has been used to operationalize electrical and chemical biological processes as information states.[7] This was developed further into a network metaphor of weighted nodes in the successful artificial intelligence paradigms of connectionism and parallel distributed processing.[8] The computational metaphor of mental states as information states could be rendered as a set of algorithms containing logical statements. This enabled a straightforward application of computer science engineering to the study of the brain and vice versa. The pragmatic benefit of identifying the metaphor of computational processes was the creation of a simple frame for applying theory to empirical inquiry. This led to plenty of tractable research questions as well as opportunities for the application of findings into new technological products and interfaces, for example in the field of human–computer interaction. This use of psychology emerged as a burgeoning research empire in academic, military, and private institutions in the latter half of the 20th and early part of the 21st century. The influence went

52 A SUSPICIOUS SCIENCE

in two directions: from studying humans to modifying computers, and from information theory to the modification of people's day-to-day behaviors, for example in Fitts's law.

Central to the theoretical foundations of cognitive science is a functionalist description of the mind as a set of interlinked adaptive mental processes.[9] Embedded at the core of cognitive science, the computational theory of mind (CTM) portrays the mind as a collection of modular processors, in which each module is a dedicated algorithm for information processing of a particular content, for example visual object detection. Philosopher Jerry Fodor's (1935–2017) description of basic perceptual processing based on seminal work by cognitive scientist David Marr (1945–1980) is the foundational interpretation of modularity of mind, which cognitive psychologists use to conceptualize mind as a device consisting of transducers, modules, and central processors. Transducers transform perceptual input, modules process this transduced input via algorithmic equations, and central processors integrate the various module-processed signals.[10] This good old-fashioned artificial intelligence (GOFAI) with the mind portrayed as a set of mental representations in the form of algorithmic information processors has led to a diverse series of applications, for example in robotics and machine learning. With the neuroscience revolution afoot, cognitive science served as the theoretical underpinning for the interpretation of evidence derived through nascent brain imaging technologies. The CTM that underlies GOFAI has itself come to form the consensual basis of the interpretation of experiments in social and developmental psychology as well.[11]

Basic Critiques and Formulation of an Interdisciplinary Multilevel Scheme

The main trouble with prevailing cognitive paradigms is that this logical, systematic view of human cognition does not adequately describe very much ecologically valid human thought and behavior.[12] Specifically, the computer metaphor of mind enacted in formal modeling and nomothetic analysis does not integrate the crucial idiographic factors of context, culture, and history.[13] Indeed, the framework of cognitivism is bound to the formalism of modeling and thus not set up to capture individual nuances. Commitment to CTM may be at the heart of its inability to account for the intentionality of mental content, semantics, and normativity.[14] The language of algorithms and representations employed in cognitive science is bound between two levels that do not use the same explanatory constructs. At the lower limit, neuroscience is about the wet matter of biology, and anthropology at the upper limit is a human science about values and meaning embodied in cultural forms.[15] This conundrum has led some to question whether psychology is a tentative field simply waiting for its reduction to neuroscience or its subsumption into a critical anthropology.

In response to these concerns about its goals and position relative to other forms of inquiry, there has been a systematic set of critiques inside the field that led to a new cognitive science in the 21st century. The new multilevel focus takes into account the following: (a) concern with the role of time, change, and coupling in dynamical cognition,[16] (b) the contextual nature of knowing and doing in situated cognition, (c) the role of the body for thought in embodied cognition,[17] (d) the extended mind theory whereby mind is built out into the environment,[18] and (e) the role of extended, embedded, enacted, and embodied factors.[19] There has also been a nagging push to shift from laboratories to real-life settings in pursuit of more ecological validity.[20]

In response to the basic critiques described above, multilevel integrative and interdisciplinary approaches have been formulated based on the principle that analysis of the phenomenon at one level can inform, refine, or constrain inferences at another level of analysis.[21] Multilevel analysis entails that events are multiply determined, demonstrate reciprocal influences, and that an understanding of higher levels of organization ameliorates understanding of the parts. This approach can be used to conceptualize a wide range of descriptions, for example, how seemingly nonmental phenomena such as gut-brain peptides influence affective disorders, or how emergent social factors such as weight-conscious fashion trends or technology can recalibrate mental habits in adolescents. A sort of triangulation of methods, of subjective and objective, perception and reality, theory and data has been suggested to surmount prevalent critiques.[22] These developments signal important steps toward an interdisciplinary psychology, though they still require the fusion of horizons which anthropology and history would provide. According to Carl Craver, different fields ultimately "contribute constraints on multilevel mechanistic explanation."[23] My notion of the levels which psychology must integrate posits the mind as a result of the brain and the person at the middle levels, with biology, chemistry, and physics at the lower levels, and history and anthropology as environmental factors at the higher levels. While the remainder of this chapter will be critical of current practices in empirical psychology, there is plenty to be hopeful about how multilevel integrative and interdisciplinary approaches can be united with a fusion of horizons that allows researchers to contextualize their knowledge practices by understanding the benefits and limitations of their use of metaphorical frames.

Since emergent behaviors and the coalescing of mental abilities form the focus of social and developmental psychology, multilevel approaches have long been integral to their methodology. Rather than positing explanations of what the mind is, these fields are respectively concerned with social interaction and how and why humans change across their lifetimes. In seeking description and explanation at higher levels of organization (i.e., people) rather than pursuing lower levels (i.e., neurotransmitters) through reductive principles, their strategies are therefore more akin to other human sciences.[24]

In the next section, I focus on methodology in contemporary empirical uses of psychology to bring out the relation between epistemology and knowledge practices.

Issues in Methodology

In the last 500 years, the scientific method clarified mysteries in the study of biology, chemistry, medicine, physics, and astronomy. Yet this approach and its protocols are not perfectly suited for all phenomena. The science of love, of why a piece of literature is successful, of the power of faith is ultimately not as fulfilling, neither as an explanation nor in accentuating our pleasure, as the respective activities or works themselves. Similarly, ethics is an aspect of human experience that despite many valiant efforts by bioethicists and others has been difficult to treat empirically.[25] The lure of attaining objective or normative answers to age-old questions about the human form by employing the scientific method was and remains tantalizing. But the move to adopt the methods, aspirations, nomenclature, and above all the social position of the natural sciences may have been a crucial misjudgment in the case of empirical psychology. During the cultural, economic, and political shifts that took place during industrialization in the early 20th century, the prestige that came along with the moniker and institutional status of "science" were difficult to resist for founders of the field. The language and methods of science seemed to offer ways to solve an outstanding number of organizational problems. In a context of secularization, science seemed to be

CONTEMPORARY EMPIRICAL PSYCHOLOGY   55

the new, exclusive language of explanation. Study of the mind and brain informed thinking about subjectivity with a reflected authority.[26] Yet, as we saw in Chapter 1, there were signs early on that importing scientific objectivity to the human sciences would be difficult, and even chemists emphasized the determinative role of tacit knowledge in the practice of science.[27] Translating methods from the study of the traditional subjects of the natural sciences to humans is not clear-cut. Psychology is a reflexive knowledge practice, it is thought about thought itself, and therefore in every interaction both the researcher and the subject of research bring extra-logical factors to bear on the experimental situation. For example, demand characteristics, confirmation biases, and expectation schemas relentlessly complicate the experimental situation.

One response to skepticism about the possibility that scientific methods could provide the ultimate set of tools to definitively settle foundational issues in psychology was to insist on the validity and reliability of the empirical approach to the mind and make a cult of its practice. As Stephen Toulmin and David Leary wrote:

> [T]his cult rested on three distinguishable but connected strands of argument. These had to do (1) with the nature and purpose of "scientific" observations and, more specifically, with the purpose of "controlling" those observations; (2) with the need to limit theoretical hypotheses and constructions to those arising out of, and securely supported by, the results of "controlled observations"; and (3) with the prize that could seemingly be won only by confining oneself to this particular empirical model, viz., universality (which would be expressed, for most of the neobehaviorists, as some sort of law in the upper reaches of a hypothetico-deductive system). (1985, p. 607)

In this section, I detail these methodological flaws which eventuate in a positivist cult of empiricism in psychology. First off, the greatest difficulty in postulating the mind as a universal object is the great *variability* in individual minds caused by environmental and genetic influences, context, and interpretation. Accordingly, very few effects in the laboratory are straightforwardly *replicable*. Nor is it simple to individuate or *operationally* define the appropriate behavior or data to be observed. There are complex issues involved in determining the suitable *population* and employing the correct *tool* for measurement. *Ecological validity*, that is, whether studies in the lab

56   A SUSPICIOUS SCIENCE

reflect behavior in the wild, is a perennial worry for empirical psychologists. Once the value-laden task of specifying what is worth recording and how it may be done is achieved, a new set of problems arise concerning how to *interpret* the data. The use of brain imaging technologies, for example, rests on tendentious inferences between abstract data and psychological constructs. Furthermore, data sets and *statistical* tools are easily manipulable. Finally, *sociological* factors influence which studies are published, which groups are represented, and how societal norms are reinscribed in scientific assumptions.

We begin with the variability of the phenomena under investigation. As alluded to earlier, the scope of psychology is massive, ranging from contrast frequency in the visual field to conceptual analysis of suicidal ideation, and much more. Chemists and physicists identified the atomic elements that underly the variety of physical forms, but empirical psychologists have not located the analogous elements of mind. While neuroscientists have clarified the basic functioning of neuronal transmission and intracellular processes, it is not clear how to connect the molecular level to the molar level of behavior, perception, and thought.[28] It turns out context plays an inordinate role in determining a person's behavior.[29] The variability of mental phenomena cannot be reduced easily to neural principles, nor can the causes of variation in an individual's behavior be explained by reduction to genetic factors or social scientific principles of the interaction between a person and her environment. Rather, these factors must be knitted together as a multilevel set of constraints upon the given explanandum.[30]

We have seen how uses of psychology have changed through the 19th and 20th centuries and moreover how different cultural settings shape the practice of psychology. Thus, interpretative tools, such as metaphor, that we employ to make decisions about the elements of mental life to be studied are bound to the scientist's culture and era. Knowledge of the mind is bound to its uses within the broad matrix of ideological and epistemological needs of the locale in which it is practiced. This was illustrated in the pragmatics of metaphor use which demonstrated how construals of the mind shifted along with technological developments and goals of knowledge production.[31] Furthermore, a given empirical psychologist decides on what is worth studying based on her education, employment opportunities, and disposition concerning metaphysical matters.[32] The presumption to objectivity is a way of clouding the situatedness of her practices. It is also a way of avoiding how study of the metaphysically loaded subject matter of mind has a bearing on ethics.

If psychology is a picture of reality, bound to the prevailing metaphorical frames, then researchers will be drawn to confirming familiar analogical frames in their work. It is the ideological thrust of positivism and the expectation of materialist reduction that allow empirical psychologists to actively ignore the ethical import of how this confirmation bias is enacted through a series of fluid empirical methodologies. Official knowledge practices in empirical psychology consist of specific language, acceptable questions and propositions, paradigms deemed worthy of assessment, a canon of good observations, and standards for assessing reliability.[33] Many of the shortcomings in empirical psychology's pursuit of mechanisms of mind arise from ignorance of such embedded epistemic limitations.

Replication and Ecological Validity

A standard psychology experiment requires identifying an area of inquiry, understanding how it has been studied and what is known, generating a hypothesis, designing a protocol which isolates the phenomenon of interest to test the hypothesis, administering the experiment, collecting results via a tool of measurement, and, finally, interpreting the data that were collected. Some philosophers of science distinguish here between the context of discovery and the context of justification. The context of discovery is ascertaining the appropriate inductive relation between a theory and a body of evidence, whereas the context of justification is the experimental situation and practices of interpretation.[34] In empirical psychology, hypothetico-deductive method is used for justification, while discovery is limned by cultural and contextual frames, such as metaphor use. Complex issues arise at each step, but the ambiguity involved in data interpretation (justification) is very sensitive to value-laden decisions and manipulation.[35] Indeed, empirical psychologists tend to have an inflated sense of the worth of data.[36] In addition, there are cognitive constraints on individual researchers' perception, memory systems, and propensities for logical inference which affect the process of scientific research.[37] To explore the limitations to objectivity in the practice of empirical psychologists, I describe the replication crisis, the philosophy of statistics, and questionable research practices (QRPs).

58   A SUSPICIOUS SCIENCE

Replication Crisis

Recently, empirical psychology became the focal point of a series of controversies concerning the replicability of laboratory results.[38] The "crisis" was thrust into the public eye with articles in popular publications, such as Amy Cuddy's power pose, and was considered by some to be a general reckoning for methods employed in the field. A lack of replicability would confound one of the two pillars of experimentation, namely, reliability. The deep worry was that if a given study, a purported finding about the way the mind works, could not be replicated, then there was a definitive difference between the natural sciences, which have developed a set of reliably replicable methodologies, and a wayward human science, psychology. To wit, known chemical catalytic compounds always act the same way; the finding that molecule x and molecule y generate molecule xy with the following properties will ceteris paribus always occur. If psychology is a natural science and its methods are objective, then its findings should be replicable in the same fashion. Of course, at our current state of the art, neither psychology nor even much of chemistry is that simple. This is mostly due to the fact that we consistently underestimate uncertainty.[39] Probabilistic laws are necessary to allow for uncertainty, and that is why Bayesian methods have provided a crucial adjunct to a nomothetic-deductive approach. Replicability may simply be a matter of degree and the specificity of prediction in the human sciences a far less powerful tool. A multilevel, interdisciplinary psychology may import insights from human sciences like anthropology and sociology to appropriately couch the uncertainty endemic to data collection in empirical psychology. Cultural factors or sociological formations contain norms and living conditions that dictate individual behaviors in a way that constrain the interpretative schemas or background conditions upon which researchers conceive of their experimental paradigms. For example, for hundreds of years Cartesian dualism, an extension of Christian metaphysics, has framed Western conceptions of the mindbrain.

The replication crisis controversy struck at the heart of the ambivalence and insecurities of empirical psychologists. As I detail below, especially affected were social and cultural psychology, the *Völkerpsychologie* of which Wundt wrote of as more akin to human sciences than natural sciences. This brought out an ambivalence about the scope of laboratory psychology presaged by William James who expressed doubt that a positivist empirical psychology was equipped to answer questions of deeper significance. Thus, the empirical study of social and cultural aspects of the individual, a defining focus of social psychology, was on thin ice during the crisis.

The main reason for the "replication crisis" is that adopting a structuralist positivist stance requires that the phenomena under investigation remain the same, that is, reliable, across time and across cases. When researchers have trouble replicating meaningful results reported by one laboratory at different labs in different countries at different times, they tend to blame the methods adopted rather than the nature of the subject. This strategy is due to the cult of empiricism, namely, the dogma that controlled experiments are possible if only we could control all the factors involved.

A failure to replicate may be due to known or unknown differences that moderate the size of an observed effect; the original result could have been a false positive, or the replication could be a false negative.[40] Reporting biases and publication bias favoring positive results play a role in the lower power, effect sizes, and higher p-value demonstrated in replications.[41] Unfortunately, even replication would not definitively uncover systematic bias; the number of replications across time and location necessary to reveal this would be impractically vast.[42] This complex problem has many causes, including QRPs.[43] Problems with replicability were taken to reflect deep-seated human biases and expose well-entrenched incentives that shape academic institutions and individuals involved in a highly competitive labor market.[44]

Essentially, it is theoretical justification that determines the essential conditions of a study that must be replicated.[45] This is because a well-formulated scientific theory explicitly states the conditions of its own empirical evaluations.[46] What replication failures also tell us is that there is a lack of specificity of what theory predicts of all the possible results from a given study. Experimental design is an art form; it must pick out an aspect of human behavior, create an (ethical) situation in which the research participant's behavior reflects their natural tendency in response to an experimental manipulation, and specify the appropriate measures to record and their mathematical relation to each other, given the hypotheses which shape the expectations of the experiment. In fact, it is more surprising when results are replicated, as they are regularly in workhorse paradigms like mere exposure effect and the Stroop task.[47] In these paradigms the stimulus seems causally related to the behavior elicited in participants. Can we say that liking something more if one has seen it before in the mere exposure effect or shifting attention due to incongruency of qualities in the Stroop task are

60   A SUSPICIOUS SCIENCE

psychological laws? That is, does successful replication in these paradigms entail that we have discovered structural laws of psychic causality?

Due to the contrived nature of the tasks, that is, their lack of validity as measures of naturally occurring behavior, there is reason to feel hesitant that replicability entails the revelation of structural laws of the mind. Indeed, if the effect is too tied to the particular task, then it is not the underlying phenomenon that is being investigated, but rather the test itself, which would not be a meaningful (i.e., a valid) result for the study of mind.[48] Rather, it would be another instance of the methodologism that has plagued the field since its inception. According to Stanley B. Klein (2014):

> Whether we can generalize the findings and therefore achieve reliable results is the core of the replication crisis. In short, social science often seems to be lacking scientifically credible nomological networks—that is, theoretical devices capable of clearly linking physical observation to a well-formulated, conceptually sophisticated, and rationally integrated set of abstract constructs—thereby enabling computationally rigorous predictions (as well as conceptually satisfying explanations). Absent such a guide, we have no way of knowing whether earlier studies are commensurate with, or antithetical to, whatever studies are presently under examination. (p. 332)

Theory is crippled by the difficulty of individuating or reducing the mind to elements beyond the setting of the particular experiment. Psychologists have apophenic tendencies; they focus on an apparent regularity or cluster of data within the larger population and would thereby like to claim a reliable regularity.[49] Despite the cognitive revolution that stressed algorithmic (modular) information processing systems, the issue of operationalizing the appropriate observables (a problem even the behaviorists had to face) still cows the empirical uses of psychology. To operationalize a mental phenomenon is to create a convention that consists of a setting and an evaluative protocol that are then taken to define the phenomenon.[50] That is to say, a tautology is inaugurated whereby the convention stands in for the phenomenon which itself has been selected out of the range of animal behaviors according to the values and ideological commitments of the given researcher and her intellectual milieu and education.[51] There are thus two sources of apodictic formulation: the researcher's decision about what is observed and why it has meaning (context of discovery), and the operationalized convention

CONTEMPORARY EMPIRICAL PSYCHOLOGY   61

that tautologically defines the act (context of justification). This insight was made as a critique of behaviorism in the mid-20th century, but operational conventions, such as the convention that reaction time reflects the time or effort of cognitive processing, remain at the core of the practices of empirical psychology.[52]

Due to the vast nature of mind in all its manifestations, a researcher must make decisions as to how to individuate, categorize, and subsequently choose an interpretive system to analyze the subject matter into manageable portions. One could choose Darwinian principles, or computational principles, or dynamic principles, or many others, but one must take on a methodological and theoretical apparatus. Metaphor use is crucial for this determination. The shifts between interpretive systems redound to a history of psychology littered with paradigms; it is a negative evolution of methodological knowledge practices whereby the new theory takes over from the old theory and leaves its findings to rot in bound volumes.[53] One reason there are so many shifts is that the mind does not break up into natural kinds as easily as phenomena investigated in the natural sciences.[54] The contours of mind are not clear and identifiable. As I have been arguing, our decisions as to what the mind is and how it is to be studied depend upon epistemological positions determined by extra-logical factors such as analogical thought and greater metaphysical, economic, and ideological commitments.

Once researchers identify what is worth observing and how the variable of interest is to be operationalized, the question of which group of individuals are to be run through the tests arises. As discussed in Chapter 1, the use of psychological subjects is itself a very particular social relationship.[55] The population from which researchers draw depends on who is available and what resources the researchers have at their disposal. The available population has been mostly undergraduate students in American colleges from Western, educated, industrialized, rich, and democratic (WEIRD) societies.[56] According to a popular article by Joseph Heinrich, Steven Heine, and Ara Norenzayan, "review of the comparative database from across the behavioral sciences suggests both that there is substantial variability in experimental results across populations and that WEIRD subjects are particularly unusual compared with the rest of the species—frequent outliers. The domains reviewed include visual perception, fairness, cooperation, spatial reasoning, categorization and inferential induction, moral reasoning, reasoning styles, self-concepts and related motivations, and the heritability of IQ."[57]

That is to say, the behavioral sciences overwhelmingly draw from an extremely narrow slice of human diversity and assume that their findings from this sample generalize to the entire species; this is a glaring sampling error.[58] Seventy percent of all psychology citations come from the United States, while 96% of subjects in empirical psychology experiments are from Western, industrialized societies.[59] The reason that this imbalance is detrimental to the positivist enterprise of delineating the structure of the form of the human mind is that cultural factors seem to account for significant amounts of variability. Attaining "universality" led psychologists to try to abstract from all nonuniversalizable influences, that is, historical and cultural factors, to present an objective picture of the mind, which ended up obscuring elements of interest and universal components of mind.[60] Outside of basic anatomical morphology, it has not been possible to declare an objective model of the mind because cultural factors, such as concepts of self, types of reasoning, social orientation, moral reasoning, and others, are intrinsic to the development and calibration of most aspects of mental behavior. Explaining all these factors in one system may be an ill-structured problem.[61]

The sampling error issue of finding a representative population (representative of what?) is part of another question that psychologists have faced since their inception: Does behavior in the artificial environment of the laboratory reflect natural, normal behavior in the world? This issue of ecological validity is behind the inappropriateness of using WEIRD populations, it is also implicated in the *file drawer problem* wherein studies that do not have positive results are never published, so that journal articles offer a misleading portrayal of the effectiveness and reliability of experimental psychology.[62] The variability of observed behavior and the regularity of null results are thus underestimated. Employing the appropriate tool of measurement also leads to issues with validity—that is, whether the method tests what it purports to test. That is why there are, for example, so many personality tests which use variables tautologically operationalized through the test itself. Psychologists ought to heed Jerome Kagan's words in considering experimental design, "It is useful to distinguish among the validity of a statement about nature that is based on certain observations, the truth of a conclusion that is based on the coherence of a logical or mathematical argument, and the rightness of a moral proposition based on a feeling."[63]

Neuroscience: The Real Revolution

The development of neuroscience during the late 20th century enabled heretofore unimaginable morphological and functional knowledge of the brain. New methods of investigation such as microtomes, microscopes, electroencephalogram (EEG), positron emission tomography (PET), computed tomography (CAT), electrophysiology, and various histological staining procedures have transformed medical solutions as well as inspired theories about mental function.[64] Furthermore, fascinating developments concerning the relation between neuronal networks in the gut and the brain are bringing together psychology with systems biology.[65] Whereas neurosurgery and treatment of neurological disorders has made tremendously successful strides using this technology, questions remain concerning how imaging evidence can contribute to an explanation of the mind.

The motivation for study of the brain was generally medical and thus accelerated during times of war. It often included transposition of biological findings and theories concerning electricity, chemistry, and anatomy to the study of the brain. In the 19th century, European physiologists, physicists, and naturalists slowly accrued the knowledge that would allow for the delineation of the morphology of neurons, transmitters, synaptic transmission, and glial structures. The study of neurological diseases developed in asylums and psychiatric clinics. The trajectory of brain localization carried on by Franz Joseph Gall, Paul Broca, Franz Wernicke, and others was compromised in the early 20th century by being framed in a pseudoscience of phrenology.[66] Nevertheless, the notion that the mind can be analyzed into sets of processes instantiated in neural circuits forms the metaphysical and pragmatic sediment of contemporary empirical psychology.[67]

Cognitive neuroscience is presently the consensus paradigm for empirical psychologists extrapolating empirical data on human behavior into models of neural processes. This approach has generated knowledge about the localization of perceptual processes, as well as maps of interconnections and networks of functional activity.[68] Cognition as information processing offers a pragmatic reductive strategy which enables research programs about the purported units of thought. Holistic functions of the brain remain under debate, for example whether the brain is heterarchical or hierarchical and how it instantiates iterative and self-reflexive abilities.[69]

64 A SUSPICIOUS SCIENCE

Brain imaging studies which employ functional magnetic resonance imaging (fMRI), or PET and EEG machines have emerged as an important source of data for psychologists. Assumptions about the organizational principles by which one interprets data from behavioral studies and imaging play a crucial role in the predictive accuracy of psychology.[70] In fMRI, blood oxygen level dependent (BOLD) contrast (i.e., oxidative metabolism, blood volume, and blood activity) is used to infer activity in regions of interest in the brain. Task protocols elicit changes in BOLD signal in research participants placed in imaging machines. Modifications in BOLD signal are recorded and analyzed through a set of complex statistical operations to deliver images of brain activity during the task protocol. Interpretation of the images, including subtraction of activity between control and task periods of the protocol lead to claims about which areas of the brain are implicated, or correlated with, which task behaviors as an analogue for mental activity. Sophisticated multipart studies are designed to investigate composite tasks that reveal functional networks. Brain imaging technologies have vastly extended the questions that psychologists ask and the studies that they design thereby. The range of published articles using brain imaging is vast; some studies are elegant and humble, while some are simplistic or meaningless.[71] While it is early in the development of these experimental paradigms, neuropsychologists who employ imaging techniques have been prone to misattributions wherein predicates originating in psychological measures are applied to the brain without reflection upon the nature of the analogical jump.[72] The uncanny and noisome nature of the ritual of brain scanning, not to mention the layers of convention-based statistical manipulation, is the seldom discussed context of all brain imaging data.[73] In fact, the language we use to describe intentional mental states remains of a different order than the language of the CTM as well as brain localization and neural firings. For example, neuropsychologists are hamstrung by a paucity of terms to describe the range of patterns of brain activation relative to reward incentives.[74]

Meanwhile, questions remain concerning which level of explanation we are achieving in describing cognition via the materialist knowledge practices of brain localization. The study of consciousness dramatizes the difficulty of rendering an explanation of the relation between our knowledge of the brain and our conceptualization of the mind. Not only are there issues in how we interpret neuroscientific data to understand the internal dynamics of the brain, but there is also an abundance of conceptual issues in the linguistic portrayal of physical properties within our limited epistemic categories of

CONTEMPORARY EMPIRICAL PSYCHOLOGY   65

understanding. From the identity theory to arguments for weak and strong artificial intelligence, panpsychism, and various forms of materialism, the hard problem of consciousness remains seemingly intransigent to empirical investigation.[75] Researchers still debate the nature of the relationship between brain and mind, asking questions such as these: Is it a type or token relation? What does the precision of language have to do with our formulations of the problem and the solution? Are we cognitively capable of accurately interpreting and understanding the evidence that we have collected?

It may be that the search for correlating mind and brain will remain indefinitely incomplete due to epistemological issues and that a more modest articulation of mechanisms is our best bet.[76] Psychology and neuroscience continue working on methodologically tractable issues, which are likewise daunting. From the nature of attention to prospective memory, social affiliation, and social psychology experiments which employ virtual reality, the empirical study of mind consists of a surfeit of topics of study and an arsenal of methodological implements with which to pursue their study. But will all the discrete research projects in neuropsychology add up to a grand theory of how to map mind onto brain?

Brain Imaging

Due to the negative evolution of paradigms, there is minimal consensus on theory and psychological concepts have short shelf lives. Nevertheless, the data and images produced in brain imaging have altered the public-facing nature of psychological research, not to mention the economics of research facilities. Brain imaging offers a range of opportunities to make inferences from neural activity to psychological processes. Clear explanations for using this tool of measurement were provided by Marcus Raichle (b. 1937) and collaborators, who developed ingenious methods to pair task with measurement and mapping to provide interesting experimental protocols.[77]

Jerome Kagan points out several problems with inferences from measurement of blood flow: BOLD is an index of neural input but not neural output; it does not take into account inhibitory effects on neural activity; the magnitude of change is not detected until five or six seconds after an incentive appears; fMRI cannot capture neuronal activity in areas without a rich blood supply, though it does affect blood flow by the degree to which an event is expected, this is not taken into account; different methods of assessing brain activity invite different conclusions; blood flow is influenced by instructions of the researcher to the participant; and each physical property of the stimulus influences the brain's reaction.[78] In a series of books, William R. Uttal (1931–2017) provided strong arguments against the validity of this tool of measurement.[79] He argued that psychology has failed to assert a clear taxonomy of psychological functions and therefore will not be able to localize anything valid; furthermore, he describes how experimental data using these tools are inconsistent and unreliable. Again, the shortcoming of theory (discovery) hobbles the articulation of a research protocol that tests what it purports to test (justification). Indeed, BOLD signal, which is affected by small movements like blinking and respiration, is a more accurate index of local field potentials than neuronal spiking rate. Additionally, for all its ingenuity, fMRI still has poor temporal resolution and cannot detect differential activity in the nucleus accumbens, medial orbitofrontal, cortex, or regions of the intraparietal sulcus.[80]

Relying on brain imaging as a source of evidence requires researchers not be mesmerized by the technological apparatus—it is far too easy to get lost in the data and its processing and to pay more attention to commonsense elements of experiments, such as the setting, the procedures, the participant's expectations, the evidence used as a basis for inference, and the meaning of the terms used to describe patterns of neuronal activation.[81] As neurodisciplinarians became aware of these limitations, a shift toward investigating connectional architecture is underfoot, the promised connectome of broad network maps of the brain.[82] While this strategy is more dynamic, it must be supplemented or constrained by higher-level conditions spelled out in the human sciences to avoid a crude materialism.

Philosophy of Statistics and Questionable Research Practices

I turn now to epistemological issues in the mediating instrument of data analysis and interpretation. The statistical tools used in empirical psychology consist of probabilistic descriptions of variability in inductive reasoning, analyses of procedures used during data collection, hypothesis testing, post facto prediction, and scientific inference.[83]

The use of statistical inference from data is in the service of claims about the processes and mechanisms that produce behaviors. What we hope is that statistics can also help us assess the reliability of our methods of inference—specifically, their capability to control and alert us to erroneous interpretation.[84] There are common ways that statistics has been used to misinterpret data: by claiming that association implies causation; by substituting statistical significance for substantive significance; by misconstruing how no evidence of risk is not evidence of no risk; and finally, by downplaying the feature of data interpretation that if you torture the data enough, they will confess to whatever you want them to.

The initial ritual of the use of statistics in the positivist cult of empirical psychology is the null hypothesis wherein researchers perform the following steps: "Set up a null hypothesis of 'no mean difference' or 'zero correlation' then do not specify the predictions of the research hypothesis, use 5% as a convention for rejecting the null; if significant, accept the research hypothesis, and report the result as $p < .05$, $p < .01$, or $p < .001$, whichever comes next to the obtained p value."[85] Unfortunately, what was taken as an irreproachable process to be performed for all questions and all data by psychologists was actually just a convention for statisticians. The null hypothesis, it turns out, is simply an invention of writers of statistics textbooks in the social sciences and in no way constitutes the sine qua non of scientific rigor.[86]

In most psychological experiments, researchers do not draw random samples from a population or define a population in the first place. Therefore, it is not possible, based on an experiment, to specify which population an inference actually refers to. Moreover, we do not take into account sampling error, that is, how different a sample may be from the population or how many data points are needed to approximate a population parameter. That's a bad start. A skeptical position based on the fragility of null hypothesis significance testing (NHST) is:

> [P]sychological theory typically cannot support prognostication beyond the binary opposition of "effect present/effect absent." Accordingly, the "numbers" assigned to experimental results amount to little more than affixing names (e.g., more than, less than) to the members of an ordered sequence of outcomes. This, in conjunction with the conceptual underspecification characterizing the targets of experimental inquiry is . . . a primary reason why psychologists find it difficult to discriminate between competing explanations of the effects of mind on behavior.[87]

Statistical tools affect the nature of research; they mediate the possibility of making inferences and can downplay the importance of replication,

68 A SUSPICIOUS SCIENCE

the minimization of measurement error, and other aspects of inferential statistics.[88] Interestingly, while the use of probability statistics changed theorizing in the natural sciences, the social and medical sciences clung to the ideal of simple, deterministic causes which were easier to produce using NHST.[89] The use of probability theory had a different working method in the social sciences than in the natural sciences: It was used to mechanize scientists' inferences rather than being used for modeling the phenomenon. This strategy was part of the positivism which approximated objectivity by replacing the subjectivity of experimenters' judgments with a method to temper biases of human reasoning.[90]

Two types of inferential statistics, frequentist and Bayesian, may be used in empirical psychology. The goal of frequentist inference such as NHST, which has dominated statistical practice during the 20th century, tends to be less computationally intensive and aims at constructing procedures with low error rates. It never uses or gives the probability of a hypothesis (i.e., it does not require a prior or posterior), and it depends on the likelihood $P(D \mid H)$ for both observed and unobserved data. This method can lead to many false positives because it does not specify why D given H.[91] NHST is the norm in empirical psychology; it is used by setting up experiments that pair a hypothesis and operationalized variables to deliver a method to derive a series of p-values to summarize complex study protocols and results which are then used to make categorical judgments. Little attention is paid to the magnitude of the effect or to uncertainties that arise in value-laden aspects of the design of the study, including the standard practice of generalizing from a sample.[92] A multilevel interdisciplinary psychology would require that samples be constrained by acknowledgement of their own social and cultural context; this would temper the tendency to generalize to populations, including the population of all human minds (more on this below).

On the other hand, Bayesian inference, which dominated statistical practice before the 20th century, uses probabilities for both hypotheses and data that depend on the prior (i.e., the context, the given) and likelihood of observed data.[93] Bayesian inference requires one to know or construct a "subjective prior"; for that reason, it may be computationally intensive due to integration over many parameters and require subjective decisions to set probabilities. The goal of the Bayesian approach is quantification and subsequent manipulation of degrees of beliefs; it thus concedes the value-laden nature of testing in psychology and effectively quantifies methodological error. Such a method aims to supply a formal, ideally mechanical, rule to process statements of observations and hypotheses that can then be translated into a neutral observation language. Nevertheless, "discretionary choices" made in setting the priors in probability functions for experiments are themselves "subjective" and may thus lead to unreliable subjective probabilities.[94]

Formulating a reliable universal method for scientific inference to be used by all psychologists has not been attainable and therefore surrogate protocols have been created, most notably the quest for significant p-values used in frequentist NHST. This form of statistics in science enshrines delusory notions of objectivity derived from the positivists and has lent itself to QRPs. Indeed, sophisticated use of inferential statistics, which can be used to present numbers that give the impression that the data are clear, tends to obscure the need for direct replication of studies, thus causing countless irreproducible results. Unfortunately, Bayesian methods may similarly fail by trying to supply a universal inference procedure because of their distinct localized sets of priors.[95] That is why multiple interpretative tools and informed judgment among researchers is the most hopeful path forward.[96]

A third type of inferential statistics, the error-statistical method, is now being espoused as a way out of some of the problems exposed by the statistics wars, insofar as it overcomes issues with tests for significance as well as counters some issues with Bayesian probability testing.[97] This movement, called "new statistics," urges the abandonment of NHST and the adoption of effect sizes, confidence intervals, and meta-analysis.[98] Specifically, new statistics calls for focusing on quantitative answers to quantitative questions; allowing for uncertainty in all statistical conclusions by seeking ways to quantify, visualize, and interpret the potential for error (using, e.g., frequentist confidence intervals and Bayesian credible intervals); pursuing replication; synthesizing across data sets using meta-analysis and informed priors for Bayesian analyses; and, finally, living up to the standards of open science.[99]

For the new statisticians, confidence intervals replace p-value NHST.[100] Confidence intervals are said to be more informative than p-values, as well as serving the important scientific goal of estimation, which is preferred to hypothesis testing. The error-statistical philosophy injects into the hypothetico-deductive method an account of statistical induction that employs frequentist statistical methods to detect and control for errors. The goal is to reduce overconfidence in small samples, reduce confirmation bias, and inspire more caution in judgments of consistency.[101] Confidence intervals also address the consistent issue of low power reported in psychology experiments,

70   A SUSPICIOUS SCIENCE

which tends to result in a higher frequency of false positives and makes failed replications an uninformative source of information.[102]

There is a subjective element to any knowledge practice, but sometimes personal ambitions, vanity, dishonesty, ignorance, and greed can also lead to QRPs.[103] Researchers are emboldened to provide statistics that back up improbable claims because these are rich in implications and thus more likely to be published and taken notice of in a competitive environment of ideas and opportunities.[104] QRPs like selective reporting, stopping rules, fishing expeditions, altered endpoints, changed variables, p-hacking, and cherry-picking data are, unfortunately, not uncommon practices.[105] In a survey of psychologists at major U.S. universities, almost half admitted to having selectively reported studies that "worked." Additionally, more than half declared that they decided whether to collect more data only after examining whether results were significant.[106] According to this survey, "the majority of research psychologists have engaged in practices such as selective reporting of studies, not reporting all dependent measures, collecting more data after determining whether the results were significant, reporting unexpected findings as having been predicted, and excluding data post hoc."[107] New statistics and open science standards are necessary to circumvent the sociological pressures of the profession and the deadening of creativity that methodologism enacts.

While not representative of the whole field, these ethical peccadilloes and the habits of methodologism, like NHST, have generated critical thought within the field that seeks to locate the sources of error in the broader sociocultural role played by psychology.

Critical Psychology

In addition to WEIRD populations, funny statistics, and QRPs, there are sociological issues with the role and function of empirical psychology. Some argue that psychology cannot be an objective positivist project because it is enmeshed in political ramifications that are too easily ignored or covered over.[108] Critical psychologists claim explanations in the field are in fact not universal but rather firmly grounded in particular cultural-historical contexts.[109] According to them, such social, historical, and cultural determinants affect what is studied and why; they also influence how researchers use data, methods, measurements, samples, observations, and statistics.[110] Concepts in psychology, according to a coercive model of the sociology of science, are said to be, above all, sociohistorical and cultural constructions for social purposes constitutive of power and authority à la Foucault. There is thus a looping effect between individuals and the concepts they use to understand themselves and their actions.[111] Critical psychologists, with roots in the Frankfurt school and Marxist thought, emphasize the role of control, surveillance, and power in the practice of psychology.[112] The field is said to be as socially constructed as elements of identity such as gender and race.[113] The commitment to conventions and structuralist systems that was central to shifts in the natural sciences in the early 20th century, for example in non-Euclidean geometry and Hilbert vector space, is akin to the emphasis that empirical psychology places on method.[114] Accordingly, critics like Bruno Latour (1947–2022) heaped doubt upon the type of knowledge produced in the human sciences, and there is certainly something to these sociological critiques, but at the same time all human endeavors must work reflexively toward knowledge under a host of constraints. Furthermore, ideology is not only the province of positivists; it is employed at all levels of knowledge practices, including and especially critical endeavors.

Recently, critical neuroscience has urged a shift in the neuro-disciplines away from the goal of discovering objective facts and toward a reflexive political socio-critique that brings neuroscientific practice back within the webs of their social, cultural, and historical context. For these scholars, the atomized brain facts, such as localization, and the experimental games that produce them, are products of a positivist technological attempt to exclude, cover up, or simply ignore the human, cultural, and political base implicated in such knowledge practices.[115] The basic thrust of these sociological critiques is that psychology has employed its purported status as a natural science to obfuscate intrinsic political aspects of its practice. Unfortunately, these critical approaches to psychology come off as one-dimensional, adjusting liberal and Marxist critiques of power to another aspect of society rather than using the critique as a basis to consider why psychology performs these functions and how it has been (and continues to be) used as a part of the human endeavor to know. In contrast and along with other philosophers of psychology, my critical approach validates attempts to move beyond positivism and short-sighted aspects of empirical psychology by suggesting modifications in methodology and possibilities for an interdisciplinary metalevel integration. This latter project issues a response to critical psychologists by building out ways that social and political aspects are taken into account as a way to

72   A SUSPICIOUS SCIENCE

constrain empirical uses of psychology. I will discuss the liberatory potential of the critical uses of psychology in Chapter 5.

What we can agree upon is that the study of the mind has implications for notions of human nature and thus implicitly posits functionally normative models.[116] This is due more to the sociology of knowledge in which psychology's status in the human sciences in the post-Darwinian context of "biologism" has promoted its claims to apodictic descriptions.[117] Rather than dwell on this aspect of the picture, my focus in the second part of the book will be on how the rich vision of interiority and the diverse knowledge practices of psychology allow for an engagement in rituals of selfhood which are themselves potentially empowering.

Empirical psychology, which has been the focus of the last three chapters, is the set of knowledge practices by which we perpetuate materialism. If the field is beset by difficulties, it may be because materialism is an incomplete theory of the mind or that it requires multilevel integration which we have not yet implemented convincingly. The study of consciousness has at least hinted that this is the case. This critique has deeper implications than the claim that the field is a mirror of the blinkered modes of power.[118] It is the epistemic status of psychology that gives it any weight at all in our ethical and ontological considerations; and despite its clear shortcomings as a natural science, a study of the mind remains an integral element of the human quest for self-knowledge, knowledge of the world, and knowledge of reality itself.

Reform

After this collection of critical assessments of contemporary psychology, it is fitting to reflect here on some hopeful reforms and exciting directions undertaken in recent research. First, proposals for incorporating the value-laden nature of empirical psychology into its practice have been suggested wherein observation, imaginative sense-making, and perspective-taking are used as sources of knowledge rather than as artifacts of the process.[119] This would craft a more reflexive discipline. As detailed in Chapter 2, the use of metaphor, of analogical models, enables creative and multilevel, cross-cutting solutions to research questions. Indeed, imagination is central to both art and science as problem-solving projects.[120] Narrative seems to be a crucial element of our imaginative appraisals of truth and knowledge and should be considered in its own regard as a shaping influence upon how we relate belief to explanation in psychology. The more we take imagination to be a central state of mind, the more we can change the kinds of questions that seem important in empirical psychology.

Part of the problem is that the ideal model for quantitative analysis, that is, the rational computable subject, leaves out much that defines our humanity. It also leaves out what makes us biological creatures, namely the historical nature of generative entrenchment.[121] Models should in fact allow for variability within tolerance, design limitations and failure rates. Heuristics should be understood as simply pragmatic applications that we substitute for deductive knowledge.[122] We can see how this looks in technology wherein design processes are confronted with contingencies in the material world and thus must include tolerable error rates in performance over the lifetime of the mechanism.[123] Overreliance on method has made the field overly susceptible to crisis and stultification of the imagination. Our theories should be so robust and valid that failure of replication does not threaten the foundation of the field. Secondly, psychologists should be throughgoing human scientists familiar with levels above and below the brain and the person, for example, evolutionary biology and anthropology.

The capability to approach mind from various perspectives is essential to a holistic interdisciplinarity that foregrounds the researcher as a person in whose practices rational and social processes are embedded. Theoretical psychologist Lisa Osbeck's program encourages psychologists to be more useful for solving the pressing problems of our times, which require a range of disciplinary practices, flexible technique, and complex modeling.[124] Indeed, as psychology has been used for organizational and aspirational consumer functions as discussed in Chapter 4, it may also be used to promote contextualized understanding of our behaviors.[125] I develop such an interdisciplinary multilevel psychology in the second part of the book by exploring discursive methods, historical psychology, and the use of the arts to articulate humanity. Anthropology and history as human and social sciences provide generative models for how psychology can be discursive, descriptive, and open to interfield integration in a pragmatic orientation to the human condition in the age of neuroscience.

After a long career, psychologist Jerome Kagan (1929–2021) offers the following wisdom about constraints on the predictive capacities of empirical psychology: (1) acknowledge the power of context, (2) note the importance of expectation, (3) consider the sources of evidence, (4) determine real patterns in data, and (5) fine-tune how to attribute psychological properties to neuroscientific data.[126] By acknowledging the value-laden, confused nature of much of contemporary research, the insight of these suggestions would take us a long way toward ameliorating methodological flaws in the positivist use of empirical psychology.

Exciting frontier work that considers the mind as part of the body is being undertaken in the study of affect, pain management, and the gut-brain axis.[127] Such work, though certainly part of the biological turn, expands and investigates the embeddedness and multilevel integration of mind in a neutral monism of mind and body. This approach has the potential to unify subjective/mental and objective/material aspects of mind. This might be our best way to avoid the erroneous assumptions of Cartesianism by focusing on the ecologically valid aspects of mind, in such a way as to maintain both phenomenological and quantitative reliability.[128]

Philosophy of Science

The methodological flaws described above are not the only source of trouble for empirical psychology; its imperfections are all too visible in the harsh light of metaphysics. In this concluding section, I discuss pertinent issues in the philosophy of science.

Research in empirical psychology is evaluated by the insight it offers about how the mind works and the explanations it provides of our actions and thoughts. Humans are social, enculturated animals, and thus there are layers of conditions, such as history and cultural norms, that are intrinsic to the phenomenon. The difficulty peculiar to the human sciences of extricating the analysis from the subject matter distinguishes psychology from the natural sciences. Psychological science is both more and less than a natural science.

If one were to treat empirical psychology as a natural science, the initial and essential discrimination to make is between realism, the view that our modes of investigation actually trace nature itself, and other forms of calibrating the relation between scientific practices and that protean source, reality. To adopt realism would be to propose the existence of an ideal form, an elementary particle of our speciation, human nature itself. If we are defined as *habilis*, as *sapiens*, as the rational biped, then the quarry of the study of mind is human nature. This partly organismic, partly ecological form is marked by the flexibility of cultural evolution as manifested in cultural norms, technology, and adaptability to environmental conditions.[129]

CONTEMPORARY EMPIRICAL PSYCHOLOGY 75

But can this form be specified through the means available to empirical psychology?

While some popularizers of psychology claim the quixotic pursuit of human nature is worthwhile and even on its way, most psychologists adopt a less ontologically onerous program. Human capacities and the interleaving of organism and ecology have been separated into myriad research programs. Cognitivism entailed that the mind is to be distinguished into parts based on function. This pragmatic concession is an empirical adequacy which requires simply that accepting a scientific theory is believing that it correctly describes what is observable. Acceptance of one theory over another is then acting out a commitment to a research program of operationalism and verificationism; a "dialogue with nature in the framework of one conceptual scheme rather than another."[130] The difference between theories is likewise pragmatic, which as a class of motivations does not tell us whether or not a theory is true, just that it works. The use of psychology which serves the appropriate pragmatic ends must be selected depending on the goals sought by introducing a layer of explanatory interior dynamics. The reductionist functional approach of the empirical use of psychology has esoteric, technological applications that do not hew to the aspirations of realism. In contrast, the holistic, discursive approach utilized in clinical psychology and discussed in the second part of this book is, above all, concerned with practical uses.

Karl Popper's construal of the hypothetico-deductive method through the strategy of falsificationism sought to maintain some link to realism by employing an intricate process of conjecture and refutation.[131] This strategy is frequently cited as what divides science from pseudoscience, even though were it to be followed, many outrageous theories would be admitted as valid hypotheses. In fact, methodologically, there is no single quality or set of characteristics that hold of pseudoscience as opposed to culturally defined "real" science. Rather, what makes a research program a pseudoscience is if it has a threatening or uncomfortable relation to consensus, to the holistic amalgam of accepted facts.[132]

Given the ecological factors that complicate the human sciences, I espouse a perspectival realism whereby a psychologist must do her best to explain phenomena given (a) the constraints of her value-laden perspective, and (b) how much of a theory, including the theory of human nature, is underdetermined by the evidence.[133] The pursuit of hypothetico-deductive principles outside of basic physiological principles (i.e., neural function) in empirical psychology is unlikely to prove successful. The sociological and epistemic perspectival conditions of the knowledge practice of psychology can be treated as a starting point to a deeper analysis of how the fruits of this work relate to society and the history of science.[134] Unlike reductionism, the use of expansionary analytic forms like the multilevel analysis employed in social/developmental psychology seems to admit the interlevel complexity of mind as nonreducible or at least administering constraints upon each other. For example, there is evidence that adversity caused by socioeconomic factors constrains genetic variations in serotonin and dopamine pathways.[135] In creating a multilevel integration, flow charts depict the interaction of causal layers of broad sociocultural mechanisms to reduce idiographic analysis to nomothetic predictive structures. This interlevel modeling (i.e., between, for example, demographic factors like socioeconomic class and recessive alleles) is akin to causal explanations used in sociology and other social sciences. In these fields, indicators of the social conditions in which an individual exists are the "prior" that allows for the positing of a set of probabilities concerning an individual's behavior in a salient interaction. I discuss the pragmatic benefits of taking on methods from other human sciences and the humanities in the second part of the book.

Reductionism and Mechanistic Explanation

Two fundamental strategies of scientific analysis employed in empirical psychology are the proposal of nomothetic-deductive and analogical models. I described the latter in Chapter 2. As for the former, the positivist project employs reductionism to assert the existence of atomic elements of thought. In this strategy, which is derived from the physical sciences, explanation is a matter of reducing the phenomena—in this case, thought, perception, cognition, and emotion, to a mechanical description of elements and the laws of their functional relationships.[136] The manner in which this (synchronic) reduction is achieved is through a set of bridging principles that compose the relations between theories.[137] These elements and the principles by which they function can then be used to cast deductive laws. This project is sometimes discussed as part of the unity of sciences in which higher-level disciplines come to be reduced to more fundamental levels of explanation.[138]

Reductionism requires a value-laden pragmatic perspective from and toward which the active element of reality is picked out.[139] In our day, descriptions of complex systems tend toward mechanistic reductions of decomposition into structural and functional aspects amenable to computational modeling.[140] The hopes of a unity of science entertained in the late 20th century are moribund as the complexity and possible incommensurability of different levels of analysis have split our endeavors into a series of robust special sciences.[141] Nevertheless, as discussed in regard to analogical models, the reduction of psychology to biology is the crucial perspective of our time. The tenets of biology, as the lens through which to evaluate neuroscientific data, provide the bridge principles of reductionism in psychology. Engineering, or reverse-engineering, the mind is the other pragmatic perspective that shapes empirical psychology's pursuit of functional reductionism. Models of modular algorithmic processes are the functional reduction of the systems biology of wet matter. Reductionism as a metaphysical strategy is convenient for empirical psychology as it allows the semblance of taking phenomena designated by natural language and folk psychology to be composed of more "real" biological or computational elements. While it could serve as a reversion to realism through allowing psychology to cut through the ecological thicket to the simpler haven of natural science, this strategy may add up to no more than nominalism, or, at least, a jejune pragmatism.[142]

Reductionism has its shortcomings. Namely, nonfundamental kinds like folk psychology concepts such as "thinking" are multiply realizable, and, secondly, reductionism does not cover cases of nonderivational and causal forms of scientific explanation.[143] Furthermore, as a heuristic strategy, it tends to misplace boundaries between vaguely defined levels and wholly ignores what happens outside the phenomenon.[144] There is an alternative to reductionism that more accurately reflects research practices in neuroscience; it is called new mechanical philosophy.[145] This strategy is an "ecumenical" mechanistic objective; it is a pragmatic functional approach wherein the goal of explanation is not regulative deductive ideals but rather a description of the local organization of a phenomenon.

This research program posits first of all that psychology, biology, and other life sciences have been pursuing mechanical descriptions rather than reductionism, and then suggests that mechanical explanation in fact requires the description of four basic features: (1) a phenomenon, (2) its parts, (3) its causings, and (4) its organization.[146] Carl Craver argues that mechanistic interfield integrations such as multilevel interdisciplinary neuroscience deliver a description of the productive flow of a mechanism through collating a variety of constraints on multiple elements of a level (i.e., structural and temporal elements, such as stages and components).[147] This approach emphasizes intralevel rather than interlevel relations to allow abstract mechanistic structures to scaffold interfield integration. "(D)ifferent fields elaborate the multilevel mechanistic scaffold with a patchwork of constraints on its organization, thereby revealing different hints as to how the mechanism can and cannot be organized."[148] An interesting element of this approach is how it deals with organization as a mechanistic form of emergence.[149] This idea has also been used to understand the mind-body problem and other complex physical phenomena.[150]

The study of memory offers a fruitful case study to demonstrate how explanation in empirical psychology integrates knowledge from neuroscience, cognitive science, and phenomenology to put forward a new mechanical philosophy about how the mind works. Long-term potentiation (LTP) is considered the neural mechanism of long-term memory (LTM); it consists of a phenomenon, namely long-term memories, its parts (i.e., receptors on neuron membranes in the hippocampus and associational cortices), its causings (i.e., events in time), and its organization, which is to say the relation of LTP to other cellular processes. LTP is subject to biological constraints, such as differential amounts of neurotransmitters (in particular, magnesium), network excitatory, and inhibitory connections. These intralevel constraints wherein the parts, causings, and organization are subject to their own resource limitations can be contrasted with cognitive neuroscience, which integrates data about the brain with interlevel constraints such as phenomenology and cognitive performance. A robust explanation of memory would allow researchers to understand and investigate integrated systems through top-down and bottom-up experiments.[151] Reducing long-term memory to the long-term potentiation of particular receptors in the hippocampus seems like a vindication of the reductionist program, but it may be more accurate to see it as an example of mosaic interlevel integration insofar as the explanation integrates learning and memory with the hippocampus, chemical and electrical activity of synapses, and cells and NMDA receptors. That is to say, the explanation is both upward-looking in that it specifies a higher-level mechanism and downward-looking in that it identifies the component entities, activities, relevant properties, and their organization.[152]

Ideally, scientific theories would attain the qualities of reliability, discrimination, efficiency, sensitivity, and robustness. Since they usually do not, scientists change the theories they espouse, and thus the practice of science redounds to a perspectival realism embodied in maps of reality crafted by experts across subfields.[153] The Enlightenment view of science is thus inadequate to capture the actual practices of science.[154] In fact, scientific models are partial and imperfect representational entities; they seek realism without truth and thus end up offering but conditional/instrumental rational systems for pragmatic purposes, which only need to be robust enough to work more often than not.[155] Models of biological creatures, which include those proffered in psychology, are necessarily full of tolerances, design limitations, and failure rates due to the contingencies of matter.[156] That is why integration rather than unity of science is a more reasonable aspiration.

The realities of fractures in and across disciplines and the political nature of scientific practice do not mean that science is hopelessly mired in relativism.[157] Rather, intersubjective agreement, or objectivism without illusions, is an achievable goal that is worth striving toward.[158] As I have been arguing, science is intrinsically bound to the cultural interests of the society in which it takes place; indeed, "philosophy is its own time apprehended in thought."[159] Nevertheless, progress (qua diachronic reductionism of theory succession and interlevel integration) does occur; elements of nature are understood at higher levels of complexity, and our epistemic relation to the world continues to shift with the state of the art in a range of fields of scientific endeavor. But there are limitations in tying empirical psychology to pragmatism rather than realism, and the rituals of materialism embodied in a positivistic cult of empiricism limit the potential scope of knowledge in the use of psychology. In the second part of the book, I broaden my vision of psychology into its discursive and popular uses to understand further the range of knowledge it offers for ethics and values.

Conclusion: The Limits of Pragmatism

William James was adamant that pragmatism could settle disputes through tracing the practical consequences of any given scientific statement and thus served as an alternative to the closed systems of rationalism.[160] In this way, it is wholly empirical—radically so.[161] Unlike positivism, truth in pragmatism is not equated with objectivity; rather, true ideas are those which we can assimilate, validate, corroborate, and verify. For James, true is the name for an idea that starts the process of verification; it is a leading that is worthwhile.[162] Empirical psychology's reliance on methodology—its methodologism—is a pragmatic resolution in the face of the insuperable odds of attaining the epistemological qualifications of the natural sciences. As an approach to

80 A SUSPICIOUS SCIENCE

philosophy and psychology, the legacy of pragmatism is the tautology of a methodological operationalization of mind.[163] This approach satisfices the deductive strategy of scientific analysis with heuristic, pragmatic models, while metaphorical models fulfill the analogical strategy. But pragmatism in empirical psychology must dedicate itself to the truth of the messiness of reality and pursue adequate stories about the integration of multilevel research findings.

Philosopher Richard Rorty (1931–2007) portrayed pragmatism as a post-Platonic intuitive realism founded on verificationism and trust that language specifies elements of reality. In the context of his critique of the metaphor of philosophy as a mirror of nature, Rorty worries that pragmatism pursues a different project than truth and true belief.[164] He argues pragmatists abandon the goal of discovering notions that correspond with reality for notions that simply allow us to cope with reality. Indeed, the stopping points for pragmatists are social practices or utilitarian ends rather than attainments of deeper truths. Even though most psychologists might not see it this way, a pragmatic appraisal of the field would suit empirical psychology just fine because even as it fails to attain the goals of realism and thus the status of a natural science (even if this notion of science is a legend), it may still deliver pragmatically true notions about the mind.[165]

Nevertheless, a serious issue for the pragmatic project of empirical psychology is the possibility of reification, that is, nominalism whereby empirically adequate terminology is taken to be real. Let us consider in this regard the notion of psychic unity, that all men's minds have the same structure, in other words, that there is a form of mind, a human nature.[166] The notion of universal grammar put forward by Noam Chomsky which began the cognitive revolution is central to psychic unity.[167] I argue that psychic unity is a reification of the idea of human nature which purports to be the realist end of psychology as a natural science. Individual differences in basic operations of mind observed in cross-cultural psychology (such as WEIRD populations and the variation in basic results across a range of cognitive domains) suggest that the thesis of psychic unity is not empirically corroborated.[168] It is possible that many basic conceptualizations of the mind are generalized reifications of very small data pools (regarding the ungeneralizability of samples to populations discussed above). That is to say, if psychology admits it is merely an empirically adequate pragmatic approach, then it cannot also claim to have attained any sort of conception of the human form. And if there is no human form, then there is little likelihood of discovering structural laws which dictate how a diverse range of minds work. The empirical use of psychology might therefore have no discernible, meaningful endpoint for discovering psychic causality.

As we saw in Chapter 2, metaphor use can also lead to the reification of theoretical entities. We can take, for example, the metaphor of "information" to refer to some real property of the brain without being able to specify the mechanism.[169] Similarly, terms commonly used in empirical psychology such as "mediate," "activate," "cause," "process," and others do not connote specific elements of known entities.[170] They are reifications of relations that are not well understood, placeholders for a set of mechanisms currently beyond our ken.

Through empirically adequate pragmatic tools, analogical models, brain imaging technology, and statistics, empirical psychology pursues a range of goals from engineering pharmaceuticals and machine learning technology, to suggesting ultimate causal explanations for behavior and normative claims about human nature. As I have endeavored to demonstrate, empirical psychology is not only incomplete but wracked with methodological and metaphysical issues which ultimately inhibit it in pursuing these vainglorious goals.

In the second part of the book, I explore the possibility of developing an interdisciplinary multilevel psychology in which the empirical use of psychology is supplemented by methods and ideas drawn from history, the arts, and the humanities. The hope is that expanding the tools and methods available for the study of the mind will give us a richer and more fulfilling understanding of the mind that may circumvent the methodological and metaphysical flaws specified above by constraining their uses.

Interlude
Mythology, Belief, and Superstition

Belief may be no more, in the end, than a source of energy,
like a battery which one clips into an idea to make it run.
— J. M. Coetzee, *Elizabeth Costello* (2003)

Mythology formalizes knowledge by serving as an analogical vehicle for deriving meaning and explanation in a manner that satisfies the affective and cognitive needs of belief.[1] By taking a historical perspective, we can see that treating psychology as an apodictic system for explaining the mind makes of it a mythology.

Mythology

In traditional belief practices, mythology is a collective epistemic niche composed of beliefs and rituals.[2] There is an emotional logic to myth; we are the kinds of creatures who seek stories that provide guidance as to where we came from and where we are going to cope pragmatically with the unknown.[3]

The scientific worldview, like mythology, is an epistemic niche; through it one can explain how every event is a repetition of a natural law. The empirical use of psychology thus delivers a totalizing system of technological tools by which explanation can be derived.[4] Adopting this notion of how we draw from collective epistemic niches to fix explanations makes distinctions between superstition and science less distinct. Epistemic judgments exemplified in the local uses of psychology embedded in streams of practical activity from popular psychology to therapy, drug use, and empirical psychology come to constitute a mythical system of sense and meaning.[5]

A Suspicious Science. Rami Gabriel, Oxford University Press. © Oxford University Press 2023.
DOI: 10.1093/oso/9780197513583.003.0005

MYTHOLOGY, BELIEF, AND SUPERSTITION 83

Myth is always present in the psyche as "the retrospective transfiguration of sacrificial crises . . . in the light of the cultural order that has arisen from them."[6] The story of the Flood recurs in early urban societies, marking a crisis in human–divine relations and human experience of gradual self-reliance and separation from nature.[7] However, during the Axial age (800–200 BCE), faith developed in an environment of early trade economies, at which time we observe a concern with individual conscience, morality, compassion, and a tendency to look within expressed in mythology.[8] Axial myths of interiority indicate that people felt they no longer shared the same nature as the gods who become impossibly difficult to access. These myths replaced previous notions of social order, cosmology, and human good, and represented these social transformations in macrocosmic stories.[9] Just as we consider how the myth of the Flood or Axial myths of interiority were reflections of how people tried to make sense of their rapidly changing world, our dependence on psychology can be understood as a result of shifts in modes of knowledge practices in the 20th century. Psychology currently acts as a mythological system to ground our metaphysical beliefs in positivist visions of the brain and the primacy of the individual agent. In effect, psychology is used a set of explanations and technical practices to supplant previous mythological stories about who and what we are.

Humans have an instinct to believe and materialize beliefs into their practices.[10] Belief itself is part of the suite of primate abilities to cooperate, collaborate, commit, imagine, and develop an aesthetic sense which allows for awe and transcendence.[11] They provide structure as norms and explanatory heuristics as knowledge. To believe is to make a commitment to a set of symbols, to a way of experiencing and navigating the world, that assuages doubt.[12] Individual beliefs are drawn from the collaborative imagination of society; they create expectations and patterns to believe in.[13]

Systematic classifications revealed in myth, for example, the genealogies provided in origin stories, provide an ethical model for social organization by defining logic through the moral power of society itself.[14] Residing in an epistemic niche, according to Émile Durkheim (1858–1917), is the very condition of civilization.[15] Early anthropologists used a term derived from Polynesian spirituality, *mana*, to specify this mythical, sacred force that guarantees the moral, symbolic, and cultural order.[16] Mythology, like *Mana*, manages the anxiety of the world's brute self-grounding by giving an ultimate felt meaning to why things are the way they are.[17]

Any system that provides explanatory tenets offers a means of enabling humans to face the world with greater confidence and increased energy.[18] Our emotional participation in mythology is thus fueled by doubt, desire, and perplexity. Mythology mediates an individual's understanding of those eruptions of emotion that we call the feeling of the sacred by providing narratives about the origins of mortality, sexuality, society, rules, and work; they provide a cosmology that explains why things are the way they are.[19] The epistemic niche which provides these narratives is then maintained by the practice of rites and rituals.[20]

Mythology offers explanatory frameworks that contain causal-predictive principles and origin stories, as well as therapeutic paths to salvation. In addition to reflective belief in which an agent decides what to believe, beliefs also entail practices that are nonreflective or implicit and which serve to enact and entrain myths in rituals and knowledge practices.[21] Mythology and its rituals are a pragmatic charter that expresses and justifies our beliefs and shared activities.[22] Together they provide the platform for creating meaning through commitments. The particular symbols adopted in a given human semiotic niche depend upon local historical and cultural factors. Our affective need for belief is situated in the complex of a technically advanced, positivist society. I suggest that psychology serves as our mythological origin story of human nature by articulating our commitment to individualism and materialism.

Belief and Emotion

From the unreflective and instinctive to consciously constructed meta-beliefs that we hone continuously, our actions are motivated by beliefs.[23] Both the reflective and unreflective beliefs by which we engage questions of meaning and significance are subject to emotional influences.[24] We distinguish three levels of emotion: a primary suite of subcortical survival drives, a secondary level of upper limbic learned social emotions, and a tertiary neocortical space of culturally mediated cognitions which exert top-down regulation.[25] The lowest level permeates and animates the higher levels which, in their sociocultural embeddedness, involve executive control. Calibrated by conditioning and constrained by social and cultural pressures, tertiary-level decision-making is itself subject to emotional factors like fear, hope, prejudice, and imitation.[26]

The Greeks had a nuanced set of terms for our concept of belief. *Doxa* refers to belief and opinion, to probable knowledge, while *episteme* refers to justified, or true, certain knowledge.[27] Each term is a type of argument, a connection between internal motivation, imagination (*eikasia*), and behavior. Ultimately, what we seek is *episteme*, but in light of the limitations of human understanding, what we end up with is *doxa* and various sources of knowledge taken on good faith (*pistis*). This is because under the guiding desire for explanation, our passional nature determines what we believe.[28] Doubt is the ground for all belief; belief in truth is thus a passionate affirmation of our desire to know shaped by the social system and local knowledge practices in which one is embedded.[29] The empirical and discursive uses of psychology illustrate how the social conditions of modernity shape our beliefs about and practices around the mind.[30] The Reformation loosened the partition between Christian belief and secular ways of knowing such that modern belief has come to be above all else a form of autonomy.[31] A humanist alternative to faith, that is, opinion (*doxa*) or autonomous belief, became emblematic of the liberal subject. To believe now in a liberal capitalist democracy is to commit to the sense of your own autonomy through self-fashioning, through consciously deciding between options of beliefs as matters of taste.[32] That is why rather than an expected desiccation in the face of secularization, modernity is characterized by a proliferation of belief. Beliefs about the mind, whether they are made in the laboratory or in popular psychology, loop into knowledge and narratives of personal agency.[33] Psychology stands between science and superstition as a reflexive play of belief and explanation.[34]

The substantive space occupied by a Judeo-Christian deity and public religious belief was partially filled with humanist ethical percepts, such as civility, self-fashioning, and romantic paeans to creativity on one side, and the causal explanatory stories of science on the other.[35] Together, these provide building blocks for the autarkic, expressive individual, which is the sociological frame of the Self as liberal subject in our era.[36] The "totemic void" integral to secularism in which there is a distinct disconnection between the human and the natural was traditionally filled by mythology.[37] Now, "the only locus of thoughts, feelings, spiritual élan is what we call minds . . . and minds are bounded, so that these thoughts, feelings, etc., are situated 'within' them."[38]

Psychology has come to encapsulate epistemological spheres heretofore reserved for spirits, demons, and gods. What the world has lost in becoming disenchanted, the mind has gained in epistemological status.[39] It is not that we no longer believe in transcendence; it is that many of us can only

86 A SUSPICIOUS SCIENCE

imagine the influence and causal power of enchanted processes to occur in the mind.[40] The perceived sense of autarky in the modern expressivist subject plays against the premise that psychology is an applied methodology of scientific materialism.[41]

In this "mental episteme" we go to any length to explain behavior through mental processes and concepts. We can cover any behavior by any creature with a mental term.[42] One explanation for this exhaustive pragmatism is that in psychology we possess a system of discourse that allows for a plethora of explanations. These serve as adjunctive rituals to ennoble us with agency and reflexivity in the face of the existential crisis of determinism.[43] It may be that in the 20th century, the personal and societal crises caused by industrialism and cybernetics battered us toward a superstitious framework that allows for control over our minds through some colony of reflexive terms.

Immanence, Desire, and Explanation

The impulse to believe and the desire to know find in explanation the feeling of immanence that signals epistemic closure.[44] This knot of knowledge and belief was remarked upon during the Classical age, most vividly in depictions of Proteus by the epic poets Homer and Virgil. The immortal old man of the sea, Proteus, was thought to possess all knowledge. In this way, he is comparable to contemporary views of science as the elusive center of order qua nature. But Proteus practices the art of delusion; he shape-shifts to occlude the truth and block those who seek it. In Book IV of the *Georgics*, we find this advice concerning how to entrap Proteus and learn the truth:

> *This seer, my son, you must bind in fetters before he'll tell you/ the whole truth ...*
>
> *Except to violence he yields not one word of advice; entreaties have no effect: you must seize him, offer him force and fetters, on which in the end his wiles will dash themselves to waste ...*
>
> *But when you have him fast ... then with the guise and visage of various wild beasts he'll keep you guessing ... But the more he transforms himself,*
>
> *The tighter, my son, you must strain the shackles that bind his body,*
>
> *Until at last it changes back to the first likeness ... when his eyes were closing down in sleep.*
>
> (Virgil, Book IV, lines 396–416, R.O.A.M Lyne, Trans.)

MYTHOLOGY, BELIEF, AND SUPERSTITION   87

Like the elusive Nature targeted by empirical psychology, Proteus must be ambushed with clever designs. In Book IV of the *Odyssey*, he replies to Menelaus:

Why do you ask me that? Why do you need to know? Why probe my mind?
You won't stay dry-eyed very long/ I warn you, once you have heard the whole
story

> (Homer, Book IV, lines 459 passim, R. Fagle, Trans.)

Similarly, Goethe in Act II of *Faust* conjures Proteus:

Proteus, when he's found, will promptly melt away;
Even if he answers, what he says only leaves you astonished and perplexed.
Still, his kind of advice is what you need

> (Goethe, *Faust*, Act II, line 8155 passim, S. Atkins, Trans.)

In these appearances of Proteus, we sense insight into the ambiguity of knowledge, how the desire to know can outstrip the affective drive to understand. This can be accounted for by the mimetic nature of knowledge whereby the values and significances (the method) with which we ask questions determine the format through which we attain and present our answers.[45] A historical psychology admits that during our current ambush of Proteus, we may not be able to see Nature itself; rather we could be looking at "a great bearded lion—a panther—a ramping wild boar—a torrent of water—a tree with soaring branchtops" (Fagle, Book IV, lines 454–459).

Not only does Proteus, the Old Man of the Sea, warn us against knowing, he is also an old wizard, a master of metamorphic illusion. Like Faust, we want to acquire knowledge, but we are perplexed by what we learn. Like Aristaeus in the *Georgics* and Menelaus in the *Odyssey*, we watch with horror the discomfiting Protean face of the phenomenon we try to grasp. Data and statistics, statement and refutation, imaging and images. Perhaps Proteus plans to wait us out with his disguises? From the phrenologists to the Freudians, from positivism to pharmaceuticals, we ambush the mind and cannot decipher the disguises for the truth. Considering our affective nature and the knowledge we expect to derive from psychology, we are unlikely to come into contact with the mind-in-itself. Rather, as Kant put it, the power of the mind to make sense is by virtue of the fact that the world is in the mind.[46]

88 A SUSPICIOUS SCIENCE

Expressing Explanation

Psychology as a fundamental explanation of our reality must then include in its portrayal of the mind a primordial motivation or depth commitment that is, like the *Eros* of Plato and Freud, a life-affirming, life-perpetuating drive.[47] This projection of value onto the goal or practice of control over the mind is a "primordial psychology." One's sense of agency is coincident with her psychological temperament, to the emotional needs that justify her search for truth and the ideals afforded by the society in which she exists.[48] Humans are creative when striving with love toward an understanding of the world precisely because their efforts are obscured from themselves by a wishful faith in the positivist possibility of a perfect knowledge.[49] The magical thought embodied in this mythical hope of order and necessity is ultimately a superstition.[50]

If psychology aims to portray reality and there is no singular human nature, then each iteration is most appropriately understood as an emotionally useful embodiment of local knowledge practices. Essentially, human nature as viewed through the uses of psychology is the reification of historical moments of empirically adequate practices about the mind. The uses of psychology are then the ways we enact our commitments as knowledge practices.

Humans are ventriloquists of order; we throw our voice into vessels of epistemic certainty. The nature of the vessel will depend on the respective symbols of authority, that is, the mythology employed in a given society. For us, order is rendered in the practices of science. Our sense of awe toward the power of technology and scientific analysis legitimates the authority of psychology to determine the human condition. The voice of authority is written, told, and enacted in our local knowledge practices.[51] The sacred double, the uncanny one who speaks our truth, like *mana* or Durkheim's *society*, is simultaneously in us and beyond us. This transubstantiation into order is actuated through analogical thought, which assembles a suitable pragmatic set of symbols to satisfy our affective need for explanation.[52] The uses of psychology are thus rituals of that mythological belief.[53] In the end, we are only talking to ourselves about ourselves around the well of hope.

Summary

Psychology as the study of human nature is a mythological system that serves the liberal subject. Two elements are central to its lore: the story of personhood—what it means to be an individual and have an identity—and the story of our physical constitution in the brain. While the empirical use of psychology explored in the first part of the book offers the latter ontological foundation of our materiality, the humanist vision of individualism, of the dignity of the human as a political subject embedded in the discursive uses of psychology described in the second part of the book, articulates the former notion of what it means to be a person.[54] Psychology provides a rich discursive space of personhood in the reflexive analogical orders of the natural and human sciences.[55] Through the locus of the pragmatic, affective ends that psychology offers, we find that descriptive explanations establish a materialist logos, while discursive explanations suggest a story about the individual. The ways in which psychology is used, for example in experiments and brain scans, in self-help literature, discourse, drug use, personality tests, and in reflexive practices in the arts, are then rituals to enact the myths of personhood and materialism.

4

Popular Psychology

This is science, that's buffoonery.

—Albert Brooks, *Real Life* (1979)

Since the empirical use of psychology does not adequately acknowledge mysterious aspects of the mind such as the transformative powers of love and mystical experience, an industry of popular psychology arose to fill this space of speculation and aspiration. The contrasting knowledge industries offer differing visions of control: empirical psychology is Promethean, seeking to explain the human condition by the virtues of rational and empirical truth-seeking, while popular psychology has Narcissus as its model, providing superstitious rituals to enact the purportedly limitless power of the self. In this chapter, I explore how the popular use of psychology melds science and desire to provide succor through the prescription of ritualized actions.

Popular psychology, also called self-help, is a suite of cultural products (books, seminars, videos, apps, etc.) comprised of practical and ethical strategies for changing our behaviors and mental habits.[1] They deliver principles that—with the requisite hope, practice, and belief—promise to deliver a sense of control and allow us to achieve our aspirations. Self-help is a continuation of—and contemporary substitute for—ancient wisdom traditions, philosophy, theology, and religion. It provides advice from wise teachers and role models, and like philosophy frames for rethinking experience, such as religion dictums to believe in, and like theology vague notions of quasi-divine presences, such as destiny. Practices that predate psychology and serve a similar function also include ceremonial sacrifice, oracularism, rituals, and moral philosophy. If psychology serves as a mythology of modernity, then popular psychology is its explicitly ethical canon.

Ritual practices and magical thinking in esoteric "spiritualities of life" comprise the core teachings in popular psychology. Recurring themes include the utopia of therapeutic recovery; the importance of positive thinking; the

A Suspicious Science. Rami Gabriel, Oxford University Press. © Oxford University Press 2023.
DOI: 10.1093/oso/9780197513583.003.0006

attainability of happiness; and the possibility of transforming the self. These inspirational and educational materials tend toward the use of personal anecdotes that read like profound moral fables. From this literature, we learn formulas both prescriptive ("You ought to show up on time") and descriptive ("Look how great Einstein was and *he* believed . . ."). Today, popular psychology increasingly includes smatterings of statistics drawn from empirical psychology to ground its explanations and provide a sense of authority.

The goal of popular psychology is the setting out of practices by which one may achieve attainment of sought-after aspirations and a sustained state of happiness. The rites and beliefs delivered therein pragmatically navigate the human condition by materializing order in this-worldly, inner-directed mystical wisdom.[2] We can trace the metaphysical background of popular psychology to several trajectories, including the synthetic hermetic *philosophia moralia* of the Renaissance when humanists fused Christian allegory with pagan symbolism. The formless mysticism of Plotinus and the neo-Gnostics of the Hellenistic and Roman mystery schools provided a sense of the *mysterium* foundational to Western notions of the sacred and mysticism.[3] Neoplatonists of various eras have also played a part in creating systems of hidden meanings that conceive mythical substratum to moral genealogy.[4] Study of the mind before the era of empirical psychology generally dwelled on its spiritual nature within the context of religious and medical traditions. Indeed, mystical traditions central to popular psychology literature consistently make a distinction between appearance and reality; this numinosity is exploited to put forward various metaphysical claims.[5]

As I argued in the Interlude, contemporary psychology offers modes of construing the mind that express our emotional and rational needs within the set of available cultural symbols. In his magnum opus, philologist Erich Auerbach (1892–1957) engages in readings of the Western canon to demonstrate how, from syntactical structure to rhetorical style, the metaphysical beliefs of a society determine how writers use language to mimetically depict reality.[6] I adopt this approach to interpret how psychological terms (i.e., mentalizing language) represent the mind in the scientific era as emotionally useful embodiments of local knowledge practices. By focusing on popular psychology, it is apparent that expressive individualism and ethical humanism constitute dominant representations of human nature in our time.[7]

Popular psychology employs the frame of humanism to define its core concept, the self. Humanism here refers to an emphasis upon the individual and in particular their rational capacities and autonomy. Furthermore, this historical concept of the self includes expressivism—that is, the notion that every person holds inside him a deep reservoir of feelings, thoughts, and impulses, and that these deep elements can and should be expressed. This aspect encapsulates the aesthetic and philosophical movement of Romanticism (approximately 1770–1830) that was characterized by an emphasis on individuality, an interest in innate, intuitive, and instinctive behaviors, the value of self-development, and an understanding of the self in terms of psychological depth. Individualism in this context is built around notions of dignity, privacy, autonomy, and self-development. Individuals have private interests, wants, purposes, and needs, while society and the state are considered secondary sets of actual or possible arrangements that respond to the requirements of individuals.[8] The interplay between the individual and their context is thus often misunderstood and so an interdisciplinary multilevel analysis which connects common tropes in popular psychology to its historical and cultural setting will clarify it as a use of psychology.

What impels a person to assess that something is not working in their life and how that person decides on the best way to fix it is dependent upon their local knowledge practices. People turn to popular psychology because they are anxious about how adaptive and efficient their thoughts and actions are. We seek wisdom and, in consulting psychology, we believe there is a way to help ourselves. In the end, there is an achievement of control over one's thoughts and actions through believing in their controllability as laid out in the rituals of popular psychology.

A review of traditional self-help bestsellers in the United States today reveals that individuals who use popular psychology want to achieve a sense of control over their minds and lives through the efficacy of will.[9] They seek rituals to match their anxieties. According to Max Weber and Ernst Troeltsch, the social context for this-worldly mysticism is the experience of alienation felt by educated middle-class moderns in response to the secularization of Judeo-Christianity.[10] The general function of spiritualities in popular psychology we will encounter is thus to infuse individual moments with a sense of totality, wonder, and gratitude.[11] The focus on this world rather than the world of the hereafter is part of the legacy of Socrates and the Roman Stoics, particularly Epictetus.[12] Reference to the supernatural also abounds in the New Age segment of popular psychology literature.

The main criticisms of self-help have been that it lacks external validation and disregards the importance of individual differences in their application.[13] Critics argue the genre can be reduced to nothing more than a gross extension of consumerism and wishful thinking. In consumer society, the rites of desire are collecting and consuming. Spirituality in this context becomes a cultural trope appropriated to promote efficiency and extend the market as a cultural addiction to some panacea for the angst of modern living.[14] On the other hand, British sociologist Paul Heelas argues that while New Age esotericisms have an economic component, they are also "much more than that" as individuals invest their hopes and dedicate their time to inner-directed changes.[15]

Traditional Wisdom Versus Popular Psychology

Looking to the written word of experts and virtuosi for guidance is nothing new, of course: Ancient "self-help" such as the *Tao Te Ching*, the *Analects* of Confucius, the *Bhagavad Gita*, the *Meditations* of Marcus Aurelius, the Holy Quran, and the Holy Bible loom large as tried-and-true, one-stop wisdom shops. Their messages speak to the human condition: our existential, psychological, and emotional needs for hope and a sense of purpose and control. These books provide not only ethical prescriptions but also mythological descriptions of the origin and fate of life; in effect, they are portable moral universes.

Just like religion, self-help mimics the concerns of the community by matching appropriate rituals to prevalent anxieties. If one were to summarize this literature, our aspirations constellate around becoming more efficient, falling in love, and becoming financially secure. Other prevalent genres include the esoteric metaphysics of New Age spiritualities and the anecdotal moral fables of inspiration literature. Self-help books from the last decade are no different, despite being presented as in-line with empirical claims that purport to leapfrog narcissism and superstition through the unassailability of data. In this case, data are interpreted into knowledge and knowledge into dogma.

A telling difference between the notions of praxis employed in traditional systems versus that of popular psychology is that practices in earlier ethical systems were part of the sacralized condition of knowledge. There has always been secret knowledge, secret societies, and power seems to accrue for those who have access to them.[16] This is so even when the content of the practices, for example some complex rituals memorized by brahmins in the Vedas, could be considered meaningless.[17] What is sacred here is attaining the position whereby you are allowed to know something that others do not know. Knowledge is also sacred in that it has traditionally been seen as the rational capacity that distinguishes humans from other animals; we can know and therefore have power to act competently as well as secure an advantage over those who do not know.

The knowledge imparted in traditional systems suffuses the practices expected of devotees. Receiving an oracle at Delphi or walking to Santiago de Compostela or making Hajj is not only a practice; it fulfills broader soteriological and doctrinal narratives in addition to serving as the space for fulfilling important social practices. Another example is the landscape of the *Rigvedas*, which offers metaphysical knowledge while also functioning as a sociological treatise about the interaction between caste and food practices.[18] More recently, we can think of the moral philosophy written during the Enlightenment as not only an ethical system but also a practical reflection upon the political transformation of liberal subjects in the context of the burgeoning secular state. In the context of a technological scientific liberal society, we consider our rights as individuals and the "truths" of science to be sacred. Popular psychology combines these elements in its methods and prescriptive practices.

Similar to ancient wisdom traditions, popular psychology tends to rely on magical thinking about the outsized strength of one's own thoughts in believing the universe will hear your wish. Popular psychology embodies a message about the possibility of surmounting obstacles through personal will. Its continual exhortations to practice hopeful optimism serve to disable despair and hopelessness. In all, the mimetic practices of popular psychology reflect an individualistic, even narcissistic, culture.[19] This can be contrasted with the reliance on *karma* and *samsara* in Indian religions wherein the will and the individual are of less import.[20]

Differences between genres of popular psychology books can be secondary to the inspirational purpose they share: to enable individuals to gain more control over mind, career, and libido. What is needed is not only a metaphysical story to believe in, but an accompanying ethic to live by. The majority of popular psychology focuses exclusively on the role of the individual, while ignoring all other factors in a person's fate, such as poverty, family conflict, or political exclusion. Hyperindividualism is integral to consumer society and accordingly plays a significant role in New Age paradigms.[21] The emphasis on sole authorship of one's life engendered by Enlightenment notions of the individual and the political economy of capitalism in effect diminishes consideration of contextual factors. Western child-rearing similarly emphasizes separation and exaggerates the importance of autonomy. When paired with the hypercompetitive nature of economic life, object relations psychologists claim that individuals respond with schizoid and narcissistic mystical experiences to form a basis for their own self narratives.[22] This form of religion qua popular psychology perpetuates a space for the liberal subject to create meaning and significance to order with symbols from local knowledge practices.

Individualism masks the social dimension of our existence.[23] Yet we can understand how it functions in popular psychology as emblematic of the power of the will as a counter to nihilistic doubt and utilitarian reason. This-worldly mysticisms allow an individual to mediate her situation through personality/character and meta-empirical metaphorical frames of meaning.[24] Inner-worldly mysticisms devolve upon the strength, joy, and power of exercising individual autonomy in response to the sense of isolation, social fragmentation, and loneliness of modern life.[25] The portrayal of mind as an individual agent with expressive powers is a prevailing popular representation of psychology in our times.

Self Help

Each subgenre of popular psychology provides succor to different needs. Business self-help has the purpose of mediating professional relationships and fiscal ambitions. Love self-help offers manuals for intimate relationships and, secondarily, salves of hope for an end to loneliness within a national mythology of romantic love. New Age ministers to the need for metaphysical myths that give meaning and hope to daily life. Inspirational self-help cultivates self-confidence amid personal insecurity caused by social and economic pressures. Scientific popular psychology tends to deliver similar therapeutic advice for love, business and self-esteem purposes—although rather than listening to spiritual virtuosi, prescriptions come from scientists and rely upon data.

Business books such as Tony Robbins's *Awaken the Giant Within* (1991) or David Allen's *Getting Things Done* (2001) describe a format for success through organizing one's efforts and career moves efficiently toward attaining fiscal success. Meanwhile, love books such as John Gray's *Men Are From Mars, Women Are From Venus* (1992) and Phil McGraw's *Love*

96 A SUSPICIOUS SCIENCE

Smart (2006) address emotions that arise in intimate relationships and the personal insecurities that keep us alone. New Age books such as Don Miguel Ruiz's *The Four Agreements* (1997) or Eckhart Tolle's *The Power of Now* (1999), on the other hand, speak directly to people who have turned their backs on the religious dogma they grew up with but still need something to believe in and a community of believers. The inspirational genre exemplified by Joel Osteen's *Break Out!* (2013) and Bruce Wilkinson's *A Life God Rewards* (2002) weds traditional Christian values with the financial ambitions of business books; this genre became more prevalent after 2001. Indeed, inner-worldly formats of mysticism reinvent themselves each generation.[26]

According to Wouter Hanegraaff, New Age provides the same thing as religion: It ritually maintains contact with larger frameworks of meaning in terms that contextualize experiences in daily life.[27] The mystical claims commonly put forward in the New Age and inspirational genres are an amalgamation of Neoplatonic numinosity, Judeo-Christian ethics, and Hindu metempsychoses; Brian Weiss's *Many Lives, Many Masters* (1988) is a clear example. Some claims said to be drawn from Eastern traditions insist on the efficacy of sending one's wishes out into the world, for example Rhonda Byrne's *The Secret* (2006) and Chopra's *The Book of Secrets* (2004). The metaphysical ideas presented in popular psychology—either explicitly in Chopra's *The Seven Spiritual Laws of Success* (1994), or implicitly in Ruiz's *The Four Agreements*—assume a philosophical position of idealism, namely that mind is stronger than matter, or the will trumps all. Currently, the dominant paradigm in New Age is well-being spirituality. It is characterized by its holism; that is, it is about the whole person, which includes conceiving of life as art, stressing relations to the environment and others, being practical, and staying away from politics.[28]

This is dramatized in the three main tropes of popular psychology: that there is a power of thought; that there are effective habits for mental organization; and that there are benefits to be gained from a self-help book. Maybe, as in the *Rigveda*, rituals or incantations are themselves the embodiment of wisdom. Frits Staal argues ritual is pure activity without meaning or goal; rather the meaninglessness of mantra and ritual allows the mind to enter a mystical state by dissolving meaning.[29] Simultaneously, ritual creates bonds and solidarity between participants that boost morale and constitute a link with the tradition of ancestors.[30]

For J. C. Heesterman, the function of ritual is to create a closed artificial space in which the participants are in total control. The purpose of this is for humans to split away from the terrifying, uncontrollable space of life-and-death contests in ceremonies of sacrifice.[31] Sacrifice was a way of experiencing nature as sacred in its inscrutability and thus facing it with fear and awe.[32] Ritual is then the stage after sacrifice's esoteric symbolic shadow battle with mortality and toward the post-Enlightenment notion of the sacred as tied up with inner-directed this-worldly mystical experience. Whereas the ancients saw a spirit world speaking through nature, modern humans see the spirit as an inner sense of life projected outward.[33] Such individualism and belief in the expressive nature of the "spiritual journey" lends itself to the self-help mind-frame of *seeking*: that ritual of perpetually "trying on" beliefs and practices to satisfy an indescribable lack.[34]

When we speak or write or act according to a set of conventions concerning the nature of reality, that is to say, within a particular language game, we in effect put into practice a mythological system. According to Ludwig Wittgenstein, "that which is characteristic of ritual action is surely not a view, or opinion, whether it is now correct or false, although an opinion—a belief—itself can be ritualistic, can belong to the rite."[35] Belief in the power of individualism, expressivism, and such Enlightenment notions of humanism is a form of ritual action. I argue it is an example of the mythology of psychology as a mimetic representation of reality.

In implementing a system—whether it be "the Secret" or "the Tao"—belief becomes embodied in our actions.[36] It is within this universal tradition of achieving a sense of control through manifesting beliefs in ritualistic thoughts and actions that popular psychology stakes out its position. With the requisite hope, practice, and faith, popular psychology conveys practicable methods for personal management toward fulfilling aspirational, emotional, and social needs. Insofar as it relies upon religious thinking and fulfills an analogous cultural role, popular psychology serves as a wisdom tradition in our time. The whole of human cultural and religious history may be better conceptualized as a history of the practices we develop, the ritual shells which provide us a sense of symbolic immunity.[37] If that is the case, popular psychology crafts individualism and expressivism into practices of symbolic immunity. These convey meaning because of the context of modernity and its mythology of psychology. Psychology is used in this popular context to articulate agency, desire, and emotions.

98　A SUSPICIOUS SCIENCE

The Message

In the New Age genre of popular psychology, the central message concerning the power of thought is really a claim about how the will can change the world through putting the individual in touch with ultimate symbolic forces, such as the universe, god, past lives, the great potentiality, love, karma, enchantment, new levels of being, or, simply, the true nature of reality. Prescriptions in this vein are generally derived from a syncretic collection of sayings by wise men like the Buddha and Gandhi, or past-life revelations, Eastern wisdom, miracles, pure faith, and enlightening shifts in the way we perceive the world around us. For example, *The Inner Game of Tennis* by W. Timothy Gallwey (1974) promotes a Taoist approach to the tendency to judge one's own strokes, so as to allow the deeper parts of the self to act in Zen freedom. These borrowings from Eastern traditions are common; cultural syncretism allows for the evasion of common arguments against Western religion as well as providing space to work around scientific materialism.[38] It was during the mid-20th century that these amalgamations of psychology, spirituality, and grifting gained prominence in the United States. To name a few culprits: Rajneesh Bhagwan, Scientology, primal scream therapy, R. D. Laing's anti-psychology, Carl Jung's transpersonal psychology, and, more recently, NXIVM. Using a disparate set of cultural symbols, individuals forge spiritual pathways based on their own deeply felt insights.[39] This bricolage of methods, beliefs, and practices is a form of expressive individualism.

The second recurring message of popular psychology is that effective habits of organization can help you to empower the self so as to influence people, work toward achievements, manage your time, improve your life circumstances, make money, and build character. Pseudo-Buddhist and Protestant practical strategies come up frequently, for example in the hardnosed economics of mental energies deployed in the business literature exemplified by early classics such as Dale Carnegie's *How to Win Friends and Influence People* (1936) and Stephen Covey's *The Seven Habits of Highly Effective People* (1989). There is an emphasis on the individual, and specifically on the existence of an element within each individual, usually referred to as the "subconscious" or the "soul," which is an invisible source of creative power that can be harnessed by using particular contemplative exercises.

Habits, of course, are the basis for ritual action. They require repetition, diligence, trust, cognitive effort, and belief in the revelations of an inspirational leader and the requirement to join (at least fiscally) his community of devotees. The psych-fiction of L. Ron Hubbard's Dianetics demonstrates that religions can be made up and that every believer is also a customer.[40] Charismatic virtuosos lead new schematizations of the numinous that keep up with dilemmas of the time.[41] As in the prevalent emphasis on the will, there is an element of expressive wish-fulfillment in the notion that one's belief in organizing habits and enactment of the rituals of organization will lead to control over the mind. For example, a popular tennis book, Brad Gilbert's *Winning Ugly* (1993), advised not only what to think about during important points and in between sets but also included a chapter describing how to pack your tennis bag. This coheres with Wittgenstein's insight that belief can be a ritualistic action in itself.

A third recurring message, on the worth of therapeutic practices, emphasizes how belief will ameliorate one's self-confidence, help manage one's sense of victimization, and create a feeling of empowerment. There is again a focus on the individual here in the invitation to a journey of transformative self-revelation. This process promises to succor one's yearning for a reconstructed inner life.[42] Such a message aims to engender in the reader a belief that foolproof strategies exist to succor emotional needs; it is a type of spiritual positivism based in the promise of order (*logos*). A range of esoteric methods are presented in popular psychology; they include meditation skills, learning how to break bad mental habits, multiple forms of expressive catharsis, how to remember past lives, and how to encounter moments of transcendental revelation about one's own character and traumas. These methods require the use of our capacity for abstract self-awareness, which itself draws on metaphors of physical phenomena to frame and situate our explanations.[43] This message bears on care of the self, that personal regime in the mold of stoicism which reflects a dynamic inward turn from understanding problems out there to "taking care of yourself first."[44]

The wisdom imparted in popular psychology suggests the cure is to be found in how we manage our mental lives. Toward some broader goal, popular psychology delivers ways to align the reader's beliefs with new ways of behaving. Authors stress the effects that understanding oneself has on becoming an adaptable creature in control of her patterns of thought and behaviors. It may be that the simple act of participation makes a difference in that the experience infuses one's outlook on life and values. One of the ways this change is effected is by setting new horizons that take one out of one's usual routine and thus enrich one's experience.[45]

100 A SUSPICIOUS SCIENCE

Scientific popular psychology relies upon findings derived from empirical psychology, whereby interviews with scientists—as in Malcolm Gladwell's *Blink* (2005)—or sets of psychological experiments—as in Daniel Kahneman's *Thinking, Fast and Slow* (2011)—buoy the author's assertions. Above all, this literature requires garnering trust from the reader by providing a convincing demonstration of authoritative credentials that is parasitic on the scientific aspect of empirical psychology. The results purport to constitute normative ethical precepts because the method used to derive them is rational and empirical. But there is much interpretation in between the studies cited and the message of popular psychology such that it is difficult not to see some of these books as an abuse of the position empirical psychology holds in our society. Whereas in the Vedic context, authority is derived through birth and caste discipline, the use of the *impratur* of science and its empirical method is crucial for the authority in our context.[46] Authority makes it that the scientist's interpretation of data is an apodictic wisdom. The use of psychology as a mimetic representation of ethical precepts which rest on a diverse range of data drawn from empirical psychology is a unique aspect of our epistemological situation and forces us to once again consider whether science can produce normative precepts for human behavior.

Belief and Practice

Believing that there is an answer might be, at least emotionally, more important than whether or not the specific practice is actually efficacious. In Abraham Maslow's hierarchy of needs, the need for safety and security (in this case, the belief that there is an answer) is prior to the need for self-actualization. Ultimately, the utility of popular psychology may be as a placebo that confirms beliefs and provides rituals to enact them; in this light, popular psychology is a spiritual self-medication.

Like the ancient Brahmanic texts that dictate ritual processes to put the universe in order, popular psychology coaches one into feeling more in control of their thoughts and actions through both therapeutic practices (i.e., rites and rituals) and the broader explanatory scheme of a metaphysical narrative (regarding the mythology of psychology).

The general claim in this popular aspect of psychology is that one's hopes and dreams—as materially substantiated in the form of job opportunities, romantic relationship partners, spiritual pacification, calming the demons of desire, and just plain making the most of life—can be fulfilled through simply thinking such wishes true. This is a mix of magical thinking and commitment to expressive individualism.

Popular psychology has taken on a similar function to receiving oracular insights; since to name one's affliction is to gain some control over it. Indeed, classifying a phenomenon takes some terror out of the disease or calamity.[47] Oracles in ancient cultures served as predictions that could change your life if you knew how to handle them. That is, within the mysteries of fate there remained space for an individual's ability to avert the prediction through knowledge. As Richard Stoneman points out, the Greek term *logos* means not only "account, explanation" but also "story."[48] If success is conceived as a method to bridge the gap between aspirations and dissatisfactions, then a story can be helpful. For many, the practical strategies and principles that constitute the philosophical and ethical core of self-help provide the symbols necessary to create self-narratives that satisfy the need for hope and empowerment over self-assessed shortcomings.

Religious knowing resembles the ordinary workings of the human mind when it deals with emotionally compelling (and mysticism-inducing) problems such as birth, aging, death, and love.[49] Like popular psychology, religious literature minimally violates ordinary intuitions while appearing to solve existential problems in a way that simultaneously grabs attention, activates intuition, and mobilizes inferences in such a manner as to facilitate retention in memory and be socially transmittable through cultural products.[50] If the purpose of ritual action is to validate one's beliefs by satisfying the very emotions that motivate belief, then self-help is a type of religious thinking, and belief is the engine of magical thinking.

Indeed, self-help and religion not only play similar roles providing belief states and accompanying ritual practices; they also recruit common mental processes, such as emotions, social bonding, and agency. The main facets of religious belief, namely the experiential (feelings), the ideological (beliefs), the ritualistic (method), the intellectual (knowledge), and the consequential (effects), are duplicated in the format of popular psychology. The latter tends to the reader's feelings through providing data as knowledge and dogma that can be believed in the form of practices that effect noticeable changes in one's sense of control.

In the face of uncertainty, animals in a laboratory placed in helpless positions will respond by engaging in activities that have been previously associated with a reward.[51] They engage in this adjunctive behavior to manage their anxiety; it is a form of magical thinking, and it may be helpful in relieving or directing latent energy. Humans, too, must manage the anxieties of life and the knowledge of death through behaviors and practices that provide a sense of meaning, purpose, and relief. Yet there is much we can never know. In those fields of unknowingness, magical thinking drawn from shared cultural symbols fills in the gaps in our knowledge.[52]

Consider how the efficacy of magic rests wholly on the sorcerer's belief in his techniques, the patient's belief in the sorcerer's powers, and the faith and expectations of the social group.[53] Analogously, in popular psychology, practitioners believe in their method, patients believe in a cure, and the social group has invested faith in the logos of science as embodied in empirical psychology. The magical thinking made possible by these acts of belief thus provides new systems of reference within which contradictory elements can be integrated.[54] Magical thinking that is apparent in rituals and religious belief produces an overflow of emotional interpretations and overtones that supplement our normal thought with a surfeit of meaning. William James and John Dewey noted this affective dimension of our need for explanation in paradigms of belief illustrated in the magical thinking that powers much of popular psychology.

The way we assess our lives and the ways we go about finding a cure are in lockstep; the form of the question holds its own answer. While the truth in religion for believers is the Word of God, the truth of traditional self-help is locating and then materializing or expressing the desires of the self.

Despite its credentials, the new wave of scientific popular psychology is playing the same tune on a different instrument: the power of thought, the importance of organization, and the reliability of the messenger remain the core messages. The truth now comes in details and data; God has been replaced by the physical universe that science can poke and prod, and the secular liberal individual is now the locus of our power as well as discontent. Our hopes of accurate self-assessment are built around a core of magical thinking: that the will is stronger than the flesh. Locating a complete narrative of human experience in the self is a type of sedative of explanation, a transitory pleasure of self-affirmation.[55]

Practice is always more important, and therefore more time-consuming and rigorous, than promiscuous belief.[56] While Prometheus steals fire from the gods, Narcissus just stares at his reflection mesmerized by its own ritual enactment, which unceasingly enchants but, in the end, only reflects his own desires.

Conclusion

Psychology is essentially in the service of our need for control over our own minds through the reinforcement of order. The belief and order by which we are possessed are two sides of the coin of civilization. Empirical psychology can give us a sense of control by presuming psychologists have devised the means to answer our need for explanation through a set of pragmatic technical methods and discursively helpful metaphors.

The emotional need to possess explanations worthy of the commitment of belief is greater than what we can ever know. Conceiving of psychology as a mythology enables us to perceive that popular psychology is a fairly transparent mimetic portrayal of the expressive individualist society we live in and suggests what we want to understand about reality. It also demonstrates the ultimately pragmatic forms such knowledge qua popular psychology has taken in ritual prescriptions.

If popular psychology demonstrates the *confirmation bias* of our frames of meaning, then empirical and clinical psychology may also be a function of our psychological need for belief and ritual. That is to say, the differences between Promethean and Narcissistic forms of psychology may very well just be a difference of discourse and of emphasis. The gray area between science and superstition expands indefinitely when the epistemology of psychology is grounded in individual emotional needs and cognitive patterns.[57]

5

The Discursive Uses of Psychology

Paoli analyzed my urine in my presence. The mixture turned black and Paoli looked grave. At last I was going to have a true analysis after all this psychoanalysis. I felt quite touched as I remembered the time, now long past, when I was myself a chemist and made true analyses; I thought fondly of retorts and reagents. The element that is being analyzed sleeps till it is summoned imperiously to life by the reagent... Here was only the truth. The thing that had to be analyzed was imprisoned in the phial and, incapable of being false to itself, awaited the reagent. When that came it always responded in the same way. In psychoanalysis, on the other hand, neither the same images nor the same words ever repeat themselves. It ought to be called by another name; psychical adventure, perhaps. Yes, that is just what it is. When one starts such an analysis, it is like entering a wood, not knowing whether one is going to meet a brigand or a friend. Nor is one quite sure which it has been, after the adventure is over. In this respect, psychoanalysis resembles spiritualism.

—Italo Svevo, *Confessions of Zeno* (1923)[1]

Psychology as a human science has come to hold an exalted position in our hierarchy of knowledge practices because in addition to being allied with science it is the study of that intimate interior space of subjectivity. In the first part of the book I described empirical psychology's alliance with the natural sciences. In this chapter, I depict the discursive articulation of subjectivity in clinical psychology. I argue that the discursive use of psychology allows for the integration of history and anthropology as the social context of individualism, and thus as constraints on an interdisciplinary multilevel psychology. In the second part of the chapter. an exploration of individualism across various contexts is presented to illustrate how culture shapes the uses of psychology.

A Suspicious Science. Rami Gabriel, Oxford University Press. © Oxford University Press 2023.
DOI: 10.1093/oso/9780197513583.003.0007

Introduction

Psychodynamic approaches were invented in the late 19th and early 20th centuries as a technology to manage pathology. In this model, people were conceived of as subjects that could be treated through discourse. At its center is the individual, with her life history, drives, and agency. This liberal subject assumed in discursive uses of psychology is a product of Enlightenment humanism wherein individual interests, wants, purposes, and will are the primary unit of analysis. The constellation of dignity, autonomy, privacy, and the centrality of self-development is deemed essential to equality and liberty in Enlightenment humanism.[2] Yet the assumption of individualism has led us to underplay the social constitution of the subject and confuse our understanding of the cultural embeddedness of mind.[3]

Individualism is an ideological position which includes a set of epistemic and political practices and that enforces notions of agency whereby the will is a determinant moral factor for the liberal subject.[4] It is part of what I call the mythology of psychology. In the first section, I describe individualism and how it is reinforced in the rituals of psychoanalysis. In the second section, I explore the liberatory potential of the discursive use of psychology.

Individualism

The self holds a central position in discourse about the mind; the narrativization of an individual's thoughts and feelings is the preeminent ritual of the liberal subject. The self serves as the locus for personality, memory, and agency and is thus embedded in our social practices. Possession of a self, or at least its availability as a platform for discourse about the mind, allows for a pragmatic encapsulation of character traits, episodic memories, and the sense of free will.[5]

As a seat for personality characteristics and dispositions that allow us to define ourselves and each other and make predictions about future behavior, the self allows us to sustain a social identity which provides an effective platform for bonding.[6] Compared to the concept of the soul, which is considered immaterial and outside of time, the self is a more useful psychological construct for secular and political purposes. It is easily embedded in cultural and social norms as the bearer of legal responsibility and political franchise; it is fungible and thus amenable to the play of identity common in mass society.[7]

In contrast to the brain, the self is a discursive concept, which is neither mechanically specified nor anonymous. The self is a social reality that exists by virtue of its interactions in systems of naming and situating within hierarchies and genealogies. The self allows for the practical interactions central to the maintenance of social bonds by contextualizing a person. The self as a social construct is thus an ideal example to demonstrate how psychology can be shaped by historical and cultural circumstances.[8] As it internalizes relational influences, such as identity and hierarchy that become "metabolized" into motives and other activities that sustain the social world, the self dramatizes the constraining role of culture upon the uses of psychology.[9]

The self is used to establish continuity in our expectations and understanding of ourselves and others.[10] The social identity function of the self serves as a platform for reputation and relations within the social hierarchy, and it allows a person to project herself into the past and the future in such a way as to infuse our behaviors and goals states with meaning and values. These autobiographical aspects of the self, referred to as identity, form the basis of notions of agency and the core of significances that suffuse an individual's actions with context.[11] As we saw in popular psychology, the "inner" space of consciousness, of subjectivity, is also a preeminent source for the expression of feelings and thoughts.

Positing an entity that remains the same across time allows not only for social interaction but also as a locus for discursive interpretation. As we saw in early experimental psychology, subjectivity can be tapped through introspection and verbal measures. Empirical psychology fixed on this use through the design of experimental protocols for research subjects by which data could be collected and aggregated as a basis for inferential statistics and nomothetic-deductive statements about how the mind works.[12]

In the empirical use of psychology, the consciousness of the participant in an experiment is collected and mined as data for patterns within the context of the researcher's agenda. The data points that emerge in this process are generally not amenable to a discursive arena of discussion and mediation. Rather, as we saw in the first part of the book they are entered into statistical equations toward testing a set of models that may explain the particular data points or trends in the aggregated data. Due to cultural and contextual factors involved in this form of data collection, issues of reliability and validity consistently plague the ambitions of an empirical study of the mind.[13] Subjectivity consistently intercedes on our attempts to furnish objective explanations of human nature.[14] The mind seems to make more meaning than we know what to do with; it is driven toward explanation and associates meaning with the feeling of salience.[15]

It is this uroboros between belief and explanation that wraps itself through our attempts to understand the uses of psychology. If we are indeed prodded by a compulsion to create accounts of how the mind works, then for psychology to achieve a fusion of horizons that is more objective, it must adopt a reflexive stance. It must catalogue and question those layers of meaning we are possessed to produce. The most appropriate approach for such reflexive analysis is qualitative discourse, principally consisting of conversation and interpretation of thoughts, habits, and actions.[16] Psychodynamic methods employ these practices to develop a flexible, creative sense of how individuals navigate their particular historical circumstances.

On a broader scale, it is through recognizing the value-laden, historical, cultural nature of the frames (metaphorical and otherwise) we employ that psychology can be reflexive. For example, to account for the disjunct between data derived through physiology and data collected through introspection, Wilhelm Wundt developed a *Völkerpsychologie* (roughly, ethnopsychology) about the shared social sphere of culture and how it informed and sculpted the mind and our conceptions of it.[17] Wundt framed cultural and social aspects of mind as being crucial to achieve the moral functions of humans but outside the purview of the experimental laboratory.[18] Another reflexive strategy that will discussed in Chapter 8 is the analysis of cultural products as collective trans-individual artifacts that fundamentally influence individuals' conceptions of self and society.[19] This notion of the collective construction of individual minds from cultural products, including language, myth, and customs, was left out of early empirical psychology in order to enable the notion of a hermetically sealed, private, individual consciousness. Individualism was central to this latter enterprise because it enabled quantitative methodologies as well as perpetuating notions of liberal subjectivity. Below, I describe how reflexive, discursive uses of psychology that are social interactionist or emphasize the unconscious can transcend individualism to enable integration of multiple levels of analysis of the mind.

The Unconscious

The work of Karl Robert Eduard von Hartmann (1824–1905) offered a type of solution to questions raised by *Völkerpsychologie* about how culture shapes

108 A SUSPICIOUS SCIENCE

the mind by positing the existence of an unconscious psychological repository.[20] There are elements of Kant's notion of the noumenal embedded in this approach, namely, that there is a reality which is whole but consistently out of reach for us. This *noumena* serves as a way to operationalize the unknowingness of the human condition and the limits of dialectical knowledge.[21] In the 19th century, there were two ways to conceive of the unconscious: (a) analytically, in the burgeoning field of psychology, as a set of processes and structures, and (b) within the contemplation of the dynamics of feeling explored by the Romanticists, Idealists, and Hegelians.[22] As von Hartmann's ideas were taken up by post-*naturphilosophers* like the ur-discursive psychologist Sigmund Freud (1856–1939), the historical and causal model of the unconscious became wedded to the concept of individualism. In this psychodynamic synthesis, the unconscious donated depth to subjectivity. For Freud, the unconscious was a reservoir of repressed memories, drives, and emotions; it was a link between infancy and adult behavior, an omnipresent background that exerts continuous causal influence, and the name of a system of instinctual and primary processes.[23]

This concept of the unconscious allowed for a range of discursive programs of investigation, articulation, and exploration. These technologies of the mind motivate therapeutic practices that elaborate upon the unconscious and the individual as real entities.[24] In the 20th century, and beyond, the concept of the unconscious is well-suited to discursive interrogation in both artistic endeavors and therapeutic encounters.[25] The unconscious can serve as a hypothetical site for storage of everything that ever happened to you. It can also be conceived as the metaphorical space for hidden powers and primordial instincts. For example, humanistic psychology stresses the potential for actualization located in an individual's unconscious.[26] Cognitive-behavioral approaches similarly developed principles by which to manage unconscious thought patterns caused by traumatic emotional episodes.[27]

An individualism that includes unconscious depths is also amenable to esoteric formats for narrativizing the self which in transpersonal psychology inspire the use of mythical and religious exegetics.[28] As we saw in Chapter 4, strategies from these systematic interventions into the self and its unconscious are employed regularly in the popular psychology and self-help literature.[29] Psychoanalysis spurred a wild range of such interpretative formats in the context of the changing social and political landscape of modern Europe.[30]

THE DISCURSIVE USES OF PSYCHOLOGY   109

Freud and Josef Breuer's ideas were seeded with theories about associations and dissociations, the role of heredity, sexology, and Jean Charcot and Pierre Janet's theories about psychic automatism, fugue states, and pathology.[31] These theories did not cohere neatly with the scientific work undertaken by German psychophysiologists like Helmholtz, Brücke, Meynert, Weber, Fechner, and Stevens. Therefore, two major lineages arose: One is the neuro-anatomists and sensation-perception psychologists who provide the basis for behavioral and cognitive neuroscience which we discussed in the first part of the book. The other strand is the plight of Sigmund Freud to use the same deductive principles of causality and systematic organization to describe consciousness and its unconscious tributaries. Mind and brain were, as Schelling wrote in 1802, different ways of approaching a unified essence.[32] While empirical uses of psychology were drawn to physical evidence and especially the study of the brain, discursive uses of psychology explored thought and the mind. The distinctions made in German nomenclature between "science" (*Wissenschaft*), the natural sciences (*Naturwissenschaft*), and the human sciences (*Geisteswissenschaft*) bear out this distinction and remain at the core of psychology's ambivalent relationship with scientific methodology. In the absence of complete understanding of the brain, discursive uses of psychology pursued a systematization of the mind that could capture its dynamics and provide practical methods for alleviating symptoms and suggesting causal stories that explained pathologies. The most fecund system to emerge from this encounter between scientific methodology and clinical practice was psychoanalysis.

Psychoanalysis

Sigmund Freud formulated a model of the mind as an active, self-regulating, and guarded consciousness.[33] The field he created was simultaneously a mode for therapy, a theory of human nature, and a toolbox for cultural criticism.[34] Legitimating dreams, forbidden desires, and other aspects of experience important to the Romantics, Freud developed a mechanistic logic in which the mind followed causal principles of energetic transfer that were amenable to naturalistic and systematic, if not necessarily scientific, study. He eventually posited a system of instinctual drives, Eros and Thanatos, which provided a basic directedness and motivation to the mind that sought to align psychoanalysis with the biological sciences. Along with Richard von Krafft-Ebing

110 A SUSPICIOUS SCIENCE

(1840–1902) and Havelock Ellis (1859–1939), Freud focused on the nature of sexuality as it allowed for discursive investigation of how intimate aspects of the mind came to be shaped by urbanization and the shifting social and cultural bourgeois norms.[35] From "hysterical" women subject to domestic abuse, like Dora, to the shell-shocked men, like the Rat man, returning from the Prussian War, there was an influx of cases upon which psychoanalysts developed methods to express subjectivity and assuage suffering.

Notable discursive formats developed in early psychoanalysis include the dynamic processes of free association, transference, reaction formation, defense mechanisms, repetition, cathexis, and catharsis.[36] The defense mechanism of displacement, for example, is an analytical tool to decipher how the mind makes associations that link disparate ideas in order to avoid the pain of repressed memory. For the same purpose, condensation is the process of superimposing ideas together.[37] Freud considered these analogical mechanisms to be innate responses to trauma, thereby suggesting that the mind naturally employs metaphor to create meaning. These dynamic processes are expressive: They articulate the individual in her historical, cultural setting. According to the discursive techniques of psychoanalysis, the mind creatively expresses its situatedness through dream, symptom, and desire. Notably, while psychoanalysis developed discursive methods to disentangle these analogical processes, early empirical psychology pursued ways to portray the mind as an associational network of meaning.

Psychoanalysis provided a method for individuals to serve as potential subjects for exegesis. The context for this interpretative hermeneutics was secular modernity at the *fin de siècle*, and the format was the character and development of the individual. Psychoanalysis offered a solution to the ontological problem of how an individual comes to think as she does.[38] Yet the function and meaning of this discursive template may be consistently reformatted in various exegetical contexts.

As other Europeans such as Welshman Ernest Jones (1879–1958), Hungarian Sándor Ferenczi (1873–1933), and German Karl Abraham (1877–1925) formed an International Psychoanalytic Association in the early 20th century, psychodynamic methods created by Freud were developed through clinical work and engagement with theory. While there was an orthodoxy maintained by Freud during his lifetime, the basic insight that the mind could be understood and mapped through causal principles was interpreted in myriad ways by those who came after him. Carl Gustav Jung's (1875–1961) work in Switzerland on reaction time and word associations

THE DISCURSIVE USES OF PSYCHOLOGY   111

was a harbinger of methods to be adopted in empirical science and scientology. He developed these insights into the associative mind through psychoanalytic methods to describe the esoteric functions of mythology and the collective unconscious in his later analytical psychology.[39] And Austrian Alfred Adler (1870–1937) in his Society for Individual Psychology used discursive psychoanalytic methods to focus on feelings of inferiority, neurosis, and aggression.

The forms of interiority generated through these discursive practices had implications for ethics, economy, and political engagement. One of these consequences was the liberatory potential that came along with a sense of agency in the possibility of self-making. Reflexive self-grounding is one of the aspects of modernity that psychology perpetuates in its practices and the language it makes available.[40] For example, from Freud through fellow Austrian Wilhelm Reich (1897–1957), a focus on sexuality served to bring intimate spaces and practices of pleasure and shame into discourse. These explorations of the affectively charged space of sexual life and identity dramatize the status of psychology as a powerful conduit for discourse and meaning. The political nature of this "movement-sect-guild-profession-faith-discipline" can also be observed in how the New Left creatively restored and consolidated psychoanalysis as a form of political subjectivity in Western and Central Europe, as well as Latin America between the 1960s and 1980s.[41]

Familiar institutional issues arose for psychoanalysis: Was it a subdiscipline of biological psychiatry or empirical psychology? Was it a natural or a human science?[42] These questions were to be answered by how its methods were adapted to particular settings. As a discursive method, psychoanalysis had the flexibility to adapt to local knowledge practices and thus take on various uses for individuals. To take one example, the child psychology debates between Anna Freud (1895–1982) and the Austrian-British psychologist Melanie Klein (1882–1960) pitted Viennese bourgeois principles against social welfare techniques in postwar Britain.[43] Another example of this flexibility is how ego psychology became ascendent in the context of a postwar capitalist boom in mid-20th century America.[44] Psychoanalysis developed other uses in response to the competition of other explanatory systems, for example during the latter half of the 20th century when it became apparent that neuroscience had developed a biomedical model of mind that offered its own rich descriptive explanatory network. The conflict between discursive, agentive systems of interpretation of the mind, like psychodynamic models, and mechanistic descriptive biomedical models plays out in contemporary

112 A SUSPICIOUS SCIENCE

balances between pharmacology and therapy, as we will see in the next chapter.

Discourse is a rich format that allows for interdisciplinary multilevel analysis because it is constructed and constructive, situated and action oriented.[45] Sandór Ferenczi and Otto Rank (1884–1939) drew attention to the analytic situation as a new secular space for discourse about the self and agency. In the space of conversation and analysis, the analysand undertook a shared exploration of the reasons for his actions. This sense of sussing out causal webs within an individual's personal history was scientific in that it adhered to a methodology buttressed by theory, but it was also open to various interpretative systems that allowed for creative ontological schematizations of inner life.[46] Creating a store of techniques to articulate the self and to be able to draw from one's personal store of historical causal narratives provided the community with a strong base for assuming the usefulness of psychoanalysis.[47] In line with the rise of science in the 20th century, psychoanalysis offered personalized discursive explanations based on methodologies in line with rationalism, empiricism, scientific naturalism, and ethics.[48] It also offered the tools and necessary beliefs about human nature for discursive interpretation of motivation, meaning, and the relationships between interiority and social context.[49] Psychoanalysis provided a cornerstone for the advent of psychological society (or the *mental episteme*), in which representation of life as a psychological drama became the norm.[50]

In his emphasis on the importance of transference, Freud was cognizant of the mediation of self-knowledge by a therapist who guides the patient into insights about how and why they act as they do. The possible irrationality and subjectivity of the analyst himself alerts us toward the social nature of the process of self-making.[51] In this intimate Socratic dialogue, there is a relation of power between analyst and analysand whereby talking and listening are pathways to healing. Psychoanalysis offers both conceptual space for the unconscious depth of subjectivity and practical space for the social process of confession and self-making. Psychoanalysis is thus used as an apparatus to discover, trace, and ultimately, through discourse, explain the self in a way that may alleviate suffering through self-knowledge.

First, an individual must admit a need for help with her mind. Then, she chooses a therapist who espouses a methodology that suits her ability and desire to engage. The therapeutic use of psychology is a platform for discourse about how the self developed in the context of the ultimate other over which it has no control, namely, the family unit.[52] British neo-Freudians developed object-relations theory in the mid-20th century to describe how the self comes to be formed in relation to object positions created through internalization of family members.[53] The family that shapes us is both self and other; it determines our basic developmental characteristics, and yet we must also be part of another world of relations and individuals.[54] This greater world we enter and over which we again do not have control then shapes us further, both delimiting and making available new tools for the exercise of agency.[55] We now turn to the social context of the discursive uses of psychology.

Social Interactionism and Self

Imitation, the mediating role of language, and other mimetic processes are crucial to self-making in society. The *socius* anthropologists and British object-relations theorists exposed the limits of Cartesian individualism by describing how identity is in fact not under the control of the individual but created in a space of symbolic interaction.[56] This can be encapsulated in the notion of a dialogical self in which many voices, influences, and desires are chained together to form a contextualized identity.[57] In particular, these approaches emphasize how the self is created in and through the discourse of the other. George Herbert Mead (1863–1931) portrayed the self as dynamically formed through the coordinated relations of social positions, roles, and cultural imaginaries.[58] Erik Erikson (1902–1994) described how the self comes to be through a process of development he called psychosocial.[59] Harry Stack Sullivan (1892–1949) investigated pathologies endemic to relationships and developed a theory about interpersonal explanations for individual behaviors.[60] Alfred Schutz (1899–1959) suggested a method to bring the social sciences into phenomenological analysis by emphasizing the shared world-making of our encounters with others.[61] According to Schutz's approach, identity is a social product that is collectively developed and imagined, and which has meaning for self and other through a sociogenetic process of active internalization. In this model, symbols are reflexive vantage points from which individuals can assess the implications of their own behavior as well as of other people's behaviors in such a way as to secure the source of the motivation for their actions. In these social interactionist schemes of discursive psychology, culture in the guise of the stories we tell, the artifacts we use, and identity constructs like nationality, institutions, and socioeconomic class is the ground for symbolic interaction.[62]

114　A SUSPICIOUS SCIENCE

The way individuals employ symbols in acts of self-definition and identity formation, such as taste in consumer society, establishes their socialization.[63] The liberal subject, the individual who expresses herself through language, ethics, consumption, and voting, and the way in which demographic information is used to characterize and predict our behaviors illustrates how individualism developed in the 20th century as a set of practical uses of individualism.[64] For Karl Mannheim (1893–1947) of the Frankfurt school, we must therefore acknowledge the situation-bound, socially conditioned context for any truth claims.[65] We are thus each required to discursively adapt to our situations and are shaped thereby in that intertwining of multiple levels of constraints described respectively in psychology, biology, sociology, political science, and anthropology.[66] This social interactionist portrayal of the self allows for a more practical, sophisticated, and empathetic analysis than the notion of the executive process in cognitive neuroscience. These multiple constraints of discursive analysis, at the level of the unconscious, the individual, the family, the culture, and the social relational renders a more generous and accurate picture of the mind than the descriptive use of psychology alone. This is because context, history, agency, and reflexivity are constitutive aspects of being a human actor. The discursive use of psychology is the set of methods by which we render the aspect of meaning that is described by metaphors and mechanical structures in empirical psychology. All these levels of analysis must be interleaved to constrain each other in an ideal interdisciplinary humanistic psychology.

Culture as Text

Cultural uses of psychoanalysis proved useful beyond the interpretation of individual behavior and pathology; they enabled political and theoretical critiques of society and models with which to reflect upon the process of artistic creation.[67]

Psychoanalysis came to be used as a rich analytic system to interpret cultural symbols located not in individuals but in cultural products. Literary theorists from the New Criticism, psychologists like Jacques Lacan (1901–1981), and Marxist philosophers like Slavoj Zizek (b. 1949) have used psychoanalysis as a framework with which to "read" ideology in literature, cinema, and advertisements.[68] The method of this practice is to analyze cultural products as symptoms of neurosis, of the unconscious repressions, transferences, and sublimations of the society in which they were produced. Instances of such interpretative activity abound in the semiology of marketing, spectacle, and postcolonial critiques.[69] Poststructuralists and deconstructionists took psychoanalysis and other forms of systematization to be ideological, which allowed them to use psychology as a lens by which to tease out the historical foundations of the cultural landscape.[70] Civilization was portrayed as the field of the Symbolic by Lacan, and after the critiques of Deleuze and Guttari, the situationists depicted culture itself as a space for creative political discourse.[71] For postwar intellectuals, psychoanalysis was more fruitful than Marxism for creating and discussing culture because it allowed for more aesthetic connections between psychic and political reality.[72]

Psychoanalysis also served as a generative system to expand structural interpretations of cultural products, particularly for French poststructuralists, such as Roland Barthes (1915–1980).[73] Lionel Trilling (1905–1975) articulated the uses of psychology for reading literature; in "Freud and Literature," he positions Freud as part of the Romantic tradition that claims the mind is inherently poetic, that is to say, naturally discursive. André Breton (1896–1966) and the Surrealists similarly ran with their sketchy understanding of Freud to create a fecund strategy for artistic production.[74]

Indeed, psychoanalysis was taken up with fervor by artists and humanists more than by empirical psychologists during the postwar period. This is because the discursive model of the mind as inherently poetic, analogical, and active was effective in generating the conditions for creativity. If our dreams are intrinsically dramatic, if the family situation is a play of object relations, then the mind is naturally a creative, analogical organ geared towards artistic production. The discursive use of psychology was thus not necessarily tied to pathology and its cure, it could also be a source for creative exploration.

The discursive use of psychology celebrates agency and subjectivity, and thus it constitutes one of the final bulwarks of humanism. We turn now to how the discursive use of psychology as humanism enabled liberatory political struggle in the postcolonial context.

The Liberatory Potential of Discursive Psychology

While the world in which psychoanalysis was created was destroyed during the Second World War, the tools that it provided for structuring, theorizing,

116 A SUSPICIOUS SCIENCE

and articulating inner space played a role in the postcolonial projects of the 20th century. The liberatory potential of elaborating discourse on the nature of one's trauma and specifying elements of the world that have been internalized to create them were used for political purposes to make multidimensional critiques of the structures of power. Psychology in this guise was used as a discursive language for agency, mastery, the expression of suffering, and the exploration of subjectivity. In this section, I describe the ways in which psychodynamic theories of mind were put to the use of resistance. My examples are drawn from a wide range of settings so as to demonstrate how malleable the discursive use of psychology has been during the 20th century.

For some, psychoanalysis inaugurated an epistemic violence in the postcolonial context by forcing subjects toward the totem of a Western model of subjecthood.[75] But it is perhaps more accurate to say psychology is an adjunct to prevailing cultural projects; its use is determined by its context, which can be domination or creativity and resistance. Psychology has been used to commit violence by labeling people degenerate, but it has likewise been used to craft notions of agency, liberation, and power. Karen Horney (1885–1952), for example, used the tenets of psychoanalysis to reject Freud's misogyny and build another form of subjectivity which took the female as its own starting point.[76]

Critical agency and double consciousness for example are reflexive forms of agency that employ the technology of psychoanalysis.[77] The Martinican psychologist Frantz Fanon (1925–1961) used discursive psychology to conceptualize and articulate the neuroses created by the equation of evil and threat with black skin.[78] In his home country and in French-colonized Algeria, he observed how racism had the psychological effect of denying personhood, even subjectivity itself, to create a sense of depersonalization in the colonized subject. Fanon analyzes the tools of this psychic oppression and alienation through the conceptions of sexuality, desire, and taboo developed by Sigmund Freud and Alfred Adler.[79] Fanon's purpose in his use of psychology is to delineate the psychic trauma of racism and generate pride in blackness through knowledge of the toxic socialization of Negroes in the colonies and the metropole.[80] Fanon's use of psychoanalysis merged with the politicization of his vocation as a doctor in Algeria during the overthrow of the French colonial administration (1954–1962). His dislocation from Martinique to Algeria and his assimilation of psychoanalytically charged French existentialist philosophy enabled insight into the conditions of racial trauma. In this context, psychology was used as a tool for revolutionary critique; as a

THE DISCURSIVE USES OF PSYCHOLOGY   117

revelatory mode of analysis that can trace the causes of suffering and then articulate pain, alienation, and fury. Fanon was able to conjure the external conditions of oppression through a depiction of mental states in the vocabulary of psychoanalysis. This use of psychology served therapeutic and political ends; it was a tool to help reveal sources of discord in enforced normative interpretations of subjectivity. For example, in his position at the psychiatric hospital at Blida-Joinville, Fanon developed techniques to give patients back a sense of agency and remove subtle forms of stigma by modifying the relationship between doctor and patient.[81]

In the psychodynamic apparatus, subjectivity is a platform for the analysis of feelings and their causes. It employs discursive knowledge practices in the analytical dyad to buttress one's sense of agency towards ultimately alleviating suffering. This can be done by aiding the analysand to understand why she acts as she does, including the triggers, the moments of trauma, and alternative ways to think of one's self. Fanon took these principles of psychoanalysis beyond the psychiatric ward to assess how the colonized mind suffers from continuous oppression and thus becomes a stranger to itself.[82] He clarified the intimate psychological causality of this harsh reality and then was able to connect the tools of oppression of subjectivity to the Algerian struggle for recognition and liberty under French colonial rule.[83] It was partly his understanding of the process of psychic oppression which pushed him to espouse violent seizure of power by anti-colonialists as the appropriate manner through which to establish a sense of power and agency.[84] The use of discursive psychology in Fanon's political analysis and practice was a means to promote liberatory subjectivity by strengthening the sense of agency through self-knowledge as analysis of the culture and practices of colonial racism.

India

The work of Bengali psychoanalyst Girind Sekhar Bose (1887–1953) under British rule and after liberation is an important example of how psychology can be used as part of the transformation of ontological systems. His writings dramatize a creative synthesis of Freud with Advaita Vedānta and, correlatively, the use of Viennese psychology to interpret Vedic texts.[85] Bose's leadership of the first department of psychology in India at the University of Calcutta and as president of the Indian Psychological Association underlines the significance of his letter correspondence with Freud. Bose's use of psychoanalysis in syntheses and interpolations located psychology at the core of Vedāntic metaphysics, despite the differences between Western metaphysics and Hindu notions of nondualism, *karma*, and *kāma* (desire). Discursive psychology was more conducive to the early forms of academic psychology in India partly because the conceptual framework of Wundtian experimentalism is not intrinsic to Indian society.[86] There are also a number of ancient Vedic texts, like the Upanisads, which offer rich psychological and ethical systems that sufficiently fulfill the same functions as empirical psychology.

Unlike Jung, Freud was in the grip of Enlightenment positivism and thus could not conceive of religion as anything other than illusion. He consistently used psychology to dismantle human motivation for succor and meaning in religious ontologies.[87] In contrast, Bose, as a Bihari *vedāntist*, could only conceive of religion as a useful palliative.[88] In the context of Hinduism, mystical intuitions play an important role in how we interpret our own minds.[89] The practical, devotional needs embodied in Vedānta and Mimamsa dogma and practice served as the motivating condition for Bose's use of psychology. Bose was thus in an appropriate position to discover alignments in the introspective methodology of psychoanalysis and the tenets of Hindu philosophy. For instance, he interprets Vedic ritual in the light of Freud's reading of ritual as adjunctive behavior and concludes that the Vedas are not the only way to arrive at Brahman; on the other hand, he developed a notion of the "theoretical ego," which was a unique contribution to psychoanalysis.[90]

Similar to how Fanon used psychology to relieve the colonial yoke through knowledge of the condition of psychological trauma, Bose was able to respond to the colonial imposition of scientistic knowledge from the West by embedding psychoanalysis in fundamental Hindu philosophical systems about the means of knowledge (*pramānas*).[91] Context determines the uses of psychology. A notable shift that arises therefrom is that the success of a theory in Indian psychology is more often based on the usefulness of application, on existential benefits, and spiritual progress, particularly through yoga and health.[92] Bose's use of psychology is an example of how psychoanalysis as a discursive system allows for syncretic interpretation for the postcolonial subject. Bose was able to demonstrate that psychoanalysis could itself be framed in the older and more successful palliative technologies of Vedānta and yogic practices.

Egypt

Psychoanalysis as an empirical and theoretical discipline played an important role in redefinitions of subjecthood, spirituality, and sexuality in several post-colonial projects.[93] In the middle of the 20th century, a circle of intellectuals in Cairo demonstrated a unique use of psychology that synthesized elements of Freudian theory with mystical Islam. We can learn about the historical embeddedness of the reflexive practices of discursive psychology through this example, as it demonstrates how psychology can be used to enable and enact the values generated in the interstices between traditional religion and the projects of modernity.

Egypt is a populous, gregarious collectivist society in which the sociality of the individual is central.[94] Psychology in the new Egypt around the time of the revolution of 1952 was used as a tool of mediation between individual and other (*socius*) because it provided ways to interrogate how the self is socialized in its various encounters. The platform of psychology was also an important middle ground to engage with the differences between the ethical traditions of Islam and Western modernity. Psychology has always been part of the ethical program of Islam: The *tareeq* (way, road) of the Sufi traveler is a form of battle against the base instincts of humans.[95] In the mid-century circle of psychologist Yousef Mourad, psychoanalysis was integrated with the postcolonial modernist project in such a manner that it was continuous with prior traditions of spiritual insight, visions, and direct affective perception (i.e., gnosis) in Sufist Islam as well as Bergsonian intuition.[96]

Mourad's circle of intellectuals maintained a view of Europe as the bearer of Enlightenment humanist values, but they were also pulled in the direction of a radical rejection of colonialism through existentialism, engagement, and socialist realism.[97] In mid-century Egypt, popular and academic psychology was constituted of a set of knowledge practices located between biological traditions such as medicine, on the one hand, and prescriptive traditions such as the law, on the other. That meant psychology could have applied uses in normative institutions within the modernizing state. Indeed, the Free Officers attended lectures on psychoanalysis and integrated this information into their organizational plans.[98] Psychoanalysis was a way to talk about psychosexual development with a scientific language that was not ethically forbidden. For example, it was used to rethink Al-Ghazali's (1058–1111) notion of instinct (*ghariza*) in a post-Darwinian space of liberal subjectivity.[99] Yousef Mourad turned to psychoanalysis because he claimed positivism was

120 A SUSPICIOUS SCIENCE

unable to encompass human complexity in the all-important relation between self and other, while phenomenology and introspection did not offer
enough of an explanatory view.[100] For Cairene intellectuals during this period, discursive psychology was thus used as a systematic language with
which to synthesize introspection, positivism, and phenomenology with
Islam. For religious and mystical practitioners, the notion of the unconscious
offered a science of the hidden similar to the concept of the hidden (*batin*)
crucial to Sufism. Mourad and his circle were able to modify elements of this
theoretical discipline to fit the context of Islamic ethics, in particular ideas
of proto-psychologists like Andalucian scholar Ibn ʿArabi (1165–1240) and
Abu al-Wafa al-Ghunaymi al-Taftazani (1322–1390), to make sense of the
role of hidden factors in psychic life.

Both the use of psychology in India and in Egypt demonstrate that discursive technologies are flexible and served as a conceptual language to enact
transitions involved in modernity and postcolonial adaptation. The language
of psychoanalysis allowed intellectuals in Martinique, Algeria, India, and
Egypt to craft a sense of subjectivity that synthesized native and imported
knowledge practices. Discursive psychology is not a normative description; rather it gives the subject the power to not only understand their own
motivations but also to craft their own epistemological framework by which
to navigate ethical matters. The discursive use of psychology is thus open
to the context of time and place in a way that empirical psychology is not.
This suggests that an interdisciplinary multilevel psychology that takes into
account historical and cultural elements through the discursive use of psychology can be more useful than positivist-pragmatist approaches alone for
assimilating contextual constraints.

Other Examples

The ethnopsychiatry employed by anthropologist Margaret J. Field (1899–
1971) in Ghana allows us to observe how psychology can be applied to the
context of animistic systems of belief. Field's use of psychology renders magic,
science, and religion together on the same plane in their attempts to understand and control people's beliefs, expectations, and soteriological actions.[101]
To understand how multilevel constraints work in an interdisciplinary psychology, it serves us well to clarify historical context in this example in which
colonialism glued together Christianity, identity, and local practice. Ghana

became a colony of Britain in 1874 as part of the Gold Coast and gained independence in 1957 under Kwame Nkrumah (1909–1972). The independence project of Ghana under Nkrumah emphasized a pan-African political platform and was an inspiration for other nationalist projects, which held more ambivalent positions concerning the colonial heritage and maintenance of regional traditional practices in the modern nation state.[102] Part of the Western colonial project in the Gold Coast was introducing Methodist and Presbyterian cosmologies through missionary work. The main traditional religion of Ghana is Akan, which centers on a supreme deity, though there are many variations and subgroups, such as Fanti, Ashanti, and Akuapem. These cultural forms serve as the basis of communitarian, collectivist identities that persist throughout the country.[103] Akan religion has been syncretized with Christianity since the earlier waves of European colonialists starting in the 15th and 16th centuries, though it also remains a distinct set of cultural practices in certain communities.[104] In those contexts, the priest serves crucial functions, as exemplified in the life of Okomfo Anokye and his influence on local identity.[105]

Field imports a use of psychology based in individualist Judeo-Christian traditions, even though Christianity is not the same ground as Akan cosmology or disparate animisms. The unifying phenomenon is the psychological practice by which individuals act out their guilt. The way in which pathological and ritualistic behaviors are explained can take many shapes, but in this case, Field writes, "(W)itchcraft meets ... the depressive's need to steep herself in irrational self-reproach and to denounce herself as unspeakably wicked."[106] In particular, Field describes how rural Ghanaians are embedded in a belief system that relies upon witchcraft and employs concepts like *kra* (soul) and *sunsum* (mind, spirit) to explain psychiatric disturbances.[107] In this context, like those of biblical narratives, there is a prevalence of spirit possessions wherein the possessed individual emits prophesy. Here, magic and medicinal rituals are enacted through the apparatus or technical instrument of the *suman*.[108]

This brief example illustrates how discursive psychology can be lined up with animistic conceptions of pathology. Witchcraft seeks similar goals of alleviating suffering and removing trauma and stigma from the individual in their local context. Yet the similarities theorized in human sciences like psychology obfuscate the historical and experiential fact that these traditions create drastically distinct inhabited worlds.[109] Akan practice can be portrayed as witchcraft for the purposes of psychological purging, but

122   A SUSPICIOUS SCIENCE

it has other uses for identity, emotional coping, and metaphysical practices that involve mystical states of mind in distinct cosmological systems. It is the historical crafting of identity and metaphysical concepts such as the complicated strands of Akan, Christian, and animist practices which then make up an individual's way of life. This cultural context is not captured by a positivist-pragmatic use of psychology, though it can be articulated and possibly analyzed using a discursive psychology.

Toward incorporating such historical, cultural factors into the discursive use of psychology, the ethnopsychoanalysis of Paul Parin (1916–2009), Goldy Parin-Matthèy (1911–1997), and Fritz Morgenthaler (1919–1984) combined ethnographic methods and psychoanalysis to explore the social interactionist relation between self and society.[110] Their extensive interviews and consultations in Mali in the 1950s led to a new way of assessing how social practices, especially concerning sexual mores and the anxieties they produce, shape ego identity. For example, they theorized how so-called sexual perversions of adolescent polygamy served as creative solutions to psychological difficulties arising in early development.[111] Morgenthaler was led by this work to consider how the deeply interpersonal nature of psyche required mutual knowing to engender emotional healing.[112]

As a set of therapeutic practices, or technologies of the self, psychology can restructure subjectivity in a political context because its practices align individuals through shared values. In this way, psychology can come to shape the agency and potential of the political subject. We saw how this came to be accomplished by Fanon, Bose, and Mourad. This process can be also be observed in the psychotherapeutic turn that took place in post-Soviet Russia (1991–present) in which psychological services for affluent children as well as municipal social services came to play a role in sculpting private spaces and political rationalities.[113] The ways in which success, aspiration, and mental health were defined through these therapeutic programs of community service conditioned the consciousness of individuals; "psychotherapeutic practices were made commensurable with the aims of Putin's political-economic agenda . . . the success complex."[114] As a set of practices of self-management, discursive psychology constitutes a type of *habitus*, of knowing oneself in the categories of class and gender within the context of a political imaginary.[115] Practices by which individuals learn aspirational notions of health and success enact a form of subjectivity informed by local cultural values. Specifically in this example of psychotherapy in Moscow, it was after a visit in 1986, that Carl Rogers's (1902–1987) school of humanistic psychology came to provide the basis of a generation of postsocialist therapists. And so, the space for confession took on the format of training sessions in municipal and private practices which allowed individuals to develop new forms of sociality and empathy.[116] The availability of these local knowledge practices inaugurated a form of subjectivity in which discourse about creativity, coping, and aspiration framed burgeoning bourgeois lifeways for parents and children.

In Chapter 1, I discussed how Alfred Luria, Lev Vygotsky, and Ivan Pavlov provided a foundation for the Marxist materialist vision of mind developed in Soviet Russia. What is interesting here is how subsequent shifts in political programs, or ideological motivations in post-Soviet Russia, set forth alternative modes in which subjectivity could be expressed and enacted. During the reign of Stalin, many of the dialectical insights of *new psychology* were pushed out of view to make room for a biomedical model. After subsequent shifts, a notion resembling the human potential movement came to dominance.[117] As Marxist-Leninists argued that material conditions define consciousness, it seems that top-down organization of psychotherapeutic community programs can redefine the position of the subject relative to the state. Similarly to the cases discussed above, the colonial system can play a determining role in how individuals develop their interior spaces. That is to say, the discursive uses of psychology by which individualism is enacted take place within a discourse, or episteme, determined by historical and political factors. Subjectivity itself can be formatted through cultural practices.[118] Psychology is thus inescapably an historical science within which local conditions furnish constraints.

In sum, each culture uses the discursive practices of psychology and the available shared symbols to minister to their prevailing needs. Psychology thus fulfills functions formerly held by religion, metaphysics, and philosophy to satisfy the human need for sense and purpose and provide techniques to promote agency and mastery over the mind. The symbols it uses to this end are drawn from the given culture's metaphysical well. Psychoanalysis offered a rich systematic description of inner experience in the 20th century.[119] The examples provided above suggest that the discursive use of psychology articulates cultural and historical epistemic constraints on the empirical uses of psychology. This interdisciplinary multilevel set of constraints produces a more robust and accurate discipline.

The picture delivered through this method is a complex causal net of constraints. It is helpful toward securing discursive understanding as well as self-knowledge that can lead to reflexive contemplation and modification of behavior. But the treatment of pathology ideally requires an explanation that offers predictive consequences. We would still need to know at which levels/interactional loci causal intervention would be effective and which modifications would lead to relief/resolution. In many ways, an interdisciplinary analysis yields an extraordinarily rich and complex scientific image which due to the interactions between levels includes a significant portion of uncertainty. Despite the accurate reflection of lived experience and bodily integrity of an interdisciplinary multilevel approach, we are still often turned back to a mechanistic analysis that allows for control in therapeutic settings. The main limitation of integrating levels of analysis is that it does not negate the value of knowing and exploiting knowledge of unique causal processes within levels.

The mechanical positivist-pragmatic stance toward the mind discussed in the first part of the book is generally applied with a moral autism because it does not flesh out the mind in its context. What I have endeavored to show is that the intersubjective mirrors of history, development, and social interaction are a necessary component of psychology because they flesh out the mechanistic image to deliver a moral science which includes the immanence of subjectivity and thus affirms the value and complexity of human life. Intersubjectivities that allow for the development of the moral sense and in their application provide space for this irreducible aspect of the human experience also include friendship, play, mimesis, culture and imagination, social interactionism, empathy, psychoanalysis, and reflexivity engendered through art (see Chapter 7).[120]

In contrast to the discursive model, there is a competing biomedical model espoused in positivist-pragmatist empirical psychology. This horn limns the discursive use of psychology by positing the person as an electro-chemical machine. The biomedical model is reinforced by neuropsychology and the rituals of drug use; namely, our propensity to employ chemical modification to treat mood, malady, and personality. The biomedical model eclipsed the discursive model in the late 20th and early 21st centuries. In the next chapter, I discuss how the moral dimension of psychology is tested in this tension between subjectivity and mechanistic explanation.

6

Drugs and the Technology of Agency

It's not the drugs, it's you.

Introduction

In the late 20th century, the efficacy of pharmaceutical drugs legitimated a descriptive, mechanistic explanation of the mind (a biomedical model) that superseded the discursive uses of psychology. In this chapter, I describe drugs as a widespread practical use of psychology and reflect upon how it transforms our notions of agency. In the second section, through the example of addiction, I illustrate how an interdisciplinary multilevel psychology can unite biomedical and psychodynamic models.

Every day millions of people actively modify their minds by ingesting chemicals to alleviate symptoms, find respite from pain, open opportunities for mental exploration, and escape from—or into—altered states. From medication to recreational and spiritual substances, drugs are the most widely available formal and informal implements we have for tweaking the mind. Consider the harsh reality of a shot of whiskey, the softening effect of a reefer stick, the jolt from a midday espresso, and the relief of the cigarette break. College students and cross-country truck drivers chew uppers, and millions take painkillers to dull their chronic pain. There are antidepressants to counter the sense of meaninglessness and benzodiazepines for the endless anxieties of modernity. Drugs function below the jurisdiction of the discursive use of psychology as a pragmatic employment of the findings derived through the empirical use of psychology. Drug use is a set of practices that enact the materialist aspect of the mythology of psychology. They act as tools for the exercise of agency to exert control over the mind, even when the goal is to lose control.

Drugs implement the discoveries of neuroscience and the positivist-pragmatic empirical use of psychology; their main targets are mood, malady,

A Suspicious Science. Rami Gabriel, Oxford University Press. © Oxford University Press 2023.
DOI: 10.1093/oso/9780197513583.003.0008

126 A SUSPICIOUS SCIENCE

and personality. With limited resources of time, support networks, money, and patience, enacting the positivist sense of control over the mind offered by imbibing drugs is regarded as more efficient than therapeutic discourse. When drugs work, they work well and can aid individuals through their suffering. Evidence supports that there are molecular foundations for psychiatric illness.[1] Unfortunately, pharmaceuticals don't always work; they usually bring along a raft of side effects, and sometimes drug use can torpedo the healing process or enable abuse.

Nevertheless, from loneliness to boredom, and from anxiety to depression, drugs are used to counter everyday suffering. The way individual users understand their drug use in the context of their "abnormality" is part of an inchoate, often illogical, "neurobiological imaginary" which is replacing previously dominant psychodynamic contextualization.[2] Through biologizing their suffering in the biomedical health landscape, terms such as "chemically imbalanced" have become part of the way individuals find meaning in their lives.[3] In this chapter, I will explore how materialism and individualism interact in this practical use of psychology.

The Biomedical and the Psychodynamic

How we portray the mind entails how we come to enact and embody this representation. That is to say, the way the mind is portrayed, in the biomedical or psychodynamic discursive model, and how we enact the models in our practices is mimetic.[4] Practical uses of psychology thus dramatize various mimetic representations of mind and agency. In regards to drug use, I am interested in how psychopharmacology enacts a biomedical model and how this bears on the discursive model.

The biomedical and psychodynamic (i.e., discursive) approaches are "two different ways to identify, understand, and respond to mental anguish."[5] In the latter, biology serves as a moral loophole wherein the individual is rendered blameless for their thoughts and behaviors because there are mechanistic accounts for how and why they come to act as they do. In the former, psychiatry is part of the social process of self-making and the interpretation of symptoms is woven into the prognosis.[6] Practitioners of either ilk enact different treatments: psychodynamic therapy consists of teaching patients to listen and look in different ways, whereas biomedical intervention is primarily concerned with assessing the proper diagnosis on the way to determining the appropriate psychopharmaceutical regiment.[7]

An important distinction in psychiatry is between "illness," the patient's experience, and "disease," the abnormality in the structural and functional systems of the body.[8] To convey the reflexive nature of the relation between the individual, the mind, the body, and society, mental illness is caused by a complex set of factors referred to as "bio-psycho-social."[9] Since there is no way to test for most diseases, the therapeutic model becomes centered on the problematic symptoms, assembling a diagnosis, and suggesting a form of treatment. There is a sense in which drugs treat symptoms rather than the disease itself; at the same time, there is an equally persistent sense in which symptoms are the maladaptive behaviors which lead to the need for treatment. Drugs are more effective to treat symptoms because they can quickly terminate them. But the therapeutic use of drugs is bound up with side effects, stigma, and a transformation of how an individual understands her body and herself as an agentive psychological subject.

What I would like to focus on here is the epistemological shift implied in a biomedical model which shifts treatment from a discursive use of psychology to a mechanical, positivist-pragmatist use of psychology. The latter implies that drugs are reliable chemical levers between mental states. In this way, drugs are treated as tools, as technologies to manipulate the mind. They seem to offer a theodicy of grace beyond the limits of our conscious abilities to create change in our lives.[10] Drugs then become the technology by which we ensure adherence to social norms of behavior and achievement. This implies a modicum of control or agency achieved by the careful, conscious user and her doctors, but it is not entirely clear whether the user is augmenting or occluding her agency in employing drugs as a tool to control the mind. The main question I would like to address is, is there a place for agency and autonomy, those bulwarks of individualism and humanism, in a biomedical model?

Is appropriate use of drugs a type of self-mastery, or is self-knowledge only possible when one uses discursive practices, such as insightful reflection and intersubjectivity? Are all forms of coping equally in line with broader values of humanist individualism? If they work, does it matter if one grows dependent on chemical tools? Is there a *meaning* behind every mental illness? In the biomedical model, meaning is essentially beside the point. Mechanical description, while being practical and functional, does not itself constitute an ethical position. Agency, on the other hand, is a discursive moral concept.

So what is really at stake is how the therapeutic use of psychology functions as a moral science, how it portrays individuals as moral actors, and how these commitments are built out into our social institutions.[11]

Drug use is embedded into local knowledge practices and thus fosters the values of its cultural context. For example, consider the use of caffeine and alcohol for amplifying or attenuating our gregariousness and productivity throughout the workday. In this way, drugs come to serve as release valves for labor and social relations. Socially acceptable drugs such as nicotine, caffeine, and alcohol are embedded into common social practices and have come to structure many of our public spaces.[12] The coffee shop is to work culture what the bar is to sociability. These practices coincide with the working week: In the morning we need to be alert, and in the evening we ought to relax. In effect, drugs are highly accessible as a form of self-medication for self-diagnosed states of stress, boredom, restlessness, anxiety, loneliness, and discomfort. They also foster the cultural values of work, efficiency, and community.

In regular use since the 1960s, pharmaceuticals serve to modify our thought patterns, undesirable behaviors, and the sensation of pain.[13] They purport to treat the mechanical chemical cause rather than the social, interpersonal, or psychodynamic causes of affective and personality pathology. These drugs are said to target the root of the experiential state, even though it remains unclear how neurotransmitters are responsible for the wide set of issues that arise in clinical disorders.[14] Self-knowledge gained by introspection and dialogue, that is, the discursive uses of psychology, are no longer our primary means for modifying pathological psychological states. By prescribing medication the medical field is implicitly promoting the position that cognitive and behavioral training is not enough and that "the brain" (another term in the "neurobiological imaginary"), of which nonspecialists have little explicit understanding, is in fact the level where issues are really happening.[15] Indeed, drugs are reliable and effective because they implement the findings of neuroscience; their very use is a type of proof of, or at least evidence for, the biomedical model.[16] Drugs, like Prozac, are said to supplement or in many cases substitute for our humanist discourse about self-development and agency. They help us "get better," or "get over" our issues. In eschewing discourse for chemical levers, we become transhuman hybrid beings who build drugs as ready-to-hand tools into the plant of the body.

The cultural practices of drug use seem to embody our historical moment in which human nature is increasingly considered to be controllable through technology.[17] The implementation of empirical psychology into medical interventions, into the biomedical model, belies a belief that biology and chemistry are the true loci of mind. How does this pertain to the ability to modulate one's own thought processes, to agency itself? This is important because the less agency we include in our reflexivity, the less ethics come to bear upon our decisions. Self-medication through use of the hedonic tools of recreational drugs that diminish our inhibition and sense of responsibility can be conceived of as deliberate manipulation of one's own *sense* of agency. In this case, one decides for oneself when he wants to augment or diminish his attention.

Finally, there is a Dionysian, or spiritual, purpose in recreational inebriation that enables revelations that succor the emotional need for existential reflection. In this sense, drugs serve as doorkeepers for access to restricted metaphysical spaces of mythical time qua creativity or depersonalization. For example, shamans in a range of cultures have employed drugs for ritualistic reliving of the mythology of their tribe.[18] A masterful experience of control is available through taking a stimulant, or one may run roughshod over inhibitions by deranging the senses and loosening the reins of agency in a state of euphoria. In both cases, the habit of using the tool may become engrained and spiral out of control until one can be said to be addicted to the effects of the drug. Addiction has traditionally been portrayed as a loss of agency, and this is one of the reasons it is deemed unethical.[19] Overindulgence of recreational drugs and socially acceptable stimulants seems to negate or distortedly inflate one's sense of agency, but determining the point at which an individual becomes dependent on drugs to cope in professional and social situations is not always easy.[20] In such cases, drug use is counterproductive; it occludes agency and compromises self-development. Yet, when recreational drug use is effective and appropriate, for many users it is considered a great source of relief.

Is the mind a mechanism to be modified by chemicals or is it, as the discursive use of psychology would have it, an organ of meaning-making? The language, or code, of neurotransmitters is mechanical and deterministic, whereas the language of pleasure, trauma, or neurosis is humanistic and historical. The positivist-pragmatist use of psychology exemplified by empirical psychology and psychopharmacology does not deal directly with agency and discourse. Yet discourse and agency clearly matter for an individual's sense of herself as a moral actor in the world. Reflexivity is part of what we take the human experience to entail; discourse seems to be a condition for

130 A SUSPICIOUS SCIENCE

self-knowledge. The discursive uses of psychology continue the tradition of humanism, but how must humanism be transformed in the light of our understanding of our biological being?[21] The answer to this question devolves upon consideration of the nature of agency and thus we can focus on how agency is said to be compromised in pathology.

Pathology and Medication

When medication is tied into the institutionalization of psychiatric prescription, as it is in the *Diagnostic and Statistical Manual of Mental Disorders* (*DSM*), there is an implication that distinct mental illnesses are natural kinds of personality formations. In fact, to define mental illnesses and to codify them as pathological is a historically contingent process.[22] Pathology contextualizes an individual's behaviors within a totalizing condition that requires a medicinal cure beyond their capacities of introspection and the intervention of their social support network. The categorization that follows is thus also an appraisal of the extent of an individual's agency. The development of the *DSM* dramatizes this shift from classification of disorders with underlying etiology rooted in the discursive perspectives to classification based on a biomedical model wherein drug action is the technical detail of the etiological theory.[23] Not only does the *DSM* purport to treat suffering, but it also serves as a reliable document to bring together disparate diagnoses with the practices of billing and insurance. It enshrines the opinions of power players in the financially resplendent medical industrial complex.[24] Standardized, easily identifiable criteria nudge patients and doctors to reframe interiority and pathology in those terms.[25] The *DSM-V* remains, like *DSM-III* and *DSM-IV*, based around defining disease by its symptoms; this tautology lacks validity and hampers the development of a more progressive understanding of mental illness which would seek to address psychosocial causality. For example, the deluge of attention deficit disorder (ADD) diagnoses and their suggested treatments is not sufficiently attentive to the changed nature of media in the last thirty years. The way the youth is socialized within the technology, sociology, and anthropology of communication devices seems to be the causal context of the diagnosis of ADD. Addressing developmental and behavioral issues as part of these cultural constraints would surface more valid, nontautological observations and therapeutic criteria than the *DSM* pipeline of checking off symptoms and following them with pharmaceutical treatment. This is not to say that drug treatment is not effective, just that it does not help us work toward a holistic, progressive understanding of this use of psychology.

The heuristics offered by the *DSM* have, by dint of being embedded in therapeutic, economic, and rhetorical practices, come to be treated as real entities, as natural kinds.[26] This has led to changes in treatment; for example, use of pharmaceuticals for mental illness is now more long term, individuals are prescribed more than one drug, children are prescribed psychoactive drugs, and psychodynamic therapies are increasingly being abandoned as too time-consuming and costly.[27] Worse, nomothetic systems of diagnosis and treatment of the biomedical model like the *DSM* can occlude one's sense of agency and thus alienate her from a sense of being a moral actor.

The experience of an individual who feels (and is diagnosed as) mentally ill often teeters among notions of normal, ill, and different.[28] One's self-image and social standing are imperiled not only by the illness but also by how the diagnosis relates to internalized social norms. The norm I have been stressing is agency, which refers to everything from Freud's claim that "where id was ego shall be," to the humanistic psychologists' notions of potential, freedom, and autonomy, to business popular psychology books which equate agency with entrepreneurship, efficiency, and organization. Recently, terms like "living intentionally" and "optimization" promote some of the meaning of agency.[29] There are also the vectors of authenticity and sense of confidence that are intimately related to agency.[30] What is at stake is that an individualism without agency is rendered hollow when it lacks a sense of moral responsibility. Individualism is founded on notions of autonomy and dignity; without them the discursive use of psychology is reduced to the empirical use of psychology in a biomedical model.

On the other hand, complete agency, or unfettered freedom, is a pipe dream. The biomedical model paradoxically fits well into a culture of the liberal consuming subject because it suggests that control is possible, that, like anything else, it can be bought.[31] In reality, we all live within the limits of our particular circumstances. Drugs or discourse simply offers enough agency to feel it is your life and that the decisions you make are your own. Some individuals use drugs as a form of self-medication for self-diagnosed issues vis-à-vis their psychological needs as social beings; for example, feelings of loneliness and alienation are highly correlated with alcohol and opiate use. Medical practitioners and other purveyors of drugs are then de facto technicians of the mind who dole out tools that effect the efficacy of agency itself. Drugs are then just one of many tools, including the technology of talk therapy, that serve to secure an appropriate sense of agency for the individual within her cultural context. In sum, the discursive tools that served to exfoliate self-actualization through agency may one day be relegated to the dustbin of obsolescent technology because drugs incisively effect carefully selected occlusions of agency that shift our sense of being moral actors. Our transhuman future could be a matter of coping with a self-prescription of helplessness by concocting the drug cocktail that best engenders a latticed sense of agency and escape.

Entheogens

The recent turn to entheogens as a mode of therapy for treatment-resistant depression, addiction, obsessive-compulsive disorder, end-of-life psychological distress, and posttraumatic stress disorder signals a shift in treatment models.[32] Entheogens like psilocybin, LSD, ketamine, and mescaline incite intense reflection upon meaning, value, and existential questions. Taking entheogens is necessarily experiential and discursive; it is the kind of thinking and sensing that takes place under the influence of the drug which leads to changes in perspective for the user. How and why entheogens have their effects can be described using a biomedical view of mind, but the effectivity of the substance is wholly due to the discursive nature of the experience in which the user explicitly reflects upon their situation. Entheogens are then clearly invitations to ethical contemplation. The assumption behind their medical use to treat pathology is that changing how one thinks about basic concepts that determine one's orientation and form of life will be transformative for coping with mood and personality disorders.[33]

Characteristics of altered states engendered by these drugs include transformations in thinking, disturbed sense of time, loss of control, change in emotional expression, change in body image, perceptual distortion, change in meaning or significance (specifically the attribution of heightened significance to subjective experiences, ideas, or perceptions), sense of the ineffable, feelings of rejuvenation, and hypersuggestibility.[34] Entheogens manifest the mind by instating the experience of immanence, in which time, identity, and the sacred are brought to immediate attention. This experience is sometimes referred to in terms of ego dissolution in the research literature, though the effect of such experiences is intimately connected to how an

DRUGS AND THE TECHNOLOGY OF AGENCY   133

individual interprets the experience in terms of their sense of identity, goals, and values.[35] In altered states of consciousness, thoughts and objects in the world gain salience; they become inescapably present.[36] Here is R. G. Wasson on the experience of the sacred mushroom (*Amanita muscaria*):

> It is hardly surprising that your emotions are profoundly affected, and you feel that an indissoluble bond unites you with the others who have shared in the sacred agape. All that you see during this night has a pristine quality: the landscape, the edifices, the carvings, the animals—they look as though they had come straight from the Maker's workshop. This newness of everything—it is as though the world had just dawned—overwhelms you and melts you with its beauty. Not unnaturally, what is happening to you seems fraught with significance, beside which the humdrum events of every day are trivial. All these things you see with an immediacy of vision that leads you to say to yourself, "Now I am seeing for the first time, seeing direct, without the intervention of mortal eyes" . . . The divine mushroom introduces ecstasy to us. Your very soul is seized and shaken until it tingles, until you fear that you will never recover your equilibrium. After all, who will choose to feel undiluted awe, or to float through that door yonder into the Divine Presence?[37]

The return of entheogens for therapeutic purposes suggests that discursive experience may indeed be crucial for coping with the great ethical problems of the human condition, such as pathology. Reflexive dimensions of experience like immanence and the sense of agency remain the basis of the discursive exploration of personhood. That is because meaning is tied in to how we discursively and experientially navigate our individuality through a world marked by affective signals like salience. Our memories, our internalization of cultural symbols, and our process of self-making within a set of local knowledge practices, determine the values that give meaning to our lives. This includes acculturation to religious and mythological background stories as well as social norms and aspirational narratives. Discursive uses of psychology, including the sense of immanence derived through entheogens and other psychoactive drugs, promote engagement with this meaningful material. The timeless, nomothetic models of the empirical use of psychology are ill-equiped to represent the value-laden context of individual experience. For many people, the positivist-pragmatic approach lacks a sense of comprehensibility since it is not couched in the cultural symbols and personal memories

134 A SUSPICIOUS SCIENCE

within which they enact their practical quotidian lives. The empirical uses of psychology coexist with the popular uses of psychology partly because the truths we believe in need to be meaningful to us.[38] It is for this reason that expressive individualism, ethical humanism, and the discourses of subjectivity play a more fundamental role than positivist-pragmatist, biomedical, and materialist uses of psychology for questions of meaning and ethics. The link between spiritual and recreational use of drugs and discursive solace thus leads us back to the experience of value. The feeling that occurs upon understanding an explanation ignites the affective dimension of belief in the sense of satisfaction, of relief from doubt.

In the next chapter, I discuss how this satisfying feeling of salience is intrinsically tied to the process of belief fixation. The experience of immanence we have referred to in the search for explanation and meaning through the mythology of psychology, religion, and as experienced in altered states of consciousness is the key affective aspect of an individual's epistemic niche. I turn now to an example which attempts to bring together the multiple levels of analysis discussed thus far.

Example of an Interdisciplinary Multilevel Psychology

From empirical uses to discourses of individualism and agency, I have endeavored to describe the utility and shortcomings of our mimetic representations of the mind. The time has come to attempt an integration of these cultural and biological levels. If neuroscience can specify functional systems in the brain which are correlated with experiential states, and the discursive use of psychology can *speak through* the perplexities of the heart, then connecting the layers of discourse, and neuropsychopharmacology in the liberal subject would amount to a nonreductionistic interdisciplinary picture of the mind. The illustration I offer below is one way in which the discursive elements of psychology can be maintained within a neuroscientific model. In particular, I suggest how salience, pleasure, and cultural constraints can be interleaved to offer psychological explanation which does not negate either the biomedical or the psychodynamic approach. This sketch focuses on how discursive psychology can provide the historical, contextual constraints that are missing from pragmatic neuroscientific conceptions.[39]

The crucial concepts for characterizing the sense of meaning are motivation and agency because they engage why and how an individual behaves in the world. Both concepts were of great interest to early psychologists but have subsequently been fragmented into an array of processes and frameworks in contemporary cognitive science, developmental psychology, and social psychology.[40] For our purposes, motivation refers to the conative striving of the organism in the context of bodily homeostasis.[41] Placing the causes of motivation into relation with the way an individual navigates the world requires the further step of enlisting ecological psychology, or the extended evolutionary synthesis (EES), to portray the organism in a symbiotic motivated relationship with its environment.[42] EES allows us to conceive of the environment as a set of meaningful objects and symbols with which an individual interacts. Agency, usually conceived of as a matter of conscious deliberation, can also be linked to nonconscious organismic striving motivated by the homeostatic system.[43]

But what determines how an organism makes decisions; how do depth psychological discursive models elaborate mechanistic neuroscientific explanation by providing a story about the specificity of motivation? The drive theory of psychoanalysis posits Eros as an instinct through which life is invested with motivational value and meaning.[44] Eros can be equated with the conative drive of motivation as it constitutes an engaged form of striving.[45] In the brain, primarily the periacqueductal gray (PAG), these notions are embodied in (a) a master emotion dubbed SEEKING which acts as a "goad without a goal," and (b) a definable set of neurotransmitter and neuroanatomical stages that correspond with the phenomenology of pleasure ("liking") and SEEKING ("wanting").[46] The psychodynamic concept Eros is a metaphorical, discursive name for the cognitive-behavioral concept motivation, which is the same as the neuroscientific concept SEEKING. This complex has clear experiential as well as neural trademarks.[47] In particular, the motivational goad of affect is experienced as bias, or salience toward or in conjunction with the content of a perception or an idea. For example, a glass of water is perceived in an affectively motivating manner on a hot day when one is thirsty. The conatively motivated nature of situated perception has consequent effects on attention in line with the adaptive role of the SEEKING system. Specifically, attention is accentuated toward content that generates salience because emotion and cognition share the same system-wide resource of attention.[48]

One way to unite motivation with the actions of an animal in an ESS environment is the affordance competition model.[49] In this model, direct perception activates a set of possible reaction behaviors. These possibilities are solicited as the product of a competition between the parallel processing of possible actions in the dorsal visual system of the frontoparietal cortex. The way in which the selection of an action is determined is via the influence of bias embodied in the feeling of salience and the consequent shifts in attentional resources.[50] In the brain, these reward and expectation variables seem to be derived from prefrontal regions, like the orbitofrontal cortices (OFC) and the basal ganglia communicating with executive and motor areas.[51] The brain processes for how to do a set of possible actions, and selection of the particular appropriate action, occur simultaneously in a hierarchical affordance competition with the dorsal stream specifying parameters of potential actions and the ventral stream providing further information toward selection.[52]

A vast number of associations are learned during the process of development to allow for appropriate responses to a variety of ethological situations. The affordance competition model can help us account for this neural process in ecological terms. That one or more pathways are put into use rather than others is a description at the level of a physical system that functions via connections between sensory and motor areas, assemblies, and neuromodulation. These associations are cathected with an affectively charged pull that may be experienced by the actor. This level at which associations and bias meet is where the historical setting of the individual and her environment is essential. Taking into account affective weighting of associations and predictive processes is crucial to understanding how and why particular objects are appealing.[53] Individuals are drawn into motivated action through interaction with a web of objects in the world which are associated with other objects within the context of social norms, historical situatedness, and individual development. Discursive psychology can explain and expand upon how each individual came to have the associated web of meaningful connections in a way that neuroscience cannot. Through discussion, reflection, and interpretative tools, discourse offers exploration of how and why certain objects, experiences, and symbols carry meaning for the actor. This is because discursive uses of psychology are about objects, ideas, and experiences for the individual in the context of the social world she inhabits; they are intersubjective. These aspects of the mind seem to be coded in the brain, but, as we saw earlier, discourse about this mechanistic embodiment can be highly esoteric. That is precisely why discourse is necessary to unfold the meaningfulness of neuronal associations.

An integration of the phenomenological experience of motivation and agency with the neuroscientific bases of the stages of pleasure and affect is possible. Inspired by the capaciousness of Eros (or, SEEKING) and the concept of desire, I suggest an integration that would allow us to build out a psychodynamic platform for how preconscious motivation and unconscious wanting come to be experienced as narrowly targeted conscious "liking." Freudian Eros, or desire, provides a language to describe the complex, idiosyncratic causal story of pleasure and object associations.[54] For Deleuze and Guttari, desire is not only sexual but also invested directly in the social field. Wilhelm Reich similarly had the insight that desire and its energies structure how bodies interact on the plains of capitalism, hierarchy, and the violent struggles of ideology.[55] This discursive notion of desire as an embodied, historically produced motivation takes us beyond moribund Oedipal stories of how desire is configured to the economic, racial, and political flows of libidinal cathexis.[56] Emotions must be conceived of as tools that motivate action and interpretation by orienting us in the world.[57] SEEKING is the basis of an affective intentionality that comes to be tied to a set of object relations through association and conditioning across the individual's development. Since humans are adaptable and since cultural objects are made by us and for us, our affective intentionality can be tuned to any object, from a team logo to a flavor of ice cream, the chorus of a song, the smell of apricots, and so on. This range of experience and exposure is why idiographic methods are necessary to supplement nomothetic methods. The former allows us to specify the contents of an individual's psychological map of the world and thus talk about actual motivations in all their affective idiosyncrasies.

Herein I sketch a method that can bring together the theory that all pleasure has a common neural currency with the notion that culturally extended pleasures and motivations (beyond the pleasure principle) are discoverable through discourse.[58] The neuropsychological process of pleasure has three components: an appetitive wanting (or SEEKING) phase mediated by mesolimbicortical dopamine, a consummatory "liking" phase mediated by opioids and cannabinoids in hedonic hotspots, and a satiation refractory phase in which learning occurs.[59] In the initial wanting phase, urges are triggered in neural pulses by reward-related cues or vivid imagery about the reward.[60] The urge for a given object that incites the wanting is based largely upon associations attached to the cue.[61] This phenomenon is dramatically illustrated in the incentive salience that particular drugs generate for addicted individuals.

138   A SUSPICIOUS SCIENCE

One is sensitized to reward cues within the context of emotional drives as well as a personal affective *umwelt* that is developed over time.[62] Through the course of an individual's development, objects—from the most basic to highly complex cultural artifacts—come to carry an affective aura for the individual.[63] It is this emotional mode of apperception to which we develop a learned motivating sensitization, which is experienced as "liking," or desire to seek for the purpose of satisfaction.[64] This is best captured by the discursive use of psychology, by looking at the individual's developmental history and their environment as a contingent context.[65] It is best explored or analyzed through discourse in which the individual expresses their thoughts, sensations, and reflections upon the situation or object. Questions like why did you approach the situation like that or why are you drawn to this object, in addition to biographical information, provide solid idiographic ground for explanation.

The discursive use of psychology theory offers a rich theoretical platform to frame the particular compulsions of wanting as associations of cathected nodes of libidinal desire learned in the course of development.[66] For example, object-relations theorists developed ideas about how we attach desire and dread to parts of objects and ideas. Furthermore, Lacanian psychology deals explicitly with desire and its vicissitudes in the context of the symbolic order of language and culturally mediated associations. Notions of ego-libido and object-libido have also been elaborated to provide a frame for how to approach the relation between desire and objects. Psychodynamics thus frames a useful discussion of how intense motivation for pleasure as preconscious and unconscious "wanting" comes to be experienced as conscious "liking" narrowly focused on specific targets. This process is applicable to drug use and addiction wherein the substance, the ritual by which it is ingested, and the experiential state thus achieved can all be marked with various aspects of desire.[67]

Addiction like many other human behaviors is best characterized in the context of the multiple functions served by objects for given individuals vis-à-vis personal history, socioeconomic opportunity, psychological comorbidity, decision-making, and identity.[68] An appropriate understanding of addiction requires an interdisciplinary multilevel psychology which takes into account (at least) genetic proclivity, personality dispositions, anthropology, sociology, pharmacology, and neuroscience. For example, alcoholics will have a genetic predisposition, specifically ADH1B and ALDH2.[69] They are also more likely than nonaddicted individuals to have a personality disorder.[70] Sociological factors like gender, economics, and cultural setting play a role in the likelihood of developing an addiction to alcohol.[71] Finally, these factors which determine the discursive understanding and approach that the individual has to the situations in which alcohol are involved have downstream effects on an individual's receptors throughout the brain because of the pharmacological nature of ethanol and its effects on glutamate, GABA, dopamine, serotonin, and other aspects of neuron function.[72] These downstream effects shape the affective *umwelt* of the user and thus shape the biases that are involved in decision-making, agency, and identity. Each of these levels constrains the other levels: Genetics constrains personality, sociological variables constrain psychodynamics, anthropology constrains personality, and all the human science levels constrain neuroscience, while pharmacology, the brute shape of the molecules, constrains the human sciences, and so on.

A biomedical approach is important, useful, and effective, but with human beings, it is not the whole story. The whole story is a mosaic of explanatory methods applied to a jungle of factors, perspectives, and contexts.[73] To leave out the history or cultural context of an addicted individual is to ignore individual motivations and agency, or at least the situatedness of agency. These literally shape an individual's perception of their environment by calibrating the SEEKING system that colors one's *umwelt* with affective signals that determine how to act through an affordance competition model. To neglect empirical uses of psychology is to ignore hard-won methodological advances and the physical basis upon which culture and psychodynamics are wrought. It is crucial that we understand that the mechanistic account offered by neuroscience is not the same kind of mechanistic account as would be given of a human-made machine. As discussed in Chapter 3, the reason that we are not able to deliver a deterministic or positivist vision of the mind is because of the amount of uncertainty involved in the human frame and the syncretistic amalgamation of multiple levels of analysis which furnish predictions about behavior. This brief description of alcoholism hints at the kinds of syncretism that may allow for a situated, robust science of humans which integrates discursive and empirical uses of psychology.[74]

To summarize, the discursive uses of psychology cluster around individualism and intersubjectivity. As demonstrated in Chapter 5, our practices are historically and culturally embedded forms of agency and moral action. The enactment of materialism in the biomedical model and drug use described in this chapter can occlude agency, but there are ways to integrate discursive approaches by interleaving methods and concepts in an interdisciplinary multilevel psychology.

In the next chapter, I follow up on some consequences of these considerations of how to bring discursive and empirical uses of psychology together by discussing the creative uses of psychology.

7

Art and Reflexivity

Creative Uses of Psychology

The imagination is man's power over nature.

—Wallace Stevens (1930)

Introduction

My exploration of the uses of psychology has emphasized the roles it fulfills within broader cultural projects. The scientific explanations embodied in empirical psychology are one such project, and the individualism enacted in discursive psychology is another. If descriptive explanation tells us how, culture is the technology through which we consider why. In this final chapter, I describe how art and the humanities are creative uses of psychology that furnish us with reflexive knowledge such as contextual modes of contemplation and coping in a range of expressive formats.[1] They accomplish this through engendering mimetic and transcendent experiences that are both analogical and discursive.

Art as Self-Knowledge

The arts consist of techniques to craft objects, and ideas to play with emotions toward the contemplation of space, place, identity, thought, and belief.[2] Ranging from simple pleasures to torture to laughter, pushing one to the edge of confusion or the fog of the sublime, the affective states achievable through art and ritual are accomplished through multiple means.[3] Art articulates humanity in a way that is informative as well as pleasurable, a *utile dolci*. It is through artworks that we may reflexively consider the human condition, including the nature of mind and self.

A Suspicious Science. Rami Gabriel, Oxford University Press. © Oxford University Press 2023.
DOI: 10.1093/oso/9780197513583.003.0009

142 A SUSPICIOUS SCIENCE

Cultural conventions such as ethical norms come to be considered through the mimetic function of representation in Art. The art object is a way we depict ourselves. It serves as both a discursive and analogical mode for exploration and interaction through intersubjectivity. Whereas norms are often communicated didactically or prescriptively as dogma, they can also be adjudicated through simulations and fantasies. Imaginative culture is thus comprised of various aesthetic forms of affect management.[4] The depiction of mythological stories, like those of Hercules, or the glorification of Oba in the Benin bronzes, serves to present norms of heroism and greatness. The depiction of legendary figures, like Aeneas who founded Rome, allows for the concentration of affective power upon a symbol, in this case a character. Through social practices materialized in imaginative culture, our emotional lives come to be domesticated into shared norm-governed group relations. It is through symbolic activities of public memory like these that individuals adapt to live in culturally defined cooperative groups.[5]

Art that equips us with a motivated understanding of ourselves in the world is thus a form of self-knowledge.[6] It requires aesthetic attending, that is to say, an imaginative seeing of the work.[7] Artists manipulate their audience's well of symbols that engage acquaintance knowledge through aesthetic comprehension. By materializing experience in formal content, art allows for acts of interpretation and is thus implicated in the manipulation of conventionally constructed symbolic systems.[8] We observe this process, for example, in digitally manipulated memes, like Pepe the frog, that symbolically represent ideas and affiliations and can be (de)constructed according to various ideological platforms.

G. W. F. Hegel (1770–1831) considered art, along with philosophy and religion, to be an essential aspect of our collective attempt to gain self-knowledge. We learn what we really think about shame, for example, by attending to its display.[9] The mimetic function of art in tragedy and subsequently in the Socratic dialogues is a form of moral psychology because it instigates reflection upon ethical norms. We learn about ourselves, about our condition through watching others like us endure. For German Romantics like Friedrich Schiller (1759–1805), art achieves a means of self-completion through which we cultivate and ennoble the human condition. The aesthetic understanding achievable through art allows for the totality of human potential, partly through extending our notions of what is possible and learning from simulations of reality.[10] Similarly, for poet Rosanna Warren, literature is that symbolic space in which we make formal, imaginative experiments in consciousness and conscience.[11] One technique by which literature accomplishes the experience of deeper meanings is the use of metaphor to enrich and offer affectively powerful resonances.[12] Recall, analogical thinking through metaphor is one of the main tools used by empirical psychologists to discover, form hypotheses, and make novel interpretation of data out of disparate empirical facts. As we saw in Chapter 2, the mimetic representation of mind through metaphor allows us to see ourselves under some description. This aspect of scientific explanation is continuous with the role of mimesis in art. Art as a creative use of psychology fulfills a similar service to the organization of discursive understanding.

The communication at the core of artistic practices is special not because the artist has something to express, but because what she has to express can be shared intersubjectively.[13] We are sense-making animals and thus we are attentive to the ways in which an artist leads the viewer to make connections, for example through narrative or musical effects. This manner of manipulating our proclivities to suggest particular reflexive perspective is a fundamental aspect of the shared experience of art. In viewing a work, we acknowledge the artist's portrayal of the world. Such a conversation quite often leads to knowledge about the self, society, customs, ethics, aesthetic techniques, aesthetic objects, and much more.

Culture as Extended Ecological Niche

Like our environmental niche, culture is an epistemic niche that structures the way we think by soliciting and directing thought.[14] Cultural artifacts such as names, totems, techniques, norms, hierarchies, and ontologies are traditions communicated through symbols.[15] The cultural establishment of conventions that shape the way individuals approach the world is reified by habit, repetition, and ideology that can be modified by language, and it is made into real things by social actions, such as ritual.[16] These, in turn, have a significant effect upon how individuals structure their goals, fears, and aspirations.[17]

Art is a natural human activity and imagination accordingly plays a crucial role in cultural arrangements.[18] Through the context of imaginative culture, religion and ritual charge shared symbols with emotional power.[19] For instance, paintings, songs, and story-telling materialize a community's belief in supernatural agents and idiosyncratic concepts.

144   A SUSPICIOUS SCIENCE

Art materializes experience, bringing a cast of mind into the world through objects.[20] These objects shape our beliefs because they depict norms and articulate social order. "It is out of participation in the general system of symbolic forms we call culture that participation in the particular we call art, which is in fact but a sector of it, is possible."[21] For example, so as to present the metaphysical beliefs of their community, shamans recite stories, songs, and create parietal art to materialize the mystic visions they experience through trance and altered states of consciousness.[22] Communal rituals like seasonal festivals commonly include events in which individuals experience emotional saturation, for example, through dancing and singing during feast days and rites of passage. Communal participation in costly ritual often includes building costumes and effigies to be burned. Through such experience of being empathetically subsumed into the group, these events stabilize the social order.[23]

Art also enables reflexive depiction of the separation of the sacred and the profane. Ancestor worship is implicit in many ritual objects such as the wine vessels and bronze pots of the ancient Chinese Bronze age (c. 1700 BCE). These objects perpetuate the liturgical order by materializing it in an object. In the case of the bronze pots, the depictions engender the feeling of awe toward mortality through nature and spirit worship. Religious art generally depicts mythic stories and allegories that underlie ethical precepts. The grandeur with which we see parables represented in the high period of Christian art in Western Europe, in the Cathedrals of Italy or the wooden votives of Prussia, testifies to the awe-inducing spiritualism of objects that materialize belief. Additionally, there is the nameless sensation engendered by landscapes and abstract patterns and images which nudge the mind to consider the existence of the unknown and experience a numinous unknowingness. Much of modern art seems to be engaged in signifying such a sense of confusion and alienation in the clattering plenitude of our times.

Saturated by the emotional experience generated through the immanent encounter of imaginative culture, information made salient in the sacred experience can become the basis for reflexive contemplation unto belief fixation.[24] It is thus central to the acculturation process that takes place during adolescence, the life history phase most appropriate for the transmission of religious beliefs and values.[25] Immanence implies complete presence. This feeling serves as an anchor for the feeling of salience which phenomenologically and pragmatically signals the correctness of the belief associated with the event. Individual belief then serves as a reflection of the social sacred. This is true both for the artist (or shaman) as well as the other participants who are compelled through the artistic object or event into spiritual emotive states wherein they become receptive to the fixation of metaphysical belief. The feeling of immanence experienced during rituals, carnivals, concerts, dramas, and cinema acts as a liminal zone of time and space.[26] In the power of drama, we surrender and are changed.[27] Liminality and marginality are conditions in which myths, symbols, rituals, philosophical systems, and works of art are particularly potent.[28] Good stories "in addition to the pleasure they bring us, serve to file down and better sharpen our judgment, such that pleasure does not remain pointless."[29] Artists are thus responsible for constructing cultural modes that motivate affective experience and reflexive consideration of local symbols. In contemplating the products of imaginative culture, humans use mimetic representations to reflect on the social order, ontology, beauty, and truth.[30] In the next section, I argue that the kind of reflexive knowledge that creative uses of psychology offer are mediated by emotions and the senses.

Sensible Affective Forms of Knowledge

While philosophy is a discursive rational project, art additionally enables analogical knowledge through engaging affective and sensory modalities.[31] A Hegelian approach treats artworks as "rendering matters of concern more intelligible to us in a distinctly sensible affective way—treats artworks as instances of determinate, and certainly not accumulating, knowledge claims or as evidence or justification for knowledge claims."[32] Hegel deepened Kantian notions of the kinds of content that can be communicated through art by claiming that sensible affective self-understanding is itself a form of insight that is philosophically and historically sensitive.[33] For Enlightenment thinkers, art was a way of relating to the world, a free play of faculties and noncognitive recognition of the purposiveness of nature relative to the moral agentic being of humans. This type of knowledge was not eclipsed or replaced by rationalism, yet these thinkers did not clarify or schematize its function. Indeed, the format of mimetic and immanent arts is not the same as discursive or descriptive explanation. The former evolved

146   A SUSPICIOUS SCIENCE

for the purpose of exploration and derivation of other kinds of knowledge, the latter to offer mechanistic explanation. I argue the elusive form of reflexive knowledge enabled by art is intrinsically tied to emotions, the body, and the imagination.

Aesthetic and materialist approaches to art are couched in Hegel's project to identify how Geist, the collective spirit, comprehends an age in thought by assessing the rationality of its norms.[34] In Hegel's scheme, art is the way humans realize freedom by establishing a self-understanding that aligns rational social relations within the context of the community. An aesthetic approach consists of analyzing how beauty and its production allow us to understand the reality of freedom in the world.[35] A materialist approach on the other hand is to understand the context of our historical moment through the art object.[36]

The broader Hegelian project is not essential to my argument. For my intents and purposes, what Hegel means by Geist, I take to mean the power of *reflexivity*: how we can represent ourselves to ourselves within a situated system of symbols. My thesis has been that psychology, the study of mind, is in essence a reflexive project wherein we question how and why we think the way we do using symbols drawn from a secular, technological society, namely mechanistic and discursive explanation. I would like to suggest that at the same time that the project of empirical psychology was unfolding, artists have also been contributing to the study of the mind. Yet their goal was never nomothetic; rather artworks are idiographic reflections, crystallizations, interpretations, judgments, and ethical considerations about local cultures. Rather than pursue psychic laws of causality, the humanities are concerned with questions of interpretation, aesthetic judgment, and ethical evaluation.[37] Interpretation and understanding require a reflexive turn in self-interpretation because knowing is intertwined with questions of value and significance.[38] This is dependent upon our intelligibility to each other as social agents and maintaining the following qualities in the artwork: credibility, compellingness, and conviction.[39]

In between intuition and conceptual thought, art enables self-knowledge through the mediation of sensible affective knowledge.[40] In addition to imagination and sensation-perception, knowledge by acquaintance is a sensible affective mode crucial for the arts of immanence.[41] Crucially, sensible affective knowledge's boundedness to context and contingency is precisely what allows it to provide knowledge that nomothetic projects cannot.[42]

Emotions and Direct Perception

Emotions are most accurately conceived as affective systems hierarchically structured in layers of interpenetrating functions.[43] The evolution of mind is the developmental story of how these layers emerged in relation to each other. Such feedback between layers is an embodied, enactive, embedded, and sociocultural process. This is what makes for the indelible richness of experience, formed of multiple strands of memories, emotions, ideas, and glimpses. It is only with great difficulty and incompleteness that we attempt to trace the complexity of our conscious experiences. That is why we place such faith in knowledge from acquaintance upon which we can say we know something because we are conscious of it and, language, because it allows us to articulate, abstract, and reflect upon our experience.

There are plenty of things that the body knows that cannot be stated propositionally, that is, procedural or muscle memory, for example how to ride a bike or how to dance the ska. Direct perception is a school of empirical psychology which describes how perception–action systems, such as visual or auditory senses, are constituted of relational loops with the environment wherein perception produces dispositions to act.[44] Effectivities in the percept provide the animal bodily dispositions in relation to a perceived surface; they thus seize and actualize affordances, which are the indicative and imperative elements of a sensory percept.[45] The imperative aspect of a percept dictates how the animal can respond; for example, spatial navigation relies on local cues that designate possible routes.[46] An organism's exploration of the environment requires prospective control that modifies its relation to the perception of particular affordances in the context of its goals.[47]

In addition to physical ecology, we can extend the notion of the niche occupied by humans to its sociocultural constituents, the epistemic niche of culture that includes symbols and other social actors. From neonatal care relationships to coalition building, to apprentice learning of sophisticated skills to cultural institutions, interaction takes place in a niche wherein communication and social position provide social affordances.[48]

The elements of direct perception which may mediate sensible truths when applied to the aesthetic intelligibility of art are affordances, effectivities, imperative representations, social and spatial navigation, and emotional contagion. These processes are all hooked in to affective reactions to the environment.[49] Emotions are manifested as evaluative and expressive actions or dispositions toward objects in the environment. Emotional contagion, that

148 A SUSPICIOUS SCIENCE

is, the sharing of emotions via nonverbal means, is widespread in mammals and begins in infancy in humans, could possibly be the basis of empathy unto feelings of alterity and metamorphosis that occur in the mimetic arts and the shared ritual experience of performance.[50]

The crucial connection between sensible and affective knowledge is the imagination: a precognitive simulation system that mediates between perception and cognition. Imagination is the creative sphere of playful adumbrations of image, sound, and movement. Voluntary imagination evolved from earlier involuntary imaginative states such as dreams.[51] There are other evolutionarily early forms of imagination which produce knowledge that is not declarative but rather poised between concept and intuition. They include image-based inferential processes, image grammar, body-task grammar, nonconceptual content, unconscious bundling, prototypes, and analogical modeling.[52]

Through sensible affective means that include the affective system, direct perception, imagination, and knowledge by acquaintance, various forms of art can engender reflexive knowledge. To illustrate these conjectures, I discuss the following: (a) mimetic arts (such as drama, cinema, and literature), in which individuals empathize and undergo ethical transformations, and (b) arts of immanence (such as music, dance, painting, and cinema), in which reflexive knowledge is generated through trance and play.

Mimetic Arts

Drama and Literature

Plato tells us in the *Republic* that art is imitation, that the artist holds a mirror up to nature.[53] Mimesis is also a moral form of imitation; the manner in which an artist renders nature is through his or her aesthetic education and intentions brought to bear on the task. We also know that imitation is a form of bodily identification in which we internalize and mirror the body grammar that we observe. Let us review further forms of imitation involved in the practice of art. Art and ritual share the mimetic impulse to express "a strongly felt emotion or desire by representing, by making or doing or enriching the object or act desired."[54] Viewers are drawn in to the ritual or performance through emotional contagion, including the activity of mirror neurons.[55] Seeing another person cry or erupt in a rage is an imperative

ART AND REFLEXIVITY   149

representation; it forces us to go along with the emotion being expressed or actively ignore the impulse. Such affordances and effectivities abound in mimetic arts. Actors in theater in particular are trained in simulating recognizable social behaviors and forms of bodily and vocative expression to draw the viewer into the situations they are representing.[56] These sensory perceptions of actors and characters can be ratcheted up to levels of great complexity when symbols and words are also loaded with emotions and associated ideas through the developmental process of acculturation. This is one of the reasons that art is such a potent tool for political expression and ideology.[57]

The traditional manner of presenting mythology through oral recitation was expanded into dramatic tragedy and, subsequently, the novel. Each development allowed for further complexity and reflexivity between the work, the viewer, and the artist. Whereas ritual specifies a liturgical order, Greek tragedy elicits reflection upon that order by the audience.[58] Dramas like the Greek tragedies were an enactment of myth, which, unlike ritual, did not indicate acceptance per se. Rather, tragedy allowed the audience to reflect upon the meaning of divine justice and the integrity of the hero.[59] Ancient Greeks fashioned tragedy to incite mimesis in an emotive ritual about social norms and the nature of compassion. Through engaging the emotional states of guilt and shame, characters like Orestes provide a focus for social expectations to consider how actions alter relations to the world. Actors imitate action, which is then observed by the audience, who, rather than enact ritual participation in the drama, engage in mimetic contemplation.[60] They see themselves in the drama, as the Greeks did in Aeschylus's *The Persians*, which depicts recent martial events from another angle, thereby soliciting reflection upon perspective, justice, and fate. In Greek tragedy, the viewer must locate a source of necessity beyond divine order in the internalized other.[61] This occurs, for example, in *The Eumenides* when justice is located in Athena itself. The genuine social reality of the limitations of metaphysical freedom is thus dramatized; this is especially clear in Attic tragedy, which addressed crises in the basic institutions of society. For example, consider the conflict between filial piety and civic responsibility in Sophocles's *Antigone* at the end of the trilogy in which we come to understand Oedipus not only for his hubris but for his blindness and powerlessness. Antigone then is trapped between norms, between modes of justice. We feel her plight and reflect upon her actions in a way that illuminates our own sense of responsibility to filial and civic norms.

150   A SUSPICIOUS SCIENCE

The novel, on the other hand, is comprised of subgenres which create models for mimetic reflection: a celebratory, idealist view of human life in the epic and chivalric stories, and a derogatory, anti-idealist attitude in picaresque stories, and novellas.[62] The 19th-century European novel refines drama into more involved narrative elements.[63] During this period of positivist optimism, and urbanization/industrialization of the economy, Honoré de Balzac (1799–1850) and Emile Zola (1840–1902) sought to provide a mythic description of their times. They achieve this in *La Comédie Humaine* and the saga of the *Rougon-Macquart* through reflections on society and the role of the individual within it.[64] Rather than reduce lived reality to laws and processes as the empiricists were wont to do in their nomothetic practice, the project of the novel is stoutly idiographic, resting on the notion that portrayals of individuals as in Marcel Proust's *À la Recherche du Temps Perdu* through their detail and insight may deliver the human form. Novels thus align with the project of humanism; they provide material for discursive contemplation of individual lives. Great novelists of the 19th century were chroniclers of the human heart.[65] Indeed, the novel provides a format for writers to assay the major conflicts of their time in the form of increasingly self-conscious narrative structures in which literary technique followed changes in social structure.[66] Literature allows for narratives that explore how individuals relate to the society in which they live, with all their tensions, aspirations, and constraints.[67] Readers mimetically sense the conditions through the rhetoric of realism and the artful presentation of the situation rendered by the writer. This leads to reflexive knowledge which is analogical and discursive but also infused with emotion. The ambition and popularity of 19th-century literature suggest that it provided a superior way for the artist and the reader to consider the world they lived in. Ethical transformations could take place through this encounter; for example, Fyodor Dostoyevsky's (1821–1881) depiction of revolutionary foment in *The Possessed* (1872) engendered public reflection upon political and existential crisis.

Generating knowledge by acquaintance is a crucial tool in the artist's arsenal. It can be achieved, for example, in how memory is regained through the artful exploration of thought, nostalgia, and ethics. From Marcel Proust to John Milton, a paradise is rendered in the *utile dolci* of imagined worlds. There is a mimetic function to moral literature; it provides a simulation of the social imaginary in which we can conceive of our ethical pursuits.[68] Because narratives enact ideals and norms, they propose hypotheses about human life and imagine fictional worlds in which characters like the readers exist

ART AND REFLEXIVITY   151

with qualified autonomy.[69] From the epic to chivalric tales, tragedy, and a vast array of narrative formats, imagination allows us to understand ourselves and others through the reflexive experience of mimetic participation.

Cinema

Cinema has become an effective medium for portraying complex stories that enable viewers to participate in, and reflect upon, the myths of our times.[70] Archetypal characters, or types, bring to life finely wrought scripts wherein storylines illustrate moral reflections, aspirational narratives, and the dramatization of historical events. Patterns of social action are represented in the form of a story grounded in aesthetic and sensory-perceptual forms, historical settings, and interpretational structures.[71] By presenting ideas in this manner, film provides an epistemological platform for consideration of ethical issues. The ways in which this is materialized can take an almost infinite range of forms. To take one example, Alfred Hitchcock's *Vertigo* (1958) brings the audience to consider our mutual interpretability: how to make sense of each other's motivations in the broader context of our fears and desires.[72] John Ford's *The Man Who Shot Liberty Valance* (1962) provides a way to understand how the law is established, how a city comes to be founded through the ambiguity of moral claims. The character John Wayne plays in the classic Ford Western is an epistemological foundation to consider core issues in political theory, such as the uses of violence, coercion, colonialism, assimilation, liminality, and foundation narratives in the Wild West.[73]

Cinema regularly causes a sense of immanence in the viewer through several means; it takes place in a mythic time of heroes and is enacted in an immersive atmosphere not unlike the ritual arena. The movie theater is a closed room, dark but for the light burning through translucent celluloid, in which we sit among strangers with whom we share emotions to spectral events in "speculative solitude."[74] By sharing our reactions, we consider and often reinforce cultural values. Cinema is larger than life—that is how it can represent life to us in a mimetic ritual of drama. We understand something about ourselves by becoming other or anonymous; by being taken in by the story, a space for reflexivity is opened. Narration by the camera, the filmmakers, the unity of interpretive meaning behind the selection of shots, give cinema its reflective form.[75] The overwhelmingly melodramatic format of the journey, the love triangle and skepticism, the violent conflict, the play of trust, and so

152   A SUSPICIOUS SCIENCE

on pushes us to identify with the characters. This mimetic form of interaction with fictional characters allows the viewer to enter into the social situation, to think of her reactions and proclivities relative to the characters on screen. For example, In Jean Renoir's *La Règle du Jeu* (1939), through entering the circle of friends one is led to consider the decadence of leisure and the fickleness of fun. We are brought into empathy and ethical reevaluation by considering human motivation in diverse moral contexts.[76] Knowledge is here mediated by the emotions; the ways in which we derive meaning from the perception of moving pictures ultimately depends upon our shared sense of symbolic content. Emotions motivate us to be reflexively present, to question, to reconsider, to decide.

We employ image-based grammar, like prototypes of characters based on physiognomy, to understand the images that flicker on the screen. Slight cues, like the shot of a building or the shadow over a face, compel us to refer to mnemonic schemas and scripts, like the femme fatale or the lonely drifter, the one-horse town or the bustling newsroom. Unconsciously, we bundle images together as situations, settings, forms of life, and draw inferences thereby. The mind is thus engaged in analogical modeling, wherein connections are made between images and sounds across memories of other films and lived experience. The emotional associations that arise then cue us to the mimetic relation between cinema and life, forcing both conscious and subterranean reflections. From romance to violence, through cinema we learn prototypes of possible encounters that sculpt our predictive capacities.

The liminality of being out of time in a dark room seemingly 'doing nothing' allows for separation from time that binds us. We are freed from speaking, from the dense maze of active interactions that make up public life. Here we are voyeurs who nevertheless, like James Stewart in *Rear Window* (1954), participate emotionally in the spectacle. Through montage a story comes together, through casting we are directed to recognize characters, and through lighting and sound we are immersed in environments. We spot prototypes of narrative arcs that draw our expectations and further participation in the immanent art.[77]

After the liminal, anonymous space of the ritual, we leave the arena, discombobulated, and sensitive to light and motion. We reaggregate ourselves after having imaginatively become part of a different reality. We reflect upon what we saw and heard. The movie becomes memory, remembered as if in a dream.[78] Cinema offers moments of alterity in which we can be ethically transformed through the power of imagination and the intimate acquaintance of mimetic emotion.

Arts of Immanence

Participation in rituals and aesthetic attendance to various forms of art engender states of alterity where we lose ourselves, and it elicits emotional experiences that transform our belief states. In addition to image-based inferential processes, sensible affective knowledge engaged by art often relies on the feeling of immanence.[79] Here I suggest some ways in which art conjures sensible affective knowledge through the feeling of immanence.

The role of participatory ritual is to edge us toward a state of receptivity, of liminality, confusion, emotional saturation, and maybe most importantly, the state of surrender. This attentive state allows for absorption; a state in which stories, characters, environments, emotions, and ideas become powerfully present. There are many methods by which such absorption can be elicited—from low lighting to repetitive or assaultive sounds to transfixing actors and actresses, compelling narratives, addictive plotlines, and so on. Participation through attention and belief is the key to engagement in ritual. The quasi-sacred spaces in which art articulates cultural dramas of meaning can come to resemble the arena of sacrifice.[80] The concert hall, the movie theater, the church, the after-hours club, all direct our attention and through their extended ecological niche provide a context for our emotional responses. Bodily tacit knowledge gained from the affordances and effectivities of the space and social affordances frame our interactions and prime us for certain kinds of experiences.

The ultimate forms of immanence occur when an individual enters the trance state.[81] These experiences resemble the states directed by shamans in rituals of spirit possession.[82] As creative uses of psychology, they fulfill a similar function of making space for reflexive contemplation through metamorphosis, by becoming other and then returning. Artists like jazz musicians themselves habitually report the sensation of being absorbed in the flow of the performance or creation of the art object. In the aesthetic experience, one enters a state of reflective play in which pleasant sensations accompany aesthetic attendance and reflection upon the work.[83] Artists experience a state of immanence in which their sensitivities are transformed; this is manifested in changes to their relation to time, space, other people, and the rehearsed or

154 A SUSPICIOUS SCIENCE

improvised content of the performance. Often, a sense of profundity ensues; it is fecund and leaves traces worthy of reflection. As William James wrote:

> (M)ystical states seem to those who experience them to be also states of knowledge. They are states of insight into depths of truth unplumbed by the discursive intellect. They are illuminations, revelations, full of significance and importance, all inarticulate though they remain; and as a rule they carry with them a curious sense of authority for after-time.[84]

Participation is a state in which one is rendered amenable to transformation. You sacrifice yourself, your memories, preoccupations, and sense of individuality to escape your particular world, with its frames, habits, and familiarity. You escape *into* another world, you enter the mind of the people who produced the spectacle or the characters represented and, while it lasts, this imaginary world is overwhelmingly present. One can become other by identifying with characters on the stage; one could become other by losing herself in the world, or soundworld, of the spectacle. This metamorphic merging with the spectacle constitutes a form of reflexivity in which forms of mimetic empathy, built upon emotional contagion, transform our notions of others and ourselves relative to them.[85] This state of alterity is the ultimate state of reflexivity in which you become other than yourself and therefore observe yourself as it were from the outside, as in a reflection. The kind of knowledge gained thereby is acquaintance knowledge that is analogical, discursive, and sensible-affective.

Music and Trance

Trance is a mental and physical dissociation characterized by a lack of voluntary movement and by automatisms of act and thought exemplified by hypnotic and mediumistic conditions. Adepts claim that riddles are solved and crises are resolved through the catharsis of the phenomenological space of trance. Individuals experiencing trance surrender themselves and thus enter a state of involuntary imagination in which, mediated by perception and cognition, their *habitus* is used as the material for the play of images, memories, neural-somatic states, and image-based inferences. This is similar to the dream state in which symbols loaded with affective content populate involuntary image-based thinking.[86]

Some likely sensible affective truths that emerge include shifting the emotional content between symbols or exaggerating/diminishing the significance of a symbol. Part of the knowledge that is produced is a self-consciousness of one's context. This reflexive illumination arises from the heightened emotional saturation of the experience. There is also the mimetic empathy of communal participation. The affordances made available in social spaces like dance festivals thrust one into a state of immanent acknowledgment of oneself as a body in space related to other bodies. Our spatial abilities are piqued by this nonverbal experience in which body task grammars are engaged.[87] Social navigation is activated in these situations and can also eventuate in changes in the evaluative tenor of social memory.[88]

Trance is an altered state of consciousness that plays an important part in the ecstatic religious tradition. It asserts the confident and egalitarian relation between humans and the divine.[89]

Techniques for achieving trance include hypnotic suggestion, rapid overbreathing, inhalation of smoke and vapors, music, dancing, alcohol, and imbibing psychoactive drugs. Sensory deprivation and hypnosis have also been implicated as inducers of trance.[90] Shamans and holy men regularly display their mastery of spirits by introducing them into their own bodies during trance states.[91] The mystical experience includes feelings of profundity, which lead to the adoption or strengthening of belief; trance is accordingly often described as divine possession.[92] Examples of such practices can be observed in Nubian *zar* ceremonies, Haitian *voudoun* communities, Sufi *dhikr* ceremonies, as well as Pentecostal traditions of speaking in tongues. The sensible affective knowledge derived from such liminal states is directly dependent upon the public and socially sanctioned shared symbols of the trancer's culture. In this way, trancers enact the dominant beliefs of the community through being possessed by them in the ritual arena. These events serve therapeutic purposes as well; the possessing personality forces an identification with the trancer in the light of his personality needs, life situation, and cultural background to either act out a wish fulfilment or directly manipulate other people.[93] The alterity introduced by trance initiates changes in the trancer's perspective on herself and generally instigates reflection upon discursive questions of value and meaning.[94]

Music is an art of immanence which exteriorizes and socializes trance.[95] It has the capacity to engender trance through several characteristics, including rhythmic entrainment of the autonomic nervous system and subsequent structural coupling between the individual and other social agents in

156 A SUSPICIOUS SCIENCE

supra-individual syntheses.[96] Direct perception of sound as affordance and effectivity makes a body move; whether it is dancing, swaying, or launching into participatory sound-making, the affordances are lodged in the sensation of hearing. The absorptive state of sound-induced trance allows for imaginative involvement and hypnotic suggestibility. This includes an escape from the bounded Cartesian self and thus makes possible a radical reflexivity.[97] Monoamines and peptide neurotransmitter systems are implicated in such arousal states and seem to have an effect on one's sense of self, expanding it out and into the world. The skill of listening allows for all this to lead to emotional arousal, depersonalization, amnesia, and cessation of inner monologue.[98] The autobiographical self may be occluded in trance by spirit possession or reversion to a more basic core bodily self.[99] What might be occurring is that bottom-up arousal is being interpreted by top-down cognition, which contains learned social and cultural symbols.[100] Trance and other forms of immanent participation are the space for the play of cultural symbols in which image-based thinking predominates. The transformations in notions of significance within the individual's system of symbols can be modified by unconscious bundling when the autobiographical self is reappointed after the liminal state of trance. Fundamental beliefs are often drawn up in and around these cathartic reflexive experiences of altered states of consciousness.[101]

Conclusion

In this chapter, I sketched various ways in which the arts engender reflexivity, which allows for contemplation of norms, values, and meaning. The arts thereby constitute creative uses of psychology and demonstrate how analogical and discursive forms of explanation introduced in my discussion of metaphor use and psychodynamic approaches can be supplemented by sensible affective knowledge. Consideration of imaginative culture extends our understanding of how psychology is used to engage in reflexive thought.

Conclusion

mans feedback is fear
and superstition his homeostasis
and religion his lifebelt
at end of his tether man lives by myths and dies by daring
ignorance

—Taban Lo Liyong (1971)

Summary

I distinguish three uses of psychology: empirical of the positivist-pragmatic suasion, discursive modes which promote expressive individualism, and reflexive creative practices. In the first part of the book, I described the origins of empirical psychology in Germany, America, and Soviet Russia, focusing on their positivist and pragmatic aspirations and providing a critical appraisal of their reliance on methodology. I elaborated on how psychologists refined their approaches in the 20th century to pursue a mechanistic account of the mind which draws equally from neuroscience, biology, and philosophy of mind. In the second chapter, I argued that in addition to empirical evidence, the process of discovery, interpretation, and hypothesis formation requires the use of analogical frames, specifically metaphors of mind, to collate and interpret various methods and results.

In the Interlude, I took a historical perspective to claim that a limiting case of analogical frames is that they tend to become mythologies. The affective nature of belief itself reveals how the study of the mind bears directly on meaning and values. Psychology is particularly susceptible to being treated like a mythology and a superstition due to its position between the human and natural sciences.

In the second part of the book, I described discursive explanations of the mind which exfoliate the individual, with a focus on popular psychology

A Suspicious Science. Rami Gabriel, Oxford University Press. © Oxford University Press 2023.
DOI: 10.1093/oso/9780197513583.003.0010

and psychoanalysis. I discussed several global, historical examples of the liberatory potential of discursive psychology so as to articulate the importance of context as well as the epistemic constraints of culture upon uses of psychology. I explained the practical uses of psychology through the example of how drugs affect agency so as to elaborate on the differences between biomedical and discursive models of the mind. In the final chapter, I described how art and the humanities are creative uses of psychology which allow for intersubjective reflexive knowledge about the self, norms, and social order.

My positive project is to articulate an interdisciplinary multilevel psychology that is a humanistic human science which takes into account history, ethics, and context. I describe how collating levels of analysis of the mind together to constrain each other provides a robust and more complete set of explanations than either the descriptive or discursive uses of psychology which are currently dominant.

The critical project of the book is to bring together a compendium of the methodological and epistemological issues in empirical psychology as constraints on what we can know about the mind through positivist and pragmatist methods. I highlight how the emotional nature of belief and the sociology of knowledge have led us to frame psychology as a mythology. This epistemic drive toward explanation is particularly susceptible to becoming a superstition when method becomes ritual and the hope of gaining control over the mind occludes the real limits of a science of the mind. I have endeavored to show how an interdisciplinary psychology is thus not only constrained by ontological levels of analysis but also by the vicissitudes of our epistemic needs.

Psychology endows us with a complex explanatory grip over thought and behavior. Yet, like the superstitious approach to deities and auguries before it, the psychological frame is uncomfortably apodictic.

Indeed, superstition provides a sense of control over the uncontrollable.[1] Positive self-deception to protect the ego is useful, because losing the power to explain leads to hopelessness and depression.[2] We are acculturated to believe the mind is the locus of causality because it is the level at which we can reliably build a story about behavior.[3] Psychology is the ideal level of discourse at which we can gain an emotional, rational, and linguistic, grasp on our condition. It provides coherence within our context. It looks like a science, it talks like an explanation, and it is pitched at a satisfying level of discourse, but psychology is a suspicious science; it is incomplete.

CONCLUSION   159

The interpretative frameworks by which we designate the soul or psyche are subject to radical historical change.[4] That which remains the same is that each vision of the mind reflects commitments to norms. Psyche can thus be considered the name for a collective historical achievement, a mode of self-understanding; what we have made ourselves into at one point or other in the service of some commitment.[5] Psychology is then the set of knowledge practices that makes manifest our aspirations for the human; it is a historically achieved manner of holding ourselves and others to account through our commitment to norms.

Psychology has been used to offer widely divergent images of human nature. Freud's vision of humans as driven by erotic and destructive drives captured the imagination in the early 20th century. It completed an older picture of the human as the animal who strives through civilization to attain rational control of their mind and body. But the humanist picture that psychoanalysis offers of the human as the animal who creates more meaning than it knows what to do with was eclipsed by the epistemological frames which have arisen in conjunction with the practical successes of neuroscience and pharmacology.[6] In the latter half of the 20th century, we thus reoriented our desire for knowledge into a paradigm that allows for chemical and therapeutic modification. We grew attached to the proliferation of technological tools used in a positivist science that also promoted the autonomy of the liberal self.[7] Thus, we adapted the modern sense of knowledge as control over nature to the study of the mind.

When we use the methods of history and anthropology to analyze our own uses of psychology, we observe a proliferation of mental terms constellating around the concepts of individualism and materialism. The behavioral sciences seem committed to notions of function and efficiency in a naturalist, neo-Darwinian frame. Subsequently, the metaphorical frames we employ to portray the mind draw extensively from the discourses of biology and engineering. But our commitment to naturalism is obscured by the fact that the data do not add up.[8] Some of our commitments are promissory notes for materialism.

Moreover, despite the political difficulties of building a society of liberal subjects, psychology reifies the individual. This commitment is enacted in popular psychology, discursive therapy, drug use, and cognitive science toward the practical ideals exemplified by economic flourishing and desire. In this sense, psychology is a set of practices that mediate the psychic health of the individual within a complex capitalist state.[9]

160   A SUSPICIOUS SCIENCE

How do we adequately capture a sense of *our* culture, of the social setting of our uses of psychology? The great philosopher of modernity, Friedrich Nietzsche, claimed that we do not have a living culture, that we exist in an ingestion—without digestion—of our own past.[10] We live in the ruins of the dreams, ideals, successes, and failures of those who came before. In this case, history is not a coherent narrative and can only serve as a contingent source of meaning.[11] It has been said that we are part of a civilization that must strive self-consciously without any confidence that we know what civilized life is for.[12] Charles Taylor and Max Weber both argue that an abandonment of comprehensive visions of reality is entailed by secular modernity.[13] The context within which we exist, ambivalent and in between, is then hostile to the possibility of developing, and living by, an action-guiding depth commitment.[14]

Towards addressing this aporia, psychology suspiciously bores a human-size hole in the wall between belief and explanation. The reflexivity that mentalizing bestows promotes a sense of agency (a ventriloquism of control), and thus we sculpt our vision of human nature through the flexible, functional, and reliable language of psychology.

Thus, human nature in its flexibility allows for a plethora of historical ontological frames and their coincident knowledge practices. Psychology as our study of mind, of psychic health, of human nature must enact our commitments, our ethical universe. That is why it can serve as the mimetic language for mass ethics in popular psychology and fulfill the machine metaphor in psychopharmacology. And yet, this scenario forces upon us the issue of the historical relativism of psychology. How can we develop a naturalist story for a historical entity? How can the mind be portrayed and understood as a natural phenomenon when its context and functions are contingent? The key insight is that humans are self-defining animals, and thus the human sciences are intrinsically hermeneutical, historical, and moral.[15] I argue psychology would be less suspicious if it was framed as an interdisciplinary multilevel investigation that takes into account findings from the other human sciences and history.[16]

The purpose of this book is not to dismiss psychology but rather to focus on its uses as examples of how belief and emotions create culturally specific concoctions to satisfy our need for knowledge and meaning in a world full of mystery and danger. Psychology delivers epistemic closure in response to our need to know in and through the techno-fetishist crises of the 21st century.[17]

CONCLUSION 161

Our attention to a reified, half-theorized notion of mind will seem superstitious many years hence. As a secular pantheon, it is host to the druids of the pharmaceutical and empirical professions, to the magicians of the unconscious in clinical psychology. The charismatic aspect of leadership used by big chiefs and shamans has been diffused into the hierarchy of knowledge in contemporary society which favors scientific and technological achievement. Psychology is the language game of our episteme. Just like the Romans had a system to explain the meaning of the flight of birds and read the entrails of sacrificed animals in haruspicy, our analogical systems of mentalizing are delivered through the currently most prestigious set of knowledge practices.

The deeper implication of making order by putting forward theories and collecting data is that we implicitly assume analogical knowledge will reveal hidden variables. Instead, the wide range of facts, reductions, and analogies often leads to fragmentation, to the loss of the sense of the world's wholeness. Measurement marginalizes subjectivity, and materialism seems committed to the reduction of basic phenomenal contents of consciousness.[18] Objectivity and fact are often hostile to the sacred, to traditional manners in which humans founded order. In the mad hunt for explanation, it has been easy to overlook that the slippery eel of reflexivity is the foundational quality of the human mind. And so, we build belief on fleeting orders.

Acknowledgments

This culmination of my work on psychology is an ideal opportunity to thank my parents, Olfat and Hani, not only for their love and companionship but also for their patience and forbearance in supporting the dedication of my formal education to the study of psychology. I thank my sister, Dina, and her family, Jeremy, Roger, and Francis, for their love and for introducing me to the madcap psychology of the developing mind. The kindness and dedication of my family continue to console me. Thanks to Mihad, Layal, Nada, Khaled, Widad, Kais, Sandra, Kamel, Dahlia, Karim, Christiane, Ramy, Magdi, Farah, Alan, and my kin in Toronto, Cairo, and Beirut.

Friendship and music travel well together; accordingly, respect and gratitude to Stephen Asma, Gary Guichard, Alfonso Ponticelli, Scott Ligon, Alex Hall, Casey McDonough, Joel Paterson, Jon Doyle, Tim Mulvenna, Karim Nagi, Steve Gibons, Beau Sample, and Nick Coventry.

I would like to thank Columbia College Chicago and the department of Humanities, History, and Social Sciences for a year-long sabbatical in 2020–2021, which allowed me the time and space to write this book. Many scholars and friends contributed to this project by providing insight, thoughtful conversation, and inspiration. Kim McCarthy, Joan Erdman, Jaak Panksepp, and Tom Greif are no longer with us but shaped my thought and relation to the world. I would like to warmly thank the following colleagues for their continued support and friendship: Stephen T. Asma, Andrew Causey, Robert and Valerie Hanserd, Maya Schechtman and John Marko, Owen Flanagan, Nadine Naber, Atef Said, Zayna Zaatari, Oscar Valdez, Krista Rogers, Rich King, Steve Corey, Teresa Prados, Rojhat Avsar, Bongrae Seok, Cecilea Mun, Muhammad Ali Khalidi, Michael Rescorla, Aaron Zimmerman, Kate Hamerton, Michael Gordin, Michael Teague, Colbey Reid, Kevin Henry, Anthony Madrid, Sebastian Huydts, Eric Ederer, Andrea Fishman, Scott Marcus, MJH, Peter Khooshabeh, Phil O'Sullivan, Piotr Szpunar, Glennon Curran, and Sharon Rutledge. I would like to thank some of my teachers, Donald Hoffman, Jack Loomis, Stanley B. Klein, and Michael Gazzaniga, for leading me into psychology, though they bear no responsibility for the eccentricity of my views.

Appreciation to the following individuals for reading and commenting on drafts of the chapters: Michael Teague, Adrian Ivakhiv, Sean Victory, Peter Khooshabeh, Marya Schechtman, and Noor Shawaf.

I thank the following institutions for allowing me to consult scholarly material during my sabbatical: Chicago Public Library, Columbia College Chicago Library and Interlibrary Loan, the Seminary Co-op in Hyde Park, and the Center for Black Music Research. Elements of chapters were published in *Aeon*. I would like to thank the following editors for their collaboration on these essays: Brigid Hains, Sam Dresser, and Pamela Weintraub.

An early paper on metaphors of mind was presented at the Department of Psychology at University of Illinois at Chicago in 2017. I thank K. K. Szpunar for the invitation. I thank M. A. Khalidi and Jacob Beck for their invitation to present at the Cognitive Science Department at York University, Canada, in 2019. A paper on the affective dynamics of pleasure was presented at the International Neuropsychoanalysis Congress in Brussels, Belgium, in 2019. I thank Mark Solms and the organizers of the conference. Thank you to Helen Lindberg and the Department of Government at Uppsala University, Sweden, for their wonderful invitation to lecture in 2021. A paper on mythology was presented at the International Conference on Myth Criticism in Madrid in 2022 hosted by José Manuel Losada.

The following journals and respective peer reviewers and editors helped strengthen ideas that found their way into the book: Chris Millard at *History of the Human Sciences*, Joseph Carroll at *Frontiers in Psychology,* and Bennett L. Schwartz at *New Ideas in Psychology*.

I acknowledge Joan Bossert for taking on this project and Abby Gross, Nadina Persaud, and everyone else at Oxford University Press for following it through to publication. The anonymous referees were exceedingly helpful in focusing the manuscript, and I thank them.

Finally, I offer love and gratitude to my wife, partner, in-house editor, and playmate, Noor Shawaf, to whom I dedicate this book, for her insight, her support, and the joy and kindness she brings to the world.

Notes

Preface

1. I will often use the term "mindbrain" to avoid confusions caused by vestigial dualism.
2. Dennett, D. (2005). Two steps closer to consciousness. In B. L. Keeley (Ed.), *Paul Churchland* (pp. 193–209). Cambridge: Cambridge University Press..
3. Churchland, P. (2007). Neurophilosophy: The early years and new directions. *Functional Neurology, 22*(4), 185–195. .
4. Churchland, P. (2008). The impact of neuroscience on philosophy. *Neuron, 60*, 409–411. doi:10.1016/j.neuron.2008.10.023
5. See Gabriel, 2012; Kaplan, D. M., & Craver, C. F. (2011). The explanatory force of dynamical and mathematical models in neuroscience: A mechanistic perspective. *Philosophy of Science, 78*(4), 601–627. doi:10.1086/661755
6. Foucault, M., Lagrange, J., Burchell, G., & Davidson, A. I. (2008). *Psychiatric power: Lectures at the College de France, 1973–1974.* New York: Picador.
7. For example, see Gabriel, 2013, in which I describe how the self in America is sculpted by economic and metaphysical forces.
8. See Gabriel, 2021a, in which emotions are conceived as a set of interconnected layers of motivation based around a core of homeostatic drives. For a full presentation of the emotional mind, see Asma & Gabriel (2019).
9. See Gabriel, 2021b.
10. Modernity is taken to mean an industrial epoch that entails particular political and personal conditions of living. See Charles Taylor, Anthony Giddens, and Robert Pippin on modernity. See Karin Knorr-Cetina on Epistemic cultures.

Introduction

1. Smith, R. (2013). *Between mind and nature: A history of psychology.* London: Reaktion Books.
2. Armstrong, K. (2005). *A short history of myth.* New York: Canongate.

Chapter 1

1. Klein, R. G. (2009). *The human career: Human biological and cultural origins* (3rd ed.). Chicago: University of Chicago Press.

166 NOTES

2. Koch, S. (Ed.). (1959). *Psychology: A study of a science.* New York: McGraw-Hill.
3. Adams, G. (1931). *Psychology: Science or superstition?* New York: Covici Friede e-publisher.
4. The distinction between methods in the natural sciences, the human sciences, and the humanities is at the root of why empirical psychology seeks law-like principles. Briefly, the natural sciences seek to "discover" transition laws which consist of systematic representations of target phenomena and systematic ways to transform the phenomena from time *t* to *t'* (Cummins, 1983). On the other hand, the humanities explore the idiosyncrasies of individual stories, events, and schools of thought, they are largely idiographic. The human sciences are in the awkward position of trying to appease both conditions of knowledge and thus as in sociology, economics, and anthropology often demonstrate a bifurcation in research between quantitative and qualitative methods. Psychology in this sense bears this ambivalent mark of the human sciences. I will be arguing that the field must become more interdisciplinary to integrate across levels to coordinate disparate methods and sources of evidence. Collingwood, R. G. (1972). *The idea of history.* New York: Oxford University Press.
5. As we will see in Chapter 3, starting in the late 20th century, probabilistic and mechanistic models in the neurosciences come to supplant the rigidity of the Hempelian model adhered to by early psychologists. Robinson, D. (1976). *An intellectual history of psychology.* Madison: University of Wisconsin Press.
6. The strategy of localization or cognitive modeling is central to a biologically based psychology and exemplifies the standards of explanation in empirical psychology. Kandel, E. R., & Pittenger, C. (1999). The past, the future and the biology of memory storage. *Philosophical Transactions of the Royal Society of London. Series B, Biological Sciences, 354*(1392), 2027–2052. https://doi.org/10.1098/rstb.1999.0542
7. Wilhelm Dilthey laid out the debate with great force and clarity in the 19th century. See Smith, R. (1997). *The Norton history of the human sciences.* New York: W.W. Norton and Company.
8. Robinson, 1976, p. 19.
9. Craver, C. F. (2007). *Explaining the brain: Mechanisms and the mosaic unity of neuroscience.* New York: Oxford University Press.
10. Robinson, 1976, p. 434.
11. Kuhn, T. (1962). *The structure of scientific revolutions.* Chicago: University of Chicago Press.
12. Robinson, 1976, p. 27. Danziger, K. (2013). Psychology and its history. *Theory & Psychology, 23*(6), 829–839. https://doi.org/10.1177/0959354313502746
13. The term "science" refers to disciplined inquiry in Europe, while in the United States it means hypothetico-deductive physicalist models. See Koch, S. (1999). *Psychology in human context: Essays in dissidence and reconstruction.* Chicago: University of Chicago Press.
14. Foucault, M. (1966/2019). *Les mots et les choses: Une archéologie des sciences humaines.* Paris: Gallimard.
15. In *Seven Theories of Human Nature* (1974), Leslie Stevenson argues that the way we view human nature leads to different determinations about what we ought to do and

how we can do it. She describes, for example, how Marxists or Existentialists motivate their political programs and readings of history through their views of human psychology. For example, Christian notions of what is wrong with humankind suggest humans are born with original sin. That vision of humanity then calls for particular ways of organizing society so as to tend to this aspect of human nature. Marxists claim that man's alienation through economic conditions requires that we reorganize society so that the fair and peaceable aspect of our nature can shine through. Existentialists like Jean-Paul Sartre focused on the human ability to define themselves, on the power of agency and good faith, and this led to allegiance with progressive political organizations. B. F. Skinner took Locke's idea of the blank slate as the basis of the behaviorist paradigm of shaping behavior through theories of learning, which he dramatized in a brave new world in *Walden Two* (1948). Plato's emphasis on the importance of wisdom and the nature of knowledge dictated how he portrayed politics and history in *The Republic*. That is to say, beliefs about the mind have implications for how we structure society through politics and how we interpret our successes and failures in history.

16. The list of progenitors of the field is voluminous; John Stuart Mill and Alexander Bain, for example, could have similarly been highlighted. An important dichotomy of rationalism versus empiricism is woven through the history of psychology; building on Kant's foundational *Critique of Pure Reason* (1781), contemporary psychology manages a compromise between the two poles. The reader is referred to the following titles for thorough histories of psychology: Boring, E. G. (1950). *A history of experimental psychology*. New York: Appleton-Century-Crofts. Leahey, T. H. (2003). *A history of psychology: Main currents in psychological thought* (6th ed.). Upper Saddle River, NJ: Pearson Prentice. Hall. Richards, G. (2010). *Putting psychology in its place* (3rd ed.). London: Routledge. Flanagan, O. (1984). *The science of the mind*. Cambridge, MA: MIT Press. The six volumes of Koch, S. (Ed.). (1959). *Psychology: A study of a science*. New York: McGraw-Hill. This book uniquely unites historical, conceptual, and contextual elements of the international story of psychology: Smith, R. (2013). *Between the mind and nature: A history of psychology*. London: Reaktion Books.

17. Nehamas, A. (1998). *The art of living*. Oakland: University of California Press.

18. For more on these antecedents to modern/contemporary psychology, the reader is referred to Robinson's (1976) *Intellectual history of psychology* and Greenwood, J. D. (2015). *A conceptual history of psychology: Exploring the tangled web*. Cambridge: Cambridge University Press.

19. See, for example, the *Sabbasava sutta* on clearing the mind of defilements and the *Salayatana-vibhanga sutta* on the emotions. Al-Ghazzali also wrote about belief, happiness, and other psychological topics in a series of treatises.

20. Robinson, 1976, p. 97.

21. Shapin, S. (1994). *A social history of truth: Civility and science in seventeenth-century England*. Chicago: University of Chicago Press.

22. Logical positivism entails that only empirical evidence is meaningful and only logical analysis is clarifying. There is a line from this philosophical approach developed in Vienna and Berlin through early philosophers of mind like Ludwig Wittgenstein and

168   NOTES

Gottlob Frege to psychologists like Clark Hull and the adaptation of operationalism by Percy Bridgman. See Koch, S. (1999). *Psychology in human context: Essays in dissidence and reconstruction.* Chicago: University of Chicago Press.

23. Pragmatism entails that the meaning of a proposition is to be determined by its consequences, that a proposition is true if it works satisfactorily.

24. James, W. (1890/1950). *The principles of psychology.* New York: Dover, p. vi.

25. James, 1890/1950, p. 8.

26. Danziger, K. (1983). Origins and basic principles of Wundt's Völkerpsychologie. *British Journal of Social Psychology, 22,* 303–313. 10.1111/j.2044-8309.1983. tb00597.x.; Luria, A. (1979). *The making of mind: A personal account of Soviet psychology* (M. Cole & S. Cole, Eds.). Cambridge, MA: Harvard University Press; Danziger, 1990, p. 37.

27. This is similar, of course, to the famous distinction between Aristotle, the protoscientist, and Plato, the arch-rationalist. Gardner, H. (1973). *The quest for mind: Piaget, Lévi-Strauss, and the structuralist movement.* New York: Vintage.

28. Danziger, K. (2008). *Marking the mind: A history of memory.* Cambridge: Cambridge University Press, p. 118.

29. Koch, 1999, p. 414.

30. Robinson, D. (1976). *An intellectual history of psychology.* Madison: University of Wisconsin Press. The full paragraph (p. 391) reads: "Physiological psychology, little more than the product of polemicism in the eighteenth century, became a science in the hands of Flourens, Gall, Bell, Magendie, Helmholtz, and Wundt. Comparative psychology was invented by Spencer, Darwin, Romanes and Morgan. The psychology of individual differences is the creation of Binet and Francis Galton, as are several of the statistical procedures needed for such studies. Cognitive and Gestalt psychologies are so intimately tied to phenomenology that only a purist could deny Hegel and the neo-Hegelians the title of founders. Freud, Janet, Jung and the unconscious are near-synonyms. Our sense of what an experimental science is and ought to be is taken over, with only the slightest modifications, from J. S. Mill, and the general attitude toward the status of science remains largely the one advocated by Auguste Comte and his positivist disciples. Our fascination with hedonistic ethics, with the possibility of shaping the world through the processes of reward and punishment, is linearly traceable to Jeremy Bentham and the Utilitarian movement. Even our 'humanistic' psychologies, with their focus on 'self-actualization, personal growth, and individual freedom, have never improved upon the original formulations by the German Romantics."

31. Similarly, earlier civilizations like the Brahmanic Vedics established a system of ritual action to quell the anxiety of unknowing and ambivalence by circumscribing an arena of control in which only their system of logic worked. As I argue in the Interlude, post-Enlightenment Western societies can be said to similarly isolate scientific knowledge practices to instate an arena of control in the laboratory.

32. Santayana, G. (1922/2009). *The genteel tradition in American philosophy and character and opinion in the United States.* New Haven, CT: Yale University Press, p. 10.

33. Koch, 1999, p. 128.

NOTES   169

34. This characteristic auto-critique was intrinsic to William James's institutionalization of the discipline in *The Principles of Psychology* (1890) in which he shifts among rationalist, literary, and spiritual stances. The ambivalence may be attributable to psychology's ambiguous position between metaphysics and natural sciences. See also Adams, G. (1931). *Psychology: Science or superstition?* New York: Covici Friede e-publisher. "Almost all the questions of most interest to speculative minds are such as science cannot answer." Bertrand Russell as quoted in Koch, 1999, p. 403.

35. Adams, 1931.

36. At the time, psychology was called the moral science by John Stuart Mill, which suggests that there were ethical aspects of the subject matter which distinguished the field from the physical sciences.

37. Robinson, 1976, p. 398.

38. Danziger, 2008, pp. 127–133.

39. Danziger, 1990, p. 47.

40. Validity and reliability are the cornerstones of operational psychology. Validity is a measure of whether the concept refers to what it purports to refer to, while reliability is a measure of the generalizability of the concept, method, and results.

41. Smith, 2013, p. 90. In particular, this view is expressed by Wilhelm Dilthey, who considered that being human entailed a continuous appraisal and reappraisal of our situation and ourselves. See Gadamer, H.-G., Weinsheimer, J., & Marshall, D. G. (2004). *Truth and method.* London: Continuum.

42. Smith, 2013, p. 84. This accords with the post-Darwinian challenge of how to portray the mind as a set of functions in service of the goal of survival (and thriving).

43. Robinson, 1976, p. 378. As an arch-phenomenologist, even with all the dialectical abstractions entailed in his system, Hegel was committed to the validity of experience, of *geist*.

44. Wundt's methodology of introspection itself has roots in Protestant theology, which dictates that methodical self-examination of one's conscience leads to enlightenment. See Trilling, L. (1950). *The liberal imagination: Essays on literature and society.* New York: Viking Press. From a historical perspective, we can see how introspection coincides with the values and epistemological thrust of liberal individualism. See Smith, 2013, p. 102.

45. Danziger, 1990, pp. 18, 23, 31. Individual difference is crucial within an age of liberal individualism and rights; it has political ramifications. See Gabriel (2013) on how individual differences became the basis for self-presentation in consumer society in the 20th century.

46. See the statistical biometry of Francis Galton (1822–1911) and Karl Pearson (1857–1936), as well as Alfred Binet (1857–1911) and chapter 7 of Danziger, 1990.

47. Smith, 2013. Intelligence testing, which resulted in measures like Charles Spearman's (1863–1945) general factor g or William Stern's (1871–1938) IQ, were used as a way of quantifying rationality and then justifying the political, economic, and social orders whereby individuals could be placed in the labor market according to their differences.

48. Smith, 2013, pp. 102–103.

170 NOTES

49. See, for example, the work of James McKeen Cattell (1860–1944).
50. Foucault, M., Lagrange, J., Burchell, G., & Davidson, A. I. (2008). *Psychiatric power: Lectures at the Collège de France, 1973–1974*. New York: Picador.
51. Smith, 2013.
52. Astrology leans on a notion of inborn personality traits which reflect zodiac signs, for example that earth signs (Taurus, Virgo, and Capricorn) are practical and grounded. This is an example of how character traits can be assembled and given apodictic status as reliable sources of determining individual behavior and disposition.
53. The history of hysteria is an example of how psychological institutions can be used to dismiss legitimate claims of abuse and structural gender inequities, and even cast blame on the victims of injustice by pathologizing their behavior and institutionalizing their reactions to disempowerment. Tasca, C., Rapetti, M., Carta, M. G., & Fadda, B. (2012). Women and hysteria in the history of mental health. *Clinical Practice and Epidemiology in Mental Health: CP & EMH, 8*, 110–119. https://doi.org/10.2174/1745 017901208010110
54. Danziger, 1990. Historically, children and adults who were not undergraduate students maintained their identity in the data collected, whereas the latter category, which constitutes the source of the lion's share of collected data, are anonymized and entered into statistical calculations as pure data. This practice has finally in the last decade been highlighted as a limitation of empirical psychological research; see discussion of WEIRD populations in Chapter 3.
55. Santayana, G. (1922/2009). *The genteel tradition in American philosophy and character and opinion in the United States*. New Haven, CT: Yale University Press.
56. Robinson, 1976, p. 375.
57. Perry, 1938. "It is . . . true that all search for truth is a practical activity, with an ethical purpose . . . the attainment of truth means success . . . but the genuine success that we demand is an ethical success . . . we need unity of life. In recognizing that need my own pragmatism consists" (quoted in Perry, 1938, p. 32). Also, "the ultimate test for us of what a truth means is indeed the conduct it dictates or inspires" (quoted in Perry, 1938, p. 59).
58. "Thought is true in proportion as its purpose is realized, and ideas are true in proportion as they serve the purpose for which thought employs them" (Perry, 1938, p. 29). Also see Flanagan, 1984. William James claimed that truth in many cases was felt intuitively, that the sense of acquaintance was required for a radical empiricist to arrive at certitude. Belief and familiarity do indeed color our sense of what seems right and what seems wrong, and yet this sense is not entirely reliable and often leads to confirmation bias.
59. Perry, 1938, p. 72.
60. Perry, 1938, p. 172.
61. "(T)he mental state as an inward activity or passion from all the objects with which it may cognitively deal. I regard this belief as the most fundamental of all the postulates of Psychology" (James, 1890, p. 185).
62. James, W. (1904). Does consciousness exist? *The Journal of Philosophy, Psychology and Scientific Methods, 1*(18), 477–449.

NOTES   171

63. James, 1890.
64. James, 1890, p. 193.
65. James, 1890, p. 197.
66. Mills, J. A. (1998). *Control: A history of behavioral psychology.* New York: New York University Press.
67. Flanagan, 1984.
68. Kendler, H. M. (1985). Behaviorism and psychology: An uneasy alliance. In S. Koch & D. E. Leary (Eds.), *A century of psychology as science.* New York: McGraw-Hill.
69. Ideologically, the emphasis on the malleability of our behaviors, on nurture rather than nature, was aligned with notions of capitalist self-making and perpetual adjustment within an urbanizing nation of individuals on an equal footing. See Smith, 2013.
70. Skinner, B. (1984). Behaviorism at fifty. *Behavioral and Brain Sciences, 7*(4), 615–621. doi:10.1017/S0140525X00027618
71. Flanagan, 1984, p. 90.
72. Skinner, 1984, p. 121. Also, on p. 134, he writes, "It adds nothing to an explanation of how an organism reacts to a stimulus to trace the pattern of the stimulus into the body."
73. Robinson, 1976, p. 452. Skinner considered private events ("within the skin") to be behavior as well. While the earlier iteration of behaviorism espoused by Watson sought law-like relations between stimulus and response, Skinnerian behaviorism admitted the role of an organism's response to the conditions based on Thorndike's "law of effect," thus building in a role for the animal in selecting circumstances that mold the acquisition and shaping of their behavioral palette. Such a process of reinforcement and scheduling has provided substantial reliable information about why nonhuman animals engage in a wide range of behaviors and how they may be trained. The addition of operant conditioning aspect allows behaviorists to explain novel behaviors and purpose-driven actions. Barrett, L. (2011). *Beyond the brain: How body and environment shape animal and human minds.* Princeton, NJ: Princeton University Press. See Flanagan, 1984, pp. 106–107.
74. Flanagan, 1984, p. 113.
75. Robinson, D. N. (1985). Science, psychology, and explanation: Synonyms or antonyms? In S. Koch & D. E. Leary (Eds.), *A century of psychology as science* (pp. 60–74). New York: McGraw-Hill.
76. Koch, 1999.
77. Barrett, 2011.
78. Koch, 1999.
79. Gardner, H. (1985). *The mind's new science: A history of the cognitive revolution.* New York: Basic Books.
80. See the work of Max Wertheimer, Kurt Koffka, and Wolfgang Köhler, also Kurt Lewin, who were all students of German philosopher Carl Stumpf (1848–1936), who himself had studied with Franz Brentano (1838–1917) and Hermann Lotze (1817–1881). This work naturally leads to Edmund Husserl's (1859–1938) phenomenological bracketing of experience in epōche. Phenomenology has a long and important afterlife in the work of Continental philosophers, most notably, Martin

172 NOTES

Heidegger, Maurice Merleau-Ponty, Jean Paul Sartre, Simone de Beauvoir, and Jacques Derrida.

81. Kimble, G. A. (1985). Conditioning and learning. In S. Koch & D. E. Leary (Eds.), *A century of psychology as science* (pp. 284–321). New York: McGraw-Hill.

82. The study of emotions was central to this project, see Solomon, R. (2003). *What is an emotion? Classic and contemporary readings.* Oxford: Oxford University Press.

83. Newell, A., & Simon, H. A. (1972). *Human problem solving.* Englewood Cliffs, NJ: Prentice-Hall.

84. Crosson, F. J. (1985). Psyche and the computer: Integrating the shadow. In S. Koch & D. E. Leary (Eds.), *A century of psychology as science* (pp. 437–451). New York: McGraw-Hill.

85. I cannot at this point offer anything of an adequate analysis of these latter fields and refer the reader to the following sources for a start: The work of Charlotte Bühler (1893–1974), Baldwin, J. M. (1897/1902). *Social and ethical interpretations in mental development.* New York: MacMillan. Erikson, E. (1950). *Childhood and society.* New York: Norton. Sullivan, H. S. (1953). *The interpersonal theory of psychiatry.* New York: Norton. Piaget, J. (1923/1950). *The language and thought of the child.* London: Routledge & Kegan Paul. Adler, A. (1929). *The practice and theory of individual psychology.* New York: Harcourt, Brace. Lewin, K. (1935). *Dynamic theory of personality.* New York: McGraw-Hill. Bandura, A., & Walters, R. (1963). *Social learning and personality development.* New York: Holt. Allport, G. W. (1937). *Personality: A psychological interpretation.* New York: Holt. Mischel, W. (1968). *Personality and assessment.* New York: Wiley. McGuire, W. J. (1985). Toward social psychology's second century. In S. Koch & D. E. Leary (Eds.), *A century of psychology as science* (pp. 284–321). New York: McGraw-Hill.

86. Perry, R. B. (1938). *In the spirit of William James.* New Haven, CT: Yale University Press.

87. Luria, A. (1979). *The making of mind: A personal account of Soviet psychology* (Eds. M. Cole and S. Cole). Cambridge, MA: Harvard University Press.

88. Vygotsky, L. S., van der Veer, R., & Valsiner, J. (Eds.). (1994). *The Vygotsky reader* (T. Prout, Trans.). Oxford: Basil Blackwell.

89. This approach can be distinguished from the structuralist approach to the role of language in development formulated by French psychologist Jean Piaget (1896–1980).

90. Smith, 2013.

91. Luria, 1979.

92. Koch, 1999.

93. This can be further demonstrated by looking at the syntheses created in the adoption of psychoanalysis in India and Egypt, as well as Frantz Fanon's postcolonial strategy. See Gabriel, in press.

94. Danziger, K. (2013). Psychology and its history. *Theory and Psychology, 23*(6), 829–839.

95. While Freud sometimes uses the term *unerkannten* (the ungraspable) rather than *unbakannten* (the unknown), he and other psychologists remain on the trail of an "embryology of the soul."

NOTES 173

96. Lear, J. (1998). *Open minded: Working out the logic of soul*. Cambridge, MA: Harvard University Press. See p. 257 on late Wittgenstein.

97. Kagan, J. (2009). *The three cultures: Natural sciences, social sciences, and the humanities in the 21st century*. Cambridge: Cambridge University Press.

98. Osbeck, L. (2019). *Values in psychological science*. Cambridge: Cambridge University Press.

99. Koch, 1999, p. 416.

Chapter 2

1. Hoffman, R. R., Cochran, E. L., & Nead, J. M. (1990). Cognitive metaphors in experimental psychology. In D. E. Leary (Ed.), *Metaphors in the history of psychology* (pp. 173–229). Cambridge University Press.

2. Kearns, 1987.

3. Rorty, 1979, p. 12.

4. Fischer, 2014.

5. Danziger, 1990.

6. Giere, 1999, 2006.

7. Harré, 2004.

8. The study of metaphor and its use in psychology reached its zenith between the mid-1980s and early 2000s. Classic texts in the field include Lakoff and Johnson (1980/2003), Gentner & Grudin, (1985), Kearns (1987), Leary (1990), Bradie (1999), Montuschi (2000), Brown (2003), Ruse (2005), and Draaisma (2000). Currently, consideration of metaphor use is a focus in the field of embodied cognition, phenomenal consciousness, and reasoning and mental models. See Barsalou, 1999; Gibbs, 2006; Asma & Gabriel, 2019; Fincher-Kiefer, 2019; Gentner et al., 2004; Fischer & Curtis, 2019; Klein, 2020; Boroditsky, 2000; and Thibodeau & Boroditsky, 2011.

9. The topic or tenor (i.e., principal subject) is conceived in the context of a vehicle (or modifying term) against a ground that serves as the semantic basis of the metaphor. Black, 1962, 1977; Hoffman, Cochran, & Nead, 1990; Richards, 1965.

10. Boyd, 1979; Lakoff & Johnson, 1980/2003.

11. Thagard, 1992.

12. Kearns, 1987.

13. Kandel & Pittenger, 1999.

14. Baddeley, 2007.

15. Magnani, 2002.

16. Squire, 2004.

17. Bowdle & Genter, 2005.

18. Pribram, 1990.

19. MacLeod & Neressian, 2013; Squire, Stark, & Clark, 2004.

20. This is the basis, for instance, of studies of dissociation in patients with lesions, such as patient H. M. who had extensive damage in the hippocampus which was used as

174 NOTES

a way to chart memory deficits and functional brain localization (Clement, 2013; Squire, 2009).

21. Magnani, 2002.

22. Barrett, 2011. For example, neuropsychologist Giulio Tononi uses the term "phi," which is also used in quantum mechanics to specify wave functions, to stand for how information is integrated in the brain. Implicit in this catechresis is the claim that consciousness is a specifiable physical magnitude that is analogous to, or even identical with, information integration.

23. Ryle, 1949; McGinn, 1989. Klein (2020) argues that metaphor cannot be applied to the problem of phenomenal consciousness without becoming tautological.

24. Craver, 2005.

25. Flanagan, 1984.

26. Vaihinger, 1924/2009.

27. Freud quoted in Leary, 1990.

28. Appiah, 2017, p. 3.

29. James, 1907, pp. 286–302; C. S. Pierce, 1878.

30. James, 1907.

31. Giere, 1999.

32. Kagan, 2017.

33. Hoffman, Cochran, & Nead, 1990.

34. Berggren, 1963.

35. Children are said to use such practical systems as they explore and learn about their environment. Gopnik, A. (1996). The Scientist as Child. *Philosophy of Science*, *63*(4), 485–514. http://www.jstor.org/stable/188064.

36. Guenther, 2015.

37. Lakoff & Johnson, 1980/2003.

38. Chemero, 2009. Furthermore, while a scientist employs an explicit surface-level metaphor in his thinking, a deeper, more implicit metaphor may also be in use throughout his oeuvre (Leary, 1990). Freud, for example, could explain dreams at the manifest level through linguistic contrivances and associations, while returning to the hydraulic and topographical models of mind to draw deeper inferences (Freud, 1915).

39. Kearns, 1987.

40. Harré, 2004.

41. Lakoff & Johnson, 1980.

42. Kenneth J. Gergen. (1993). A realist psychology revealed. *Contemporary Psychology*, *38*(7), 698–699. doi:10.1037/033493

43. Panksepp, 1998.

44. Gentner, 1983; Bowdle & Gentner, 2005.

45. Kearns, 1987.

46. Locke, 1689/2004.

47. Kearns describes, for instance, how mentally ill people were thought to have immutable souls but diseased, immoral bodies which needed to be reshaped by new customs. Kearns, 1987.

48. Kearns, 1987; Black, 1962. George Henry Lewes portrayed the mind as a web of sentient neural tremors grouped into sensations (Kearns, 1987, p. 129).
49. Kearns, 1987, p. 98.
50. Jacyna, 1981.
51. Robinson, 1976.
52. See review and tables in Gentner & Grudin, 1985.
53. Locke, 1689/2004; Watson, 1924/2007; Skinner, 1951; Barrett, 2012; Herken, 1995; Gardner, 1985.
54. Gabriel, 2012.
55. Barrett, 2012.
56. On the history of "information," see Garson, 2015; Gardner, 1985; Fodor, 1983.
57. Metzinger, 2002; Klein, 2017.
58. Danziger, 1990.
59. Draaisma, 2000. K. Danziger, 2008.
60. Douglas, 1977.
61. Draaisma, 2000.
62. Jaynes, 1976/2000.
63. Draaisma, 2000.
64. Araujo, 2017.
65. Tibell & Harms, 2017; Ruse, 2005.
66. Carey, 2012.
67. Kaufman, 1993.
68. Carroll, 2005; Nagel, 2012.
69. Hurst, 1999.
70. Tooby & Cosmides, 1990.
71. Colombetti, 2017.
72. Pessoa, 2013.
73. See Damasio, 2018; Boyd, 2017; Kahneman, 2013; Panksepp, Biven, & Siegel, 2012; Davidson, R. J., Scherer, K. R., & Goldsmith, H. H. (Eds.). (2003). *Handbook of affective sciences*. Oxford University Press; Marcus, 2009; Ekman, 1999.
74. Panksepp, 1998.
75. de Waal, 2001.
76. Though likening an object of study to natural processes has been used in the past as a way to normalize social construals and legitimate imbalanced power relations, as it did with the notion of gender in primatology.

    Haraway, D. J. (1989). *Primate visions: Gender, race, and nature in the world of modern science*. New York: Routledge.
77. Uttal, 2011; Pribram, 1990.
78. Guenther, 2015.
79. See Gibson, 1979/2014; Varela, Thompson, & Rosch, 1991; Chemero, 2009; Hutto & Myin, 2013; Manzotti, 2019.
80. Wilson, 2002.

176 NOTES

81. Laland et al., 2015. The mind is said to have been built out into the world since the objects we created store aspects of mind, like the built environment and technological gadgets (Barrett & Rendall, 2002).

82. Loomis & Beall, 1998.

83. Chemero & Silberstein, 2008.

84. See Eliasmith & Andersen, 2003; Colombetti, 2017; van Gelder, 1995; Cosmelli, Lachaux, & Thompson, 2007, see Bechtel, 2008; Bechtel & Richardson, 2010; Pessoa, 2013.

85. Simon, 1982; Oaksford & Chater, 1994; Serre et al., 2007; Gigerenzer, 2015, Barsalou, 2009.

86. Brette, 2019.

87. Gigrenzer, 2010.

88. Gallistel, 1990.

89. For example, Chemero, 2009; Colombetti, 2017; Carruthers, 2008; Proust, 2015; Gabriel, 2021.

90. Bechtel & Abrahamsen, 2010; Craver, 2005.

91. Uttal, 2011; Klein, 2017.

92. Gentner & Grudin, 1985.

93. James, 1907, p. 83.

94. Asay, 2018.

95. Bechtel & Richardson, 1993; Bechtel & Abrahamsen, 2010.

96. Smith, 1997. Although, starting with Wilhelm Wundt there has been a correlative effort to distinguish psychology as more than a mere adjunct to physiology.

97. Though drawing from biology may entail a hasty commitment to scientific naturalism (Klein, 2020).

98. Rieff, 1959; Chemero & Silberstein, 2008.

99. Bandura, 1991; Cervone, 2004.

100. Lo Dico, 2018; Mead, 1934; Hermans, 2001.

101. Freud, 1915.

102. Chemero & Silberstein, 2008; Craver, 2005.

103. Bechtel, 2008; Craver & Bechtel, 2007.

104. Gigrenzer, 2010.

105. Gigrenzer & Todd, 1999.

106. Todd, 2001.

107. Bechtel & Abrahamsen, 2010.

108. Gigrenzer, 2010.

109. Dawkins, 1989. In fact, both psychoanalytic and psychiatric theories minimize the role of intention, the former by locating it in the unconscious, and the latter by reducing it to neurochemistry (Luhrmann, 2000). More on this in Chapter 6, where I contrast talk therapy with psychopharmacology.

110. Gould, 1997.

111. Lakoff & Johnson, 1980; Hoffman, 1979.

112. Putnam, 1975.

113. Vidal & Ortega, 2017.

NOTES 177

114. Stafford, 1999, p. 176.
115. Stafford, 1999, p. 137.
116. Asma & Gabriel, 2019.
117. Lima, 2013.
118. Leary, 1990, p. 364.
119. Cassirer, E. (1946). *Language and myth*. New York: Harper.
120. Bhaksar, 1975.
121. Harré, 2004, p. 124.
122. Lima, 2014.
123. Leary, 1990.
124. Khalidi, 2013; Greenberg, 2013.
125. Uttal, 2011.
126. Kuhn, 1962/2012; Jasanoff, 2004.
127. Shapiro, 1985; Scheffler, 1967.
128. Giere, 1999; Van Fraassen, 1980.
129. Rorty, 1979.
130. Bloor, 1976.
131. Leary, 1990.
132. James, 1897; James, 1907; Asma & Gabriel, 2019.
133. Lakoff & Johnson, 1980.
134. Heyes, 2018.
135. Giere, 2006.
136. Lewontin, 2000. Some argue that this is precisely the corner into which empirical psychology has painted itself by adopting a materialist, mechanistic metaphor to explain the inherently subjective phenomenon of mind (Klein, 2014b, 2017).
137. Frazzetto & Anker, 2009; Smith, 2019; Vidal & Ortega, 2017.
138. Chemero & Silberstein, 2008.
139. Smith, 2019.
140. Smith, 2019, p. 15.
141. Gadamer, H.-G., Weinsheimer, J., & Marshall, D. G. (2004). *Truth and method*. London: Continuum. (See pp. 300–305, 367.) For Gadamer, working out the hermeneutical situation entails acquiring the appropriate horizon of inquiry for the questions raised by an encounter with tradition (p. 302). We need to project a historical horizon that is different from that of the present (p. 305).
142. "Historical knowledge contributes narrative, and the understanding of narrative is fundamental to the notion of being human; human self-knowledge and action are mutually constitutive, or, belief changes a person and what a person does changes belief" (Smith, 2019, p. 17).
143. Henrich et al., 2010; Muthukrishna, Henrich, & Slingerland, 2021. I discuss this at length in Chapter 5.

Chapter 3

1. Gardner, H. (1985). *The mind's new science: A history of the cognitive revolution.* New York: Basic Books.
2. Barrett, L. (2012). Why behaviorism isn't Satanism. In J. Vonk & T. K. Shackelford (Eds.), *The Oxford handbook of comparative evolutionary psychology* (pp. 17–38). Oxford University Press.
3. Green, C. D. (1996). Where did the word "cognitive" come from anyway? *Canadian Psychology, 37,* 31–39. Adams, F., & Aizawa, K. (2001). The bounds of cognition. *Philosophical Psychology, 14,* 43–64.
4. Frege, G. (1984). "Thoughts." In B. McGuinness (Ed.), *Gottlob Frege: Collected papers on mathematics, logic, and philosophy* (pp. 351–372). Oxford: Basil Blackwell.
5. Refinements of these models continue—for example, the coding metaphor of neural communication and storage has been criticized as not sufficiently taking into account the causal structure of the brain and the informational requirements of cognition. See Brette, R. (2019). Neural coding: The bureaucratic model of the brain. *Behavioral and Brain Sciences, 42,* e243. https://doi.org/10.31234/osf.io/tgcn9
6. See Fodor, J. (1975). *The language of thought.* New York: Thomas Y. Crowell; Fodor, J., & McLaughlin, B. P. (1990). Connectionism and the problem of systematicity: Why Smolensky's solution doesn't work. *Cognition, 35*(2), 183–204. doi:10.1016/0010-0277(90)90014-B; Schneider, S. (2011). *The language of thought: A new philosophical direction.* Cambridge, MA: MIT Press; Rescorla, M. The language of thought hypothesis. In Edward N. Zalta (Ed.), *The Stanford encyclopedia of philosophy* (Summer 2019 edition). https://plato.stanford.edu/archives/sum2019/entries/language-thought/; Rescorla, M. (2017). Maps in the head. In K. Andrews & J. Beck (Eds.), *The Routledge handbook of philosophy of animal minds.* New York: Routledge.
7. Chalmers, D. J. (1996). *The conscious mind: In search of a fundamental theory.* New York: Oxford University Press.
8. Rumelhart, D. E., McClelland, J. L., & the PDP Research Group (Eds.) (1986). *Parallel distributed processing, volume 1: Explorations in the microstructure of cognition: Foundations.* Cambridge, MA: MIT Press.
9. Breedlove, S. M., & Watson, N. V. (2013). *Biological psychology: An introduction to behavioral, cognitive, and clinical neuroscience* (7th ed.). Somerville, MA: Sinauer Associates.
10. For issues with this theory, see Gabriel, R. (2012). Modularity in affective neuroscience and cognitive psychology. *Journal of Consciousness Studies, 19*(3–4), 19–25.
11. Cacioppo, J. T., Berntson, G. G., & Decety, J. (2010). Social neuroscience and its relationship to social psychology. *Social Cognition, 28*(6), 675–685. https://doi.org/10.1521/soco.2010.28.6.675
12. Fodor, J. A. (1998). *Concepts: Where cognitive science went wrong.* London: Clarendon Press.
13. While social psychology has maintained a focus on situational and dispositional factors in the emergence of social behaviors, it still imports cultural assumptions, for example taking for granted that the individual must be the basis of its models.

See Berntson, G. G., & Cacioppo, J. T. (2008). The neuroevolution of motivation. In J. Shah & W. Gardner (Eds.), *Handbook of motivation science* (pp. 188–200). New York: Guilford; Allport, G. W. (1947). Scientific models and human morals. *Psychological Review, 54*(4), 182–192.

14. Putnam, H. (1975). The meaning of "meaning." In K. Gunderson (Ed.), *Language, mind, and knowledge* (pp. 131–193). Minneapolis: University of Minnesota Press.

15. Some critics, like the eliminative materialists Churchlands and Dan Dennett discussed in the Preface, argue that the neuroscientific level of explanation effectively negates the psychological level; see Coltheart, M. (2006). What has functional neuroimaging told us about the mind (so far)? *Cortex, 42*(3), 323–331.

16. Van Gelder, 1998.

17. Wilson, M. (2002). Six views of embodied cognition. *Psychonomic Bulletin and Review, 9*(4), 625–636.

18. Barrett, L., & Rendall, D. (2010). Out of our minds: The neuroethology of primate strategic behavior. In M. L. Platt & A. A. Ghazanfar (Eds.), *Primate neuroethology* (pp. 570–586). New York: Oxford University Press.

19. Osbeck, L. M. (2009). Transformations in cognitive science: Implications and issues posed. *Journal of Theoretical and Philosophical Psychology, 29*(1), 16–33.

20. Neisser, U. (1976). *Cognition and reality: Principles and implications of cognitive psychology*. New York: W. H. Freeman.

21. Cacioppo, J. T., & Berntson, G. G. (1992). Social psychological contributions to the decade of the brain: Doctrine of multilevel analysis. *American Psychologist, 47*(8), 1019–1028.

22. Campbell, D. T. (1988). *Methodology and epistemology for social science: Selected papers* (E. Samuel Overman, Ed.). Chicago: University of Chicago Press.

23. Craver, C. (2007). *Explaining the brain: Mechanisms and the mosaic unity of neuroscience*. New York: Clarendon Press of Oxford University, p. 246.

24. Developmental psychologists do engage in reduction when they employ perceptual explanations of infant mentality, for example, how depth perception emerges from binocular vision. Although social neurosciences and developmental neurosciences have recently adopted methods from the neurosciences to seek neural correlates. Though interdisciplinary practices carry their own issues; see Osbeck, L. M., & Nersessian, N. J. (2017). Epistemic identities in interdisciplinary science. *Perspectives on Science, 25*(2), 226–261.

25. For example, see the work of Owen Flanagan, Alisdair MacIntyre, Bernard Williams, Martha Nussbaum, Richard Rorty, and Charles Taylor.

26. Guenther, 2015.

27. Polanyí, M. (1958). *Personal knowledge: Towards a post-critical philosophy*. Chicago: University of Chicago Press.

28. The question of what constitutes a level is itself highly contested. One answer is that a level contains all factors that are constitutively relevant, that is, all factors that are mutually manipulable. In fact, the study of the mind occurs at multiple levels and thus the putative mechanism that will serve as explanations in psychology will require integration across levels, for example, neuronal assemblies, behavior, phenomenology,

180 NOTES

and physics. See the work of Wimsatt, W., & Craver, C. F. (2005). Beyond reduction: Mechanisms, multifield integration and the unity of neuroscience. *Studies in History and Philosophy of Biological and Biomedical Sciences*, *36*(2), 373–395. https://doi.org/10.1016/j.shpsc.2005.03.008

29. Kagan, J. (2012). *Psychology's ghosts: The crisis in the profession and the way back*. New Haven, CT: Yale University Press. It is in fact possible that context sensitivity undermines the possibility of reductive explanation in psychology, though there are ways to build this sensitivity into the explanatory schema. See Craver, C. (2007). *Explaining the brain: Mechanisms and the mosaic unity of neuroscience*. New York: Clarendon Press of Oxford University.

30. The explanandum is a description of the phenomenon, while the explanans is description of a mechanism. Craver, 2007, p. 139. Indicating the relevance of the constitutive elements is itself a serious challenge for explanation in psychology, especially a multilevel analysis in which, among other levels, physiological and cultural factors must be integrated.

31. These models that subsume scientific results under representations, like metaphors, to aid understanding may not be sufficient to capture an objective explanation of the phenomenon itself because they cannot serve as a guide to the norms that distinguish good from bad and complete from incomplete explanations. See Craver, 2007, p. 28.

32. Polanyí, 1959.

33. Kitcher, P. (1993). *The advancement of science: Science without legend, objectivity without illusions*. New York: Oxford University Press, p. 31.

34. Reichenbach, H. (1938). *Experience and prediction: An analysis of the foundations and the structure of knowledge*. Chicago: University of Chicago Press. https://doi.org/10.1037/11656-000

35. Resnik, D. B. (2014). Data fabrication and falsification and empiricist philosophy of science. *Science and Engineering Ethics*, *20*(2), 423–431. https://doi.org/10.1007/s11948-013-9466-z

36. Machery, E. (2021). A mistaken confidence in data. *European Journal for Philosophy of Science*, *11*(2), 1–17.

37. Kitcher, 1993.

38. Earp, B. D., & Trafimow, D. (2015). Replication, falsification, and the crisis of confidence in social psychology. *Frontiers in Psychology*, *6*, 621. https://doi.org/10.3389/fpsyg.2015.00621

39. Polanyí, 1958; Machery, E. (2021). A mistaken confidence in data. *European Journal for Philosophy of Science*, *11*(2), 1–17.

40. Aarts, A. A., & Lin, S. C. (2015). Estimating the reproducibility of psychological science. *Science*, *349*(6251), 943–950. Research Collection Lee Kong Chian School of Business. https://ink.library.smu.edu.sg/lkcsb_research/5257

41. Aarts & Lin, 2015. Power refers to the probability of obtaining a statistically significant p-value, given a set alpha, sample size, and population effect size. Effect size is a quantitative measure of the magnitude of the experimental effect. The larger the effect size, the stronger the relationship between two variables. p-value is the probability that the results from an experiment are due to chance and not the experimental

NOTES 181

conditions; it determines the significance of the empirical findings relative to the null hypothesis.

42. Mayo, 2018.

43. Simmons, J. P., Nelson, L. D., & Simonsohn, U. (2011). False-positive psychology: Undisclosed flexibility in data collection and analysis allows presenting anything as significant. *Psychological Science*, *22*, 1359–1366.

44. Pashleer, H., & Wagenmakers, E. (2012). Editors' introduction to the Special Section on Replicability in Psychological Science: A crisis of confidence? *Perspectives on Psychological Science*, *7*(6), 528–530.

45. Klein, S. B. (2014). What can recent replication failures tell us about the theoretical commitments of psychology? *Theory Psychology*, *24*, 326. doi:10.1177/ 0959354314529616

46. Recall the discussion of validity in Chapter 1. See Klein, 2014.

47. Zajonc, R. B. (1968). Attitudinal effects of mere exposure. *Journal of Personality and Social Psychology Monograph Supplement*, *9*(2/2), 1–27. MacLeod, C. M. (1991). Half a century of research on the Stroop effect: An integrative review. *Psychological Bulletin*, *109*, 163–203.

48. Klein, 2014.

49. Mayo, 2018.

50. Flanagan, 1984.

51. Osbeck, L. M. (2019). *Values in psychological sciences*. Cambridge: Cambridge University Press.

52. Koch, S. (1999). *Psychology in human context: Essays in dissidence and reconstruction*. Chicago: University of Chicago Press.

53. Koch, 1999.

54. Khalidi, M. A. (2013). *Natural categories and human kinds: Classification in the natural and social sciences*. Cambridge, MA: Cambridge University Press.

55. Danziger, 1990.

56. Henrich, J., Heine, S. J., & Norenzayan, A. (2010). The weirdest people in the world?. *The Behavioral and Brain Sciences*, *33*(2–3), 61–135. https://doi.org/10.1017/S01405 25X0999152X

57. Henrich, Heine, & Norenzayan, 2010, p. 1.

58. Henrich et al., 2010.

59. May, R. M. (1997). The scientific wealth of nations. *Science*, *275*, 793–796; Arnett, J. (2008). The neglected 95%: Why American psychology needs to become less American. *American Psychologist*, *63*(7), 602–614.

60. Toulmin, S., & Leary, D. E. (1985). The cult of empiricism in psychology, and beyond. In Sigmund Koch & David E. Leary (Eds.), *A Century of Psychology as Science* (pp. 594–617). New York: McGraw-Hill.

61. Simon, H. A. (1973). The structure of ill structured problems. *Artificial Intelligence*, *4*, 181–201.

62. Rosenthal, R. (1979). The file drawer problem and tolerance for null results. *Psychological Bulletin*, *86*(3), 638–641. https://doi.org/10.1037/0033-2909.86.3.638

63. Kagan, 2017, p. 63.

64. Brazier, M. A. B. (1988). *A history of neurophysiology in the 19th century*. New York: Raven Press.

    Jacobson, M. (1995). *Foundations of neuroscience*. New York: Plenum Press.

65. Carabotti, M., Scirocco, A., Maselli, M. A., & Severi, C. (2015). The gut-brain axis: Interactions between enteric microbiota, central and enteric nervous systems. *Annals of Gastroenterology, 28*(2), 203–209.

66. Finger, S. (2000). *Minds behind the brain: A history of the pioneers and their discoveries*. New York: Oxford University Press. According to Shapin (1982), the phrenologists of late Victorian Edinburgh sought to imply a hereditarianism of human nature to oppose the introspection-heavy methodology of academic philosophy. In Britain, the same phrenology was used to suggest the changeability of character within the broader goals of eugenics. This system was then employed by bourgeois social reformers in America as a scientific naturalist basis for generally racist and sexist ideological social programs.

67. Raichle, M. E. (2000). A brief history of human functional brain mapping. In A. W. Toga & J. C. Mazziotta (Eds.), *Brain mapping: The systems* (pp. 33–77). San Diego, CA: Academic Press.

68. Many of these insights are collected in Gazzaniga, M. S., Ivry, R. B., & Mangun, G. R. (2019). *Cognitive neuroscience: The biology of the mind*. New York: W.W. Norton and Company. Also see Guenther, K. (2015). *Localization and its discontents: A genealogy of psychoanalysis and the neuro disciplines*. Chicago: University of Chicago Press.

69. Llínas, R. R. (2001). *I of the vortex*. Cambridge, MA: MIT Press; Pessoa, L. (2013). *The cognitive-emotional brain*. Cambridge, MA: MIT Press.

70. Kagan, J. (2017). *Five constraints on predicting behavior*. Cambridge, MA: MIT Press.

71. Uttal, W. R. (2001). *The new phrenology: The limits of localizing cognitive processes in the brain*. Cambridge, MA: MIT Press.

72. A good example of this is the purported study of the self in Kelley, W. M., Macrae, C. N., Wyland, C. L., Caglar, S., Inati, S., & Heatherton, T. F. (2002). Finding the self? An event-related fMRI study. *Journal of Cognitive Neuroscience, 14*(5), 785–794. https://doi.org/10.1162/08989290260138672

73. Modern, J. L. (2021). *Neuromatic, or, a particular history of religion and the brain*. Chicago: University of Chicago Press.

74. Kagan, J. (2017). *Five constraints on predicting behavior*. Cambridge, MA: MIT Press.

75. Though creative philosophical and neuropsychoanalytic approaches have recently managed to restate the mind-body problem into manageable research questions, see Solms, M. (2021). *The hidden spring: A journey to the source of consciousness*. New York: W.W. Norton and Co.

76. McGinn, C. (1989). Can we solve the mind-body problem? *Mind*, New Series, *98*(391), 349–366.; Wimsatt, W. C. (2006). Reductionism and its heuristics: Making methodological reductionism honest. *Synthese, 151*(3), 445–475.

77. Raichle, M. E., & Mintun, M. A. (2006). Brain work and brain imaging. *Annual Review of Neuroscience, 29*, 449–476. https://doi.org/10.1146/annurev.neuro.29.051605.112819

NOTES 183

Raichle, M. E. (2009). A brief history of human brain mapping. *Trends in Neurosciences, 32*(2), 118–126. https://doi.org/10.1016/j.tins.2008.11.001

Raichle M. E. (2015). The brain's default mode network. *Annual Review of Neuroscience, 38*, 433–447. https://doi.org/10.1146/annurev-neuro-071013-014030

78. Kagan, 2009, pp. 61–64.

79. Uttal, W. R. (2001). *The new phrenology: The limits of localizing cognitive processes in the brain.* Cambridge, MA: MIT Press.

80. Kagan, 2017; Kim & Ress, 2016; Buxton, 2013. These areas in particular are important in determining motivation states of the organism and thus the inability to image them is significant. For more on the role of the nucleus accumbens and orbitofrontal cortex for the crucial activity of value generation, see Gabriel, R. (2021). The motivational role of affect in an ecological model. *Theory and Psychology, 31*(4), 1–21.

81. Kagan, 2017; Rose, N. S., & Abi-Rached, J. M. (2013). *Neuro: The new brain sciences and the management of the mind.* Princeton, NJ: Princeton University Press.

82. Guenter, K. (2015). *Localization and its discontents: A genealogy of psychoanalysis and the neuro disciplines.* Chicago: University of Chicago Press.

83. Brown, E. N., & Kass, R. E. (2009). What is statistics? *The American Statistician, 63*(2), 105–110. doi:10.1198/tast.2009.0019

84. Mayo, D. (2018). Beyond probabilism and performance. In *Statistical inference as severe testing: How to get beyond the statistics wars* (pp. 3–29). Cambridge: Cambridge University Press. doi:10.1017/9781107286184.002

85. Gigerenzer & Marewski, 2015, p. 427.

86. Gigerenzer, & Marewski, 2015.

87. Klein, S. B. (unpublished manuscript). Quantification, conceptual reduction and theoretical under-determination in psychological science, p. 1.

88. Gigerenzer & Marewski, 2015.

89. Krüger, Gigerenzer, & Morgan, 1987.

90. Gigerenzer & Marewski, 2015.

91. P(D l H) means the conditional probability of D, given H. Open Science Collaboration. (2015). Estimating the reproducibility of psychological science. *Science, 349*, aac4716. doi:10.1126/science.aac4716

92. Kline, R. B. (2004). *Beyond significance testing.* Washington, DC: American Psychological Association.

93. Bayes' rule is: posterior odds = likelihood ratio × prior odds, where the likelihood ratio p(D|H1)/p(D|H2) is also known as the Bayes' factor.

94. Mayo, D. (2018). The myth of "the myth of objectivity." In *Statistical inference as severe testing: How to get beyond the statistics wars* (pp. 221–238). Cambridge: Cambridge University Press. doi:10.1017/9781107286184.009.

95. Gigerenzer, G., & Marewski, J. N. (2015). Surrogate science: The idol of a universal method for scientific inference. *Journal of Management, 41*(2), 421–440. https://doi.org/10.1177/0149206314547522

96. Kirschner, S. R. (2006). Psychology and pluralism: Toward the psychological studies. *Journal of Theoretical and Philosophical Psychology, 26*(1–2), 1–17. However, the author quotes Richard Shweder's notion of confusionism that "reality is only knowable

184 NOTES

partially through any given lens or perspective—if you try to put them all together you get incoherence—so it is best to stay on the move between different points of view to see what each illuminates and what each leaves out or obscures" (Shweder, 2001, p. 222). Indeed, ultimate knowledge that takes into account the wide range of data must itself be split up across individuals; it is the community that knows while any individual who is part of the community has incomplete knowledge (see Kitcher, 1993).

97. Haig, B. D. (2020). What can psychology's statistics reformers learn from the error-statistical perspective? *Methods in Psychology*, 2, 2590–2601. According to Haig, error-statistical approach breaks down a research question into a set of local hypotheses that can be investigated using reliable methods. Experimental models structure the particular models at hand and link primary models to data models. Data models generate and model raw data and check whether the data satisfy the assumptions of the experimental models. This hierarchy of models facilitates piece-meal testing of local hypotheses rather than broad theories, and it employs the model hierarchy to move back and forth between statistical and scientific hypotheses. The error-statistical perspective insists on maintaining a clear distinction between sta-tistical and scientific hypotheses. Psychologists are quick to tie tests of significance in particular data sets to direct implications for substantive hypotheses and theories.

98. Calin-Jageman, R. J., & Cumming, G. (2019). The new statistics for better sci-ence: Ask how much, how uncertain, and what else is known. *The American Statistician*, 73(Suppl. 1, 271), 280. doi:10.1080/00031305.2018.1518266

99. Eich, E. (2014). Business not as usual. *Psychological Science*, 25, 3–6. doi:10.1177/ 0956797613512465

100. A confidence interval is the mean of your estimate plus/minus the variation in that estimate. This indicates the range of values one expects the estimate to fall between with replication with a particular level of confidence. Confidence is thus used as an-other way to describe probability.

101. Calin-Jageman & Cumming, 2019.

102. Szucs, D., & Ioannidis, J. P. (2017). Empirical assessment of published effect sizes and power in the recent cognitive neuroscience and psychology literature. *PLoS Biology*, 15(3), e2000797. https://doi.org/10.1371/journal.pbio.2000797; Machery, 2021.

103. Recent high-profile cases include Marc Hauser's fabrication of data in primate studies, Diederik Stapel's social psychology, and the controversy over Amy Cuddy's claims about the power pose. See, for example, the following analysis of such "ghost literature": Simmons, J. P., & Simonsohn, U. (2017). Power posing: P-curving the evidence. *Psychological Science*, 28(5), 687–693. http://dx.doi.org/10.1177/09567 97616658563; Carney, D. R., Cuddy, A. J. C., & Yap, A. J. (2010). Power posing: Brief nonverbal displays affect neuroendocrine levels and risk tolerance. *Psychological Science*, 21, 1363–1368.

104. Kunda, Z. (1990). The case for motivated reasoning. *Psychological Bulletin*, 108, 480–498.

105. Selective reporting and cherry picking are divulging or using only the data that fit one's hypothesis; stopping rules and altered endpoints are conventions to only count

data within a certain range that accord with one's hypothesis; fishing expeditions are when a researcher surveys the data and tries a host of tests fishing for one that will render a significant p-value; changed variables are when researchers change the variables or their range after the data have been collected so as to create a narrative to explain the data; p-hacking is the outcome-dependent strategy of modifying the range of data used in inferential statistics until a significant p-value is achieved.

106. John, L. K., Loewenstein, G., & Prelec, D. (2012). Measuring the prevalence of questionable research practices with incentives for truth telling. *Psychological Science, 23*(5), 524–532. https://doi.org/10.1177/0956797611430953; Gigerenzer & Marewski, 2015.

107. John, Loewenstein, & Prelec, 2012, p. 527.

108. Smith, R. (2013). *Between mind and nature: A history of psychology.* London: Reaktion Books.

109. Latour, B., & Woolgar, S. (1986). *Laboratory life: The construction of scientific facts.* Princeton, NJ: Princeton University Press.

110. Teo, T. (2015). Theoretical psychology: A critical-philosophical outline of core issues. In I. Parker (Ed.), *Handbook of critical psychology* (pp. 117–126). New York: Routledge.

111. Hacking, I. (1999). *The social construction of what?* Cambridge, MA: Harvard University Press.

112. Teo, 2015.

113. Gergen, K. J. (1985). The social constructionist movement in modern psychology. *American Psychologist, 40*(3), 266–275. https://doi.org/10.1037/0003-066X.40.3.266. However, see Longino, H. (2002). *The fate of knowledge.* Princeton, NJ: Princeton University Press, on how the vagueness of constructionism and the ways in which social factors are helpful elements in interaction with rational and cognitive elements toward building robust knowledge.

114. Isaac, J. (2012). *Working knowledge: Making the human sciences from Parsons to Kuhn.* Cambridge, MA: Harvard University Press.

115. Fitzgerald, D., Matusall, S., Skewes, J., & Roepstorff, A. (2014). What's so critical about critical neuroscience? Rethinking experiment, enacting critique. *Frontiers in Human Neuroscience, 8,* 365. https://doi.org/10.3389/fnhum.2014.00365; Slaby, J. (2010). Steps towards a critical neuroscience. *Phenomenology Cognitive Science, 9,* 397–416. doi:10.1007/s11097-010-9170-2; Choudhury, S., Nagel, S. K., & Slaby, J. (2009). Critical neuroscience: Linking neuroscience and society through critical practice. *Biosocieties, 4,* 61–77. doi: 10.1017/s1745855209006437; Slaby, J., & Choudhury, S. (2012). Proposal for a critical neuroscience. In S. Choudhury & J. Slaby (Eds.), *Critical neuroscience: A handbook of the social and cultural contexts of neuroscience* (pp. 27–35). London: Wiley-Blackwell.

116. Koch, 1999; Martin, 2000.

117. Isaac, 2012.

118. According to Klein (2015), "To maintain that all reality submits to current scientific method is to maintain without evidential or conceptual warrant that reality consists in its entirety of aspects capable of being fully grasped by a particular set of techniques and theoretical assumptions" (p. 52).

186   NOTES

119. Osbeck, 2019.
120. Asma, S. (2017). *The evolution of imagination*. Chicago: University of Chicago Press.
121. Wimsatt, William C. (forthcoming). Evolution and the metabolism of error: Biological practice as a foundation for a scientific metaphysics. In William C. Bausman, Janella Baxter, & Oliver M. Lean (Eds.), *From Biological Practice to Scientific Metaphysics. Minnesota Studies in the Philosophy of Science.* Minneapolis: University of Minnesota Press.
122. Wimsatt, forthcoming.
123. Wimsatt, forthcoming.
124. Osbeck, 2019, p. 110.
125. See for example, Thaler, R. H., & Sunstein, C. R. (2008). *Nudge: Improving decisions about health, wealth, and happiness.* New Haven, CT: Yale University Press.
126. Kagan, J. (2017). *Five constraints on predicting behavior.* Cambridge, MA: MIT Press.
127. Damasio, A. (2018). *The strange order of things.* New York: Vintage; Panksepp, J. (1998). *Affective neuroscience.* Oxford: Oxford University Press; Asma & Gabriel, 2019; Carabotti, M., Scirocco, A., Maselli, M. A., & Severi, C. (2015). The gut-brain axis: Interactions between enteric microbiota, central and enteric nervous systems. *Annals of Gastroenterology, 28*(2), 203–209.
128. Klein, S. B. (2015). A defense of experiential realism: The need to take phenomenological reality on its own terms in the study of the mind. *Psychology of Consciousness: Theory, Research, and Practice, 2*(1), 41–56.
129. Merlin Donald portrayed human nature in terms of flexibility via conscious processes and our use of distributed cognitive cultural networks. He singles out mimesis as the basic human thought-skill. Of relevance to our purposes, he describes mythic imagination as the second important aspect of mind, emphasizing the use of metaphor in narrative to codify social customs and norms. Donald, M. W. (2004). The definition of human nature. In D. Reese & S. Rose (Eds.), *The new brain sciences: Perils and prospects* (pp. 34–60). Cambridge: Cambridge University Press.
130. Van Fraassen Bas, C. (1980). *The scientific image.* Oxford: Oxford University Press, p. 4.
131. Popper, K. (1963). *Conjectures and refutations: The growth of scientific knowledge.* London: Routledge.
132. See Gordin, M. D. (2021). *On the fringe: Where science meets pseudoscience.* New York: Oxford University Press. I thank Dr. Gordin for steering me through this vexatious knot.
133. Giere, R. (2006). *Scientific perspectivism.* Chicago: University of Chicago Press.
134. Shapin, S. (1982). History of science and its sociological reconstructions. *History of Science, 20*, 157–211.
135. Mitchell, C., Hobcraft, J., McLanahan, S. S., Siegel, S. R., Berg, A., Brooks-Gunn, J., Garfinkel, I., & Notterman, D. (2014). Social disadvantage, genetic sensitivity, and children's telomere length. *Proceedings of the National Academy of Sciences of the United States of America, 111*(16), 5944–5949. https://doi.org/10.1073/pnas.1404293111
136. Bechtel, W. (2008). *Mental mechanisms: Philosophical perspectives on cognitive neuroscience.* London: Routledge. Here is Ernest Nagel on reductionism: "A reduction

NOTES   187

is effected when the experimental laws of the secondary science (and if it has an adequate theory, its theory as well) are shown to be the logical consequences of the theoretical assumptions (inclusive of the coordinating definitions) of the primary science." Nagel, E. (1961). *The structure of science. Problems in the logic of explanation*. New York: Harcourt, Brace & World, p. 352.

137. See van Riel, R., & Van Gulick, R. Scientific reduction. In Edward N. Zalta (Ed.), The Stanford encyclopedia of philosophy (Spring 2019 edition). https://plato.stanford. edu/archives/spr2019/entries/scientific-reduction/.

138. Oppenheim, P., & Putnam, H. (1958). Unity of science as a working hypothesis. *Minnesota Studies in the Philosophy of Science, 2*, 3–36.

139. Shaffner, K. (1993). *Discovery and explanation in biology and medicine*. Chicago: The University of Chicago Press. Of course, reality can simultaneously sustain a range of diverging accounts we give of it (Shapin, 1982). The boundaries we choose determine the bias in reductionism: "This systematic bias operates relative to the system boundary chosen, so changing the system boundary will change what simplifications are made and appear acceptable" (Wimsatt, 2006, p. 468). Wimsatt describes twenty biases in reductionist heuristics that affect model-building, observation and experimental design, functional localization, and other elements of the scientific process; see Wimsatt, 2006, pp. 469–473.

140. Bechtel, W., & Richardson, R. C. (1992). Emergent phenomena and complex systems. In A. Beckermann, H. Flohr, & J. Kim (Eds.), *Emergence or Reduction? Essays on the prospects of nonreductive physicalism* (pp. 257–288). Berlin: Walter de Gruyter Verlag; Bechtel, W., & Abrahamsen, A. (2010). Dynamic mechanistic explanation: Computational modeling of circadian rhythms as an exemplar for cognitive science. *Studies in History and Philosophy of Science Part A, 1*, 321–333.

141. Fodor, J. (1974). Special sciences (or: The disunity of science as a working hypothesis). *Synthese, 28*(2), 97–115. http://www.jstor.org/stable/20114958

142. Rorty, 1982.

143. Fodor, 1974; Salmon, W. C. (1989). Four decades of scientific explanation. In P. Kitcher & W. C. Salmon (Eds.), *Scientific explanation* (pp. 3–219). Minnesota Studies in the Philosophy of Science, XVIII. Minneapolis: University of Minnesota Press.

144. Wimsatt, 2006.

145. Machamer, P., Darden, L., & Craver, C. F. (2000). Thinking about mechanisms. *Philosophy of Science, 67*(1), 1–25.

146. Craver, C., & Tabery, J. Mechanisms in science. In Edward N. Zalta (Ed.), *The Stanford encyclopedia of philosophy* (Summer 2019 edition). https://plato.stanford. edu/archives/sum2019/entries/science-mechanisms/.

147. Craver, C. F. (2005). Beyond reduction: Mechanisms, multifield integration and the unity of neuroscience. *Studies in History and Philosophy of Biological and Biomedical Sciences, 36*(2), 373–395. https://doi.org/10.1016/j.shpsc.2005.03.008

148. Craver, 2005, p. 393.

149. Wimsatt, W. C. (1976). Reductionism, levels of organization, and the mind-body problem. In G. Globus, G. Maxwell, & I. Savodnik (Eds.), *Consciousness and*

188 NOTES

the Brain: A Scientific and Philosophical Inquiry (pp. 202–267). Plenum Press: New York.

150. Bechtel, W., & Abrahamsen, A. (2005). Explanation: A mechanist alternative. *Studies in History and Philosophy of Biological and Biomedical Sciences, 36*(2), 421–441. https://doi.org/10.1016/j.shpsc.2005.03.010

151. Kandel, E. R., & Pittenger, C. (1999). The past, the future and the biology of memory storage. *Philosophical Transactions of the Royal Society of London. Series B, Biological Sciences, 354*(1392), 2027–2052. https://doi.org/10.1098/rstb.1999.0542

152. Craver, 2007, pp. 256–257.

153. Giere, 1999.

154. Kuhn, T. (1962/2012). *The structure of scientific revolutions.* Chicago: University of Chicago Press.

155. Giere, R. (1999). *Science without laws.* Chicago: University of Chicago Press.

156. Wimsatt, 2021.

157. Gross, P. R., & Levitt, N. (1994). *The academic left and its quarrels with science.* Baltimore, MD: The Johns Hopkins University Press.

158. Kitcher, 1993.

159. Hegel quoted in Rorty, 1982, p. 28

160. James, W. (1907). *On pragmatism.* London: Longmans, Green and Co.

161. James, W. (1912). *Essays in radical empiricism.* London: Longmans, Green and Co.

162. "Any idea that helps us deal, whether practically or intelligibly, with either the reality or its belongings, that doesn't entangle our progress in frustrations, that fits, in fact, and adapts our life to reality's whole setting . . . it will hold true of that reality" (James, 1907, p. 82).

163. Rorty, R. (1982). *Consequences of pragmatism.* Minneapolis: University of Minnesota Press.

164. Rorty, R. (1979). *Philosophy and the mirror of nature.* Princeton, NJ: Princeton University Press.

165. See Kitcher (1993) on the legend of science.

166. The term is drawn from the early generation of anthropologists like Adolf Bastian, Franz Boas, and Edward B. Tylor, as they sought a method to draw together comparative cultural projects and evolutionary theories about humankind.

167. Donovan, J. M., & Rundle, B. A. (1997). Psychic unity constraints upon successful intercultural communication. *Law Faculty Scholarly Articles, 431.* https://uknowle dge.uky.edu/law_facpub/431

168. Sapir, E. (1949). *Selected writings of Edward Sapir in language, culture and personality.* Berkeley: University of California Press; Berlin, B., & Kay, P. (1991). *Basic color terms: Their universality and evolution.* Berkeley: University of California Press; Rosch, E. (1977). Human categorization. In N. Warren (Ed.), *Studies in cross-cultural psychology* (Vol. 1, pp. 1–49). New York: Academic Press; Henrich, Heine, & Norenzayan, 2010; Muthukrishna, M., Henrich, J., & Slingerland, E. (2021). Psychology as a historical science. *Annual Reviews in Psychology, 72,* 717–749

169. Brette, 2019.

170. Craver, 2005.

NOTES 189

Interlude

1. Tambiah, S. J. (1990). *Magic, science, religion, and the scope of rationality* (Lewis Henry Morgan lectures). Cambridge: Cambridge University Press.
2. Mazzarrella, W. (2017). *The mana of mass society.* Chicago: The University of Chicago Press. Malinowski, B. (1948). *Magic, science and religion and other essays.* Glencoe, IL: The Free Press (Reissued by Long Grove, IL: Waveland Press, 1992). Beattie, J. (1964). *Other cultures: Aims, methods and achievements in social anthropology* (1st ed.). London: Routledge. https://doi.org/10.4324/9781315017648. Armstrong, K. (2005). *A short history of myth.* New York: Grove Atlantic. Myths are therefore a form of discursive psychological solution to interior crises, to the tragic facts of life that are beyond our comprehension. Keith Thomas claims magic ritualizes optimism when there is a hiatus in knowledge. Thomas, K. (1971). *Religion and the decline of magic.* New York: Scribner.
3. Armstrong, K. (2005). *A short history of myth.* New York: Grove Atlantic.
4. Indeed, mythology entails the use of symbols to represent and thus understand reality. "Explanations of the world as all or nothing are mythologies, and guaranteed roads to redemption are sublimated magic practices" (p. 54). Horkheimer, M., & Adorno, T. (1944/72). On the concept of enlightenment. In W. Shirmacher (Ed.), *German 20th century philosophy: The Frankfurt School* (pp. 60–85). New York: The Continuum Publishing Group. See also Deacon, D. (1997). *The symbolic species.* New York: W.W. Norton and Co. Barthes, R. (1972). *Mythologies.* New York: Hill and Wang. Even arguing that modernity is characterized by the loss of myths is itself a myth; see Josephson-Storm, J. A. (2017). *The myth of disenchantment: Magic, modernity, and the birth of the human sciences.* Chicago: University of Chicago Press.
5. These come to shape ethics, intimacy, and ontology by being enacted in social, political, and economic knowledge practices. Shapin, S. (1994). *A social history of truth: Civility and science in seventeenth-century England.* Chicago: University of Chicago Press.
6. Eliade, M. (1957/67). *Myths, dreams, and mysteries.* New York: Harper Torchbooks, p. 27. Girard, R. (1977). *Violence and the sacred.* Baltimore: Johns Hopkins University Press, p. 64.
7. Armstrong, 2005.
8. Taylor, C. (1989). *Sources of the self.* Cambridge, MA: Harvard University Press. Also see Siegel, J. (2005). *The idea of the self: Thought and experience in Western Europe since the seventeenth century.* Cambridge: Cambridge University Press.
9. Taylor, 2007.
10. Mythology remains important in Western culture. Take, for instance, heroic role models, from Hercules and Aeneas to contemporary revolutionaries, martyrs, and dictators. Eliade, M. (1963). *Aspects du Mythe.* Paris: Gallimard. These ideal figures exemplify models of human achievement. Even notions of salvation, change, and ethics are so constitutive of our notions of reality that they are often communicated through the format of mythology. There is a surfeit of cultural products that fulfill the function of myth whereby characters and stories give us the means to

190   NOTES

understand the world we live in. See Deacon, T. W. (1998). *The symbolic species: The co-evolution of language and the brain* (No. 202). New York: WW Norton & Company. In the imaginary world we enter, be it through novels or the weightless experience of desire that is consumerism, we draw from shared symbols to create meaning that is both social and personal. Through superhero comic books, to the obscure immanence of modern art, from visions of paradisiacal vacations to computer games and the self-mythologizing of social media production, we seek a higher ground beyond the banal and the profane (cf. Eliade, 1963). We have even replaced the effervescent experience of sacred rites, not in blood sacrifice or vision quests, but in our engagement with art, drugs, dance, and the spectacles of cinema and rock music. (Armstrong, K. (2005). *A short history of myth*. New York: Grove Atlantic). Individuals have developed self-narratives that include mythical transitions in pilgrimages or personal quests to their ancestral lands. Likewise, some seek inner spaces wherein faith and meaning can be transformed into experience. Taylor, C. (2007). *A secular age*. Cambridge, MA: Belknap Press of Harvard University Press.

11. Fuentes, A. (2019). *Why we believe: Evolution and the human way of being*. New Haven, CT: Yale University Press. https://doi.org/10.2307/j.ctvnwbx97

12. Pragmatically speaking, no religions are false, because any belief that a person holds is true insofar as it serves as justification for that person's behaviors. Due to the personal stakes involved in our beliefs about the mind, they cannot be affirmed by any higher authority than our own affective predilections. Any given set of beliefs is real to anyone who adopts it. Compare Durkheim, E. (1915). *The elementary forms of the religious life: A study in religious sociology*. New York: Macmillan. Skorupski, J. (1976). *Symbol and theory: A philosophical study of theories of religion in social anthropology*. Cambridge: Cambridge University Press.

13. Fuentes, 2019; Deacon, T. (1997). *The symbolic species*. New York: W.W. Norton.

14. Durkheim, E. (1915). *The elementary forms of the religious life: A study in religious sociology*. New York: Macmillan, pp. 85, 257.

15. Society is both external and intimate: We live in it and it lives in us and our practices. The collective epistemic niche is thus *extimate* in Jacques Lacan's neologism.

16. Mazzarella, 2007.

17. Mazzarella, 2007.

18. Durkheim, 1915, p. 219.

19. Eliade, M. (1963). *Aspects du Mythe*. Paris: Gallimard.

20. These rites are rules of conduct in the presence of the sacred, which is thus protected and insulated from the profane. (Durkheim, 1915). The sacred fascinates and attracts us while at the same time evoking horror and awe. In myths and the rituals that grow out of them we search for a sense of intimacy with transcendent sources. See Bataille, G. (1973). *Theory of religion* (R. Hurley, Trans.). New York: Zone Books. The sacred, which is immanent in totemic images, relics, and hallowed spaces, is codified into rituals and mythical symbols. See Hanegraaff, W. J. (1999). New Age spiritualities as secular religion: A historian's perspective. *Social Compass, 46*(2), 145–160. doi:10.1177/003776899046002004

NOTES 191

21. Phillips, D. Z. (1993). *Wittgenstein and religion*. London: Macmillan. Siwiec, J. A. (2004). Philosophy of religion as hermeneutics of contemplation according to Dewi Z. Phillips. PhD diss., McGill University.

22. Malinowski, 1949/1992.

23. As John Dewey wrote, "the problem fixes the end of thought, and the end controls the process of thinking." Dewey, J. (1910). *How We Think*. Lexington, MA: D.C. Heath and Company. https://doi.org/10.1037/10903-000. Also see James, W. (1897). *The Will to Believe, and Other Essays in Popular Philosophy*. New York: Longmans, Green, and Co. Belief is not just what we think, it is what we do; it brings together mind and body, practice and thought in local knowledge practices. Wittgenstein, L., &Anscombe, G. E. M. (1997). *Philosophical investigations*. Oxford: Blackwell.

24. Belief is often and maybe always riding on emotional factors like "lively conceptions" and "instinctive liking." (James, 1897).

25. Panksepp, J. (1998). *Affective neuroscience*. New York: Oxford University Press.

26. A pragmatic approach to belief must thus take into account not only how we verify our beliefs through observable action but also the various subtypes of implicit and explicit belief, and the influence of other taxonomic choices like the passions, volition, positive illusions, and play. The latter conditions are generally considered beneath scientific considerations in the hierarchy of normativity, but the more we learn about emotions, the more it seems that these conditions of belief are fundamental. Zimmerman, A. (2018). *A pragmatic picture of belief*. New York: Oxford University Press. Cf. Bain, A. (1865). *The emotions and the will* (2nd ed.). New York: Longmans, Green and Co. https://doi.org/10.1037/12264-000

27. Shagan, 2019. Moss and Schwab (2019) argue that Aristotle's *hupolêpsis* is the closest ancient precursor to modern belief as the generic attitude of taking-to-be-true of the intellectualist analytic philosophers. *Hupolêpsis* has been translated as interpret, understand, conceive, suppose, opine, and assume. For Aristotle, *hupolêpsis* includes episteme, doxa, and practical wisdom (*phronesis*). *Pistis* means knowledge taken on good faith, in the sense of trustworthy and reliable; this is practical knowledge that could serve as a foundation for how to live ethically.

28. Dewey, 1910. Indeed, when reason is overwhelmed, we resort to confabulation. See Bergson, H., Audra, R. A., Brereton, C., & Carter, W. H. (1954). *The two sources of morality and religion*. Garden City, NY: Doubleday.

29. James, 1897; Durkheim, 1915.

30. There are immense consequences to how we categorize knowledge; this is especially pertinent in psychology's position between the natural and social sciences. Explanations generally fulfill the four Aristotelian causes: efficient, material, final (teleological or functional), and formal. The quality of an explanation of the mechanism by which something came to be is generally judged by its simplicity, scope, and power. See Lombrozo, T., & Vasilyeva, N. (2017). Causal explanation. In M. Waldmann (Ed.), *Oxford handbook of causal reasoning*. Oxford: Oxford University Press. Inference to the best explanation and Bayesian probability are other ways to determine the relative quality of an explanation. See Lombrozo, T. (2016). Explanatory preferences shape learning and inference. *Trends in Cognitive Sciences*,

192 NOTES

20(10), 748–759. https://doi.org/10.1016/j.tics.2016.08.001. In the English-speaking world, science refers to natural science, while in continental Europe, science refers to a body of knowledge grounded on rational principles and thought to be true. Smith, R. (2013). *Between mind and nature: A history of psychology.* London: Reaktion Books. On the dominance of scientific ways of knowing in our epistemic cultures, see Knorr-Cetina K. (1999). *Epistemic cultures : how the sciences make knowledge.* Cambridge, MA: Harvard University Press.

31. Shagan, E. (2019). *The birth of modern belief.* Princeton, NJ: Princeton University Press.

32. Gabriel, R. (2013). *Why I buy: Self, taste, and consumer society in America.* London: Intellect Press.

33. Smith, R. (1997). *The Norton history of the human sciences.* New York: W.W. Norton. See also Foucault, M. (1966). *Les mots et les choses: Une archéologie des sciences humaines.* Paris: Gallimard. According to Smith (2013, p. 16), we become what we think we are.

34. Weisberg, D. S., et al. (2015) Deconstructing the seductive allure of neuroscience explanations. *Judgment and Decision Making, 10,* 429–441; Hopkins, E. J., et al. (2016) The seductive allure is a reductive allure: People prefer scientific explanations that contain logically irrelevant reductive information. *Cognition, 155,* 67–76

35. Taylor, 2007.

36. Gabriel, 2013.

37. The order we currently provide draws from the diachronic narratives of history—we live in the drafts of the past. Lévi-Strauss, 1961/2021, p. 263. Weber, M. (2004). *The vocation lectures* (D. Owen & T. Strong, Eds.; R. Livingstone, Trans.). Indianapolis: Hackett.

38. Taylor, 2007, p. 30.

39. Indeed, "the imagination of religion by neuro and cognitive scientists in this secular age is as much, if not more so, about the intensities of psychic investment, epistemic certitude, and passionate sociality that these same scientists dismissively ascribe to religion." Modern, J. (2021). *Neuromatic: Or, a particular history of religion and the brain.* Chicago: University of Chicago Press, p. 41.

40. Storm, J. J. (2017). *The myth of disenchantment.* Chicago: University of Chicago Press. See also Berman, M. (1981). *The reenchantment of the world.* New York: Cornell University Press. In an enchanted world, things can impose meanings and exert causal power; meaning is not only a power of mind, the mind is porous to the enchanted world of objects (cf. Taylor, 2007).

41. Taylor, 1989; Gabriel, 2013. Rose, N., & Abi-Rached, J. M. (2013). *Neuro: The new brain sciences and the management of the mind.* Princeton, NJ: Princeton University Press.

42. Consider the range of concepts at our disposal—working memory, decision-making, perseveration, intuition, repression, and so on. To take an example at random: while common sense suggests bodies read bodies, the appraisal theory of emotions states that we act toward other people based on our inferences about their goals and receptivity displayed in facial expressions. See de Melo, C. M., Carnevale, P. J., Read, S. J., & Gratch, J. (2013). Reading people's minds from emotion

expressions in interdependent decision making. *Journal of Personality and Social Psychology, 106*(1), 73–88. . doi:10.1037/a0034251

43. Adams, G. (1931). *Psychology: Science or superstition?* New York: Covici Friede. Indeed, the scientific method is one such ritualized response to the hazard of ignorance. Foss, J. (2007). The rituals of explanation. *Behavioral and Brain Sciences, 29*(6), 618–619.

44. Rhetorical tools I use throughout the book like the Uroboros and ventriloquism illustrate this loop between the desire to know and frames of belief.

45. For Stanley Cavell, "knowledge has replaced the world as the object of our passion. So science turns back into magic, theory becomes incantation, and intellectual caution produces psychic promiscuity." Cavell, S. (1979). *The world viewed* (enlarged ed.). Cambridge, MA: Harvard University Press, p. 65.

46. Tallis, 2018.

47. According to Nietzsche, the Platonic search for truth through explanation is an erotic striving. Also see Lear, 1999.

48. What is needed is for psychology to constitute a self-sustaining civilizational project that affirms the limits of our knowledge as well as the ethical import of the frameworks we construct. In the latter part of the book, I argue that this may be possible if we draw together an interdisciplinary psychology which in addition to the analogical modes of explanation employed in the empirical uses of psychology draws on discursive and creative uses of psychology employed in history and anthropology. Cf. Pippin, 2010, p. 20. In the *Gay Science* (1882), Nietzsche argued that to find oneself in one's deeds and to experience them as genuinely one's own is the ideal freedom. To become the poet of your own life is to embody a hierarchically unified being. The power achieved through this ethical approach requires indifference to holding and gaining power and furthermore understanding that people's happiness and misery depend on their beliefs about their motives, not the actual motives themselves. How do the attachments to ideals that orient our inquiry become possible? Since this process is unstable and potentially incoherent, Zarathustra maintained we must rather sustain a commitment to an ideal but also a willingness to overcome such a commitment in altered circumstances. To say yes to all things and follow a Spinozist acknowledgment of necessity is the sign of a free spirit that takes leave of all faith and hopes for certainty nevertheless. Nietzsche, F. W., & Kaufmann, W. (1995). *Thus spoke Zarathustra: A book for all and none.* New York: Modern Library. Tambiah, 1990. See also Austin, J. L. (1962). *How to do things with words.* Cambridge, MA: Harvard University Press; Wittgenstein (1997).

49. "Human nature just is a disaffection with its own nature." Pippin, 2010, p. 61.

50. A Maslovian desire for safety is built out into a need for the security of totalizing knowledge, whether or not it is attainable. Psychology as a science is our erotic striving toward truth about ourselves; it is the agglomeration of attempts to furnish depth commitments for human nature through technical tools. Our safari through contemporary psychology in this book displays the creativity humans have exercised in mimetically creating discursive, descriptive, and positivist approaches

194 NOTES

to ultimate meaning. See also Nietzsche, F. (1882/2010). *The gay science: With a prelude in rhymes and an appendix of songs* (W. Kaufman, Trans.). New York: Vintage, pp. 7, 35.

51. Consider, for example, the incarnation of Vishnu in the *Bhagavad Gita* who reveals the truth to Arjuna on the fields of Dharmakshetre Kurukshetre. Krishna is an embodiment of Vishnu, the god who preserves order. He speaks the tragic truth of how and why Arjuna has come to the field of battle. On the shores of Troy in *The Illiad*, Athena or Apollo alternately embodies the wishes of the Trojans and Achaeans. With the gods on his side, Hector or Achilles's voice is legitimated as the voice of truth. In these myths, as in the Vedic arena, the field of sacrifice, of the sacred, has demarcated barriers, in which a particular order reigns. Rites of witchcraft similarly employ figures to embody order. The masks used in Akan or Benin rituals, for instance, allow the society to throw legitimating order into reigning deities. Zeus, Agni, Vishnu, Onyame, and Yahweh speak in the thrown voices of order. It is a Durkheimian socialization of the soteriological imagination. Cf. Jaynes, J. (1976). *The origin of consciousness in the breakdown of the bicameral mind*. Boston: Mariner Books. On the voice of the gods, see Williams, B. (1993). *Shame and necessity*. Berkeley: University of California Press.

52. Lévi-Strauss, C. (1961/2021). *Wild thought* (J. Mehlman and J. Leavitt, Trans.). Chicago: University of Chicago Press.

53. Rituals are meaningful schematized, repeatable actions that serve as a language for social interaction within a given society's mythological grounding of meaning. Burkert, W. (2006). Ritual between ethology and post-modern aspects: Philological-historical notes. In E. Stavrianopoulou (Ed.), *Ritual and communication in the Graeco-Roman world* (pp. 23–35). Presses universitaires de Liège. doi:10.4000/books.pulg.1132. Yet we should be suspicious of any epistemological system that promises to catalogue exceedingly diverse and vague phenomena within a predetermined arena of order. Cf. "The proscription of superstition has always signified not only the progress of domination but its compromise," p. 68. Horkheimer, M., & Adorno, T. (1944/72). On the concept of enlightenment. In W. Shirmacher (Ed.), *German 20th century philosophy: The Frankfurt School*. New York: Continuum.

54. Individualism in the modern ethos is self-inflating, whereas the pervasive uneasiness with truth is self-deflating. Pippin, R. (1991). *Modernism as a philosophical problem: On the dissatisfactions of European high culture*. Oxford: Blackwell, p. 165.

55. One's framework beliefs and values constrict one's theoretical imagination (Taylor, 2007), this is especially true in the empirical uses of psychology, which tend to ignore or exclude such discussions of mythology and cultural frames. But see Danziger, K. (1990). *Constructing the subject: Historical origins of psychological research*. Cambridge: Cambridge University Press. https://doi.org/10.1017/CBO9780511524059

NOTES 195

Chapter 4

1. Popular psychology is literally more popular than academic, applied, and clinical psychology.
2. Heelas, P. (2008). *Spiritualities of life: New Age romanticism and consumptive capitalism*. Oxford: Blackwell.
3. Hunt, H. T. (2003). *Lives in spirit: Precursors and dilemmas of secular Western mysticism*. Albany: SUNY Press
4. Seznec, J. (1953/1981). *The survival of pagan gods*. Bollingen series. Princeton, NJ: Princeton University Press.
5. Staal, F. (1975). *Exploring mysticism: A methodological essay*. Los Angeles: University of California Press. In America, the numinous has been exploited for a wide variety of revivalisms, including transcendentalism and born-again fundamentalisms.
6. Auerbach, E. (1946/2003). *Mimesis: The representation of reality in Western literature* (50th anniversary ed., W. Trask, Trans.). Princeton, NJ: Princeton University Press. Mendelsohn, D. (2020). *Three rings: A tale of exile, narrative, and fate*. Charlottesville: University of Virginia Press.
7. Heelas, 2008.
8. I describe the historical and philosophical antecedents of this model of the self in Gabriel, R. (2013). *Why I buy: Self, taste, and consumer society in America*. London: Intellect Press.
9. Sean Victory and I read forty books, with a focus on books published since 2001. Previous eras are well covered in Starker, S. (2002). *Oracle at the supermarket: The American preoccupation with self-help books*. New York: Transaction; and Greenberg, G. (1994). *The self on the shelf: Recovery books and the good life*. Albany: SUNY Press.
10. Weber, M. (1922/1978). *Economy and society*. Los Angeles: University of California Press; Molendijk, A. L. (2019). Ernst Troeltsch and mysticism. *Interdisciplinary Journal for Religion and Transformation in Contemporary Society*, 5(1), 8–32. https://doi.org/10.30965/23642807-00501002
11. Hunt, 2003.
12. Hunt, 2003.
13. Shermer, M. (2006). SHAM scam. *Scientific American*, May 1, 2006. Though one could similarly argue that belief in any doctrinal system requires faith.
14. Carrette, J., & King, R. (2005). *Selling spirituality: The silent takeover of religion*. New York: Routledge.
15. Heelas, P. (2008). *Spiritualities of life: New Age romanticism and consumptive capitalism*. Oxford: Blackwell
16. Hayden, B. (2018). *The power of ritual in prehistory: Secret societies and origins of social complexity*. Cambridge: Cambridge University Press.
17. Staal. F. (1982). *The science of ritual*. Poona, India: The Bhandarkar Institute Press.
18. Malamoud, C. (1996). *Cooking the world: Ritual and thought in sncient India*. Oxford: Oxford University Press.
19. Greenberg, 1993.

196 NOTES

20. Danto, A. C. (1988). *Mysticism and morality: Oriental thought and moral philosophy.* New York: Columbia University Press.
21. Carrette & King, 2005.
22. Hunt, 2003. See Herzog, D. (2017). *Cold War Freud: Psychoanalysis in an age of catastrophes.* Cambridge: Cambridge University Press. For more on the British school of object relations, see the work of Melanie Klein, and for more on self psychology, see the work of Heinz Kohut.
23. Carrette & King, 2005.
24. Hanegraaff, 1998. This-worldly mysticisms are also known as radical phenomenologies.
25. Hunt, 2003.
26. Hunt, 2003; Heelas, 2008.
27. Hanegraaff, W. J. (1999). New Age spiritualities as secular religion: A historian's perspective. *Social Compass, 46*(2), 145–160. doi:10.1177/003776899046002004
28. Heelas, 2008.
29. Staal, F. (1979). The meaninglessness of ritual. *Numen, 26*, 2–22.
30. Rappaport, R. A. (1999). *Ritual and religion in the making of humanity.* Cambridge: Cambridge University Press.
31. Heesterman, J. C. (1993). *The broken world of sacrifice: An essay in ancient Indian ritual.* Chicago: University of Chicago Press.
32. Hanegraaff, W. (1998). Reflections on New Age and the secularization of nature. In J. Pearson, R. H. Roberts, & G. Samuel (Eds.), *Nature religion today: Paganism in the modern world* (pp. 22–32). Edinburgh: Edinburgh University Press.
33. Taylor, 1989.
34. Shermer, M. (2006). SHAM scam. *Scientific American*, May 1, 2006.
35. Quoted in Stoneman (2011) and Tambiah, S. J. (1990). *Magic, science and religion and the scope of rationality.* Cambridge: Cambridge University Press.
36. The Chinese sage Mencius (372–289 BCE) similarly conceived an ethics of actions employing the four germs, not as rational precepts like Kant and Aristotle, but as ritualized actions formulated as part of earlier traditions that promulgated order and proportion in the social structure. This ritualized virtue ethic bears a similarity to Confucian ethics and stands in contrast to its competitor, the spiritualistic Daoism of Chuang Tzu, which is a far more common touchstone in contemporary popular psychology. See Seok, B. (2008). Mencius's vertical faculties and moral nativism. *Asian Philosophy, 18*(1), 51–68.
37. Sloterdijk, P. (2013). *You must change your life: On anthropotechnics* (W. Hoban, Trans.). London: Polity Press. See also Hanegraaff, W. (2016). Reconstructing "religion" from the bottom up. *Numen, 63*, 577–606.
38. Hunt, 2003.
39. Taylor, C. (2007). *A secular age.* Cambridge, MA: The Belknap Press of Harvard University.
40. Sloterdijk, 2013.
41. Hunt, 2003.

42. Roof, W. C. (1999). *Spiritual marketplace: Baby boomers and the remaking of American religion*. Princeton, NJ: Princeton University Press.
43. Hunt, 2003.
44. Compare the third volume of Michel Foucault's *History of sexuality* on care of the self.
45. Taylor, C. (1989). *Sources of the self*. Cambridge, MA: Harvard University Press.
46. Danto, 1988.
47. Stoneman, R. (2011). *The ancient Oracles: Making the gods speak*. New Haven, CT: Yale University Press.
48. Stoneman, 2011, p. 25.
49. Staal, 1973.
50. Atran, S. (2002). *In gods we trust: The evolutionary landscape of religion*. New York: Oxford University Press.
51. Burghardt, G. M. (2017). The origins, evolution, and interconnections of play and ritual: Setting the stage. In C. Renfrew, I. Morley, & M. Boyd (Eds.), *From play to faith: Ritual and play in animals, and in early human societies* (pp. 23–39). Cambridge: Cambridge University Press.
52. Tambiah, S. J. (1990). *Magic, science, religion, and the scope of rationality* (Lewis Henry Morgan lectures). Cambridge: Cambridge University Press.
53. Cf. the concept of Mana. Lévi-Strauss, C. (1963). *Structural anthropology*. New York: Basic Books.
54. Durkheim, 1915.
55. Carrette & King, 2005.
56. Crawford, M. (2015). *The world beyond your head: On becoming an individual in an age of distraction*. New York: Farrar, Straus and Giroux.
57. Modern, J. (2021). *Neuromatic: Or, a particular history of religion and the brain*. Chicago: University of Chicago Press.

Chapter 5

1. Svevo, I. (1923/1958). *Confessions of Zeno* (B. de Zoete, Trans.). New York: Vintage Books, p. 379.
2. Macpherson, C. B. (1969). *The political theory of possessive individualism: Hobbes to Locke*. Oxford: Clarendon Press.
3. Shweder, R. A., LeVine, R. A., & Social Science Research Council (U.S.). (1984). *Culture theory: Essays on mind, self, and emotion*. Cambridgeshire, UK: Cambridge University Press. Gabriel, R. (2013). *Why I buy: Self, taste, and consumer society in America*. Bristol, UK: Intellect Press.
4. Dumont, L. (1986). *Essays on individualism: Modern ideology in anthropological perspective*. Chicago: University of Chicago Press.
5. The self may have evolved as a result of interaction between social habitat and the affective motivations of *Homo sapiens*. Damasio, A. (2010). *Self comes to mind: Constructing the conscious brain*. New York: Pantheon/Random House. Asma,

198 NOTES

S. T., & Gabriel, R. (2019). *The emotional mind: The affective roots of culture and cognition.* Cambridge, MA: Harvard University Press. See pp. 231–234.

6. This approach makes sense for the trait theory of personality, in which traits are dispositions that individuals have across their lives. Klein, S. B., German, T. P., Cosmides, L., & Gabriel, R. (2004). A theory of autobiographical memory: Necessary components and disorders resulting from their loss. *Social Cognition, 22*(5), 460–490.

7. Martin, R., & Barresi, J. (2006). *The rise and fall of soul and self.* New York: Columbia University Press. This is not to say that the self is ontologically real; in fact, it may be the central conceit of humanity, offering the hopeful illusion of continuity and unique individuality. The Buddha and David Hume famously argued that the self does not exist because there is no entity that continues across time or at least no way to individuate such an entity. Their arguments are strong, but regardless of the theoretical veridicality of the self, it is a de facto entity in social life, and it is in this spirit that I discuss it herein.

8. The self has been taken to be everything from a machine to an immaterial soul; see Martin & Barresi, 2006.

9. Lear, J. (1998). *Open minded: Working out the logic of soul.* Cambridge, MA: Harvard University Press, p. 175.

10. The stability of the self seems to be a result not only of cultural functions it plays but also of cognitive processes like memory for events, places, and things (i.e., episodic memory). Klein, S. B., Gabriel, R. H., Gangi, C. E., & Robertson, T. E. (2009). Reflections on the self: A case study of a prosopagnosic patient. *Social Cognition, 26*, 766–777.

11. Klein et al., 2004.

12. Danziger, K. (1990). *Constructing the subject: Historical origins of psychological research.* Cambridge: Cambridge University Press. Smith, R. (2013). *Between the mind and nature: A history of psychology.* London: Reaktion Books. The conceptualization of the individual as the subject of psychological research can be traced to the British empiricists, who grounded philosophical speculation in the experience of individual minds. The theoretical commitment to this model usually entailed a philosophy of liberal individualism and its attendant notion of agency. The notion of the liberal individual entails the possession of agency (Danziger, 1990, p. 23).

13. According to Auguste Comte, self-observation of thought, feeling, and desire is precisely subjectivity and therefore psychology can never be objective. Comte, A. (1855/1974). *The positive philosophy of Auguste Comte* (H. Martineau, Trans.). New York: AMS Press.

14. "It is for love of the world that we try to understand it" (p. 9). Lear, J. (1998). *Open minded: Working out the logic of soul.* Cambridge, MA: Harvard University Press.

15. Kringelbach, M. L., & Berridge, K. C. (2017). The affective core of emotion: Linking pleasure, subjective well-being, and optimal metastability in the brain. *Emotion Review: Journal of the International Society for Research on Emotion, 9*(3), 191–199. https://doi.org/10.1177/1754073916684558;

16. Lear, 1998, pp. 12, 18.

NOTES 199

17. Danziger, K. (1983). Origins and basic principles of Wundt's Völkerpsychologie. *British Journal of Social Psychology, 22*, 303–313. 10.1111/j.2044-8309.1983.tb00597.x

18. Danziger, 1983, p. 307. As a corollary to his work on motivational drives, Wundt focused on the mimetic nature of nonverbal communication and expression. See Gabriel, R. (2021). The motivational role of affect in an ecological model. *Theory & Psychology, 31*, 1–21.

19. Danziger, 1983, p. 309.

20. Hartmann, E., & Coupland, W. C. (1869/1893). *Philosophy of the unconscious.* London: K. Paul, Trench, Trübner, & Co.

21. Pippin, R. B. (2017). *The philosophical Hitchcock: Vertigo and the anxieties of unknowingness.* Chicago: University of Chicago Press.

22. Ffytche, M. (2011). *The foundation of the unconscious: Schelling, Freud and the birth of the modern psyche.* Cambridge: Cambridge University Press.

23. Freud, S. (1915/2004). *The unconscious.* New York: Penguin Classics.

24. Foucault, M. (1966). *Les mot et les choses.* Paris: Plon.

25. Many artists, from the Dadaists to Franz Kafka, Maya Deren, and the action painters, employed the concept of the unconscious when describing the inspiration of their work. Ellenberger, H. F. (1970). *The discovery of the unconscious: The history and evolution of dynamic psychiatry.* New York: Basic Books.

26. Maslow, A. (1998). *Towards a psychology of being* (3rd ed.). New York: Wiley.

27. Currently, notions of trauma and posttraumatic stress disorder (PTSD) loom large in popular culture. Beck, J. S. (2011). *Cognitive behavior therapy: Basics and beyond* (2nd ed.). New York: The Guilford Press. Cognitive psychologists developed notions of the cognitive unconscious, a set of modules whirring away in the darkness. See Baars, B. J. (1988). *A cognitive theory of consciousness.* Cambridge: Cambridge University Press. Kihlstrom, J. F. (1987). The cognitive unconscious. *Science, 237*, 1445–1452.

28. Carl Jung developed a model of the unconscious which was not individualist. He and his followers are sometimes referred to as transpersonal or analytical psychologists; they often discuss esoteric cultural examples as elements of a collective unconscious. Jung, C. G. (1912/1916). *Psychology of the unconscious: A study of the transformations and symbolisms of the libido.* New York: Routledge.

29. Many of these methods also form the basis of applied uses of psychology in the fields of organizational and industrial psychology. This institutionalization of techniques for motivating and punishing labor provided a rubric of evaluation within the context of industrial production. See Smith, 2013.

30. Makari, G. (2008). *Revolution in mind: The creation of psychoanalysis.* New York: Harper Perennial.

31. Makari, 2008, p. 20.

32. Schelling, F. M. J. (1802–3/1989). *The philosophy of art.* Minneapolis: Minnesota University Press. Though see recent work by Mark Solms (2020) which aims to fulfill Freud's dream of a metapsychology that integrates science and psychodynamics.

33. Makari, 2008, p. 80.

34. Herzog, D. (2017). *Cold War Freud: Psychoanalysis in an age of catastrophes.* Cambridge: Cambridge University Press, p. 2.

200 NOTES

35. Schorske, C. E. (1981). *Fin-de-siècle Vienna: Politics and culture*. New York: Vintage Books. As Robert Musil wrote in his opus *The Man Without Qualities*, man is nothing but a little channel washed out by the trickling streams of his various identities. From professional to geographic and sexual elements of character, the trickling of these streams during modernity leads to a diffuse and uneasy sense of existence.

36. Freud, S., Strachey, J., & Richards, A. (1991). *Introductory lectures on psychoanalysis*. London: Penguin.

37. Lear, 1998, p. 85.

38. The self as a tradition is transformed into a sheath of concentric exegetic enterprises.

39. Jung, C. G., Franz, M.-L., Henderson, J. L., Jaffé, A., & Jacobi, J. (1964). *Man and his symbols*. New York: Doubleday.

40. Lears, J. (1995). *Fables of abundance: A cultural history of advertising in America*. New York: Basic Books; Siegel, J. (2005). *The idea of the self: Thought and experience in Western Europe since the seventeenth century*. Cambridge: Cambridge University Press; Taylor, C. (1989). *Sources of the self*. Cambridge, MA: Harvard University Press.

41. Herzog, 2017, pp. 7, 17.

42. Makari, 2008, p. 411.

43. Makari, 2008.

44. Ego psychology argues that ego defenses serve both instinctual drives as well as adaptive functions. See Hartmann, H. (1958). *Ego psychology and the problem of adaptation* (D. Rapaport, Trans.). New York: International Universities Press.

45. Edwards, D., & Potter, J. (2001). Discursive psychology. In Willig/Stainton-Rogers (Eds.), *The Sage handbook of qualitative research in psychology* (pp. 73–90) New York: Sage publications.. https://hdl.handle.net/2134/9485

46. In Vienna, all it took to become an analyst was to have been analyzed. This led to one of the major conflicts in the field between the orthodox Viennese school and their associates in the *Berlin Poliklinik* who required didactic analysis, theoretical training, and practical training, and the American branch, which leaned toward requiring a medical degree to practice. Although these distinctions were put in abeyance during the years of the Second World War so that analysts who were part of the community but endangered by the policies of the German national socialists could leave their countries to safety (Makari, 2008, pp. 370–372). The debate about credentials continues in how psychiatrists are trained; see Luhrmann, T. M. (2000). *Of two minds: The growing disorder in American psychiatry*. New York: Alfred A. Knopf.

47. Rieff, P. (1968). *The triumph of the therapeutic: Uses of faith after Freud*. Chicago: University of Chicago Press.

48. Hartmann, H. (1927). *Die Grundlagen der Psychoanalyse*. Leipzig: G. Thieme.

49. Trilling, L. (1950). *The liberal imagination: Essays on literature and society*. New York: Viking Press. Herzog, 2017, p. 17.

50. Smith, 2013, p. 102.

51. Makari, 2008, p. 408.

52. Greenberg, G. (1994). *The self on the shelf: Recovery books and the good life*. Albany: State University of New York Press.

NOTES 201

53. Makari, 2008, p. 435. Klein, M. (1930). The importance of symbol-formation in the development of the ego. *International Journal of Psycho-Analysis, 11*, 24–39. Also see the work of Joan Riviere, Susan Isaacs, James Strachey, and Ernest Jones.

54. Interoceptive processes and affective touch are also ways in which the self is formed during infancy. See Damasio, A. (2010). *Self comes to mind*. New York: Pantheon Books. Fotopoulou, A., & Tsakiris, M. (2017). Mentalizing homeostasis: The social origins of interoceptive inference. *Neuropsychoanalysis, 19*(1), 3–28. doi:10.1080/15294145.2017.1294031

55. This world is constituted by shared symbols, the most important of which is language, which becomes the tool of our intimacy. Lacan, J. (2007). *Écrits* (B. Fink, Trans.). New York: W.W. Norton.

56. For an introduction to object relations, see Klein, M. (1981). *Love, guilt, and reparation*. London: Hogarth Press; Winnicott, D. W. (1975). *Through paediatrics to psychoanalysis*. London: Hogarth Press; Mahler, M. (1967). *On human symbiosis and the vicissitudes of individuation*. New York: International Universities Press.

57. Vygotsky in particular emphasizes the role of language in the structuring of the mind, which is an assertion of Marxist notions of how material conditions exhaustively define consciousness. Vygotsky, L. S. (1978). *Mind in society: The development of higher psychological functions*. Cambridge, MA: Harvard University Press; Holland, D., & Lachicotte, Jr., W. (2007). Vygotsky, Mead, and the new sociocultural studies of identity. In H. Daniels, M. Cole, & J. Wertsch (Eds.), *The Cambridge companion to Vygotsky* (pp. 101–135). Cambridge: Cambridge University Press. doi:10.1017/CCOL0521831040.005

58. Mead, G. H. (1934). *Mind, self and society*. Chicago: University of Chicago Press. His work was followed by that of Charles Horton Cooley and Erving Goffman. Important progenitors are James Mark Baldwin and the moral philosopher Josiah Royce; see Perry, R. B. (1938). *In the spirit of William James*. New Haven, CT: Yale University Press.

59. This includes ego stages of development, like identity moratorium in adolescents and the search for appropriate role models. Erikson, E. H. (1980). *Identity and life cycle*. New York: Norton.

60. Makari, 2008, p. 481.

61. Schutz, A. (1954). Concept and theory formation in the social sciences. *The Journal of Philosophy, 51*(9), 257–273. doi:10.2307/2021812

62. Holland & Lachicotte, 2007, p. 103. See also Bourdieu, P. (1984). *Distinction: A social critique of the judgement of taste*. Cambridge, MA: Harvard University Press.

63. Gabriel, 2013.

64. McCracken, G. (1988). *Culture and consumption: New approaches to the symbolic character of consumer goods and activities*. Bloomington: Indiana University Press.

65. Mannheim, K. (1936). *Ideology and utopia: An introduction to the sociology of knowledge*. New York: Harvest Books.

66. Hartmann, 1958.

67. The creative interpretation of psychoanalysis is amenable to exegetical maneuvers such as Jacques Lacan's notion of civilization as the Symbolic Order into which

202 NOTES

the child is born (Lacan, 2007). These strands were synthesized in Gilles Deleuze (1925–1995) and Félix Guattari's (1930–1992) controversial *Anti-Oedipe* in which the authors develop a conceptualization of individuals as biological machines of desire within the context of late capitalism. Deleuze, G., & Guattari, F. (1983). *Anti-Oedipus: Capitalism and schizophrenia*. Minneapolis: University of Minnesota Press.

68. See, for example, Lacan's (2007). *Seminar on Edgar Allan Poe's Purloined Letter*, or Zizek's *Pervert's Guide to Cinema*. Lone star, Mischief, Amoeba films, Kasander films. (2006). *The Pervert's Guide to Cinema* [DVD]. United Kingdom. .

69. See, for example, Williamson, J. (1994). *Decoding advertisements: Ideology and meaning in advertising*. London: Marion Boyars; Khanna, R. (2003). *Dark continents: Psychoanalysis and colonialism*. Durham, NC: Duke University Press.

70. Trumbull, R. (2012). Derrida, Freud, Lacan: Resistances. *UC Santa Cruz*. ProQuest ID: Trumbull_ucsc_0036E_10030. Merritt ID: ark:/13030/m55q4tpk. Retrieved from https://escholarship.org/uc/item/9p43t6nf

71. Deleuze, G., & Guattari, F. (2013). *A thousand plateaus*. New York: Bloomsbury Academic.

72. Duong, K. (2021). *Freud in the tropics*. Working paper presented at University of Chicago, Political Science colloquium.

73. Barthes, R. (1972). *Mythologies*. New York: Hill and Wang.

74. One example is Salvador Dalí's (1904–1989) paranoid-critical method, which depicts the creative process as consisting of a stage of creative analogical connections, a wild thought, followed by a critical phase of editing and ordering by aesthetic principles. Dalí, S., & Chevalier, H. (1942). *The secret life of Salvador Dali*. New York: Dial Press. Also, see Andre Bréton's use of psychoanalysis toward building a new mythology in the second Surrealist manifesto.

75. Khanna, 2003. Also see Spivak, G. C. (1990). *Postcoloniality and value, in literary theory today* (P. Collier and H. Geyer-Ryan, Eds.). Cambridge: Polity Press, p. 228. Also consider Joseph Conrad's *Heart of Darkness* and the critique of this narrative of encounter by Chinua Achebe. Achebe, Chinua. (2016). An Image of Africa: Racism in Conrad's Heart of Darkness. *The Massachusetts Review, 57*, 14–27. 10.1353/mar.2016.0003.

76. Makari, 2008, pp. 380–381. Karen Horney rejected the idea of penis envy by demonstrating how the phallic theory was simply a psychological name for the oppressive material conditions faced by females. Compare Friedan, B. (1963). *The feminine mystique*. New York: Norton. While designating Freud an enemy, second- and third-wave feminism found his views very useful to push against and thus they served an important use for their respective liberatory projects.

77. W.E. B. Du Bois (1868–1963), who developed the notion of double consciousness, was also a student of William James at Harvard University from 1888 to 1892 and was influenced by his notion of pragmatism. Du Bois, W. E. B. (1968). *The souls of black folk; essays and sketches*. New York: Johnson Reprint Corp.

78. Butts, H. F. (1979). Frantz Fanon's contribution to psychiatry: The psychology of racism and colonialism. *Journal of the National Medical Association, 71*(10), 1015–1018.

NOTES   203

79. Fanon, F. (1952). *Black skin, white masks*. New York: Grove Press.

80. The négritude of Martinician poet Aimé Césaire (1913–2008) similarly aimed at augmenting pride in achievements and potential.

81. Fanon, 1952. Also see Abi-Rached, J. M. (2021). Aṣfūriyyeh: A history of madness, modernity, and war in the Middle East. *History of Psychiatry, 32*(4), 462–477. https://doi.org/10.1177/0957154X211028430

82. Wynter, S. (1999). Towards the sociogenic principle: Fanon, the puzzle of conscious experience, of "identity" and what it's like to be "black." In M. Durán-Cogan & A. Gómez-Moriana (Eds.), *National identity and sociopolitical change: Latin America between marginalization and integration* (pp. 30–66). Minnesota: University of Minnesota Press.

83. Fanon, F. (1963). *The wretched of the Earth*. New York: Grove Press.

84. Other Black Power thinkers came to similar conclusions in different contexts; see Cleaver, E., & Geismar, M. (1967). *Soul on ice*. New York: McGraw-Hill.

85. Hiltebeitel, A. (2018). *Freud's India: Sigmund Freud and India's first psychoanalyst Girindrasekhar Bose*. New York: Oxford University Press.

86. Nandy, A., & Kakar, S. (1980). Culture and personality. In U. Pareek (Ed.), *A survey of research in psychology, 1971–76*, Part 1 (pp. 141–158). Bombay: Popular.

87. Rieff, P. (1968). *The triumph of the therapeutic: Uses of faith after Freud*. New York: Harper Torchbooks.

88. Kapila S. (2007). The "godless" Freud and his Indian friends: An Indian agenda for psychoanalysis. In S. Mahone & M. Vaughan (Eds.), *Psychiatry and empire* (pp. 124–152). Cambridge Imperial and Post-Colonial Studies Series. London: Palgrave Macmillan. https://doi.org/10.1057/9780230593244_6

89. Heelas, P. (2008). *Spiritualities of life: New Age romanticism and consumptive capitalism*. Oxford: Blackwell.
   Calasso, R. (2016). *Ardor* (R. Dixon, Trans.). New York: Farrar, Strauss, and Giroux.

90. Hiltebeitel, 2018, pp. 137–138. See Freud, S. (1927). *The future of an illusion* (J. Strachey, Trans.). New York: W.W. Norton & Company.

91. Vahali, H. O. (2011). Landscaping a perspective: India and the psychoanalytic vista. In G. Misra (Ed.), *Psychology in India: Theoretical and methodological developments* (Vol. 4, pp. 1–91). New Delhi: Pearson Education. This thrust to maintain indigenous traditions was continued in Durganad Singha et al.'s *Pondicherry Manifesto of Indian Psychology* in 1965. Also see Rao, K. R. (2002). *Consciousness studies: Cross-cultural perspectives*. Jefferson, MO: McFarland; Rao, K. R. (2011). *Cognitive anomalies, consciousness and yoga*. New Delhi: Centre for Studies in Civilizations; Paranjpe, A. C. (1998). *Self and identity in modern psychology and Indian thought*. New York: Plenum Press. More empirical work drawing together applied psychology and the Gita is to be found in Pande, N., & Naidu, R. K. (1992). Anāsakti and health: A study of nonattachment. *Psychology and Developing Societies, 4*, 89–104. For full analysis, see Misra, G., & Paranjpe, A. C. (2012). Psychology in modern India. In *Encyclopedia of the history of psychological theories*. New York: Springer Science + Business Media. 10.1007/978-1-4419-0463-8_422

204 NOTES

92. See Mira Nair's 2001 documentary on *The Laughing Club of India*, although experimental psychology and psychometry still dominate university curriculums. See Misra & Paranjpe, 2012.
93. Khanna, 2003.
94. Hopwood, D. (1982). *Egypt: Politics and society 1945–1981*. London: George Allen and Unwin.
95. El Shakry, O. (2017). *The Arabic Freud: Psychoanalysis and Islam in modern Egypt*. Princeton, NJ: Princeton University Press.
96. Bergson, H. (1907/2008). *Creative evolution*. New York: Dover Books.
97. El Shakry, 2017, p. 40.
98. El Shakry, 2017.
99. El Shakry, 2017.
100. El Shakry, 2017, p. 30.
101. Tambiah, S. J. (1990). *Magic, science, religion, and the scope of rationality*. Cambridge: Cambridge University Press.
102. Shillington, K. (2005). *History of Africa*. Oxford: Macmillan Education.
103. Appiah, A. (1992). *In my father's house: Africa in the philosophy of culture*. New York: Oxford University Press.
104. Opokuwaa, N. A. K. (2005). *The quest for spiritual transformation: Introduction to traditional Akan religion, rituals and practices*. Bloomington, IN: iUniverse.
105. Hanserd, R. (2020). *Identity, spirit and freedom in the Atlantic world: The Gold Coast and the African diaspora*. New York: Routledge.
106. Field, M. J. (1970). *Search for security: An ethnopsychiatric study of rural Ghana*. Evanston, IL: Northwestern University Press, p. 38.
107. Field, 1970.
108. Field, 1970.
109. Appiah, 1992.
110. Parin, P., Parin-Matthèy, G., & Morgenthaler, F. (1966). *Les Blancs pensent trop: 13 entretiens avec les Dogon*. Paris: Payot. See also the work of George Devereux.
111. Herzog, 2017, pp. 179–211.
112. Herzog, 2017, p. 207.
113. Matza, T. A. (2018). *Shock therapy: Psychology, precarity, and well-being in post-Socialist Russia*. Durham, NC: Duke University Press.
114. Matza, 2018, p. 86.
115. Bourdieu, P. (1984). *Distinction: A social critique of the judgement of taste*. Cambridge, MA: Harvard University Press.
116. Matza, 2018. Note that since the 1930s, Freudian ideas were deemed insufficiently dialectical and thus did not form the basis of Russian psychotherapy (p. 230).
117. Kripal, J. (2007). *Esalen: America and the religion of no religion*. Chicago: University of Chicago Press.
118. See Gabriel (2013) on possessive individualism in how consumerism conditions the self in America.
119. Makari, 2008.

NOTES   205

120. As dramatized for instance in Maisie's coming into knowledge in Henry James's novel of 1897, *What Maisie Knew*.

Chapter 6

1. Hyman, S. E., & Nestler, E. J. (1993). *The molecular foundations of psychiatry*. Washington, DC: American Psychiatric Press.
2. Davis, J. E. (2020). *Chemically imbalanced: Everyday suffering, medication, and our quest for self-mastery*. Chicago: University of Chicago press.
3. We are initiated into this materialist imaginary through advertising, social acquaintances, public education, popular media, medical professionals, and the internet. See Davis, 2020, p. 11.
4. My use of the term "mimesis" refers to how our modes of depicting the mind in practical uses of psychology are themselves implicit representations of the mind. The classic discussion of mimesis is about how style, analogy, rhetoric, and other linguistic tools are used to represent reality. See Auerbach, E. (1957) *Mimesis: The representation of reality in Western literature*. Garden City, NY: Doubleday.
5. Luhrmann, T. M. (2000). *Of two minds: The growing disorder in American psychiatry*. New York: Alfred A. Knopf, p. 7.
6. Luhrmann, 2000.
7. Luhrmann, 2000, p. 22. The two approaches are ideally used in tandem.
8. Kleinman, A., Eisenberg, L., & Good, B. (1978). Culture, illness, and care: Clinical lessons from anthropologic and cross-cultural research. *Annals of Internal Medicine*, 88(2), 251–258. https://doi.org/10.7326/0003-4819-88-2-251
9. Bruner, J. S. (1990). *Acts of meaning*. Cambridge, MA: Harvard University Press.
10. Davis, 2020. See conclusion.
11. John Stuart Mill considered psychology to be a moral science that tells us why but also delivers the pleasure of explanation. Foucault, M. (1961/2006). *Madness and civilization*. New York: Vintage Books.
12. Cannabis is currently transitioning into a socially acceptable drug and thus is being aligned with cultural values of commodification and the pleasure industry.
13. The categories of psycho-pharmaceuticals are antipsychotics, antidepressants, psychostimulants, anxiolytics (tranquilizers), mood stabilizers, and cognitive enhancers.
14. Greenberg, G. (2014). *Manufacturing depression: The secret history of a modern disease*. New York: Simon & Schuster.
15. Kirsch, I. (2010). *The emperor's new drugs: Exploding the antidepressant myth*. New York: Basic Books.
16. Even as doctors readily admit that we do not fully understand why they work; see Kramer, P. D. (1994). *Listening to Prozac*. New York: Penguin Books.
17. Modern, J. (2021). *Neuromatic; Or, a particular history of religion and the brain*. Chicago: University of Chicago Press.

206   NOTES

18. Lewis-Williams, D. J. (2002). *The mind in the cave: Consciousness and the origins of art*. London: Thames & Hudson. Eliade, M. (1972). *Shamanism: Archaic techniques of ecstasy*. Princeton, NJ: Princeton University Press.

19. Pickard, H. (2020). Addiction and the self. *Noûs*, *55*(4), 737–761. 10.1111/nous.12328.

20. Pickard, H. (2018). The puzzle of addiction. In H. Pickard & S. H. Ahmed (Eds.), *The Routledge handbook of philosophy and science of addiction* (pp. 9–22). Abingdon, UK: Routledge.

21. Though humanism is itself a historical concept; consider how Suzanne and Aimé Césaire argued that humanism was in fact simply an abstract bourgeois apologetics belied by the colonial age of slavery and industrial production. They suggest that what we are in need of is a new situated, postcolonial humanism. Césaire, A. (1959). L'homme de culture et ses responsabilités. *Présence Africaine*, 24/25, nouvelle série, 116–122. http://www.jstor.org/stable/24349005. On a reconstituted nonracist humanism, see Wynter, S. (1984). The ceremony must be found: After humanism. *Boundary 2*, *12*(3), 19–70.

22. Foucault, M., & Howard, R. (1965). *Madness and civilization: A history of insanity in the age of reason*. New York: Pantheon.

23. Davis, 2020, p. 11, chapter 2.

24. Greenberg, G. (2013). *The book of woe: The DSM and the unmaking of psychiatry*. New York: Blue Rider Press/Penguin Group.

25. Davis, 2020, p. 15, chapter 2.

26. Luhrmann, 2000.

27. Davis, 2020, pp. 19–20, chapter 2, n. 118.

28. Davis, 2020.

29. Davis, 2020, p. 13, chapter 4.

30. Trilling, L. (1972). *Sincerity and authenticity*. Cambridge, MA: Harvard University Press. doi:10.2307/j.ctvjhzrdp

31. See Davis, 2020, chapter 5.

32. Carhart-Harris, R., & Goodwin, G. (2017). The therapeutic potential of psychedelic drugs: Past, present, and future. *Neuropsychopharmacologys*, *42*, 2105–2113. https://doi.org/10.1038/npp.2017.84; Moreno, F. A., Wiegand, C. B., Taitano, E. K., & Delgado, P. L. (2006). Safety, tolerability, and efficacy of psilocybin in 9 patients with obsessive-compulsive disorder. *Journal of Clinical Psychiatry*, *67*, 1735–1740.

33. Pollan, M. (2018). *How to change your mind: What the new science of psychedelics teaches us about consciousness, dying, addiction, depression, and transcendence*. New York: Penguin Press.

34. Ludwig, A. (1968). Altered states of consciousness. In R. Prince (Ed.), *Trance and possession states* (pp. 69–95). Montreal: R.M. Bucke Memorial Society.

35. Nour, M. M., Evans, L., Nutt, D., & Carhart-Harris, R. L. (2016). Ego-dissolution and psychedelics: Validation of the Ego-Dissolution Inventory (EDI). *Frontiers in Human Neuroscience*, *10*, 269. doi:10.3389/fnhum.2016.00269; Harrison, J. (2010). Ego death and psychedelics. *MAPS Bulletin*, *20*, 40–41.

36. Bourguignon, E. (1973). *Religion, altered states of consciousness, and social change*. Columbus: Ohio State University Press. In accord with my own analysis, some

NOTES 207

researchers characterize this state of openness as a pivotal mental state: Brouwer, A., & Carhart-Harris, R. L. (2021). Pivotal mental states. *Journal of Psychopharmacology*, 35(4), 319–352. https://doi.org/10.1177/0269881120959637

37. Wasson, R. G. (1968). *Soma: Divine mushroom of immortality*. New York: Harcourt Brace Jovanovich, pp. 197, 199.

38. There is a limit to the public's receptivity to the esoteric findings of research, especially when the narratives provided therein do not cohere with lived experience and folk intuitions. This is clearer in psychology than in other fields because each individual has developed a sense of meaning and order through their own experience.

39. Similar syntheses have been developed in the philosophy of psychiatry; see, for example, Murphy, D. (2006). *Psychiatry in the scientific image*. Cambridge, MA: MIT Press; Whooley, O. (2019). *On the heels of ignorance: Psychiatry and the politics of not knowing*. Chicago: University of Chicago Press. For more details, see Gabriel (manuscript).

40. Master theories by Wilhelm Wundt, William James, William McDougall, Abraham Maslow, Clark Hull, and the theory of homeostasis by Cannon provide the foundation for subsequent theories of motivations. For example, see work on persuasion by John Cacioppo and colleagues. In general, any textbook on developmental and social psychology will include discussion of the motivation of behavior which will similarly interleave multiple levels.

41. Conatus means striving; this concept was crucial for Baruch Spinoza's characterization of the mind and was also important in Aristotle's delineation of the teleology of biological entities. See the second chapter of Asma and Gabriel (2019). Conatus has been connected to the notion of homeostasis, or allostasis (the often unconscious regulatory physiological pursuit of equilibrium by the body) by Walter Cannon and subsequently Antonio Damasio and other philosophers of emotion; see Damasio, A. R. (2018). *The strange order of things: Life, feeling, and the making of cultures*. New York: Pantheon Press. Asma and Gabriel (2019) offer a fleshed-out model of motivation in the context of the evolution of the mind. Motivation is commonly characterized into intrinsic meaning arising from internal factors, and extrinsic, meaning arising from external factors, based on the nature of the motivator. See Deci, E. L. (1971). Effects of externally mediated rewards on intrinsic motivation. *Journal of Personality and Social Psychology*, 18(1), 105–115. https://doi.org/10.1037/h0030 644; DeCharms, R. C. (1968). *Personal causation: The internal affective determinants of behavior*. New York: Academic Press; Lepper, M. R., & Greene, D. (Eds.). (1978). *The hidden costs of reward: New perspectives on the psychology of human motivation*. Mahwah, NJ: Lawrence Erlbaum.

42. See Laland, K. N., Uller, T., Feldman, M. W., Sterelny, K., Müller, G. B., Moczek, A., Jablonka, E., & Odling-Smee, J. (2015). The extended evolutionary synthesis: Its structure, assumptions and predictions. *Proceedings of the Royal Society B: Biological Sciences*, 282(1813), Article 20151019. https://doi.org/10.1098/rspb.2015.1019

For more on the basis of this synthesis, see Gabriel, R. (2021). The motivational role of affect in an ecological model. *Theory & Psychology*, 31(4), 552–572. https://doi. org/10.1177/0959354321992869

208 NOTES

43. Synofzik et al. (2008) draw an important distinction between the feeling of agency (FOA) and the judgment of agency (JOA). FOA is a lower-level nonconceptual feeling of being an agent; it is the background buzz of control we feel for our voluntary actions when not explicitly thinking about them. JOA, on the other hand, is a higher-level conceptual judgment of agency, and it arises in situations where we make explicit attributions of agency to the self or other. The FOA is linked to low-level sensorimotor processes, while the JOA is linked to higher-level cognitive processes such as background beliefs and contextual knowledge relating to the action (Moore, 2016).

44. Freud, S. (1915/2004). *The unconscious.* New York: Penguin Classics.

   Lear, J. (1998). *Open minded: Working out the logic of soul.* Cambridge, MA: Harvard University Press, p. 133.

45. Solms, M. (2021). *The hidden spring: A journey to the source of consciousness.* New York: W.W. Norton.

46. Affective neuroscientists have observed this SEEKING system as an integrated anatomical, chemical, and behavioral system in all mammals. Panksepp, 1998; Berridge, K. C., & Kringelbach, M. L. (2013). Neuroscience of affect: Brain mechanisms of pleasure and displeasure. *Current Opinion in Neurobiology, 23*(3), 294–303. https://doi. org/10.1016/j.conb.2013.01.017

47. Panksepp, J. (1998). *Affective neuroscience.* New York: Oxford University Press.

48. Pessoa, L. (2013). *The cognitive-emotional brain.* Cambridge, MA: MIT Press.

49. Cisek, P. (2007). Cortical mechanisms of action selection: The affordance competition hypothesis. *Philosophical Transactions of the Royal Society B: Biological Sciences, 362*(1485), 1585–1599. https://doi.org/10.1098/rstb.2007.2054.

50. The somatic marker hypothesis may have something to do with how bias functions in this model. See Bechara, A., Damasio, H., Tranel, D., & Damasio, A. R. (1997). Deciding advantageously before knowing the advantageous strategy. *Science, 275,* 1293–1295. doi:10.1126/science.275.5304.1293

51. McGinty, V. B., Rangel, A., & Newsome, W. T. (2016). Orbitofrontal cortex value signals depend on fixation location during free viewing. *Neuron, 90*(6), 1299–1311. https://doi.org/10.1016/j.neuron.2016.04.045

52. Cisek, 2007.

53. Clark, A. (2013). Whatever next? Predictive brains, situated agents, and the future of cognitive science. *Behavioral and Brain Sciences, 36*(3), 181–204. doi:10.1017/S0140525X12000477

54. Solms, M. L. (2018). The neurobiological underpinnings of psychoanalytic theory and therapy. *Frontiers in Behavioral Neuroscience, 12,* 294. https://doi.org/10.3389/fnbeh.2018.00294; Carhart-Harris, R. L., & Friston, K. J. (2010). The default-mode, ego-functions and free-energy: A neurobiological account of Freudian ideas. *Brain, 133,* 1265–1283. doi:10.1093/brain/awq010

55. Herzog, D. (2017). *Cold War Freud: Psychoanalysis in an age of catastrophes.* Cambridge: Cambridge University Press, p. 159.

56. Herzog, 2017, p. 169. See also Schroeder, T. (2004). *Three faces of desire.* Oxford: Oxford University Press. In which the author posits motivation, pleasure and reward as the

three faces of desire, and has a representational theory of desire that accords in places with my own.

57. Lear, 1998, p. 194.

58. For more on the neural currency of pleasure, see Berridge, K. C., & Kringelbach, M. L. (2013). Neuroscience of affect: Brain mechanisms of pleasure and displeasure. *Current Opinion in Neurobiology, 23*(3), 294–303. https://doi.org/10.1016/j.conb.2013.01.01. For more on how to bridge the neuroscience of pleasure with psychoanalysis, see Moccia, L., Mazza, M., Di Nicola, M., & Janiri, L. (2018). The experience of pleasure: A perspective between neuroscience and psychoanalysis. *Frontiers in Human Neuroscience, 12*, 359. https://doi.org/10.3389/fnhum.2018.0035

59. For more on these three phases, including graphs and brain localization, see Kringelbach, M. L., & Berridge, K. C. (2017). The affective core of emotion: Linking pleasure, subjective well-being, and optimal metastability in the brain. *Emotion Review: Journal of the International Society for Research on Emotion, 9*(3), 191–199. https://doi.org/10.1177/1754073916684558. For more on the SEEKING system and how it is channeled into cultural uses, see Panksepp, J., & Biven, L. (2012). *The archaeology of mind: Neuroevolutionary origins of human emotions.* New York: W. W. Norton.

60. These are generated by frontal lobe regions, see Berridge, K. C. (2012). From prediction error to incentive salience: Mesolimbic computation of reward motivation. *The European Journal of Neuroscience, 35*(7), 1124–1143. https://doi.org/10.1111/j.1460-9568.2012.07990.x

61. Berridge, K. C., Robinson, T. E., & Aldridge, J. W. (2009). Dissecting components of reward: "Liking," "wanting," and "learning." *Current Opinion in Pharmacology, 9*(1), 65–73. https:// doi.org/10.1016/j.coph.2008.12.014

62. *Umwelt* is the world as experienced by a particular organism. See Brentari, C. (2015). *Jakob von Uexküll: The discovery of the umwelt between biosemiotics and theoretical biology.* Dordrecht: Springer. Also see Panksepp, 1998.

63. Asma & Gabriel, 2019.

64. Cisek, 2007. The motivational function of value resides in OFC frontostriatal dopaminergic projections from the basal ganglia. The OFC receives connections from all sensory modalities and extensive limbic connections, in addition to the autonomic nervous system (ANS) and the periaqueductal grey, though it has weak motor connections Wallis, J. D. (2007). Orbitofrontal cortex and its contribution to decision-making. *Annual Review of Neuroscience, 30*, 31–56. https://doi.org/10.1146/annurev.neuro.30.051606.094334. Biasing signals therein take the form of motivational affective nudges wherein value in the OFC is an instantiation of computationally efficient preference transitivity adapted over a range of decisions. Platt, M., & Padoa-Schioppa, C. (2009). Neuronal representations of value. In P. W. Glimcher, C. F. Camerer, E. Fehr, & R. A. Poldrack (Eds.), *Neuroeconomics: Decision making and the brain* (pp. 441–462). New York: Elsevier Academic Press. Such a conative–doxastic loop may assign a cardinal measure of values to situation-types and action modes, or ethological action maps Iberall, A. S. (1995). A physical (homeokinetic) foundation for the Gibsonian theory of perception and action.

Ecological Psychology, 7(1), 37–68. https://doi.org/10.1207/s15326969eco0701_3 Iberall, A. S., & McCulloch, W. S. (1969). The organizing principle of complex living systems. *Journal of Basic Engineering, 91*(2), 290–294. https://doi.org/10.1115/1.3571099. Economic choices may be partly based on such value signals in the OFC, wherein the three elements of the motivational value of reward are quality, quantity, and probability of reward. Criterion setting and attentional dynamics are also crucial factors in decision-making Crapse, T. B., Lau, H., & Basso, M. A. (2018). A role for the superior colliculus in decision criteria. *Neuron, 97*(1), 181–194. https://doi.org/10.1016/j.neuron.2017.12.006

65. Cf. Levy, N. (2013). Addiction is not a brain disease (and it matters). *Frontiers in Psychiatry, 4*(24). doi:10.3389/fpsyt.2013.00024

66. Freud, S. (1917). Mourning and melancholia. In *The standard edition of the complete psychological works of Sigmund Freud, Volume XIV (1914–1916): On the history of the psycho-analytic movement, papers on metapsychology and other works* (pp. 237–258). London: Hogarth Press.

67. Pickard, 2020.

68. Pickard, 2018.

69. Edenberg, H. J., & Foroud, T. (2013). Genetics and alcoholism. *Nature Reviews: Gastroenterology & Hepatology, 10*(8), 487–494. https://doi.org/10.1038/nrgastro.2013.86

70. Littlefield, A. K., & Sher, K. J. (2010). The multiple, distinct ways that personality contributes to alcohol use disorders. *Social and Personality Psychology Compass, 4*(9), 767–782. https://doi.org/10.1111/j.1751-9004.2010.00296.x

71. Bucholz, K. K., & Robins, L. N. (1989). Sociological research on alcohol use, problems, and policy. *Annual Review of Sociology, 15*, 163–186. http://www.jstor.org/stable/2083223

72. Valenzuela, C. F. (1997). Alcohol and neurotransmitter interactions. *Alcohol Health and Research World, 21*(2), 144–148.

73. Craver, C. (2007). *Explaining the brain: Mechanisms and the mosaic unity of neuroscience.* New York: Clarendon Press of Oxford University.

74. We could frame a similar analysis with regards to consumerism, and how goods depicted within a semiological system of totemized brands can function as fetishized social identity cues. See Williamson, J. (2010). *Decoding advertisements: Ideology and meaning in advertising.* London: Marion Boyars. Also see Gabriel, 2013 and Gabriel (unpublished manuscript).

Chapter 7

1. For more on the relation between broader cultural projects and psychology, also see Noë, A. (2015). *Strange tools: Art and human nature.* New York: Hill and Wang; Damasio, A. R. (2019). *The strange order of things: Life, feeling, and the making of the cultures.* New York: First Vintage Books.

NOTES 211

2. This is not a complete definition; it does not take into account traditional aesthetics as well as institutional and art-historical dimensions of art. My focus in this chapter is simply on how art allows for reflexivity, and thus the definition provided ought to be serviceable for my purposes.

3. The mystification inherent in the emotional response to many works of art and ritual ceremonies draws from the occult power of collective effervescence and the confrontation of multiple orders and disorders. See Rappaport, R. A. (1999). *Ritual and religion in the making of humanity*. Cambridge: Cambridge University Press, p. 48, n. 11.

4. Asma & Gabriel, 2019. See chapter 9.

5. Richerson, P. J., & Boyd, R. (2001). The evolution of subjective commitment to groups: A tribal instincts hypothesis. In R. M. Nesse (Ed.), *Evolution and the capacity for commitment* (pp. 184–220). Thousand Oaks, CA: Russell Sage Foundation.

6. Pippin, 2021. Or, in Cavell's words, "Painting, being art, is revelation; it is revelation because it is acknowledgment; being acknowledgment, it is knowledge, of itself, and of the world" (Cavell, 1979, p. 110).

7. Pippin, R. (2017). *The philosophical Hitchcock: Vertigo and the anxieties of unknowingness*. Chicago: University of Chicago Press, p. 2.

8. Geertz, 1983, p. 119.

9. For example, Emil Jannings in *Der blaue engel* (1930) in which Jannings's character is transformed from a respectable scholar to a clown through his infatuation with Marlene Dietrich's character. Pippin, 2017, pp. 4–6.

10. Schiller, F., Hinderer, W., & Dahlstrom, D. O. (1993). *Essays*. New York: Continuum.

11. Poetry is then "art in quest of difficult knowledge." Warren, R. (2008). *Fables of the self: Studies in lyric poetry*. New York: W.W. Norton and Company, p. xvii.

12. Rappaport, 1999, p. 393. Analogy, as Levi-Strauss claims, is also a quality of wild thought which creates order by making connections between ideas. Freud as well as the British empiricists thought that the mind is intrinsically given to making associations, whether in primary processes and the dream work or through laws of association.

13. Gabriel, 2013. See Conclusion.

14. On the landscape of affordances, see Laland, K. N., Uller, T., Feldman, M. W., Sterelny, K., Müller, G. B., Moczek, A., Jablonka, E., & Odling-Smee, J. (2015). The extended evolutionary synthesis: Its structure, assumptions and predictions. *Proceedings of the Royal Society B: Biological Sciences, 282*(1813), Article 20151019. https://doi.org/10.1098/rspb.2015.1019

15. According to Roy Rappaport: "Humanity is a species that lives and can only live in terms of meanings it itself must invent. These meanings and understandings not only reflect or approximate an independently existing world but participate in its very construction. The worlds in which humans live are not fully constituted by tectonic, meteorological and organic processes . . . but are also constructed out of symbolically conceived and performatively established cosmologies, institutions, rules, and values." Rappaport, R. A. (1999). *Ritual and religion in the making of humanity*. Cambridge: Cambridge University Press, p. 8. Also see Austin, J. L. (1962). *How to do things with words*. Oxford: Oxford University Press.

212 NOTES

16. Rappaport, 1999, p. 9.
17. Spiritual emotions, like awe, create conditions for the imprinting of metaphysical beliefs. Participation in ritual disables emotions arising from fear and anxiety, thus mediating between conflicting drives through sublimation. Rappaport, 1999, p. 49 n12. See Gabriel, R. (2021). Affect, belief, and the arts. *Frontiers in Psychology*, December 2. https://doi.org/10.3389/fpsyg.2021.757234On fear and anxiety see Malinowski, B. (1922). *Argonauts of the Western Pacific; An account of native enterprise and adventure in the archipelagoes of Melanesian New Guinea*. London: G. Routledge & Sons. On conflicting drives and emotions, see Freud, S. (1907). Obsessive acts and religious practices. In J. Strachey (Ed.), *The collected papers of Sigmund Freud*, Vol. 9 (J. Riviere, Trans.). London: Hogarth Press; on sublimation, see Turner, V. (1969). *The ritual process*. Chicago: Aldine.
18. Dissanayake, E. (1992). *Homo aestheticus: Where art comes from and why*. New York: Free Press.
19. Alcorta & Sosis, 2005.
20. Geertz, C. (1983). *Local knowledge*. New York: Basic Books, p. 99.
21. Geertz, 1983, p. 109.
22. Lewis-Williams, 2010.
23. Alterity and metamorphosis, the experience of otherness, of being subsumed into a group in an overwhelming affective experience of immanence, is central to creating a sense of *communitas*. Johnson, A. W., & Earle, T. (2006). *The evolution of human societies: From foraging group to agrarian state*. Stanford, CA: Stanford University Press; Asma, S. T, & Gabriel, R. (2019). *The emotional mind: The affective roots of culture and cognition*. Cambridge, MA: Harvard University Press.
24. Durkheim, 1915.
25. Alcorta & Sosis, 2005. Adolescence is the period when one invests the most in group affiliation. Often, the group affiliations are related to imaginative cultural products like music, movies, fashion, and so on. In the psychodynamic tradition, adolescence is referred to as the second individuation process. Blos, P. (1967). The Second Individuation Process of Adolescence. *The Psychoanalytic Study of the Child*, 22(1), 162–186, doi:10.1080/00797308.1967.11822595
26. Turner, V. W. (1969). *The ritual process: Structure and anti-structure*. Chicago: Aldine.
27. Charles Morgan quoted in Geertz, 1983, p. 28. Also, see Cavell, "To satisfy the wish for the worlds' exhibition we must be willing to let the world as such appear. According to Heidegger this means that we must be willing for anxiety, to which alone the world as world, into which we are thrown, can manifest itself; and it is through that willingness that the possibility of one's own existence begins or ends. To satisfy the wish to act without performing, to let our actions go out of our hands, we must be willing to allow the self to exhibit itself without the self's intervention. The wish for total intelligibility is a terrible one. It means that we are willing to reveal ourselves through the self's betrayal of itself" (1979, p. 159). But see Fried on theatricality and objecthood: Fried, M. (1998). *Art and objecthood: Essays and reviews*. Chicago: University of Chicago Press.
28. Turner, 1969, p. 128.

NOTES 213

29. Amyot, J. (2008). "Proesme du translateur." In L. Plazenet (Ed.), *L'Histoire aethiopique* (J. Amyot, Trans.). Paris: Champion, p. 159.

30. Turner, 1969.

31. For Hegel and the German Romantics, like Schopenhauer on music and Nietzsche on tragedy, art can be a form of collective self-knowledge in which humans externalize and self-realize their conceptions. Pippin. R. B. (2020). *Filmed thought: Cinema as reflective form.* Chicago: University of Chicago Press, pp. 3–10.

32. Pippin, R. B. (2014). *After the beautiful: Hegel and the philosophy of pictorial modernism.* Chicago: University of Chicago Press.

33. See Kant's *Critique of the power of judgment* (1790), and Hegel's *Lectures on fine arts* given between 1818–1829 and collected in Hegel, G. W. F., & Knox, T. M. (1998). *Aesthetics: Lectures on fine art.* Oxford: Clarendon.

34. Pippin, 2014, pp. 20, 24.

35. Pippin, 2014, pp. 7–8, 11, 13. For Pippin, aesthetics allow for "a reconciliation of sorts between the inescapably finite, constrained, natural embodied features of human existence and the practically undeniable, meaning- and norm-responsive, reflective, self-determining features" (p. 16).

36. Clark, T.J. (1999). *The painting of modern life: Paris in the art of Manet and his followers* (rev. ed.). Princeton, NJ: Princeton University Press.

37. Rodowick, D. N. (2015). *Philosophy's artful conversation.* Cambridge, MA: Harvard University Press, p. xii.

38. Taylor, C. (1971). Interpretation and the sciences of man. *The Review of Metaphysics,* 25(1), 3–51. http://www.jstor.org/stable/20125928

39. Pippin, 2014, p. 135.

40. Imagination and body grammar are discussed in detail in Asma and Gabriel (2019).

41. Lewis, 1989.

42. This is akin to Nietzsche's notion of genealogy of knowledge in which our consideration of the timeliness of the idea, its changing character, allows us to recognize that value and meaning are themselves relational and contextual. Rodowick, 2015, pp. xi, 301.

43. It is possible to suggest a mechanics of sensible affective knowledge now because the study of emotions in recent decades has transformed our understanding of their range and capacities. The crucial insight is that the lower layers of affect permeate, infiltrate, and animate the higher layers of emotions. Panksepp, 1998; Damasio, 2018; Davidson, R. J., Scherer, K. R., & Goldsmith, H. (2009). *Handbook of affective sciences.* Oxford: Oxford University Press; de Waal, F. (Ed.) (2001). *Tree of origin: What primate behavior can tell us about human social evolution.* Cambridge, MA: Harvard University Press; Pessoa, L. (2013). *The cognitive-emotional brain.* Cambridge, MA: MIT Press; Phelps, E. (2006). Emotion and cognition: Insights from studies of the human amygdala. *Annual Review of Psychology,* 57, 27–53. https://doi.org/10.1146/annurev.psych.56.091103.070234; Prinz, J. (2004). *Gut reactions: A perceptual theory of emotion.* Oxford: Oxford University Press. Meanwhile, ecological psychology (also referred to as direct perception) has refined our understanding of the active nature of sensation and perception. See Chemero, A. (2011). *Radical embodied*

214 NOTES

cognitive science. Cambridge, MA: MIT Press; Heft, H. (2010). Affordances and the perception of landscape: An inquiry into environmental perception and aesthetics. In C. W. Thompson, P. Aspinall, & S. Bell (Eds.), *Innovative approaches to researching landscape and health* (pp. 9–32); Reed, E. S. (1996). *Encountering the world: Toward an ecological psychology.* Oxford: Oxford University Press; Rietveld, E. (2012). Bodily intentionality and social affordances in context. In F. Paglieri (Ed.), *Consciousness in interaction: The role of the natural and social context in shaping consciousness* (pp. 207–226). Amsterdam: John Benjamins. https://doi.org/10.1075/aicr.86.11rie; Turvey, M. T. (1992). Affordances and prospective control: An outline of the ontology. *Ecological Psychology, 4*(3), 173–187. https://doi.org/10.1207/s15326969eco0403_3; Withagen, R., & Chemero, A. (2009). Naturalizing perception: Developing the Gibsonian approach to perception along evolutionary lines. *Theory & Psychology, 19*(3), 363–389. https://doi.org/10.1177/0959354309104159

44. Reed, E. S. (1986). James Gibson's ecological revolution in perceptual psychology: A case study in the transformation of scientific Ideas. *Studies in the History and Philosophy of Science, 17,* 65–99.

45. Withagen, R., & Michaels, C. (2005). On ecological conceptualizations of perceptual systems and action systems. *Theory & Psychology, 15*(5), 603–620. https://doi.org/10.1177/0959354305057265; Shaw, R. (2003). The agent–environment interface: Simon's indirect or Gibson's direct coupling? *Ecological Psychology, 15*(1), 37–106. https://doi.org/10.1207/S15326969ECO1501_04; Millikan, R. G. (1996). Pushmi-Pullyu representations. In J. E. Tomberlin (Ed.), *Philosophical perspectives: Vol. 9. AI, connectionism, and philosophical psychology* (pp. 185–200). Atascadero, CA: Ridgeview.

46. Millikan, R. G. (1996). Pushmi-Pullyu representations. In J. E. Tomberlin (Ed.), *Philosophical perspectives: Vol. 9. AI, connectionism, and philosophical psychology* (pp. 185–200). Atascadero, CA: Ridgeview.

47. Recall the discussion of salience and the affordance competition model from Chapter 6. See Pezzulo, G., & Cisek, P. (2016). Navigating the affordance landscape: Feedback control as a process model of behavior and cognition. *Trends in Cognitive Science, 20*(6), 414–424. https:// doi.org/10.1016/j.tics.2016.03.013. Warren, W. H. (1988). Action modes and laws of control for the visual guidance of action. In O. Meijer & K. Roth (Eds.), *Movement behavior: The motor–action controversy* (pp. 339–380). Amsterdam: North Holland.

48. Laland, K., Odling-Smee, J., & Myles, S. (2010). How culture shaped the human genome: Bringing genetics and the human sciences together. *Nature Reviews Genetics, 11,* 137–148. https://doi.org/10.1038/nrg2734; Warren, W. H. (2006). The dynamics of perception and action. *Psychological Review, 113*(2), 358–389. https://doi.org/10.1037/0033-295X.113.2.358

49. Gabriel, R. (2021). The motivational role of affect in an ecological model. *Theory & Psychology, 31*(4), 552–572. https://doi.org/10.1177/0959354321992869

50. De Waal, 2001. See Frans De Waal's Russian doll model of empathy.

51. Panksepp, 1998; Asma, S. T. (2017). *The evolution of imagination.* Chicago: University of Chicago Press.

NOTES 215

52. On image grammar, see Barsalou, L. W. (1999). Perceptual symbol systems. *Behavior and Brain Sciences, 22*(4), 577–660. On body-task grammar, see Barton, R. A. (2012). Embodied cognitive evolution and the cerebellum. *Philosophical Transactions of the Royal Society B, 367*(1599), 2097–2107. On nonconceptual content, see Bermúdez, J., & Cahen, A. (2015). Nonconceptual mental content. In E. N. Zalta (Ed.), *The Stanford encyclopedia of philosophy* (Fall ed.). http://plato.stanford.edu/archives/fall2015/entries/content-nonconceptual/

53. Harrisson, J. E. (1913). *Ancient art and ritual.* Oxford: Oxford University Press.

54. Harrison, 1913, p. 27.

55. Gallese, V., Fadiga, L. Fogassi, L., & Rizzolatti, G. (1996). Action recognition in the premotor cortex. *Brain, 119*(2), 593–609.

56. The Stanislavsky method (in)famously trains actors to feel like the character they are portraying.

57. Trotsky, L. (1960). *Literature and revolution.* Ann Arbor: University of Michigan Press.

58. Rappaport, 1999, p. 42.

59. Harrisson, 1913, chapter 2.

60. Rappaport, 1999, p. 137.

61. Williams, B. A. (1993). *Shame and necessity.* Oakland: University of California Press.

62. Pavel, T. G. (2013). *The lives of the novel: A history.* Princeton, NJ: Princeton University Press.

63. See Bruner, J. (1991). The narrative construction of reality. *Critical Inquiry, 18*(1), 1–21. http://www.jstor.org/stable/1343711

64. Pavel, 2013.

65. Narrative formats of drama are particularly compelling partly because they elicit emotional responses. For example, *Romance* gives narrative expression to the sexual desire and longing (i.e., LUST and SEEKING), while the typical *horror* plot is a narrative expression of terror (i.e., FEAR). *Tragedy* engages feelings of grief (i.e., separation distress system), while *mysteries* and hero stories engage tantalizing meanderings (of the SEEKING system). See Asma, S. (2021). Adaptive imagination: Toward a mythopoetic cognitive science. *Evolutionary Studies in Imaginative Culture, 5*(2), 1–32. https://doi.org/10.26613/esic.5.2.236

66. Watt, I. (1957). *The rise of the novel: Studies in Defoe, Richardson, and Fielding.* Berkeley: University of California Press.

67. Lukacs, G (1916/1971). *The theory of the novel: A historico-philosophical essay on the forms of great epic literature.* Cambridge, MA: MIT Press. Dutton, D. (2009). *The art instinct: Beauty, pleasure, and human evolution.* New York: Bloomsbury Press.

68. For example, we are shuttled between perspectives in the town of *Middlemarch* in George Eliot's classic of 1871. This navigation of the social imaginary allows readers to reflect through the prism of multiple dwellers in the city and their respective ethical quandaries which arise from communal life.

69. These imaginative projections include the depiction of human types and consideration of the meaning of life, love, and the nature of human interaction. Pavel, 2013, pp. 17–19.

216 NOTES

70. Film is magical and thus sacred for Stanley Cavell because it satisfies the wish for "the magical reproduction of the world by enabling us to view it unseen . . . to see in this way . . . the world itself." Cavell, 1979, p. 101. Jean-Luc Godard made a similar appraisal and illustrated it throughout his career, including in the *Histoire(s) du Cinéma* (1988).

71. Rodowick, 2015, p. 25.

72. Pippin, 2017.

73. Pippin, R. B. (2012). *Hollywood Westerns and American myth: The importance of Howard Hawks and John Ford for political philosophy.* New Haven, CT: Yale University Press.

74. Cavell, S. (1979). *The world viewed* (enlarged ed.). Cambridge, MA: Harvard University Press, p. 7.

75. Pippin, 2020, p. 24.

76. Pippin, 2020, p. 14.

77. "It is the knowledge . . . that we exist in the condition of myth: we do not require the gods to show that our lives illustrate a story which escapes us; and it requires no major recognition or reversal to bring its meaning home. Any life may illustrate any; any change may bring it home" (Cavell, 1979, p. 157).

78. Cavell, 1979, p. 12.

79. According to Walter Freeman, "the role of trance states was particularly important for breaking down preexisting habits and beliefs. That meltdown appears to be necessary for personality changes leading to the formation of social groups by cooperative action leading to trust. Bonding is not simply a release of a neurochemical in an altered state. It is the social action of dancing and singing together that induces new forms of behavior, owing to the malleability that can come through the altered state" (Freeman, 2000, p. 422). Gregory Bateson (1972) calls this third-level learning.

80. Heesterman, J. C. (1993). *The broken world of sacrifice: An essay in ancient Indian ritual.* Chicago: University of Chicago Press.

81. Many traditions of music maintain space for such experiences, including Arabic *tarab*, Moroccan *gnawa*, Tunisian *stambeli*, and American rock n' roll. *Tarab* is a borderline state of consciousness in which sensory and aesthetic percepts are mixed to afford a form of ecstasy, it is analogous to Spanish *duende*, Sufi *hāl*, and secular deep listening. Racy, A. J. (2003). *Making music in the Arab world: The culture and artistry of Tarab.* Cambridge: Cambridge University Press.

82. Lewis, I. M. (1989). *Ecstatic religion: A study of shamanism and spirit possession* (2nd ed.). New York: Routledge.

83. Pippin, 2014, p. 4, n. 8. This making present is called "presentness" by Michael Fried, and for Hegel art has the task of bringing the Absolute to presentness.

84. James, W. (1910/1982). *Varieties of religious experience.* New York: Penguin, pp. 380–381.

85. In pictorial art, a painting can arrest time and make present, or immanent, aspects of human action and of our condition relative to objects and nature. Photographs, with their connection to the journalistic, truth-telling project, likewise capture light

and time to bring the moment to us in all its immanent glory. Modern art can be considered a dramatization of how our condition implicates a crisis of meaning, political strife, theatricality, consumer fetishism, and a lack of coherence due to the surfeit of information that came along with technical mastery. Modern art thus discloses the immanence of such issues in the intention of the artist and in truths that transcend the artist's intentions. Pippin, 2014. See his chapter on Heidegger's view of art as a deed of unconcealment.

86. Panksepp, 1998.
87. Barton, R. A. (2012). Embodied cognitive evolution and the cerebellum. *Philosophical Transactions of the Royal Society B, 367*(1599), 2097–2107.
88. Fiebich, A. (2014). Perceiving affordances and social cognition. In M. Gallotti & J. Michael (Eds.), *Perspectives in social ontology and social cognition* (vol. 4, pp. 149–166). New York: Springer.
89. Lewis, 1989, pp. 179, 184.
90. *Penguin Dictionary of Psychology* quoted in Lewis, 1989, p. 33.
91. An epidemiology of possession indicates that individuals can modify their sociopolitical standing through their role in these rituals. Lewis, 1989.
92. Bourguignon, E. (1973). *Religion, altered states of consciousness, and social change.* Columbus: Ohio State University Press.
93. Jankowsky, R. C. (2007). Music, spirit possession and the in-between. *Ethnomusicology Forum, 16*(2), 165–208.
94. Bourguignon, 1973.
95. Herbert, R. (2011). Reconsidering music and trance: Cross-cultural differences and cross-disciplinary perspectives. *Ethnomusicology Forum, 20*(2), 201–227. Herbert quotes Nettl (2000, p. 468) in describing music as the crucial component of ritual and link to the supernatural found in some form in all societies.
96. Becker, J. (2004). *Deep listening; Music, emotion, and trancing.* Bloomington: Indiana University Press. Certain emotional states like "chills" are mediated by endogenous opioids and oxytocin which play a role in social bonding. These characteristics provide excellent grounds for sensible affective knowledge in the form of direct perception and imagination. Panksepp, J. (1995). The emotional sources of "chills" induced by music. *Music Perception, 13*(2), 171–207.
97. Herbert, 2011; Becker, 2004, p. 27.
98. Becker, 2004.
99. Panksepp, 1998.
100. Asma & Gabriel, 2019.
101. Rouget, G. (1985). *La musique et la transe.* Paris: Gallimard. Indeed, trance requires both psychophysiological modification and cultural symbols. It has been used for a wide range of purposes, especially modification or confirmation of metaphysical belief. We are physically susceptible to these receptive states and subsequently build cultural institutions like festivals and schools around the immanent arts to produce individuals who can attain trance states as well as generate them in others and who straddle the social distinction between artist and spiritual teacher.

218   NOTES

Chapter 8

1. Beliefs and practices can be groundless and yet consistent with a community's emotional needs. Under some circumstances, superstition can be said to be rational for pragmatic reasons of mental health and narrative coherence. Malinowski, B. (1948). *Magic, science and religion and other essays*. Glencoe, IL: The Free Press (Reissued Long Grove, IL: Waveland Press, 1992).

    Taylor, S. E. (1991). *Positive illusions: Creative self-deception and healthy mind*. New York: Basic Books. Indeed, metaphysics may be more intrinsic to psychology than science. Adams, 1931.

2. Adler, A. (1930). Individual psychology. In C. Murchison (Ed.), *International university series in psychology. Psychologies of 1930* (pp. 395–405). Worcester, MA: Clark University Press. https://doi.org/10.1037/11017-021; Vyse, S. (1997/2014). *Believing in magic*. New York: Oxford University Press.

3. Consider the causal planes above and below psychology to which we do not turn when in need of succoring explanation.

4. Pippin, R. (2010). *Nietzsche, psychology, and first philosophy*. Chicago: University of Chicago Press.

5. When we describe to one another what we think the soul is, we mean thereby to propose a vision of *psychic health* vis-à-vis our notion of human nature. Pippin, 2010, p. 3.

6. Lear, J. (1999). *Open-minded*. Cambridge, MA: Harvard University Press.

7. Gray, J. (2007). *Straw dogs*. New York: Farrar, Strauss, and Giroux.

8. We do not know how the mind is the brain in any but the most cursory detail, and yet we manage to act even with consciousness of this deficiency. See Pippin, 2010, p. 55, n. 18; Klein, 2016.

9. Individual commitments within a culture of course do not all coincide; the plurality of mass society, multiculturalism, and the historical palimpsest resist drawing simple lines between the uses of psychology and commitments.

10. Pippin, 2010, p. 39.

11. Lévi-Strauss, 1961/2021.

12. Nietzsche, F. (1882/2010). *The gay science: With a prelude in rhymes and an appendix of songs* (W. Kaufman, Trans.). New York: Vintage.

13. Taylor, C. (2007). *A secular age*. Cambridge, MA: Belknap Press of Harvard University Press; Strong, R. L., & Weber, M. (2004). *The vocation lectures*. Indianapolis: Hackett. Though see Storm, J. J. (2017). *The myth of disenchantment*. Chicago: University of Chicago Press, for a different take on the status of the enchanted world.

14. Philosopher Robert Pippin's portrayal of modernity emphasizes how, in a post-Darwinian climate, we are faced with the gross simplicity of any of our attempts to will a new life-affirming value reinvestment in the world. Bourgeois modernity thus suffers from what he terms an "erotic timidity" wherein health, security, prudence, and comfort of a happy life are the chief desiderata. Such living disguises from itself the lack of a sufficient depth commitment. We obscure the hidden brutalities of the

human experience, and the boring, and ultimately unsatisfying, erotic failure of the bourgeois vision of life as safety and pleasure (pp. 122–123).

15. Taylor, C. (1971). Interpretation and the sciences of man. *The Review of Metaphysics*, *25*(1), 3–51. http://www.jstor.org/stable/20125928
16. Danziger, K. (2003). Prospects of a historical psychology. *History and Philosophy of Psychology Bulletin, 15*(2), 4–10. .
17. Rose, N., &Abi-Rached, J. M. (2013). *Neuro: The new brain sciences and the management of the mind*. Princeton, NJ: Princeton University Press.
18. Tallis, 2010.

References

Preface

Churchland, P. (2007). Neurophilosophy: The early years and new directions. *Functional Neurology, 22*(4), 185–195.

Churchland, P. (2008). *Impact of neuroscience on philosophy. Neuron, 60*(3), 409–411.

Dennett, D. (2006). Two steps closer to consciousness. In Brian L. Keeley (Ed.), *Paul Churchland* (pp. 193–209). Cambridge: Cambridge University Press.

Foucault, M., Lagrange, J., Burchell, G., & Davidson, A. I. (2008). *Psychiatric power: Lectures at the College de France, 1973–1974*. New York: Picador.

Kaplan, D. M., & Craver, C. F. (2011). The explanatory force of dynamical and mathematical models in neuroscience: A mechanistic perspective. *Philosophy of Science, 78*(4), 601–627. doi:10.1086/661755

Chapter 1: Empirical Psychology: Mind in a Lab

Adams, G. (1931). *Psychology: Science or superstition?* New York: Covici Friede e-publisher.

Adler, A. (1929). *The practice and theory of individual psychology.* New York: Harcourt, Brace.

Allport, G. W. (1937). *Personality: A psychological interpretation.* New York: Holt.

Baldwin, J. M. (1897/1902). *Social and ethical interpretations in mental development.* New York: MacMillan.

Bandura, A., & Walters, R. (1963). *Social learning and personality development.* New York: Holt.

Barrett, L. (2011). *Beyond the brain: How body and environment shape animal and human minds.* Princeton, NJ: Princeton University Press.

Boring, E. G. (1950). *A history of experimental psychology.* New York: Appleton-Century-Crofts.

Collingwood, R. G. (1972). *The idea of history.* New York: Oxford University Press.

Crosson, F. J. (1985). Psyche and the computer: Integrating the shadow. In S. Koch & D. E. Leary (Eds.), *A century of psychology as science* (pp. 284–321). New York: McGraw-Hill.

Danziger, K. (1983). Origins and basic principles of Wundt's Völkerpsychologie. *British Journal of Social Psychology, 22*, 303–313. doi:10.1111/j.2044-8309.1983.tb00597.x

Danziger, K. (2008). *Marking the mind: A history of memory.* Cambridge. Cambridge University Press.

Danziger, K. (2013). Psychology and its history. *Theory & Psychology, 23*(6), 829–839. https://doi.org/10.1177/0959354313502746

Erikson, E. (1950). *Childhood and society.* New York: Norton.

Flanagan, O. (1984). *The science of the mind.* Cambridge, MA: MIT Press.

222 REFERENCES

Foucault, M. (1966/2019). *Les mots et les choses: Une archéologie des sciences humaines.* Paris: Gallimard.

Gardner, H. (1973). *The quest for mind: Piaget, Lévi-Strauss, and the structuralist movement.* New York: Vintage.

Gardner, H. (1985). *The mind's new science: A history of the cognitive revolution.* New York: Basic Books.

Greenwood, J. D. (2015). *A conceptual history of psychology: Exploring the tangled web.* Cambridge: Cambridge University Press.

James, W. (1890/1950). *The principles of psychology.* New York: Dover.

James, W. (1904). *Does consciousness exist?* New York: Longman, Green, and co.

Kagan, J. (2009). *The three cultures: Natural sciences, social sciences, and the humanities in the 21st century.* Cambridge: Cambridge University Press.

Kendler, H. M. (1985). *Behaviorism and psychology: An uneasy alliance.* In S. Koch & D. E. Leary (Eds.), *A century of psychology as science* (pp. 121–134). New York: McGraw-Hill.

Kimble, G. A. (1985). Conditioning and learning. In S. Koch & D. E. Leary (Eds.), *A century of psychology as science* (pp. 284–321). New York: McGraw-Hill.

Klein, Richard G. 2009. *The human career: Human biological and cultural origins* (3rd ed.). Chicago: University of Chicago Press.

Knorr-Cetina K. (1999). *Epistemic cultures: How the sciences make knowledge.* Cambridge, MA: Harvard University Press.

Koch, S. (Ed.) (1959). *Psychology: A study of a science.* New York: McGraw-Hill.

Koch, S. (1999). *Psychology in human context: Essays in dissidence and reconstruction.* Chicago: University of Chicago Press.

Kuhn, T. (1962). *The structure of scientific revolutions.* Chicago: University of Chicago Press.

Leahey, T. H. (2003). *A history of psychology: Main currents in psychological thought* (6th ed.). Upper Saddle River, NJ: Pearson Prentice Hall.

Lear, J. (1998). *Open minded: Working out the logic of soul.* Cambridge, MA: Harvard University Press.

Lewin, K. (1935). *Dynamic theory of personality.* New York: McGraw-Hill.

Luria, A. (1979). *The making of mind: A personal account of soviet psychology.* M. Cole & S. Cole, Eds. Cambridge, MA: Harvard University Press.

McGuire, W. J. (1985). Toward social psychology's second century. In S. Koch & D. E. Leary (Eds.), *A century of psychology as science* (pp. 284–321). New York: McGraw-Hill.

Mills, J. A. (1998). *Control: A history of behavioral psychology.* New York: New York University Press.

Mischel, W. (1968). *Personality and assessment.* New York: Wiley.

Modern, J. (2021). *Neuromatic: Or, a particular history of religion and the brain.* Chicago: University of Chicago Press.

Nehamas, A. (1998). *The art of living.* Oakland: University of California Press.

Newell, A., & Simon, H. A. (1972). *Human problem solving.* Englewood Cliffs, NJ: Prentice-Hall.

Osbeck, L. (2019). *Values in psychological science.* Cambridge: Cambridge University Press.

Perry, R. B. (1938). *In the spirit of William James.* New Haven, CT: Yale University Press.

Piaget, J. (1923/1950). *The language and thought of the child.* London: Routledge & Kegan Paul.

Richards, G. (2010). *Putting psychology in its place* (3rd ed.). London: Routledge.

REFERENCES 223

Robinson, D. (1976). *An intellectual history of psychology*. Madison: University of Wisconsin Press.

Robinson, D. N. (1985). Science, psychology, and explanation: Synonyms or antonyms? In S. Koch & D. E. Leary (Eds.), *A century of psychology as science* (pp. 60–74). New York: McGraw-Hill.

Santayana, G. (1922/2009). *The genteel tradition in American philosophy and character and opinion in the United States*. New York: Yale University Press.

Shapin, S. (1994). *A social history of truth: Civility and science in seventeenth-century England*. Chicago: University of Chicago Press.

Skinner, B. (1984). Behaviorism at fifty. *Behavioral and Brain Sciences*, 7(4), 615–621. doi:10.1017/S0140525X00027618

Smith, R. (2013). *Between the mind and nature: A history of psychology*. London: Reaktion Books.

Solomon, R. (2003). *What is an emotion? Classic and contemporary readings*. Oxford: Oxford University Press.

Stevenson, L. (1974). *Seven theories of human nature* (2nd ed.). New York: Oxford University Press.

Sullivan, H. S. (1953). *The interpersonal theory of psychiatry*. New York: Norton.

Vygotsky, L. S., van der Veer, R., & Valsiner, J. (Eds.). (1994). *The Vygotsky reader* (T. Prout, Trans.). Oxford: Basil Blackwell.

Chapter 2: Metaphor in Empirical Psychology

Appiah, K. A. (2017). *As if: Idealization and ideals*. Cambridge, MA: Harvard University Press.

Araujo, S. F. (2017). Toward a philosophical history of psychology: An alternative path for the future. *Theory & Psychology*, 27(1), 87–107.

Asay, J. (2018). The role of truth in psychological science. *Theory & Psychology*, 28(3), 382–397.

Asma, S. T., & Gabriel, R. (2019). *The emotional mind: The affective roots of culture and cognition*. Cambridge, MA: Harvard University Press.

Baars, B. J. (1988). *A cognitive theory of consciousness*. Cambridge: Cambridge University Press.

Baddeley, A. D. (2007). *Working memory, thought and action*. Oxford: Oxford University Press.

Bandura, A. (1991). Social cognitive theory of self regulation. *Organizational Behavior and Human Decision Processes*, 50(2), 248–287.

Barrett, L. (2011). *Beyond the brain: How body and environment shape animal and human minds*. Princeton, NJ: Princeton University Press.

Barrett, L. (2012). *Why behaviorism isn't Satanism 2*. In J. Vonk & T. K. Shackelford (Eds.), *The Oxford handbook of comparative evolutionary psychology* (pp. 17–38). Oxford: Oxford University Press.

Barrett, L., & Rendall, D. (2010). Out of our minds: The neuroethology of primate strategic behavior. In M. L. Platt & A. A. Ghazanfar (Eds.), *Primate neuroethology* (pp. 570–586). New York: Oxford University Press.

224 REFERENCES

Barsalou L. W. (2009). Simulation, situated conceptualization, and prediction. *Philosophical Transactions of the Royal Society of London. Series B, Biological Sciences, 364*(1521), 1281–1289. https://doi.org/10.1098/rstb.2008.0319

Bechtel, W. (2008). *Mental mechanisms: Philosophical perspectives on cognitive neuroscience.* London: Routledge.

Bechtel, W., & Abrahamsen, A. (2010). Dynamic mechanistic explanation: Computational modeling of circadian rhythms as an exemplar for cognitive science. *Studies in History and Philosophy of Science Part A, 1*, 321–333.

Bechtel, W., & Richardson, R. C. (1992). Emergent phenomena and complex systems. In A. Beckermann, H. Flohr, & J. Kim (Eds.), *Emergence or reduction? Essays on the prospects of nonreductive physicalism* (pp. 257–288). Berlin: Walter de Gruyter Verlag.

Bechtel, W., & Richardson, R. C. (2010). Neuroimaging as a tool for functionally decomposing cognitive processes. In S. J. Hanson & M. Bunzl (Eds.), *Foundational issues in human brain mapping* (pp. 241–262). Cambridge, MA: MIT Press.

Berggren, D. (1963). The use and abuse of metaphor II. *The Review of Metaphysics, 17*, 450–472.

Bhaskar, R. (1975). *Forms of realism.* Ghent, NL: Ghent University Press.

Black, M. (1962). *Models and metaphors.* Cornell, NY: Cornell University Press.

Black, M. (1977). More about metaphor. *Dialectica, 31*, 431–457.

Bloor, D. (1976). *Knowledge and social imagery.* Chicago: University of Chicago Press.

Boroditsky, L. (2000). Metaphoric structuring: Understanding time through spatial metaphors. *Cognition, 75*, 1–28. doi:10.1016/S0010-0277(99)00073-6

Bowdle, B., & Gentner, D. (2005). The career of metaphor. *Psychological Review, 112*, 193–216.

Boyd, R. (1979). Metaphor and theory change, In A. Ortony (Ed.), *Metaphor and thought* (pp. 19–43). Cambridge: Cambridge University Press.

Boyd, R. (2017). *A different kind of animal.* Princeton, NJ: Princeton University Press.

Bradie, M. (1999). Science and metaphor. *Biology & Philosophy, 14*, 159–166. https://doi.org/10.1023/A:1006601214943

Brette, R. (2019). Neural coding: The bureaucratic model of the brain. *Behavioral and Brain Sciences, 42*, e243. https://doi.org/10.31234/osf.io/tgcn9

Brown, T. L. (2003). *Making Truth: Metaphor in Science.* Urbana: University of Illinois Press.

Carey, N. (2012). *The epigenetic revolution: How modern biology is rewriting our understanding of genetics, disease, and inheritance.* New York: Columbia University Press.

Carroll, S. B. (2005). *Endless forms most beautiful: The new science of evo devo and the making of the animal kingdom.* New York: W. W. Norton.

Carruthers, P. (2008). Meta-cognition in animals: A skeptical look. *Mind & Language, 23*, 58–89.

Carruthers, P. (2013). Mindreading in infancy. *Mind & Language, 28*, 141–172.

Cervone, D. (2004). The architecture of personality. *Psychological Review, 111*(1), 183–204.

Chemero, A. (2011). *Radical embodied cognitive science.* Cambridge, MA: MIT Press.

Colombetti, G. (2017). *The feeling body: Affective science meets the enactive mind.* Cambridge, MA: The MIT Press.

Craver, C. F. (2005). *Special issue: Mechanisms in biology.* Oxford: Elsevier.

Craver, C. (2007). *Explaining the brain: Mechanisms and the mosaic unity of neuroscience.* New York: Clarendon Press of Oxford University.

REFERENCES 225

Craver, C. F., & Bechtel, W. (2007). Top-down causation without top-down causes. *Biology & Philosophy, 22,* 547–563. doi:10.1007/s10539-006-9028-8

Chemero, A., & Silberstein, M. (2008). After the philosophy of mind: Replacing scholasticism with science. *Philosophy of Science, 75*(1), 1–27.

Clement, J. (2013). *Creative model construction in scientists and students. Springer handbook of model-based science.* Dordrecht, NL: Springer.

Cosmelli, D. J., Lachaux, J., & Thompson, E. (2007). Neurodynamics of consciousness. In P. D. Zelazo, M. Moscovitch, & E. Thompson (Eds.), *Cambridge handbook of consciousness* (pp. 731–774). Cambridge: Cambridge University Press.

Damasio, A. (1994). *Descartes' error: Emotion, reason, and the human brain.* New York: Putnam.

Damasio, A. (2018). *Strange order of things: The biological roots of culture.* New York: Knopf Doubleday.

Davidson, R. J., Scherer, K. R., & Goldsmith, H. H. (2003). *Handbook of affective sciences.* Oxford: Oxford University Press.

Dawkins, R. (1989). *The selfish gene.* New York: Oxford University Press.

de Waal, Frans (Ed.). (2001). *Tree of origin: What primate behavior can tell us about human social evolution.* Cambridge, MA: Harvard University Press.

Davidson, R. J., Scherer, K. R., & Goldsmith, H. H. (Eds.). (2003). *Handbook of affective sciences.* Oxford University Press.

Douglas, M. (1977). *Rules and meanings: The anthropology of everyday knowledge: Selected readings.* New York: Psychology Press.

Draaisma, D. (2000). *Metaphors of memory: A history of ideas about the mind.* Cambridge: Cambridge University Press.

Ekman, P. (1999). Basic emotions. In T. Dalgleish & M. J. Power (Eds.), *Handbook of cognition and emotion* (pp. 45–60). Sussex, UK: John Wiley & Sons.

Eliasmith, C., & Anderson, C. H. (2003). *Neural engineering: Computational, representation, and dynamics in neurobiological systems.* Cambridge, MA: The MIT Press.

Fincher-Kiefer, R. (2019). *How the body shapes knowledge: Empirical support for embodied cognition.* Washington, DC: American Psychological Association. doi:10.1037/0000136-000

Fischer, E. (2014). Philosophical intuitions, heuristics, and metaphors. *Synthese, 191*(3), 569–606.

Fischer, E., & Curtis, M. (Eds.). (2019). *Methodological advances in experimental philosophy.* London: Bloomsbury.

Flanagan, O. (1984). *The science of the mind.* Cambridge, MA: MIT Press.

Fodor, J. A. (1983). *The modularity of mind.* Cambridge, MA: MIT Press.

Fodor, J. A. (1998). *Concepts: Where cognitive science went wrong.* Oxford: Oxford University Press.

Foucault, M. (1966). *Les mots et les choses.* Paris: Editions Gallimard.

Frazzetto, G., & Anker, S. (2009). Neuroculture. *Nature Reviews Neuroscience, 10,* 815–821. https://doi.org/10.1038/nrn2736

Freud, S. (1915/1963). *The unconscious.* Standard edition. *14:* 159–204. New York: Collier Books.

Gabriel, R. (2012). Modularity in cognitive psychology and affective neuroscience (pp. 19–25). In J. Panksepp et al., *The philosophical implications of affective neuroscience. Journal of Consciousness Studies, 19*(3–4), 6–48.

226 REFERENCES

Gabriel, R. (2021a). The motivational role of affect in an ecological model. *Theory & Psychology, 31*(4), 552–572. https://doi.org/10.1177/0959354321992869

Gallistel, C. R. (1990). *Learning, development, and conceptual change: The organization of learning.* Cambridge, MA: MIT Press.

Gardner, H. (1985). *The mind's new science: A history of the cognitive revolution.* New York: Basic Books.

Garson, J. (2015). The birth of information in the brain: Edgar Adrian and the vacuum tube. *Science in Context, 28,* 31–52.

Gazzaniga, M. (2018). *The consciousness instinct: Unraveling the mystery of how the brain makes the mind.* New York: Farrar, Strauss, and Giroux.

Gentner, D. (1983). Structure-mapping: A theoretical framework for analogy. *Cognitive Science, 7,* 155–170.

Gentner, D., & Grudin, J. (1985). The evolution of mental metaphors in psychology: A 90-year retrospective. *American Psychologist, 40,* 181–192.

Gentner, D., Loewenstein, J., & Thompson, L. (2004). Learning and transfer: A general role for analogical encoding. *Journal of Educational Psychology, 95,* 393–405. doi:10.1037/0022-0663.95.2.393.

Gergen, K. J. (1993). A realist psychology revealed. *Contemporary Psychology, 38*(7), 698–699. doi:10.1037/033493

Gibbs, R. W. Jr. (2006). Metaphor interpretation as embodied simulation. *Mind and Language, 21,* 434–458.

Gibson, J. J. (1979/2014). *The ecological approach to visual perception.* Hoboken, NJ: Taylor et Francis.

Giere, R. (1999). *Science without laws.* Chicago: University of Chicago Press.

Giere, R. (2006). *Scientific perspectivism.* Chicago: University of Chicago Press.

Gigerenzer, G. (2010). Moral satisficing: Rethinking moral behavior as bounded rationality. *Topics in Cognitive Science, 2,* 528–554.

Gigerenzer, G. (2015). *Simply rational: Decision making in the real world.* New York: Oxford University Press.

Gigerenzer, G., & Todd, P. M. (1999). Fast and frugal heuristics: The adaptive toolbox. In G. Gigerenzer, P. M. Todd, & The ABC Research Group, *Evolution and cognition. Simple heuristics that make us smart* (pp. 3–34). New York: Oxford University Press.

Gopnik, A. (1996). The scientist as child. *Philosophy of Science, 63*(4), 485–514. http://www.jstor.org/stable/188064

Gould, S. J. (1997). *Full house: The spread of excellence from Plato to Darwin.* New York: Harmony Books.

Greenberg, G. (2013). *The book of woe: The DSM and the unmaking of psychiatry.* New York: Blue Rider Press.

Gross, P. R., & Levitt, N. (1994). *Higher superstition: The academic left and its quarrels with science.* Baltimore, MD: The Johns Hopkins University Press.

Guenther, K. (2015). *Localization and its discontents: A genealogy of psychoanalysis and thee neuro-disciplines.* Chicago: University of Chicago Press.

Harré, R. (2004). *Modeling: Gateway to the unknown: A work.* New York: Elsevier.

Henrich, J., Heine, S. J., & Norenzayan, A. (2010). The weirdest people in the world? *The Behavioral and Brain Sciences, 33*(2–3), 61–135. https://doi.org/10.1017/S0140525X0999152X

Herken, R. (1995). *The universal Turing machine: A half-century survey.* Vienna: Springer-Verlag.

Hermans, H. J. M. (2001). The dialogical self: Toward a theory of personal and cultural positioning. *Culture and Psychology*, 7(3), 243–281.

Heyes, C. M. (2018). *Cognitive gadgets: The cultural evolution of thinking*. Cambridge, MA: Harvard University Press.

Hoffman, R. R., Cochran, E. L., & Nead, J. M. (1990). Cognitive metaphors in experimental psychology. In D. E. Leary (Ed.), *Metaphors in the history of psychology* (pp. 173–229). Cambridge University Press.

Hurst, K. S. (1999). *Engineering design principles*. New York: Butterworth-Heinemann. https://doi.org/10.1016/B978-0-340-59829-0.X5023-1

Hutto, D., & Myin, E. (2013). *Radicalizing enactivism*. Cambridge, MA: MIT Press.

Jacyna, L. S. (1981). The physiology of mind, the unity of nature, and the moral order in Victorian thought. *The British Journal for the History of Science*, 14, 109–132.

James, W. (1897). *The will to believe and other essays in popular philosophy (reprinted version)*. New York: Dover.

James, W. (1907/1972). *Pragmatism: A new name for an old way of thinking*. Cambridge, MA: Harvard University Press.

Jasanoff, S. (2004). *States of knowledge: the co-production of science and social order*. Abingdon, UK: Routledge Taylor & Francis Group.

Jaynes, J. (2000). *The origin of consciousness in the breakdown of the bicameral mind*. Boston: Mariner.

Kagan, J. (2017). *Five constraints on predicting behavior*. Cambridge, MA: MIT Press.

Kahneman, D. (2013). *Thinking, fast and slow*. New York: Farrar, Strauss, and Giroux.

Kandel, E. R., & Pittenger, C. (1999). The past, the future and the biology of memory storage. *Philosophical Transactions of the Royal Society of London. Series B, Biological Sciences*, 354(1392), 2027–2052.

Kaufman, S. (1993). *The origins of order: Self-organization and selection in evolution*. New York: Oxford University Press.

Kearns, M. (1987). *Metaphors of mind in fiction and psychology*. Lexington: The University Press of Kentucky.

Khalidi, M. A. (2013). *Natural categories and human kinds: Classification in the natural and social sciences*. Cambridge, MA: Cambridge University Press.

Klein, S. B. (2014a). *The two selves: Their metaphysical commitments and functional independence*. New York: Oxford University Press.

Klein, S. B. (2014b). What can recent replication failures tell us about the theoretical commitments of psychology? *Theory & Psychology*, 24(3), 326–338.

Klein, S. B. (2017). The unplanned obsolescence of psychological science and an argument for its revival. *Psychology of Consciousness: Theory, Research, and Practice*, 3(4), 357–379.

Klein, S. B. (2020). Thoughts on the scientific study of phenomenal consciousness. *Psychology of Consciousness: Theory, Research, and Practice*, 8(1), 74–80. https://doi.org/10.1037/cns0000231

Koch, S. (1999). *Psychology in human context: Essays in dissidence and reconstruction*. Chicago: University of Chicago Press.

Kuhn, T. S. (2012). *The structure of scientific revolutions*. Chicago: University of Chicago Press.

Lakoff, G., & Johnson, M. (2003). *Metaphors we live by*. Chicago: University of Chicago Press.

228 REFERENCES

Laland, K. N., Uller, T., Feldman, M. W., Sterelny, K., Müller, G. B., Moczek, A., Jablonka, E., & Odling-Smee, J. (2015). The extended evolutionary synthesis: Its structure, assumptions and predictions. *Proceedings of the Royal Society B: Biological Sciences, 282*(1813), Article 20151019. https://doi.org/10.1098/rspb.2015.1019

Leary, D. E. (1990). Psyche's muse: The role of metaphor in the history of psychology. In D. E. Leary (Ed.), *Metaphors in the history of psychology* (pp. 1–78). Cambridge University Press.

Lewontin, R. C. (2000). *The triple helix.* Cambridge, MA: Harvard University Press.

Lima, M. (2013). *Visual complexity: Mapping patterns of information.* New York: Princeton Architectural Press.

Lima, M. (2014). *The book of trees: Visualizing branches of knowledge.* New York: Princeton Architectural Press.

Lo Dico, G. (2018). Freud's psychoanalysis, contemporary cognitive/social psychology, and the case against introspection. *Theory & Psychology, 28*(4), 510–527. https://doi.org/10.1177/0959354318774854

Locke, J., & Fraser, A. C. (2004). *An essay concerning human understanding.* New York: Barnes & Noble Books.

Loomis, J. M., & Beall, A. B. (1998). Visually controlled locomotion: Its dependence on optic flow, three-dimensional space perception, and cognition. *Ecological Psychology, 10*(3/4), 271–285.

Luhrmann, T. M. (2000). *Of two minds: The growing disorder in American psychiatry.* New York: Knopf.

MacLeod, M., & Nersessian, N. J. (2013). The creative industry of integrative systems biology. *Mind & Society, 12,* 35–48.

Magnani, L. (2002). An abductive theory of scientific reasoning. In *Proceedings of the International Workshop on Computational Models of Scientific Reasoning and Applications* (CMRSA '02). Pavia, Italy.

Manzotti, R. (2019). Embodied AI beyond embodied cognition and enactivism. *Philosophies, 4*(3), 39–54.

Marcus, G. F. (2009). *Kluge: The haphazard evolution of the human mind.* Boston: Mariner Books.

Marr, D. (1975). Approaches to biological information processing. *Science, 190,* 875–876.

McGinn, C. (1989). Can we solve the mind-body problem? *Mind,* New Series, *98*(391), 349–366.

Mead, G. H. (1934). *Mind, self, and society.* Chicago: University of Chicago Press.

Metzinger, T. (2002). *Neural correlates of consciousness: Empirical and conceptual questions.* Cambridge, MA: MIT Press.

Montuschi, E. (2000). *Metaphor in science.* In: Newton-Smith, William (Ed.), *A Companion to the Philosophy of Science. Blackwell companions to philosophy* (pp. 277–282). Blackwell Publishing, Oxford.

Muthukrishna, M., Henrich, J., & Slingerland, E. (2021). Psychology as a historical science. *Annual Review of Psychology, 72,* 717–749.

Nagel, T. (2012). *Mind and cosmos: Why the materialist neo-Darwinian conception of nature is almost certainly false.* New York: Oxford University Press.

Oaksford, M., & Chater, N. (1994). A rational analysis of the selection task as optimal data selection. *Psychological Review, 101*(4), 608–631.

Panksepp, J. (1998). *Affective neuroscience: The foundations of human and animal emotions.* Oxford: Oxford University Press.

REFERENCES 229

Panksepp, J., Biven, L., & Siegel, D. J. (2012). *The archaeology of mind: Neuroevolutionary origins of human emotions*. New York: W.W. Norton & Company.

Pessoa, L. (2010). Emergent processes in cognitive-emotional interactions. *Dialogues in Clinical Neuroscience, 12*(4), 433–448.

Pessoa, L. (2013). *The cognitive-emotional brain: From interactions to integration*. Cambridge, MA: The MIT Press.

Pessoa, L. (2018). Emotion and the interactive brain: Insights from comparative neuroanatomy and complex systems. *Emotion Review, 10*(3), 204–216.

Pierce, C. S. (1878). How to make our ideas clear. *Popular Science Monthly, 12*, 286–302.

Pribram, K. H. (1990). From metaphors to models: The use of analogy in neuropsychology. In D. E. Leary (Ed.), *Metaphors in the history of psychology* (pp. 79–104). Cambridge University Press.

Proust, J. (2015). Feelings as evaluative indicators—A reply to Iuliia Pliushch. In T. Metzinger & J. M. Windt (Eds.), *Open MIND: 31(R)* (pp. 1–7). Frankfurt am Main: MIND Group.

Putnam, H. (1975). The meaning of "meaning." In K. Gunderson (Ed.), *Language, mind, and knowledge* (pp. 131–193). Minneapolis: University of Minnesota Press.

Richards, I. A. (1965). *The philosophy of rhetoric*. New York: Oxford University Press.

Rieff, P. (1979). *Freud: The mind of the moralist*. Chicago: University of Chicago Press.

Riskin, J. (2020). Review of the scientific method: An evolution of thinking from Darwin to Dewey by H.M. Cowles. *New York Review of Books*, July 2, 2020, *Vol. LXVII*, no. 11, 50–56.

Rorty, R. (1979). *Philosophy and the mirror of nature*. Princeton, NJ: Princeton University Press.

Rose, S. P. R. (2006). *The future of the brain: The promise and perils of tomorrow's neuroscience*. New York: Oxford University Press.

Ruse, M. (2005). Darwinism and mechanism: Metaphor in science. *Studies in History and Philosophy of Science Part C: Studies in History and Philosophy of Biological and Biomedical Sciences, 36*(2), 285–302.

Ryle, G. (1949). *The concept of mind*. Chicago: University of Chicago Press.

Scheffler, I. (1967). *Science and subjectivity*. New York: Hackett.

Serre, T., Wolf, L., Bileschi, S., Riesenhuber, M., & Poggio, T. (2007). Robust object recognition with cortex-like mechanisms. *IEEE Transactions on Pattern Analysis and Machine Intelligence, 29*, 411–426. doi:10.1109/TPAMI.2007.56.

Shapiro, M. (1985). Metaphor in the philosophy of the social sciences. *Cultural Critique, 2*, 191–214.

Simon, H. (1982). *Models of bounded rationality*. Cambridge, MA: MIT Press.

Smith, J. D. (2009). The study of animal metacognition. *Trends in Cognitive Sciences, 13*(9), 389–396.

Smith, R. (1997). *The Norton history of the human sciences*. New York: W.W. Norton and Company.

Smith, R. (2019). Resisting neurosciences and sustaining history. *History of the Human Sciences, 32*(1), 9–22. https://doi.org/10.1177/0952695118810286

Squire, L. R. (2004). Memory systems of the brain: A brief history and current perspective. *Neurobiology of Learning and Memory, 82*(3), 171–177.

Squire, L. R. (2009). The legacy of patient H.M. for neuroscience. *Neuron, 61*(1), 6–9. https://doi.org/10.1016/j.neuron.2008.12.023

230   REFERENCES

Squire, L. R., Stark, C. E. L., & Clark, R. (2004). The medial temporal lobe. *Annual Review of Neuroscience, 27,* 279–306.

Stafford, B. M. (1999). *Visual analogy: Consciousness as the art of connecting.* Cambridge, MA: MIT Press.

Sterelny, K. (2014). *The evolved apprentice: How evolution made humans unique.* Cambridge, MA: The MIT Press.

Thagard, P. (1992). *Conceptual revolutions.* Princeton, NJ: Princeton University Press.

Thagard, P. (2012). *The cognitive science of science: Explanation, discovery, and conceptual change.* Cambridge, MA: MIT Press.

Thibodeau, P. H., & Boroditsky, L. (2011). Metaphors we think with: The role of metaphor in reasoning. *PLoS One, 6*(2), e16782. https://doi.org/10.1371/journal.pone.0016782

Tibell, L. A. E., & Harms, U. (2017). Biological principles and threshold concepts for understanding natural selection. *Science & Education, 26,* 953–973. https://doi.org/10.1007/s11191-017-9935-x

Todd, P. M. (2001). Fast and frugal heuristics for environmentally bounded minds. In G. Gigerenzer & R. Selten (Eds.), *Bounded rationality: The adaptive toolbox* (pp. 51–70). Cambridge, MA: The MIT Press.

Tononi, G. (2012). *Phi: A voyage from the brain to the soul.* New York: Pantheon/Random House.

Tooby, J., & Cosmides, L. (1990). The past explains the present: Emotional adaptations and the structure of ancestral environments. *Ethology and Sociobiology, 11,* 375–424.

Uttal, W. R. (2011). *Mind and brain: A critical appraisal of cognitive neuroscience.* Cambridge, MA: MIT Press.

Vaihinger, H. (1911/2009). *The philosophy of as if: A system of the theoretical, practical and religious fictions of mankind.* London: Routledge.

Van Fraassen B. C. (1980). *The scientific image.* New York: Oxford University Press.

van Gelder, T. (1995). What might cognition be, if not computation? *The Journal of Philosophy, 92*(7), 345–381.

Varela, F. J., Thompson, E., & Rosch, E. (1991). *The embodied mind: Cognitive science and human experience.* Cambridge, MA: MIT Press.

Vidal, F., & Ortega, F. 2017. *Being brains: Making the cerebral subject.* New York: Fordham University Press.

Watson, J. B. (1924/2007). *Behaviorism.* New Brunswick, NJ: Transaction.

Wilson, N. (2002). Six views of embodied cognition. *Psychonomic Bulletin & Review, 9*(4), 625–636.

Withagen, R., & Chemero, A. (2009). Naturalizing perception: Developing the Gibsonian approach to perception along evolutionary lines. *Theory & Psychology, 19*(3), 363–389.

Chapter 3: Contemporary Empirical Psychology

Aarts, A. A., & Lin, S. C. (2015). Estimating the reproducibility of psychological science. *Science, 349*(6251), 943–950.

Adams, F., & Aizawa, K. (2001). The bounds of cognition. *Philosophical Psychology, 14,* 43–64.

Allport, G. W. (1947). Scientific models and human morals. *Psychological Review, 54*(4), 182–192.

REFERENCES   231

Arnett, J. (2008). The neglected 95%: Why American psychology needs to become less American. *American Psychologist, 63*(7), 602–614.

Asma, S. (2017). *The evolution of imagination.* Chicago: University of Chicago Press.

Barrett, L. (2012). Why behaviorism isn't Satanism. In J. Vonk & T. K. Shackelford (Eds.), *The Oxford handbook of comparative evolutionary psychology* (pp. 17–38). Oxford: Oxford University Press.

Barrett, L., & Rendall, D. (2010). Out of our minds: The neuroethology of primate strategic behavior. In M. L. Platt & A. A. Ghazanfar (Eds.), *Primate neuroethology* (pp. 570–586). New York: Oxford University Press.

Bechtel, W. (2008). *Mental mechanisms: Philosophical perspectives on cognitive neuroscience.* London: Routledge.

Bechtel, W., & Abrahamsen, A. (2005). Explanation: A mechanist alternative. *Studies in History and Philosophy of Biological and Biomedical Sciences, 36*(2), 421–441. https://doi.org/10.1016/j.shpsc.2005.03.010

Bechtel, W., & Abrahamsen, A. (2010). Dynamic mechanistic explanation: Computational modeling of circadian rhythms as an exemplar for cognitive science. *Studies in History and Philosophy of Science Part A, 1,* 321–333.

Bechtel, W., & Richardson, R. C. (1992). Emergent phenomena and complex systems. In A. Beckermann, H. Flohr, & J. Kim (Eds.), *Emergence or reduction? Essays on the prospects of nonreductive physicalism* (pp. 257–288). Berlin: Walter de Gruyter Verlag.

Berlin, B., & Kay, P. (1991). *Basic color terms: Their universality and evolution.* Berkeley: University of California Press.

Berntson, G. G., & Cacioppo, J. T. (2008). The neuroevolution of motivation. In J. Shah & W. Gardner (Eds.), *Handbook of motivation science* (pp. 188–200). New York: Guilford.

Brazier, M. A. B. (1988). *A history of neurophysiology in the 19th century.* New York: Raven Press.

Breedlove, S. M., & Watson, N. V. (2013). *Biological psychology: An introduction to behavioral, cognitive, and clinical neuroscience* (7th ed.). Somerville, MA: Sinauer Associates.

Brette, R. (2019). Neural coding: The bureaucratic model of the brain. *Behavioral Brain Sciences, 42,* e243. https://doi.org/10.31234/osf.io/tgcn9

Brown, E. N., & Kass, R. E. (2009). What is statistics? *The American Statistician, 63*(2), 105–110. doi:10.1198/tast.2009.0019

Buxton, R. B. (2013). The physics of functional magnetic resonance imaging (fMRI). *Reports on Progress in Physics, 76*(9), 096601.

Cacioppo, J. T., & Berntson, G. G. (1992). Social psychological contributions to the decade of the brain: Doctrine of multilevel analysis. *American Psychologist, 47*(8), 1019–1028.

Cacioppo, J. T., Berntson, G. G., & Decety, J. (2010). Social neuroscience and its relationship to social psychology. *Social Cognition, 28*(6), 675–685. https://doi.org/10.1521/soco.2010.28.6.675

Calin-Jageman, R. J., & Cumming, G. (2019) The new statistics for better science: Ask how much, how uncertain, and what else is known, *The American Statistician, 73*(Suppl.1), 271–280. doi: 10.1080/00031305.2018.1518266

Calin-Jageman, R. J., & Cumming, G. (2019). The new statistics for better science: Ask how much, how uncertain, and what else is known. *The American Statistician, 73*(Suppl. 1), 271–280.

Campbell, D. T. (1988). *Methodology and epistemology for social Science: Selected papers.* E. S. Overman, Ed. Chicago: University of Chicago Press.

232 REFERENCES

Carabotti, M., Scirocco, A., Maselli, M. A., & Severi, C. (2015). The gut-brain axis: Interactions between enteric microbiota, central and enteric nervous systems. *Annals of Gastroenterology, 28*(2), 203–209.

Carney, D. R., Cuddy, A. J. C., & Yap, A. J. (2010). Power posing: Brief nonverbal displays affect neuroendocrine levels and risk tolerance. *Psychological Science, 21*, 1363–1368.

Chalmers, D. J. (1996). *The conscious mind: In search of a fundamental theory.* New York: Oxford University Press.

Choudhury, S., Nagel, S. K., & Slaby, J. (2009). Critical neuroscience: Linking neuroscience and society through critical practice. *Biosocieties, 4*, 61–77. doi:10.1017/s1745855209006437

Coltheart, M. (2006). What has functional neuroimaging told us about the mind (so far)? *Cortex, 42*(3), 323–331.

Craver, C., & Tabery, J. (2019). Mechanisms in science. In E. N. Zalta (Ed.), *The Stanford encyclopedia of philosophy* (Summer 2019). https://plato.stanford.edu/archives/sum2019/entries/science-mechanisms/

Craver, C. F. (2005). Beyond reduction: Mechanisms, multifield integration and the unity of neuroscience. *Studies in History and Philosophy of Biological and Biomedical Sciences, 36*(2), 373–395. https://doi.org/10.1016/j.shpsc.2005.03.008

Damasio, A. (2018). *The strange order of things.* New York: Vintage.

Donald, M. W. (2004). The definition of human nature. In D. Reese & S. Rose (Eds.), *The new brain sciences: Perils and prospects* (pp. 34–60). Cambridge: Cambridge University Press.

Donovan, J. M., & Rundle, B. A. (1997). Psychic unity constraints upon successful intercultural communication. *Language & Communication, 17*(3), 219–235.

Earp, B. D., & Trafimow, D. (2015). Replication, falsification, and the crisis of confidence in social psychology. *Frontiers in Psychology, 6*, 621. https://doi.org/10.3389/fpsyg.2015.00621

Eich, E. (2014). Business not as usual. *Psychological Science, 25*, 3–6. doi:10.1177/0956797613512465

Finger, S. (2000). *Minds behind the brain: A history of the pioneers and their discoveries.* New York: Oxford University Press.

Fitzgerald, D., Matusall, S., Skewes, J., & Roepstorff, A. (2014). What's so critical about critical neuroscience? Rethinking experiment, enacting critique. *Frontiers in Human Neuroscience, 8*, 365. https://doi.org/10.3389/fnhum.2014.00365

Fodor, J. (1974). Special sciences (Or: The disunity of science as a working hypothesis). *Synthese, 28*(2), 97–115. http://www.jstor.org/stable/20114958

Fodor, J. (1975). *The language of thought.* New York: Thomas Y. Crowell.

Fodor, J. (1998). *Concepts: Where cognitive science went wrong.* New York: Clarendon Press.

Fodor, J., & McLaughlin, B. P. (1990). Connectionism and the problem of systematicity: Why Smolensky's solution doesn't work. *Cognition, 35*(2), 183–204. doi:10.1016/0010-0277(90)90014-B

Frege, G. (1984). Thoughts. In B. McGuinness (Ed.), *Gottlob Frege: Collected papers on mathematics, logic, and philosophy* (pp. 351–372). Oxford: Basil Blackwell.

Gabriel, R. (2012). Modularity in affective neuroscience and cognitive psychology. *Journal of Consciousness Studies, 19*(3–4), 19–25.

Gabriel, R. (2021a). The motivational role of affect in an ecological model. *Theory and Psychology, 31*(4), 552–572.

REFERENCES 233

Gardner, H. (1985). *The mind's new science: A history of the cognitive revolution*. New York: Basic Books.

Gergen, K. J. (1985). The social constructionist movement in modern psychology. *American Psychologist, 40*(3), 266–275. https://doi.org/10.1037/0003-066X.40.3.266

Giere, R. (1999). *Science without laws*. Chicago: University of Chicago Press.

Giere, R. (2006). *Scientific perspectivism*. Chicago: University of Chicago Press.

Gigerenzer, G., & Marewski, J. N. (2015). Surrogate science: The idol of a universal method for scientific inference. *Journal of Management, 41*(2), 421–440.

Gordin, M. D. (2021). *On the fringe: Where science meets pseudoscience*. New York: Oxford University Press.

Green, C. D. (1996). Where did the word "cognitive" come from anyway? *Canadian Psychology, 37*, 31–39.

Gross, P. R., & Levitt, N. (1994). *The academic left and its quarrels with science*. Baltimore, MD: The Johns Hopkins University Press.

Guenther, K. (2015). *Localization and its discontents: A genealogy of psychoanalysis and the neuro disciplines*. Chicago: University of Chicago Press.

Hacking, I. (1999). *The social construction of what?* Cambridge, MA: Harvard University Press.

Haig, B. D. (2020). What can psychology's statistics reformers learn from the error-statistical perspective? *Methods in Psychology, 2*, 2590–2601.

Henrich, J., Heine, S. J., & Norenzayan, A. (2010). The weirdest people in the world? *Behavioral and Brain Sciences, 33*(2–3), 61–83.

Isaac, J. (2012). *Working knowledge: Making the human sciences from Parsons to Kuhn*. Cambridge, MA: Harvard University Press.

Jacobson, M. (1995). *Foundations of neuroscience*. New York: Plenum Press.

James, W. (1907). *On pragmatism*. London: Longmans, Green and Co.

James, W. (1912). *Essays in radical empiricism*. London: Longmans, Green and Co.

John, L. K., Loewenstein, G., & Prelec, D. (2012). Measuring the prevalence of questionable research practices with incentives for truth telling. *Psychological Science, 23*(5), 524–532. https://doi.org/10.1177/0956797611430953

Kagan, J. (2012). *Psychology's ghosts: The crisis in the profession and the way back*. New Haven, CT: Yale University Press.

Kagan, J. (2017). *Five constraints on predicting behavior*. Cambridge, MA: MIT Press.

Kandel, E. R., & Pittenger, C. (1999). The past, the future and the biology of memory storage. *Philosophical transactions of the Royal Society of London. Series B, Biological sciences, 354*(1392), 2027–2052. https://doi.org/10.1098/rstb.1999.0542

Khalidi, M.A. (2013). *Natural categories and human kinds: Classification in the natural and social sciences*. Cambridge: Cambridge University Press.

Kim, J. H., & Ress, D. (2016). Arterial impulse model for the BOLD response to brief neural activation. *NeuroImage, 124*, 394–408.

Kirschner, S. R. (2006). Psychology and pluralism: Toward the psychological studies. *Journal of Theoretical and Philosophical Psychology, 26*(1–2), 1–17.

Kitcher, P. (1993). *The advancement of science: Science without legend, objectivity without illusions*. New York: Oxford University Press.

Klein, S. B. (2014). What can recent replication failures tell us about the theoretical commitments of psychology? *Theory Psychology, 24*, 326. doi:10.1177/0959354314529616

234 REFERENCES

Klein, S. B. (2015). A defense of experiential realism: The need to take phenomenological reality on its own terms in the study of the mind. *Psychology of Consciousness: Theory, Research, and Practice, 2*(1), 41–56.

Klein, S. B. (2021). Quantification, conceptual reduction and theoretical underdetermination in psychological science.

Kline, R. B. (2004). *Beyond significance testing*, Washington, DC: American Psychological Association.

Koch, S. (1999). *Psychology in human context: Essays in dissidence and reconstruction.* Chicago: University of Chicago Press.

Krüger, L., Gigerenzer, G., & Morgan, M. S. (1987). *The probabilistic revolution. Vol. 2.* Cambridge, MA: MIT Press.

Kuhn, T. (1962/2012). *The structure of scientific revolutions.* Chicago: University of Chicago Press.

Kunda, Z. (1990). The case for motivated reasoning. *Psychological Bulletin, 108,* 480–498.

Latour, B., & Woolgar, S. (1986). *Laboratory life: The construction of scientific facts.* Princeton, NJ: Princeton University Press.

Llínas, R. (2001). *I of the vortex.* Cambridge, MA: MIT Press.

Longino, H. (2002). *The fate of knowledge.* Princeton, NJ: Princeton University Press.

Machamer, P., Darden, L., & Craver, C. F. (2000). Thinking about mechanisms. *Philosophy of Science, 67*(1), 1–25.

Machery, E. (2021). A mistaken confidence in data. *European Journal for Philosophy of Science, 11*(2), 1–17.

MacLeod, C. M. (1991). Half a century of research on the Stroop effect: An integrative review. *Psychological Bulletin, 109,* 163–203.

May, R. M. (1997). The scientific wealth of nations. *Science, 275,* 793–796.

Mayo, D. (2018). Beyond probabilism and performance. In Debra Mayo (Ed.), *Statistical inference as severe testing: How to get beyond the statistics wars* (pp. 3–29). Cambridge: Cambridge University Press. doi:10.1017/9781107286184.002

Mayo, D. (2018). The myth of "the myth of objectivity." In Debra Mayo (Ed.), *Statistical inference as severe testing: How to get beyond the statistics wars* (pp. 221–238). Cambridge: Cambridge University Press. doi:10.1017/9781107286184.009

McGinn, C. (1989). Can we solve the mind-body problem? *Mind*, New Series, *98*(391), 349–366.

Modern, J. L. (2021). *Neuromatic, or, a particular history of religion and the brain.* Chicago: University of Chicago Press.

Muthukrishna, M., Henrich, J., & Slingerland, E. (2021). Psychology as a historical science. *Annual Review Psychology, 72,* 717–749.

Nagel, E. (1961). *The structure of science: Problems in the logic of explanation.* New York: Harcourt, Brace & World.

Neisser, U. (1976). *Cognition and reality: Principles and implications of cognitive psychology.* New York: W. H. Freeman.

Osbeck, L. M. (2009). Transformations in cognitive science: Implications and issues posed. *Journal of Theoretical and Philosophical Psychology, 29*(1), 16–33.

Osbeck, L. M. (2019). *Values in psychological sciences.* Cambridge: Cambridge University Press.

Osbeck, L. M., & Nersessian, N. J. (2017). Epistemic identities in interdisciplinary science. *Perspectives on Science, 25*(2), 226–261.

REFERENCES 235

Open Science Collaboration. (2015). Estimating the reproducibility of psychological science. *Science, 349*, aac4716. doi:10.1126/science.aac4716

Panksepp, J. (1998). *Affective neuroscience.* Oxford: Oxford University Press.

Pashleer, H., & Wagenmakers, E. (2012). Editors' introduction to the special section on replicability in psychological science: A crisis of confidence? *Perspectives on Psychological Science, 7*(6), 528–530.

Pessoa, L. (2013). *The cognitive-emotional brain.* Cambridge, MA: MIT Press.

Polanyí, M. (1958). *Personal knowledge: Towards a post-critical philosophy.* Chicago: University of Chicago Press.

Popper, K. (1963). *Conjectures and refutations: The growth of scientific knowledge.* London: Routledge.

Putnam, H. (1975). The meaning of "meaning." In K. Gunderson (Ed.), *Language, mind, and knowledge* (pp. 131–193). Minneapolis: University of Minnesota Press.

Raichle, M. E. (2000). A brief history of human functional brain mapping. In A. W. Toga & J. C. Mazziotta (Eds.), *Brain mapping: The systems* (pp. 33–77). San Diego, CA: Academic Press.

Raichle, M. E. (2009). A brief history of human brain mapping. *Trends in Neurosciences, 32*(2), 118–126. https://doi.org/10.1016/j.tins.2008.11.001

Raichle, M. E. (2015). The brain's default mode network. *Annual Review of Neuroscience, 38*, 433–447. https://doi.org/10.1146/annurev-neuro-071013-014030

Raichle, M. E., & Mintun, M. A. (2006). Brain work and brain imaging. *Annual Review of Neuroscience, 29*, 449–476. https://doi.org/10.1146/annurev.neuro.29.051605.112819

Rescorla, M. (2017). Maps in the head? In K. Andrews & J. Beck (Eds.), *The Routledge handbook of philosophy of animal mind* (pp. 34–45). New York: Routledge.

Rescorla, M. (2019). The language of thought hypothesis. In E. N. Zalta (Ed.). *The Stanford encyclopedia of philosophy* (Summer 2019 ed.). https://plato.stanford.edu/archives/sum2019/entries/language-thought

Resnik, D. B. (2014). Data fabrication and falsification and empiricist philosophy of science. *Science and Engineering Ethics, 20*(2), 423–431. https://doi.org/10.1007/s11948-013-9466-z

Rorty, R. (1979). *Philosophy and the mirror of nature.* Princeton, NJ: Princeton University Press.

Rorty, R. (1982). *Consequences of pragmatism.* Minneapolis: University of Minnesota Press.

Rosch, E. (1977). Human categorization. In N. Warren (Ed.), *Studies in cross-cultural psychology* (Vol. 1, pp. 1–49). New York: Academic Press.

Rosenthal, R. (1979). The file drawer problem and tolerance for null results. *Psychological Bulletin, 86*(3), 638–641. https://doi.org/10.1037/0033-2909.86.3.638

Rumelhart, D. E., McClelland, J. L., & the PDP Research Group (Eds.). (1986). *Parallel distributed processing, volume 1: Explorations in the microstructure of cognition: Foundations.* Cambridge, MA: MIT Press.

Salmon, W. C. (1989). Four decades of scientific explanation. In P. Kitcher & W. C. Salmon (Eds.), *Scientific explanation* (pp. 3–219). *Minnesota Studies in the Philosophy of Science, XVIII.* Minneapolis: University of Minnesota Press.

Sapir, E. (1949). *Selected writings of Edward Sapir in language, culture and personality.* University of California Press, Berkeley.

Schneider, S. (2011). *The language of thought: A new philosophical direction.* Cambridge, MA: MIT Press.

236 REFERENCES

Shaffner, K. (1993). *Discovery and explanation in biology and medicine.* Chicago: University of Chicago Press.

Shapin, S. (1982). History of science and its sociological reconstructions. *History of Science, 20,* 157–211.

Shweder, R. A. (2001). A polytheistic conception of the sciences and the virtues of deep variety. *Annals of the New York Academy of Sciences, 935*(1), 217–232.

Simmons, J. P., Nelson, L. D., & Simonsohn, U. (2011). False-positive psychology: Undisclosed flexibility in data collection and analysis allows presenting anything as significant. *Psychological Science, 22,* 1359–1366.

Simmons, J. P., & Simonsohn, U. (2017). Power posing: P-curving the evidence. *Psychological Science, 28*(5), 687–693. http://dx.doi.org/10.1177/0956797616658563.

Simon, H. A. (1973). The structure of ill structured problems. *Artificial Intelligence, 4,* 181–201.

Slaby, J. (2010). Steps towards a critical neuroscience. *Phenomenology Cognitive Science, 9,* 397–416. doi:10.1007/s11097-010-9170-2.

Slaby, J., & Choudhury, S. (2012). Proposal for a critical neuroscience. In S. Choudhury & J. Slaby (Eds.), *Critical neuroscience: A handbook of the social and cultural contexts of neuroscience* (pp. 27–35). London: Wiley-Blackwell.

Solms, M. (2021). *The hidden spring: A journey to the source of consciousness.* New York: W.W. Norton and Co.

Szucs, D., & Ioannidis, J. P. (2017). Empirical assessment of published effect sizes and power in the recent cognitive neuroscience and psychology literature. *PLoS Biology, 15*(3), e2000797. https://doi.org/10.1371/journal.pbio.2000797

Teo, T. (2015). Theoretical psychology: A critical-philosophical outline of core issues. In I. Parker (Ed.), *Handbook of critical psychology* (pp. 117–126). New York: Routledge.

Toulmin, S., & Leary, D. E. (1985). The cult of empiricism in psychology, and beyond. In Sigmund Koch and David E. Leary (Eds.), *A Century of Psychology as Science* (pp. 594–617). New York: McGraw-Hill.

Uttal, W. R. (2001). *The new phrenology: The limits of localizing cognitive processes in the brain.* Cambridge, MA: MIT Press.

Van Fraassen Bas, C. (1980). *The scientific image.* Oxford: Oxford University Press.

van Riel, R., & Van Gulick, R. (2019). Scientific reduction. In E. N. Zalta (Ed.), *The Stanford encyclopedia of philosophy* (Spring 2019 ed.). https://plato.stanford.edu/archives/spr2019/entries/scientific-reduction/.

William, W., & Craver, C. F. (2005). Beyond reduction: Mechanisms, multifield integration and the unity of neuroscience. *Studies in History and Philosophy of Biological and Biomedical Sciences, 36*(2), 373–395. https://doi.org/10.1016/j.shpsc.2005.03.008

Wilson, M. (2002). Six views of embodied cognition. *Psychonomic Bulletin and Review, 9*(4), 625–636.

Wimsatt, W. C. (1976). Reductionism, levels of organization, and the mind-body problem. In G. G. Globus (Ed.), *Consciousness and the brain* (pp. 205–267). New York: Plenum Press.

Wimsatt, W. C. (2006). Reductionism and its heuristics: Making methodological reductionism honest. *Synthese, 151*(3), 445–475.

Wimsatt, W. C. (2023). Evolution and the metabolism of error: Biological practice as a foundation for a scientific metaphysics. In William C. Bausman, Janella Baxter, & Oliver M. Lean (Eds.), *From Biological Practice to Scientific Metaphysics. Minnesota Studies in the Philosophy of Science.* Minneapolis: University of Minnesota Press.

REFERENCES 237

Zajonc, R. B. (1968). Attitudinal effects of mere exposure. *Journal of Personality and Social Psychology Monograph Supplement, 9*(2/2), 1–27.

Interlude

Adler, A. (1930). *Individual psychology.* In C. Murchison (Ed.), *International university series in psychology. Psychologies of 1930* (pp. 395–405). Worchester, MA: Clark University Press. https://doi.org/10.1037/11017-021

Asma, S. T. (2018). *Why we need religion.* New York: Oxford University Press.

Asma, S. T., & Gabriel, R. (2019). *The emotional mind: The affective roots of culture and cognition.* Cambridge, MA: Harvard University Press.

Atran, S. (2004). *In gods we trust: The evolutionary landscape of religion.* New York: Oxford University Press.

Bain, A. (1865). *Of feeling in general.* New York: Longmans, Green.

Banerjee, K., & Bloom, P. (2014). Why did this happen to me? Religious believers' and non-believers' teleological reasoning about life events. *Cognition, 133*(1), 277–303. https://doi.org/10.1016/j.cognition.2014.06.017

Barthes, R. (1972). *Mythologies.* New York: Hill and Wang.

Bataille, G. (1973). *Theory of religion* (R. Hurley, Trans.). New York: Zone Books.

Bergson, H., Audra, R. A., Brereton, C., & Carter, W. H. (1954). *The two sources of morality and religion.* Garden City, NY: Doubleday.

Bering, J. M. (2006). The cognitive psychology of supernatural belief. Reprinted from *American Scientist, 94*(2), 142–150. doi:10.1511/2006.58.142

Bering, J. (2006). The cognitive psychology of belief in the supernatrual. In Patrick McNamara, (Ed.), *Where God and science meet: How brain and evolutionary studies alter our understanding of religion* (pp. 123–134). Westport, CT: Praeger/Greenwood.

Berman, M. (1981). *The reenchantment of the world.* New York: Cornell University Press.

Bernal, M. (1987). *Black Athena.* New Jersey: Rutgers University Press.

Berridge, K. C., & Robinson, T. E. (2016). Liking, wanting, and the incentive-sensitization theory of addiction. *The American Psychologist, 71*(8), 670–679. https://doi.org/10.1037/amp0000059

Boyer, P. (2002.) *Religion explained: The evolutionary origins of religious thought.* New York: Basic Books.

Boyer, P., & Lienaud, P. (2006). Why ritualized behavior? Precaution systems and action parsing in developmental, pathological, and cultural rituals. *Behavioral Brain Sciences, 29*, 595–650.

Bürgi, P., & Roos, J. (2003). Images of strategy. *European Management Journal, 21*(1), 69–78.

Burghardt, G. (2018). The origins, evolution, and interconnections of play and ritual: Setting the stage. In C. Renfrew, I. Morley, & M. Boyd (Eds.), *From play to faith: Ritual and play in animals, and in early human societies* (pp. 23–39). Cambridge: Cambridge University Press.

Burghardt, G. M. (1973). Instinct and innate behavior: Toward an ethological psychology. In J. A. Nevin & G. S. Reynolds (Eds.), *The study of behavior: Learning, motivation, emotion, and instinct* (pp. 322–400). Glenview, IL: Scott Foresman.

Burghardt, G. M. (1999). Conceptions of play and the evolution of animal minds. *Evolution and Cognition, 5*(2), 115–123.

238 REFERENCES

Burkert, W. (2006). Ritual between ethology and post-modern aspects: Philological-historical notes. In E. Stavrianopoulou (Ed.), *Ritual and communication in the Graeco-Roman world* (pp. 23–35). Liège: Presses universitaires de Liège. doi:10.4000/books.pulg.1132

Chemero, A. (2011). *Radical embodied cognitive science*. Cambridge, MA: MIT Press.

Conti, N. (2012). *Her master's voice*. BBC.

Coviello, P. (2020). *Make yourselves gods: Mormons and the unfinished business of American secularism*. Chicago: University of Chicago Press.

Danziger, K. (1990). *Constructing the subject: Historical origins of psychological research*. Cambridge: Cambridge University Press. https://doi.org/10.1017/CBO9780511524059

Danziger, K. (2003). *Prospects of a historical psychology*. Address to Canadian Psychological Association.

Deacon, T. W. (1998). *The symbolic species: The co-evolution of language and the brain (No. 202)*. New York: WW Norton & Company.

de Melo, C. M., Carnevale, P. J., Read, S. J., & Gratch, J. (2013). Reading people's minds from emotion expressions in interdependent decision making. *Journal of Personality and Social Psychology, 106*(1), 73–88. doi:10.1037/a0034251

Dewey, J. (1910). *What is thought?* Washington, D.C.: Heath.

Durkheim, É. (1915). *The elementary forms of the religious life, a study in religious sociology*. London: G. Allen & Unwin; Macmillan.

Eliade, M. (1957/67). *Myths, dreams, and mysteries*. New York: Harper Torchbooks.

Eliade, M. (1963). *Aspects du Mythe*. Paris: Gallimard.

Foucault, M. (1966). *Les mots et les choses: Une archéologie des sciences humaines*. Paris: Gallimard.

Fraley, J. E. (2003). A behaviorological analysis of adjunctive behavior. *Behaviorology Today, 6*(2), 15–29.

Fuentes, A. (2019). *Why we believe: Evolution and the human way of being*. New Haven, CT: Yale University Press. https://doi.org/10.2307/j.ctvnwbx97

Gabriel, R. (2013). *Why I buy: Self, taste, and consumer society in America*. London: Intellect Press.

Gazzaniga, M. (2009). *Human: The science behind what makes your brain unique*. New York: Ecco.

Gibson, J. J. (1979). *The ecological approach to visual perception*. Boston: Houghton Mifflin.

Girard, R. (1977). *Violence and the sacred*. Baltimore: Johns Hopkins University Press.

Gray, J. (2007). *Straw dogs*. New York: Farrar, Strauss, and Giroux.

Hanegraaf, W. J. (1999). New Age spiritualities as secular religion: A historian's perspective. *Social Compass, 46*(2), 145–160. doi:10.1177/003776899046002004

Harvey, D. (1999). *The enigma of capital and the crises of capitalism*. New York: Oxford University Press.

Heesterman, J. C. (1993). *The broken world of sacrifice: An essay in ancient Indian ritual*. Chicago: University of Chicago Press.

Heilbroner, R. L. (1999). *The worldly philosophers: The lives, times, and ideas of the great economic thinkers*. New York: Simon & Schuster.

Hobsbawm, E. J. (1962). *The age of revolution, 1789–1848*. Cleveland, OH: World Publishing Company.

Hobsbawm, E. (1968/99). *Industry and empire*. New York: The New Press.

REFERENCES   239

Hopkins, E. J., et al. (2016). The seductive allure is a reductive allure: People prefer scientific explanations that contain logically irrelevant reductive information. *Cognition, 155*, 67–76.

Horkheimer, M., & Adorno, T. (1944/72). On the concept of enlightenment. In W. Shirmacher (Ed.), *German 20th century philosophy: The Frankfurt School* (pp. 60–85). New York: Continuum.

Hume, D. (1741/1963). *Essays: moral, political, and literary.* London: Oxford University Press.

Hutto, D., & Myin, E. (2013). *Radicalizing enactivism.* Cambridge, MA: MIT Press.

James, W. (1897). *The will to believe.* New York: Longmans, Green, and co.

Jaynes, J. (1976). *The origin of consciousness in the breakdown of the bicameral mind.* New York: Mariner Books.

Josephson-Storm, J. A. (2017). *The myth of disenchantment: Magic, modernity, and the birth of the human sciences.* Chicago: University of Chicago Press.

Kitcher, P. (1993). *The advancement of science: Science without legend, objectivity without illusions.* New York: Oxford University Press.

Klein, S. B. (2014). *The two selves: Their metaphysical commitments and functional independence.* Oxford: Oxford University Press.

Klein, S. B. (2016). The unplanned obsolescence of psychological science and an argument for its revival. *Psychology of Consciousness: Theory, Research, and Practice, 3*(4), 357–379. https://doi.org/10.1037/cns0000079

Knorr-Cetina K. (1999). *Epistemic cultures: How the sciences make knowledge.* Cambridge, MA: Harvard University Press.

Lear, J. (1999). *Open-minded.* Cambridge, MA: Harvard University Press.

Lévi-Strauss, C. (1961/2021). *Wild thought* (J. Mehlman & J. Leavitt, Trans.). Chicago: University of Chicago Press.

Lewis-Williams, D. J., & Challis, S. (2011). *Deciphering ancient minds: The mystery of San Bushman rock art.* London: Thames & Hudson.

Lombrozo, T. (2016). Explanatory preferences shape learning and inference. *Trends in Cognitive Sciences, 20*(10), 748–759. https://doi.org/10.1016/j.tics.2016.08.001

Lombrozo, T., & Vasilyeva. N. (2017). Causal explanation. In M. Waldmann (Ed.), *Oxford handbook of causal reasoning* (pp. 415–432). Oxford: Oxford University Press.

Malinowski, B. (1948). *Magic, science and religion and other essays.* Glencoe, IL: The Free Press (Reissued Long Grove, IL: Waveland Press, 1992).

Marmor, J. (1956). Some observations on superstition in contemporary life. *American Journal of Orthopsychiatry, 26,* 119–130. https://doi.org/10.1111/j.1939-0025.1956. tb06161.x

Mazzarrella, W. (2017). *The mana of mass society.* Chicago: The University of Chicago Press.

Modern, J. (2021). *Neuromatic: Or, a particular history of religion and the brain.* Chicago: University of Chicago Press.

Moyer, R. M. (2010). *Maintaining self-integrity through superstitious behavior.* PhD diss., Florida Atlantic University.

Nietzsche, F. (1882/2010). *The gay science: With a prelude in rhymes and an appendix of songs* (W. Kaufmann, Trans.). New York: Vintage.

Nietzsche, F. W., & Kaufmann, W. (1995). *Thus spoke Zarathustra: A book for all and none.* New York: Modern Library.

Nozick, R. (1981). *Philosophical explanations.* Cambridge, MA: Harvard University Press.

Panksepp, J. (1998). *Affective neuroscience*. New York: Oxford University Press.

Phillips, D. Z. (1970). *Faith and philosophical enquiry*. London: Routledge & Kegan Paul.

Phillips, D. Z. (1986). *Belief, change and forms of life*. New York: Macmillan.

Phillips, D. Z. (1993). *Wittgenstein and religion*. London: Macmillan.

Pippin, R. (1991). *Modernism as a philosophical problem: On the dissatisfactions of European high culture*. Oxford: Blackwell.

Pippin, R. (2010). *Nietzsche, psychology, and first philosophy*. Chicago: The University of Chicago Press.

Rose, N., & Abi-Rached, J. M. (2013). *Neuro: The new brain sciences and the management of the mind*. Princeton, NJ: Princeton University Press.

Rottman, J., Young, L., & Kelemen, D. (2017). The impact of testimony on children's moralization of novel actions. *Emotion (Washington, D.C.)*, *17*(5), 811–827. https://doi.org/10.1037/emo0000276

Shagan, E. (2019). *The birth of modern belief*. Princeton, NJ: Princeton University Press.

Shapin, S. (1994). *A social history of truth: Civility and science in seventeenth-century England*. Chicago: University of Chicago Press.

Siegel, J. (2005). *The idea of the self: Thought and experience in Western Europe since the seventeenth century*. Cambridge: Cambridge University Press.

Singer, P. (1975). *Animal liberation: A new ethics for our treatment of animals*. New York: New York Review/Random House.

Siwiec, J. A. (2004). *Philosophy of religion as hermeneutics of contemplation according to Dewi Z. Phillips*. PhD Diss., McGill University.

Skorupski, J. (1976). *Symbol and theory*. Cambridge: Cambridge University Press.

Slone, J. D., & McCorkle Jr, W. W. (2019). *The cognitive science of religion: A methodological introduction to key empirical studies*. London: Bloomsbury Academic.

Smith, R. (1994). *Between mind and nature*. London: Reaktion.

Smith, R. (1997). *The Norton history of the human sciences*. New York: W.W. Norton.

Storm, J. J. (2017). *The myth of disenchantment*. Chicago: University of Chicago Press.

Strong, R. L., & Weber, M. (2004). *The vocation lectures*. Indianapolis: Hackett.

Taylor, C. (1971). Interpretation and the sciences of man. *The Review of Metaphysics*, *25*(1), 3–51. http://www.jstor.org/stable/20125928

Taylor, C. (1989). *Sources of the self*. Cambridge, MA: Harvard University Press.

Taylor, C. (2007). *A secular age*. Cambridge, MA: The Belknap Press of Harvard University Press.

Taylor, S. E. (1991). *Positive illusions: Creative self-deception and healthy mind*. New York: Basic Books.

Thomas, K. (1971). *Religion and the decline of magic*. New York: Scribner.

Uttal, W. R. (2001). *Life and mind: Philosophical issues in biology and psychology. The new phrenology: The limits of localizing cognitive processes in the brain*. Cambridge, MA: The MIT Press.

Vyse, S. (1997/2014). *Believing in magic*. New York: Oxford University Press.

Weber, M. (2004). *The Vocation Lectures* (D. Owen & T. B. Strong, Eds.; R. Livingston, Ed.). Indianapolis, IN: Hackett.

Weisberg, D. S., et al. (2015) Deconstructing the seductive allure of neuroscience explanations. *Judgment and Decision Making*, *10*, 429–441.

Willard, A. K., & Norenzayan, A. (2013). Cognitive biases explain religious belief, paranormal belief, and belief in life's purpose. *Cognition*, *129*(2), 379–391. https://doi.org/10.1016/j.cognition.2013.07.016

REFERENCES 241

Williams, B. (1993). *Shame and necessity*. New York: University of California Press.

Wittgenstein, L., & Anscombe, G. E. M. (1997). *Philosophical investigations*. Oxford: Blackwell.

Young, K. (2017). *Bunk: The rise of hoaxes, humbug, plagiarists, phonies, post-facts, and fake news*. New York: Graywolf Press.

Zimmerman, A. (2018). *A pragmatic picture of belief*. New York: Oxford University Press.

Chapter 4: Popular Psychology

Atran, S. (2002). *In gods we trust: The evolutionary landscape of religion*. New York: Oxford University Press.

Auerbach, E. (1946/2003). *Mimesis: The representation of reality in Western literature* (50th anniversary ed., W. Trask, Trans.). Princeton, NJ: Princeton University Press.

Burghardt, G. M. (2017). The origins, evolution, and interconnections of play and ritual: Setting the stage. In C. Renfrew, I. Morley, & M. Boyd (Eds.), *From play to faith: Ritual and play in animals, and in early human societies* (pp. 22–39). Cambridge: Cambridge University Press.

Carrette, J., & King, R. (2005). *Selling spirituality: The silent takeover of religion*. New York: Routledge.

Crawford, M. (2015). *The world beyond your head: On becoming an individual in an age of distraction*. New York: Farrar, Straus and Giroux.

Danto, A. C. (1988). *Mysticism and morality: Oriental thought and moral philosophy*. New York: Columbia University Press.

Greenberg, G. (1994). *The self on the shelf: Recovery books and the good life*. Albany: SUNY Press.

Hanegraaff, W. (1998) Reflections on New Age and the secularization of nature. In J. Pearson, R. H. Roberts, & G. Samuel (Eds.), *Nature religion today: Paganism in the modern world* (pp. 22–32). Edinburgh: Edinburgh University Press.

Hayden, B. (2018). *The power of ritual in prehistory: Secret societies and origins of social complexity*. Cambridge: Cambridge University Press.

Heelas, P. (2008). *Spiritualities of life: New Age romanticism and consumptive capitalism*. Oxford: Blackwell.

Heesterman, J. C. (1993). *The broken world of sacrifice: An essay in Ancient Indian ritual*. Chicago: University of Chicago Press.

Herzog, D. (2017). *Cold War Freud: Psychoanalysis in an age of catastrophes*. Cambridge: Cambridge University Press.

Gabriel, R. (2013). *Why I buy: Self, taste, and consumer society in America*. New York: Intellect Press.

Hanegraaff, W. J. (1999). New Age spiritualities as secular religion: A historian's perspective. *Social Compass, 46*(2), 145–160. doi:10.1177/003776899046002004

Hanegraaff, W. (2016). Reconstructing "religion" from the bottom up. *Numen, 63*, 577–606.

Hunt, H. T. (2003). *Lives in spirit: Precursors and dilemmas of secular Western mysticism*. Albany: SUNY Press.

Lévi-Strauss, C. (1963). *Structural anthropology*. New York: Basic Books.

Malamoud, C. (1996). *Cooking the world: Ritual and thought in ancient India*. Oxford: Oxford University Press.

242 REFERENCES

Mendelsohn, D. (2020). *Three rings: A tale of exile, narrative, and fate.* Charlottesville: University of Virginia Press.

Modern, J. (2021). *Neuromatic: Or, a particular history of religion and the brain.* Chicago: University of Chicago Press.

Molendijk, A. L. (2019). Ernst Troeltsch and mysticism, interdisciplinary *Journal for Religion and Transformation in Contemporary Society, 5*(1), 8–32. https://doi.org/10.30965/23642807-00501002

Rappaport, R. A. (1999). *Ritual and religion in the making of humanity.* Cambridge: Cambridge University Press.

Roof, W. C. (1999). *Spiritual marketplace: Baby boomers and the remaking of American religion.* Princeton, NJ: Princeton University Press.

Seok, B. (2008). Mencius's vertical faculties and moral nativism. *Asian Philosophy, 18*(1), 51–68.

Seznec, J. (1953/1981). *The survival of pagan gods.* Bollingen series. Princeton, NJ: Princeton University Press.

Shermer, M. (2006). SHAM scam. *Scientific American,* May 1, 2006.

Sloterdijk, P. (2013). *You must change your life: On anthropotechnics* (W. Hoban, Trans.). Cambridge: Polity Press.

Staal, F. (1975). *Exploring mysticism: A methodological essay.* Los Angeles: University of California Press.

Staal, F. (1979). The meaninglessness of ritual. *Numen, 26,* 2–22.

Staal, F. (1982). *The science of ritual.* Poona, India: The Bhandarkar Institute Press.

Starker, S. (2002). *Oracle at the supermarket: The American preoccupation with self-help books.* New York: Transaction.

Stoneman, R. (2011). *The ancient oracles: Making the gods speak.* New Haven, CT: Yale University Press.

Tambiah, S. J. (1990). *Magic, science and religion and the scope of rationality.* Cambridge: Cambridge University Press.

Taylor, C. (1989). *Sources of the self.* Cambridge, MA: Harvard University Press.

Taylor, C. (2007). *A secular age.* Cambridge, MA: The Belknap Press of Harvard University.

Weber, M. (1922/1978). *Economy and society.* Los Angeles: University of California Press.

Popular Psychology Titles

Allen, D. (2001). *Getting things done.* New York: Penguin.

Atran, S. (2002). *In gods we trust: The evolutionary landscape of religion.* New York: Oxford University Press.

Byrne, R. (2006). *The secret.* New York: Atria Books.

Calasso, R. (2014). *Ardor.* New York: Farrar, Straus and Giroux.

Carnegie, D. (1936/1998). *How to win friends and influence people.* New York: Pocket.

Chopra, D. (2005). *The book of secrets.* New York: Harmony.

Chopra, D. (2015). *The seven spiritual laws of success.* New York: Amber-Allen Publishing.

Covey, S. (2004). *The seven habits of highly effective people.* New York: Free Press.

Gallwey, W. T. (1997). *The inner game of tennis.* New York: Random House.

Gray, J. (2012). *Men are from Mars, women are from Venus.* New York: Harper paperbacks.

Justman, S. (2005). *Fool's paradise: The unreal world of pop psychology.* New York: Ivan R Dee.

McGraw, P. (2006). *Love smart.* New York: Free Press.

Osteen, J. (2013). *Breakout.* New York: Faithwords.

Robbins, T. (1992). *Awaken the giant within.* New York: Simon & Schuster.

REFERENCES 243

Ruiz, D. M. (1997). *The four agreements.* New York: Amber-Allen Publishing.
Starker, S. (2002). *Oracle at the supermarket: The American preoccupation with self-help* (2nd ed.). New York: Transaction.
Taylor, C. (1989). *Sources of the self.* Cambridge, MA: Harvard University Press.
Taylor, C. (2007). *A secular age.* Cambridge, MA: Belknap, Harvard University Press.
Tolle, E. (1999). *The power of now.* New York: New World Library.
Watts, F., & Williams, M. (1988). *The psychology of religious knowing.* Cambridge: Cambridge University Press.
Weiss, B. (1988). *Many lives, many masters.* New York: Simon & Schuster.
Wilkinson, B. (2002). *A life God rewards.* Colorado Springs, CO: Multnomah.

Chapters 5 and 6: The Discursive Uses of Psychology; Drugs and the Technology of Agency

Abi-Rached, J. M. (2021). 'Aṣfūriyyeh: A history of madness, modernity, and war in the Middle East. *History of Psychiatry, 32*(4), 462–477. https://doi.org/10.1177/095715 4X211028430
Achebe, Chinua. (2016). An Image of Africa: Racism in Conrad's Heart of Darkness. *The Massachusetts Review, 57,* 14–27. doi:10.1353/mar.2016.0003.
Appiah, A. (1992). *In my father's house: Africa in the philosophy of culture.* New York: Oxford University Press.
Asma, S. T., & Gabriel, R. (2019). *The emotional mind: The affective roots of culture and cognition.* Cambridge: Harvard University Press.
Auerbach, E. (1957). *Mimesis: The representation of reality in Western literature.* Garden City, NY: Doubleday.
Barthes, R. (1972). *Mythologies.* New York: Hill and Wang.
Bechara, A., Damasio, H., Tranel, D., & Damasio, A. R. (1997). Deciding advantageously before knowing the advantageous strategy. *Science, 275,* 1293–1295. doi:10.1126/science.275.5304.1293
Beck, J. S. (2011). *Cognitive behavior therapy: Basics and beyond* (2nd ed.). New York: The Guilford Press.
Bergson, H. (1907/2008). *Creative evolution.* New York: Dover Books.
Berridge, K. C. (2012). From prediction error to incentive salience: Mesolimbic computation of reward motivation. *The European Journal of Neuroscience, 35*(7), 1124–1143. https://doi.org/10.1111/j.1460-9568.2012.07990.x
Berridge, K. C., & Kringelbach, M. L. (2013). Neuroscience of affect: Brain mechanisms of pleasure and displeasure. *Current Opinion in Neurobiology, 23*(3), 294–303. https://doi.org/10.1016/j.conb.2013.01.017
Berridge, K. C., Robinson, T. E., & Aldridge, J. W. (2009). Dissecting components of reward: "Liking," "wanting," and "learning." *Current Opinion in Pharmacology, 9*(1), 65–73. https:// doi.org/10.1016/j.coph.2008.12.014
Bourdieu, P. (1984). *Distinction: A social critique of the Judgement of Taste.* Cambridge, MA: Harvard University Press.
Bourguignon, E. (1973). *Religion, altered states of consciousness, and social change.* Columbus: Ohio State University Press.
Brentari, C. (2015). *Jakob von Uexküll: The discovery of the umwelt between biosemiotics and theoretical biology.* Dordrecht: Springer.

244 REFERENCES

Bruner, J. S. (1990). *Acts of meaning*. Cambridge, MA: Harvard University Press.

Bucholz, K. K., & Robins, L. N. (1989). Sociological research on alcohol use, problems, and policy. *Annual Review of Sociology, 15*, 163–186. http://www.jstor.org/stable/2083223

Butts, H. F. (1979). Frantz Fanon's contribution to psychiatry: The psychology of racism and colonialism. *Journal of the National Medical Association, 71*(10), 1015–1018.

Calasso, R. (2016). *Ardor* (R. Dixon, Trans.). New York: Farrar, Strauss, and Giroux.

Carhart-Harris, R. L., & Friston, K. J. (2010). The default-mode, ego-functions and free-energy: A neurobiological account of Freudian ideas. *Brain 133*, 1265–1283. doi:10.1093/brain/awq010

Carhart-Harris, R., & Goodwin, G. (2017). The therapeutic potential of psychedelic drugs: Past, present, and future. *Neuropsychopharmacologys, 42*, 2105–2113. https://doi.org/10.1038/npp.2017.84.

Césaire, A. (1959). L'homme de culture et ses responsabilités. *Présence Africaine, 24/25*, nouvelle série, 116–122. http://www.jstor.org/stable/24349005

Cisek, P. (2007). Cortical mechanisms of action selection: The affordance competition hypothesis. *Philosophical Transactions of the Royal Society B: Biological Sciences, 362*(1485), 1585–1599. https://doi.org/10.1098/rstb.2007.2054

Clark, A. (2013). Whatever next? Predictive brains, situated agents, and the future of cognitive science. *Behavioral and Brain Sciences, 36*(3), 181–204. doi:10.1017/S0140525X12000477

Cleaver, E., & Geismar, M. (1967). *Soul on ice*. New York: McGraw-Hill.

Comte, A. (1855/1974). *The positive philosophy of Auguste Comte* (H. Martineau, Trans.). New York: AMS Press.

Crapse, T. B., Lau, H., & Basso, M. A. (2018). A role for the superior colliculus in decision criteria. *Neuron, 97*(1), 181–194. https://doi.org/10.1016/j.neuron.2017.12.006

Dalî, S., & Chevalier, H. (1942). *The secret life of Salvador Dali*. New York: Dial Press.

Damasio, A. (2010). *Self comes to mind*. New York: Pantheon Books.

Damasio, A. R. (2018). *The strange order of things: Life, feeling, and the making of cultures*. New York: Pantheon Press.

Danziger, K. (1983). Origins and basic principles of Wundt's Völkerpsychologie. *British Journal of Social Psychology, 22*, 303–313. doi:10.1111/j.2044-8309.1983.tb00597.x

Danziger, K. (1990). *Constructing the subject: Historical origins of psychological research*. Cambridge: Cambridge University Press.

Davis, J. E. (2020). *Chemically imbalanced: Everyday suffering, medication, and our quest for self-mastery*. Chicago: University of Chicago Press.

DeCharms, R. C. (1968). *Personal causation: The internal affective determinants of behavior*. New York: Academic Press.

Deci, E. L. (1971). Effects of externally mediated rewards on intrinsic motivation. *Journal of Personality and Social Psychology, 18*(1), 105–115. https://doi.org/10.1037/h0030644.

Deleuze, G., & Guattari, F. (1983). *Anti-Oedipus: Capitalism and schizophrenia*. Minneapolis: University of Minnesota Press.

Deleuze, G., & Guattari, F. (2013). *A thousand plateaus*. New York: Bloomsbury Academic.

Du Bois, W. E. B. (1903/1968). *The souls of black folk; essays and sketches*. New York: Johnson Reprint Corp.

Dumont, L. (1986). *Essays on individualism: Modern ideology in anthropological perspective*. Chicago: University of Chicago Press.

REFERENCES 245

Duong, K. (2021). *Freud in the tropics*. Working paper presented at University of Chicago, Political Science colloquium.

Edenberg, H. J., & Foroud, T. (2013). Genetics and alcoholism. *Nature Reviews. Gastroenterology & Hepatology*, *10*(8), 487–494. https://doi.org/10.1038/nrgastro.2013.86

Edwards, D., & Potter, J. (2001). Discursive psychology. In Willig & Stainton-Rogers (Eds.), *The Sage handbook of qualitative research in psychology* (pp. 73–90). Thousand Oaks, CA: Sage. https://hdl.handle.net/2134/9485

El Shakry, O. (2017). *The Arabic Freud: Psychoanalysis and Islam in modern Egypt*. Princeton, NJ: Princeton University Press.

Eliade, M. (1972). *Shamanism: Archaic techniques of ecstasy*. Princeton, NJ: Princeton University Press.

Ellenberger, H. F. (1970). *The discovery of the unconscious: The history and evolution of dynamic psychiatry*. New York: Basic Books.

Erikson, E. H. (1980). *Identity and Life Cycle*. New York: Norton.

Fanon, F. (1952). *Black skin, white masks*. New York: Grove Press.

Fanon, F. (1963). *The wretched of the earth*. New York: Grove Press.

Field, M. J. (1970). *Search for security: An ethnopsychiatric study of rural Ghana*. Evanston, IL: Northwestern University Press.

Fotopoulou, A., & Tsakiris, M. (2017). Mentalizing homeostasis: The social origins of interoceptive inference. *Neuropsychoanalysis*, *19*(1), 3–28. doi:10.1080/15294145.2017.1294031

Foucault, M. (1961/2006). *Madness and civilization*. New York: Vintage Books.

Foucault, M. (1966). *Les mot et les choses*. Paris: Plon.

Foucault, M., & Howard, R. (1965). *Madness and civilization: A history of insanity in the age of reason*. New York: Pantheon.

Freud, S. (1915/2004). *The unconscious*. New York: Penguin Classics.

Freud, S. (1917). *Mourning and melancholia*. In James Strachey (Ed.), *The standard edition of the complete psychological works of Sigmund Freud, Volume XIV (1914–1916): On the history of the psycho-analytic movement, papers on metapsychology and other works* (pp. 237–258). London: Hogarth Press.

Freud, S. (1927). *The future of an illusion* (J. Strachey, Trans.). New York: W.W. Norton & Company.

Freud, S., Strachey, J., & Richards, A. (1991). *Introductory lectures on psychoanalysis*. London: Penguin.

Friedan, B. (1963). *The feminine mystique*. New York: Norton.

Ffytche, M. (2011). *The foundation of the unconscious: Schelling, Freud and the birth of the modern psyche*. Cambridge: Cambridge University Press.

Gabriel, R. (2023). *The affective psychodynamics of pleasure: Reward associations in drug use and consumer society*. Unpublished manuscript.

Gabriel, R. (2013). *Why I buy: Self, taste, and consumer society in America*. Bristol, UK: Intellect Press.

Gabriel, R. (2021a). The motivational role of affect in an ecological model. *Theory & Psychology 31*, 1–21.

Girard, R. (2016). *La violence et le sacré*. Paris: Fayard.

Greenberg, G. (1994). *The self on the shelf: Recovery books and the good life*. Albany: State University of New York Press.

246 REFERENCES

Greenberg, G. (2013). *The book of woe: The DSM and the unmaking of psychiatry.* New York: Blue Rider Press.

Greenberg, G. (2014). *Manufacturing depression: The secret history of a modern disease.* New York: Simon & Schuster.

Hanserd, R. (2020). *Identity, spirit and freedom in the Atlantic world: The Gold Coast and the African diaspora.* New York: Routledge.

Harrison, J. (2010). Ego death and psychedelics. *MAPS Bulletin, 20,* 40–41.

Hartmann, E., & Coupland, W. C. (1869/1893). *Philosophy of the unconscious.* London: K. Paul, Trench, Trübner, & Co.

Hartmann, H. (1927). *Die Grundlagen der Psychoanalyse.* Leipzig: G. Thieme.

Hartmann, H. (1958). *Ego psychology and the problem of adaptation* (D. Rapaport, Trans.). New York: International Universities Press.

Heidegger, M., Macquarrie, J., & Robinson, E. (1962). *Being and time.* Malden, MA: Blackwell.

Herzog, D. (2017). *Cold War Freud: Psychoanalysis in an age of catastrophes.* Cambridge: Cambridge University Press.

Hiltebeitel, A. (2018). *Freud's India: Sigmund Freud and India's first psychoanalyst Girindrasekhar Bose.* New York: Oxford University Press.

Holland, D., & Lachicotte, Jr., W. (2007). Vygotsky, Mead, and the new sociocultural studies of identity. In H. Daniels, M. Cole, & J. Wertsch (Eds.), *The Cambridge companion to Vygotsky* (pp. 101–135). Cambridge: Cambridge University Press. doi:10.1017/CCOL0521831040.005

Hopwood, D. (1982). *Egypt: Politics and society 1945–1981.* London: George Allen and Unwin.

Hyman, S. E., & Nestler, E. J. (1993). *The molecular foundations of psychiatry.* Washington, DC: American Psychiatric Press.

Iberall, A. S. (1995). A physical (homeokinetic) foundation for the Gibsonian theory of perception and action. *Ecological Psychology, 7*(1), 37–68. https://doi.org/10.1207/s15326969eco0701_3

Iberall, A. S., & McCulloch, W. S. (1969). The organizing principle of complex living systems. *Journal of Basic Engineering, 91*(2), 290–294. https://doi.org/10.1115/1.3571099

Jung, C. G. (1912/1916). *Psychology of the unconscious: A study of the transformations and symbolisms of the libido.* New York: Routledge.

Jung, C. G., Franz, M.-L., Henderson, J. L., Jaffé, A., & Jacobi, J. (1964). *Man and his symbols.* New York: Doubleday.

Kapila, S. (2007). The "godless" Freud and his Indian friends: An Indian agenda for psychoanalysis. In S. Mahone & M. Vaughan (Eds.), *Psychiatry and empire.* Cambridge imperial and post-colonial studies series (pp. 124–152). London: Palgrave Macmillan. https://doi.org/10.1057/9780230593244_6

Khanna, R. (2003). *Dark continents: Psychoanalysis and colonialism.* Durham, NC: Duke University Press.

Kihlstrom, J. F. (1987). The cognitive unconscious. *Science, 237,* 1445–1452.

Kirsch, I. (2010). *The emperor's new drugs: Exploding the antidepressant myth.* New York: Basic Books.

Klein, M. (1930). The importance of symbol-formation in the development of the ego. *International Journal of Psycho-Analysis, 11,* 24–39.

Klein, M. (1981). *Love, guilt, and reparation.* London: Hogarth Press.

REFERENCES 247

Klein, S. B., Gabriel, R. H., Gangi, C. E., & Robertson, T. E. (2009). Reflections on the self: A case study of a prosopagnosic patient. *Social Cognition, 26*, 766–777.

Klein, S. B., German, T. P., Cosmides, L., & Gabriel, R. (2004). A theory of autobiographical memory: Necessary components and disorders resulting from their loss. *Social Cognition, 22*(5), 460–490.

Kleinman, A., Eisenberg, L., & Good, B. (1978). Culture, illness, and care: Clinical lessons from anthropologic and cross-cultural research. *Annals of Internal Medicine, 88*(2), 251–258. https://doi.org/10.7326/0003-4819-88-2-251

Kramer, P. D. (1994). *Listening to Prozac.* New York: Penguin Books.

Kringelbach, M. L., & Berridge, K. C. (2017). The affective core of emotion: Linking pleasure, subjective well-being, and optimal metastability in the brain. *Emotion Review: Journal of the International Society for Research on Emotion, 9*(3), 191–199. https://doi.org/10.1177/1754073916684558

Kripal, J. (2007). *Esalen: America and the religion of no religion.* Chicago: University of Chicago Press.

Lacan, J. (2007). *Écrits* (B. Fink, Trans.). New York: W.W. Norton.

Laland, K. N., Uller, T., Feldman, M. W., Sterelny, K., Müller, G. B., Moczek, A., Jablonka, E., & Odling-Smee, J. (2015). The extended evolutionary synthesis: Its structure, assumptions and predictions. *Proceedings of the Royal Society B: Biological Sciences, 282*(1813), Article 20151019. https://doi.org/10.1098/rspb.2015.1019

Lear, J. (1998). *Open minded: Working out the logic of soul.* Cambridge, MA: Harvard University Press.

Lears, J. (1995). *Fables of abundance: A cultural history of advertising in America.* New York: Basic Books.

Lepper, M. R., & Greene, D. (Eds.). (1978). *The hidden costs of reward: New perspectives on the psychology of human motivation.* Mahwah, NJ: Lawrence Erlbaum.

Levy, N. (2013). Addiction is not a brain disease (and it matters). *Frontiers in Psychiatry, 4*(24). doi:10.3389/fpsyt.2013.00024

Lewis-Williams, D. J. (2002). *The mind in the cave: Consciousness and the origins of art.* London: Thames & Hudson.

Littlefield, A. K., & Sher, K. J. (2010). The multiple, distinct ways that personality contributes to alcohol use disorders. *Social and Personality Psychology Compass, 4*(9), 767–782. https://doi.org/10.1111/j.1751-9004.2010.00296.x

Ludwig, A. (1968). Altered states of consciousness. In R. Prince (Ed.), *Trance and possession states* (pp. 69–95). Montreal: R.M. Bucke Memorial Society.

Luhrmann, T. M. (2000). *Of two minds: The growing disorder in American psychiatry.* New York: Alfred A. Knopf.

Mahler, M. (1967). *On human symbiosis and the vicissitudes of individuation.* New York: International Universities Press.

Martin, R., & Barresi, J. (2006). *The rise and fall of soul and self.* New York: Columbia University Press.

Macpherson, C. B. (1969). *The political theory of possessive individualism: Hobbes to Locke.* Oxford: Clarendon Press.

Makari, G. (2008). *Revolution in mind: The creation of psychoanalysis.* New York: Harper Perennial.

Mannheim, K. (1936). *Ideology and utopia: An introduction to the sociology of knowledge.* New York: Harvest Books.

Maslow, A. (1998). *Towards a psychology of being* (3rd ed.). New York: Wiley.

Matza, T. A. (2018). *Shock therapy: Psychology, precarity, and well-being in postsocialist Russia*. Durham, NC: Duke University Press.

McCracken, G. (1988). *Culture and consumption: New approaches to the symbolic character of consumer goods and activities*. Bloomington: Indiana University Press.

McGinty, V. B., Rangel, A., & Newsome, W. T. (2016). Orbitofrontal cortex value signals depend on fixation location during free viewing. *Neuron, 90*(6), 1299–1311. https://doi.org/10.1016/j.neuron.2016.04.045

Mead, G. H. (1934). *Mind, self and society*. Chicago: University of Chicago Press.

Misra, G., & Paranjpe, A. C. (2012). Psychology in modern India. In *Encyclopedia of the history of psychological theories*. Berlin: Springer Science+Business Media. doi:10.1007/978-1-4419-0463-8_422

Moccia, L., Mazza, M., Di Nicola, M., & Janiri, L. (2018). The experience of pleasure: A perspective between neuroscience and psychoanalysis. *Frontiers in Human Neuroscience, 12*, 359. https://doi.org/10.3389/fnhum.2018.0035

Modern, J. (2021). *Neuromatic; Or, a particular history of religion and the brain*. Chicago: University of Chicago Press.

Moore, J. W. (2016). What is the sense of agency and why does it matter? *Frontiers in Psychology, 7*, 1272. https://doi.org/10.3389/fpsyg.2016.01272

Moreno, F. A., Wiegand, C. B., Taitano, E. K., & Delgado, P. L. (2006). Safety, tolerability, and efficacy of psilocybin in nine patients with obsessive- compulsive disorder. *Journal of Clinical Psychiatry, 67*, 1735–1740.

Murphy, D. (2006). *Psychiatry in the scientific image*. Cambridge, MA: MIT Press.

Nair, M. (2001). *The laughing club of India*. New York: Filmakers Library.

Nandy, A., & Kakar, S. (1980). Culture and personality. In U. Pareek (Ed.), *A survey of research in psychology*, 1971–76, part 1 (pp. 141–158). Bombay: Popular.

Nour, M. M., Evans, L., Nutt, D., & Carhart-Harris, R. L. (2016). Ego-dissolution and psychedelics: Validation of the Ego-Dissolution Inventory (EDI). *Frontiers in Human Neuroscience, 10*, 269. doi: 10.3389/fnhum.2016.00269

Opokuwaa, N. A. K. (2005). *The quest for spiritual transformation: Introduction to traditional Akan religion, rituals and practices*. Bloomington, IN: iUniverse.

Pande, N., & Naidu, R. K. (1992). Anāsakti and health: A study of non-attachment. *Psychology and Developing Societies, 4*, 89–104.

Panksepp, J., & Biven, L. (2012). *The archaeology of mind: Neuroevolutionary origins of human emotions*. New York: W. W. Norton.

Platt, M., & Padoa-Schioppa, C. (2009). Neuronal representations of value. In P. W. Glimcher, C. F. Camerer, E. Fehr, & R. A. Poldrack (Eds.), *Neuroeconomics: Decision making and the brain* (pp. 441–462). New York: Elsevier Academic Press.

Paranjpe, A. C. (1998). *Self and identity in modern psychology and Indian thought*. New York: Plenum Press.

Parin, P., Parin-Matthèy, G., & Morgenthaler, F. (1966). *Les Blancs pensent trop: 13 entretiens avec les Dogon*. Paris: Payot.

Pickard, H. (2018). The puzzle of addiction. In H. Pickard &S. H. Ahmed (Eds.), *The Routledge handbook of philosophy and science of addiction* (pp. 9–22). Abingdon, UK: Routledge.

Pickard, H. (2020). Addiction and the self. *Noûs, 55*(4), 737–761. doi:10.1111/nous.12328

Pippin, R. B. (2017). *The philosophical Hitchcock: Vertigo and the anxieties of unknowingness*. Chicago: University of Chicago Press.

REFERENCES 249

Pollan, M. (2018). *How to change your mind: What the new science of psychedelics teaches us about consciousness, dying, addiction, depression, and transcendence.* New York: Penguin Press.

Rao, K. R. (2002). *Consciousness studies: Cross-cultural perspectives.* Jefferson, MO: McFarland.

Rao, K. R. (2011). *Cognitive anomalies, consciousness and yoga.* New Delhi: Centre for Studies in Civilizations.

Rieff, P. (1968). *The triumph of the therapeutic: Uses of faith after Freud.* Chicago: University of Chicago Press.

Schelling, F. M. J. (1802–3/1989). *The philosophy of art.* Minnesota: Minnesota University Press.

Schorske, C. E. (1981). *Fin-de-siècle Vienna: Politics and culture.* New York: Vintage.

Schutz, A. (1954). Concept and theory formation in the social sciences. *The Journal of Philosophy, 51*(9), 257–273. doi:10.2307/2021812

Shillington, K. (2005). *History of Africa.* Oxford: Macmillan Education.

Shweder, R. A., LeVine, R. A., & Social Science Research Council (U.S.). (1984). *Culture theory: Essays on mind, self, and emotion.* Cambridgeshire: Cambridge University Press.

Siegel, J. (2005). *The idea of the self: Thought and experience in Western Europe since the seventeenth century.* Cambridge: Cambridge University Press.

Smith, R. (2013). *Between the mind and nature: A history of psychology.* London: Reaktion Books.

Solms, M. L. (2018). The neurobiological underpinnings of psychoanalytic theory and therapy. *Frontiers in Behavioral Neuroscience, 12,* 294. https://doi.org/10.3389/fnbeh.2018.00294

Solms, M. L. (2020). New project for a scientific psychology: General scheme. *Neuropsychoanalysis, 22*(1-2), 5–35. doi:10.1080/15294145.2020.1833361

Spivak, G. C. (1990). Poststructuralism, marginality, postcoloniality and value. In P. Collier & H. Geyer-Ryan (Eds.), *Literary theory today* (pp. 219–224). Cambridge: Polity Press.

Svevo, I. (1923/1958). *Confessions of Zeno* (B. de Zoete, Trans.). New York: Vintage Books.

Synofzik, M., Thier, P., Leube, D. T., Schlotterbeck, P., & Lindner, A. (2010). Misattributions of agency in schizophrenia are based on imprecise predictions about the sensory consequences of one's actions. *Brain, 133,* 262–271. doi:10.1093/brain/awp291

Taylor, C. (1989). *Sources of the Self.* Cambridge, MA: Harvard University Press.

Trilling, L. (1950). *The liberal imagination: Essays on literature and society.* New York: Viking Press.

Trilling, L. (1972). *Sincerity and authenticity.* Cambridge, MA: Harvard University Press. doi:10.2307/j.ctvjhzrdp

Trumbull, R. (2012). Derrida, Freud, Lacan: Resistances. *UC Santa Cruz.* ProQuest ID: Trumbull_ucsc_0036E_10030. Merritt ID: ark:/13030/m55q4tpk. Retrieved from https://escholarship.org/uc/item/9p43t6nf

Vahali, H. O. (2011). Landscaping a perspective: India and the psychoanalytic vista. In G. Misra (Ed.), *Psychology in India (Theoretical and methodological developments)* (Vol. 4, pp. 1–91). New Delhi: Pearson Education.

Valenzuela, C. F. (1997). Alcohol and neurotransmitter interactions. Alcohol health and research. *world, 21*(2), 144–148.

Vygotsky, L. S. (1978). *Mind in society: The development of higher psychological functions.* Cambridge, MA: Harvard University Press.

250 REFERENCES

Wallis, J. D. (2007). Orbitofrontal cortex and its contribution to decision-making. *Annual Review of Neuroscience, 30,* 31–56. https://doi.org/10.1146/annurev.neuro.30.051 606.094334

Wasson, R. G. (1968). *Soma: Divine mushroom of immortality.* New York: Harcourt Brace Jovanovich.

Whooley, O. (2019). *On the heels of ignorance: Psychiatry and the politics of not knowing.* Chicago: University of Chicago Press.

Williamson, J. (1994). *Decoding advertisements: Ideology and meaning in advertising.* London: Marion Boyars.

Williamson, J. (2010). *Decoding advertisements: Ideology and meaning in advertising.* London: Marion Boyars.

Winnicott, D. W. (1975). *Through paediatrics to psycho-analysis.* London: Hogarth Press.

Wynter, S. (1984). The ceremony must be found: After humanism. *Boundary 2, 12*(3), 19–70.

Wynter, S. (1999). Towards the sociogenic principle: Fanon, the puzzle of conscious experience, of "identity" and what it's like to be "black." In M. Durán-Cogan & A. Gómez-Moriana (Eds.), *National identity and sociopolitical change: Latin America between marginizalization and integration* (pp. 30–66). Minnesota: University of Minnesota Press.

Chapter 7: Art and Reflexivity: Creative Uses of Psychology

Alcorta, C. S., & Sosis, R. (2005). Ritual, emotion, and sacred symbols: The evolution of religion as an adaptive complex. *Human Nature (Hawthorne, N.Y.), 16*(4), 323–359. https://doi.org/10.1007/s12110-005-1014-3

Amyot, J. (2008). Proesme du translateur. In *L'Histoire aethiopique* (J. Amyot, Trans.; L. Plazenet, Ed.) (p. 159). Paris: Champion.

Asma, S. T. (2017). *The evolution of imagination.* Chicago: University of Chicago Press.

Asma, S. T. (2021). Adaptive imagination: Toward a mythopoetic cognitive science. *Evolutionary Studies in Imaginative Culture, 5*(2), 1–32. https://doi.org/10.26613/esic.5.2.236

Asma, S. T., & Gabriel, R. (2019). *The emotional mind: The affective roots of culture and cognition.* Cambridge, MA: Harvard University Press.

Atran, S. (2002). *In gods we trust: The evolutionary landscape of religion.* New York: Oxford University Press.

Atran, S., & Henrich, J. (2010). The evolution of religion: How cognitive by-products. adaptive learning heuristics, ritual displays, and group competition generate deep commitments to prosocial religions. *Biological Theory, 5*(1), 1–13.

Atran, S., & Norenzayan, A. (2004). Religion's evolutionary landscape: Counterintuition, commitment, compassion, communion. *The Behavioral and Brain Sciences, 27*(6), 713–770. https://doi.org/10.1017/s0140525x04000172

Austin, J. L. (1962). *How to do things with words.* Oxford: Oxford University Press.

Barsalou, L. W. (1999). Perceptual symbol systems. *Behavior and Brain Sciences, 22*(4), 577–660.

Barton, R. A. (2012). Embodied cognitive evolution and the cerebellum. *Philosophical Transactions of the Royal Society B, 367*(1599), 2097–2107.

REFERENCES 251

Becker, J. (2004). *Deep listening; Music, emotion, and trancing.* Bloomington: Indiana University Press.

Bellah, R. N. (2011). *Religion in human evolution.* Cambridge, MA: Harvard University Press.

Bennett, J. (2001). *The enchantment of modern life: Attachments, crossings, and ethics.* Princeton, NJ: Princeton University Press.

Bermúdez, J., & Cahen, A. (2015). Nonconceptual mental content. In E. N. Zalta (Ed.), *The Stanford encyclopedia of philosophy* (Fall ed.). http://plato.stanford.edu/archives/fall2015/entries/content-nonconceptual/.

Blos, P. (1967). The second individuation process of adolescence. *The Psychoanalytic Study of the Child, 22*(1), 162–186. doi:10.1080/00797308.1967.11822595

Bourdieu, P. (1984). *Distinction: A social critique of the judgment of taste.* Cambridge, MA: Harvard University Press.

Bourguignon, E. (1973). *Religion, altered states of consciousness, and social change.* Columbus: Ohio State University Press.

Bruner, J. (1991). The narrative construction of reality. *Critical Inquiry, 18*(1), 1–21. http://www.jstor.org/stable/1343711

Bulbulia, J. A., Geertz, A., Atkinson, Q. D., et al. (2013). The cultural evolution of religion. In P. J. Richerson & M. H. Christiansen (Eds.), *Cultural evolution: Society, technology, language, and religion* (pp. 381–404). Strüngmann Forum Reports, vol. 12. J. Lupp, series editor. Cambridge, MA: MIT Press.

Calasso, R. (2020). *The celestial hunter* (R. Dixon, Trans.). New York: Farrar, Strauss and Giroux.

Cavell, S. (1979). *The world viewed* (enlarged ed.). Cambridge, MA: Harvard University Press

Charles, S. J., van Mulukom, V., Brown, J. E., Watts, F., Dunbar, R. I. M., & Farias, M. (2021). United on Sunday: The effects of secular rituals on social bonding and affect. *PLoS ONE, 16*(1), e0242546. https://doi.org/10.1371/journal.pone.0242546

Chemero, A. (2009). *Radical embodied cognitive science.* Cambridge, MA: MIT Press.

Clark, T. J. (1999). *The painting of modern life: Paris in the art of Manet and his followers* (Rev. ed.). Princeton, NJ: Princeton University Press.

Damasio, A. R. (2019). *The strange order of things: Life, feeling, and the making of the cultures.* New York: First Vintage Books.

Davidson, R. J., Scherer, K. R., & Goldsmith, H. (2009). *Handbook of affective sciences.* Oxford: Oxford University Press.

de Waal, F. (Ed.). (2001). *Tree of origin: What primate behavior can tell us about human social evolution.* Cambridge, MA: Harvard University Press.

Dehaene, S., & Changeux, J. P. (2000). Reward-dependent learning in neuronal networks for planning and decision making. *Progress Brain Research, 126,* 217–229.

Dissanayake, E. (1992). *Homo aestheticus: Where art comes from and why.* New York: Free Press.

Dutton, D. (2009). *The art instinct: Beauty, pleasure, and human evolution.* New York: Bloomsbury Press.

Fiebich, A. (2014). Perceiving affordances and social cognition. In M. Gallotti & J. Michael (Eds.), *Perspectives in social ontology and social cognition* (vol. 4, 149–166). New York: Springer.

Foss, J. (2007). The rituals of explanation. *Behavioral and Brain Sciences, 29*(6), 618–619.

252 REFERENCES

Freud, S. (1907). Obsessive acts and religious practices. In J. Strachey (Ed.), *The collected papers of Sigmund Freud* (Vol. 9, J. Riviere, Trans.) (pp. 25–50). London: Hogarth Press.

Fried, M. (1998). *Art and objecthood: Essays and reviews.* Chicago: University of Chicago Press.

Gabriel, R. (2021a). The motivational role of affect in an ecological model. *Theory & Psychology, 31*(4), 552–572. https://doi.org/10.1177/0959354321992869

Gallese, V., Fadiga, L. Fogassi, L., & Rizzolatti, G. (1996). Action recognition in the premotor cortex. *Brain, 119*(2), 593–609.

Geertz, C. (1983). *Local knowledge.* New York: Basic Books.

Hammoudi, A. (2006). *A season in mecca.* New York: Hill and Wang.

Harrisson, J. E. (1913). *Ancient art and ritual.* Oxford: Oxford University Press.

Hayden, B. (2003). *Shamans, sorcerers, and saints: A prehistory of religion.* Washington, DC: Smithsonian Books.

Hayden, B. (2018). *The power of ritual in prehistory: Secret societies and origins of social complexity.* Cambridge: Cambridge University Press.

Heesterman, J. C. (1993). *The broken world of sacrifice: An essay in ancient Indian ritual.* Chicago: University of Chicago Press.

Heft, H. (2010). Affordances and the perception of landscape: An inquiry into environmental perception and aesthetics. In C. W. Thompson, P. Aspinall, & S. Bell (Eds.), *Innovative approaches to researching landscape and health* (pp. 9–32). New York: Routledge.

Hegel, G. W. F., & Knox, T. M. (1998). *Aesthetics: Lectures on fine art.* Oxford: Clarendon.

Herbert, R. (2011). Reconsidering music and trance: Cross-cultural differences and cross-disciplinary perspectives. *Ethnomusicology Forum, 20*(2), 201–227.

Gabriel, R. (2021b). Affect, belief, and the arts. *Frontiers in Psychology, 12,* 757234. https://doi.org/10.3389/fpsyg.2021.757234

James, W. (1910/1982). *Varieties of religious experience.* New York: Penguin.

Johnson, A. W., & Earle, T. (2006). *The evolution of human societies: From foraging group to agrarian state.* Stanford, CA: Stanford University Press.

James, W., & Castell, A. (1948). *Essays in pragmatism.* New York: Hafner.

Jankowsky, R. C. (2007). Music, spirit possession and the in-between. *Ethnomusicology Forum, 16*(2), 165–208.

Kant, I. (2000). *Critique of the power of judgment.* Cambridge: Cambridge University Press.

Laland, K., Odling-Smee, J., & Myles, S. (2010). How culture shaped the human genome: Bringing genetics and the human sciences together. *Nature Reviews Genetics, 11,* 137–148. https://doi.org/10.1038/nrg2734

Laland, K. N., Uller, T., Feldman, M. W., Sterelny, K., Müller, G. B., Moczek, A., Jablonka, E., & Odling-Smee, J. (2015). The extended evolutionary synthesis: Its structure, assumptions and predictions. *Proceedings of the Royal Society B: Biological Sciences, 282*(1813), Article 20151019. https://doi.org/10.1098/rspb.2015.1019

Lewis, I. M. (1989). *Ecstatic religion: A study of shamanism and spirit possession* (2nd ed.). New York: Routledge.

Levenson, R. W. (2003). Blood, sweat and fears: The autonomic architecture of emotion. In P. Ekman, J. J. Campos, R. J. Davidson, & F. B. M. de Waal (Eds.), *Emotions inside out* (pp. 348–366). New York: Annals of the New York Academy of Sciences volume 1000.

Lex, B. (1979). The neurobiology of ritual trance. In E. d'Aquili, C. Laughlin, & J. McManus (Eds.), *The spectrum of ritual* (pp. 117–151). New York: Columbia University Press.

REFERENCES   253

Lukacs, G. (1916/1971). *The theory of the novel: A historico-philosophical essay on the forms of great epic literature.* Cambridge, MA: MIT Press.

Malinowski, B. (1922). *Argonauts of the Western Pacific: An account of native enterprise and adventure in the archipelagoes of Melanesian New Guinea.* London: G. Routledge & Sons.

Millikan, R. G. (1996). Pushmi-Pullyu representations. In J. E. Tomberlin (Ed.), *Philosophical perspectives: Vol. 9. AI, connectionism, and philosophical psychology* (pp. 185–200). Atascadero, CA: Ridgeview.

Noë, A. (2015). *Strange tools: Art and human nature.* New York: Hill and Wang.

Nugent, P. (2017). Fascination. *Journal of Consciousness Studies, 24* (11–12), 118–141.

Otto, R. (1926). *The idea of the holy: An inquiry into the non-rational factor in the idea of the divine and its relation to the rational.* Oxford: H. Milford and Oxford University Press.

Otto, R. (2014). *Naturalism and religion* (J. Thomson & M. Thomson, Trans.). London: Williams and Norgate. (First published as *Naturalistische und Religiose Weltansicht.* Tubingen: J.C. B. Mohr, 1904)

Panksepp, J. (1995). The emotional sources of "chills" induced by music. *Music Perception, 13*(2), 171–207.

Panksepp, J. (1998). *Affective neuroscience.* New York: Oxford University Press.

Panksepp, J., & Biven, L. (2012). *The archaeology of mind: Neuroevolutionary origins of human emotion.* New York: W. W. Norton & Company.

Pavel, T. G. (2013). *The lives of the novel: A history.* Princeton, NJ: Princeton University Press.

Pessoa, L. (2013). *The cognitive-emotional brain.* Cambridge, MA: MIT Press.

Pezzulo, G., & Cisek, P. (2016). Navigating the affordance landscape: Feedback control as a process model of behavior and cognition. *Trends in Cognitive Science, 20*(6), 414–424. https:// doi.org/10.1016/j.tics.2016.03.013

Phelps, E. (2006). Emotion and cognition: Insights from studies of the human amygdala. *Annual Review of Psychology, 57,* 27–53. https://doi.org/10.1146/annurev.psych.56.091 103.070234

Pippin, R. B. (2012). *Hollywood Westerns and American myth: The importance of Howard Hawks and John Ford for political philosophy.* New Haven, CT: Yale University Press.

Pippin, R. B. (2014). *After the beautiful: Hegel and the philosophy of pictorial modernism.* Chicago: University of Chicago Press.

Pippin, R. B. (2017). *The philosophical Hitchcock: Vertigo and the anxieties of unknowing-ness.* Chicago: University of Chicago Press.

Pippin, R. B. (2020). *Filmed thought: Cinema as reflective form.* Chicago: University of Chicago Press.

Prinz, J. (2004). *Gut reactions: A perceptual theory of emotion.* Oxford: Oxford University Press.

Purzycki, B. G., & Sosis, R. (2013) The extended religious phenotype and the adaptive coupling of ritual and belief. *Israel Journal of Ecology & Evolution, 59*(2), 99–108. doi:10.1080/15659801.2013.825433.

Racy, A. J. (2003). *Making music in the Arab world: The culture and artistry of Tarab.* Cambridge: Cambridge University Press.

Rappaport, R. A. (1999). *Ritual and religion in the making of humanity.* Cambridge: Cambridge University Press.

Reed, E. S. (1986). James Gibson's ecological revolution in perceptual psychology: A case study in the transformation of scientific Ideas. *Studies in the History and Philosophy of Science, 17*, 65–99.

Reed, E. S. (1996). *Encountering the world: Toward an ecological psychology.* Oxford: Oxford University Press.

Richerson, P. J., & Boyd, R. (2001). The evolution of subjective commitment to groups: A tribal instincts hypothesis. In R. M. Nesse (Ed.), *Evolution and the capacity for commitment* (pp. 184–220). Thousand Oaks, CA: Russell Sage Foundation.

Rietveld, E. (2012). Bodily intentionality and social affordances in context. In F. Paglieri (Ed.), *Consciousness in interaction: The role of the natural and social context in shaping consciousness* (pp. 207–226). Amsterdam: John Benjamins. https://doi.org/10.1075/aicr.86.11rie

Rodowick, D. N. (2015). *Philosophy's artful conversation.* Cambridge, MA: Harvard University Press.

Rouget, G. (1985). *La musique et la transe.* Paris: Gallimard.

Schiller, F., Hinderer, W., & Dahlstrom, D. O. (1993). *Essays.* New York: Continuum.

Shaw, R. (2003). The agent–environment interface: Simon's indirect or Gibson's direct coupling? *Ecological Psychology, 15*(1), 37–106. https://doi.org/10.1207/S15326969ECO1501_04

Sterelny, K., Richard, J., Calcott, B., & Fraser, B. (2013). *Cooperation and its evolution.* Cambridge, MA: MIT Press.

Tallis, R. (2018). *Logos: The mystery of how we make sense of the world.* Newcastle upon Tyne: Agenda Publishing.

Taylor, C. (1971). Interpretation and the sciences of man. *The Review of Metaphysics, 25*(1), 3–51. http://www.jstor.org/stable/20125928

Trotsky, L. (1960). *Literature and revolution.* Ann Arbor: University of Michigan Press.

Turner, V. (1969). *The ritual process.* Chicago: Aldine.

Turvey, M. T. (1992). Affordances and prospective control: An outline of the ontology. *Ecological Psychology, 4*(3), 173–187. https://doi.org/10.1207/s15326969eco0403_3

Warren, R. (2008). *Fables of the self: Studies in lyric poetry.* New York: W.W. Norton and Company.

Warren, W. H. (1988). Action modes and laws of control for the visual guidance of action. In O. Meijer & K. Roth (Eds.), *Movement behavior: The motor–action controversy* (pp. 339–380). North Holland.

Warren, W. H. (2006). The dynamics of perception and action. *Psychological Review, 113*(2), 358–389. https://doi.org/10.1037/0033-295X.113.2.358

Watt, I. (1957). *The rise of the novel: Studies in Defoe, Richardson, and Fielding.* Berkeley: University of California Press.

Whitehouse, H. (2000). *Arguments and icons: divergent modes of religiosity.* Oxford: Oxford University Press.

Whitehouse, H. (2015). Explaining religion and ritual. In K. Almqvist & A. Linklater (Eds.), *Religion: Perspectives from the Engelsberg seminar 2014* (pp. 261–270). Stockholm: Axel and Margaret Axson Johnson Foundation.

Whitehouse, H., Jong, J., Buhrmester, M., et al. (2017). The evolution of extreme cooperation via shared dysphoric experiences. *Science Reports, 7*, 44292. https://doi.org/10.1038/srep44292

Williams, B. A. (1993). *Shame and necessity.* Oakland: University of California Press.

Withagen, R., & Chemero, A. (2009). Naturalizing perception: Developing the Gibsonian approach to perception along evolutionary lines. *Theory & Psychology, 19*(3), 363–389. https://doi. org/10.1177/0959354309104159.

Withagen, R., & Michaels, C. (2005). On ecological conceptualizations of perceptual systems and action systems. *Theory & Psychology, 15*(5), 603–620. https://doi.org/10.1177/0959354305057265

Conclusion

Cavell, S. (2005). *Philosophy the day after tomorrow.* Cambridge, MA: Belknap Press of Harvard University Press.

Crawford, M. (2008). *The limits of neuro-talk: On the dangers of a mindless brain science. The New Atlantis, Winter, 19,* 65–78.

Curran, G., & Gabriel, R. (2012). Affective neuroscience and the law. *Journal of Consciousness Studies, 19*(3–4), 36–48.

Danziger, K. (1990). *Constructing the subject: Historical origins of psychological research.* Cambridge: Cambridge University Press. https://doi.org/10.1017/CBO9780511524059.

Danziger, K. (2003). Prospects of a historical psychology. *History and Philosophy of Psychology Bulletin, 15*(2), 4–10.

Gabriel, R. (2012). Modularity in cognitive psychology and affective neuroscience (pp. 19–25). In J. Panksepp et al., *The philosophical implications of affective neuroscience. Journal of Consciousness Studies, 19*(3–4), 6–48.

Gergen, K. J. (1973). Social psychology as history. *Journal of Personality and Social Psychology, 26*(2), 309–320. https://doi.org/10.1037/h0034436

Goffman, E. (1967). *Interaction ritual.* New York: Doubleday.

Guenther, K. (2015). *Localization and its discontents: A genealogy of psychoanalysis and the neurodisciplines.* Chicago: University of Chicago Press.

Isaac, J. (2012). *Working knowledge: Making the human sciences from Parsons to Kuhn.* Cambridge, MA: Harvard University Press.

Kagan, J. (2009). *The three cultures: Natural sciences, social sciences, and the humanities in the 21st century.* Cambridge: Cambridge University Press.

Kagan, J. (2012). *Psychology's ghost: The crisis in the profession and way back.* New Haven, CT: Yale University Press.

Klein, S. B. (2015). What memory is. *WIREs Cognitive Science, 6*(1), 1–38.

Kleinman, A. (1988). *Rethinking psychiatry: From cultural category to personal experience.* New York: Free Press.

Koch, S. (1999). *Psychology in human context: Essays in dissidence and reconstruction.* Chicago: University of Chicago Press.

Kuhn, T. S. (1962). *The structure of scientific revolutions.* Chicago: University of Chicago Press.

Luhrmann, T. M. (2000). *Of two minds: The growing disorder in American psychiatry.* New York: Knopf.

Parsons, T., & Shils, E. A. (Eds.). (1951). *Toward a general theory of action.* Cambridge, MA: Harvard University Press.

Phillips, D. Z. (1993). *Wittgenstein and religion.* London: Macmillan.

Scruton, R. (2016). *The ring of truth: The wisdom of Wagner's Ring of the Nibelung*. London: Penguin.

Tallis, R. (2010). What neuroscience cannot tell us about ourselves. *The New Atlantis, 29, Fall*, 3–25.

Troy, A. S., Wilhelm, F. H., Shallcross, A. J., & Mauss, I. B. (2010). Seeing the silver lining: cognitive reappraisal ability moderates the relationship between stress and depressive symptoms. *Emotion (Washington, D.C.), 10*(6), 783–795. https://doi.org/10.1037/a0020262s

Wittgenstein, L., & Anscombe, G. E. M. (1997). *Philosophical investigations*. Oxford: Blackwell.

Wolfe, T. (1996). *Sorry but your soul just died*. The Independent.

Index

For the benefit of digital users, indexed terms that span two pages (e.g., 52–53) may, on occasion, appear on only one of those pages.

aesthetics
  aesthetic movement of
    Romanticism, 91–92
  aesthetic versus materialist
    approach, 146
  in arts of immanence, 153–54
  cinema and, 151
  developing aesthetic sense, 83
  drama and literature, 148–49
  emotions and direct perception, 147–48
  in imaginative culture, 142–43
  and metaphor, 46
affect
  affective states achieved through art and
    ritual, 141–43
  affect management in imaginative
    culture, 142
  failure to address in behaviorism and
    cognitive science, 34
  in interdisciplinary multilevel
    psychology, 135–37
  role of within a neutral monism, ix, 74
affective neuroscience, x–xi, 37
affordances, 147–49, 153, 155–56
agency
  contemporary metaphors and, 40–42
  drugs and the technology of, 125–40
  in early cognitive science, 23
  enabled by psychology, 88, 97, 115–17,
    122–24, 160
  individualism and, 105–6
  maintaining in the face of
    determinism, 86
  motivation and, 134–35
  neglect of in empirical
    psychology, 129–30
  psychoanalysis and, 112–13

relationship to beliefs about the
  mind, 85
role of self-help and religion in, 101
in Soviet psychology, 25
altered states of consciousness, 132–34,
  144, 155–56
American psychology, 17–23
analogical reasoning
  creating order and necessity through,
    29, 161
  treating psychology as mythology, 157
  used by empirical psychologists,
    110, 142–43
anthropology
  in contemporary empirical
    psychology, 73
  in Egyptian psychology, 120
  in German psychology, 10, 11–12
  in interdisciplinary multilevel
    psychology, 42, 47–49, 58,
    114, 138–39
  as interpretative framework, 159
  link to psychology, 25–26
  role in neuroscience, 52–54
  use of medication and, 130–31
art and reflexivity
  art as self-knowledge, 141–43
  arts of immanence, 153–54
  cinema, 151–53
  creative uses of psychology, 141
  culture as extended ecological
    niche, 143–45
  drama and literature, 148–51
  emotions and direct perception, 147–48
  music and trance, 154–56
  sensible affective forms of
    knowledge, 145–46

258 INDEX

Bayesian approach, 8, 68–69
behaviorism
  critique of, 60–61
  in early psychology, 19–23
  failure to address affect in, 34
  use of metaphor in, 31
Belief
  dictated by affective needs and
    reactions, 46
  embedded in methodological
    paradigms, 25
  and emotion, 84–86
  epistemic closure based on, 86
  excavating functional nature of, x
  goal of Bayesian approach, 68–69
  pragmatism and, 18–19
  psychology used as rituals of, 88
  reflexive process between belief and
    explanation, 8–9, 72–73, 133–34, 160
  relation to pragmatism, 80
  role in individualism, 98–99
  role in mythology, 82–84
  role in popular psychology, 90–91,
    97, 100–2
  in a useful fiction, 31–32
biology
  clarified through scientific
    method, 54–55
  in interdisciplinary multilevel
    psychology, 47, 53–54, 73, 114
  metaphors drawn from, 29, 33–34,
    35–39, 159
  as moral loophole, 126–27, 128–29
  reductionism and mechanistic
    explanation, 76–79
  rise of metaphors drawn from, 40–43
  role in cognitive science, 50, 63
biomedical approach, 126–30. *See also*
  psychopharmacology
bio-psycho-social model, 127
brain imaging, 65

causality, vii, 15, 19–21, 80–81, 109, 117,
  130–31, 146, 158
cinema, 151–53
cognitive science
  in contemporary empirical
    psychology, 50–52

critics of, 42, 52–53
history of, 22–24
motivation, agency and, 134–35
new focus of, 53
use of metaphor in, 30, 33, 34, 40
computational theory of mind (CTM), 52
consciousness
  altered states of, 132–34, 144, 155–56
  art as self-knowledge, 142–43, 155
  in early cognitive science, 22
  in empirical psychology, 106–9
  German psychology and, 14
  ideas of William James, 19
  metaphors for, 33, 51
  mind as seat of, vii–viii
  path to understanding, 43
  psychoanalysis and, 109–10, 116–
    17, 122–23
  reduction of basic phenomenal contents
    of, 161
  relation between brain and mind, 64–
    65, 72
  role in psychology, 25–26
  in Soviet psychology, 24
contemporary empirical psychology.
    See also empirical psychology;
    psychology
  brain imaging, 65
  cognitive science, 50–52
  critical psychology, 70–72
  interdisciplinary multilevel
    scheme, 52–54
  issues in methodology, 54–57
  limits of pragmatism, 79–81
  neuroscience, 63–65
  philosophy of science, 74–76
  reductionism and mechanistic
    explanation, 76–79
  reform, 72–74
  replication and ecological
    validity, 57–62
  statistics and questionable research
    practices, 66–70
control
  affective need for, vii, 29, 86, 88,
    93, 159
  animistic systems of belief and, 120–21
  behaviorism and, 21–22

drugs and the technology of agency, 125–26, 127, 128–29, 131–32
executive control, 84
and the family unit, 112–13
hope of gaining, 158
metaphors and, 40–41
in popular psychology, 94–95, 97–99, 100–2
psychology as attempt to cure lack of, 1–3, 90–92, 103, 160
role in critical psychology, 70–71
social interactionism and self, 113
in therapeutic settings, 123–24
creative uses of psychology. *See* art and reflexivity
critical psychology
anthropology and, 11–12
in contemporary empirical psychology, 70–72
CTM (computational theory of mind), 52
cult, 55–56, 59, 79
culture, as extended ecological niche, 143–45

Darwin, Charles, 20–21
Darwinian, 16, 19, 43, 61
descriptive methods
of biomedical model of mind, 111–12, 125
descriptive versus discursive explanation, 44–47
discursive and descriptive functions of metaphor, 3
versus interdisciplinary multilevel psychology, 158
materialistic logos established by, 88–89
in popular psychology, 90–91
versus sensible affective forms of knowledge, 145–46
Soviet synthesis of descriptive and explanatory goals, 24
desire, immanence and, 86–87
Diagnostic and Statistical Manual of Mental Disorders (DSM), 130–31
direct perception, 147–48
discursive methods. *See also* art and reflexivity
anthropology and, 11–12

descriptive versus discursive explanation, 44–47
discursive and descriptive functions of metaphor, 3
discursive uses of psychology, 104–5
effect of social conditions of modernity, 85
entheogen therapy, 132–34
individualism enacted in, 105–7, 141
interdisciplinary multilevel psychology and, 134–40
liberatory potential of discursive psychology, 115–17
metaphors and, 103
other examples of, 120–24
philosophy of science and, 75
psychoanalysis, 109–13
psychoanalysis in Egypt, 119–20
psychoanalysis in India, 117–18
relation to biomedical model, 125–32
social interactionism and self, 113–15
story of personhood and, 88–89
unconscious and, 107–9
drama and literature, 148–51
drives, 21, 22, 37, 41–42, 84, 107, 109–10, 138, 159
drugs
benefits and drawbacks of drug therapies, 125–26
biomedical and psychodynamic models, 126–30
entheogens, 132–34
interdisciplinary multilevel psychology and, 134–40
pathology and medication, 130–32
pharmaceutical drugs and explanation, 125
and the technology of agency, 131–32
DSM (Diagnostic and Statistical Manual of Mental Disorders), 130–31
dynamic, viii, 38–39, 40–41, 46–47, 61, 66, 99, 110

ecological psychology, 37–38, 134–35
ecological validity, 57–62
Egypt, psychoanalysis in, 119–20
emotion
and belief, 84–86

260 INDEX

emotion (*cont.*)
  and direct perception, 147–48
empirical psychology. *See also*
  contemporary empirical psychology;
  metaphor; psychology
  biomedical model and, 124, 128–29
  early methodology in, 110
  establishment of private, individual
    consciousness, 107
  experimental protocols in, 106
  history of, 5–8
  methodological and epistemological
    issues in, 158
  neglect of agency in, 129–30
  neglect of individualism in, 141
  origins of, 8–10
  perception–action systems and, 147
  psychoanalysis and, 111–12, 117–
    18, 120
  psychology as local knowledge
    practices, 25–27
  role in popular psychology, 90–91,
    100, 102
  role of positivism and methodology
    in, 10–17
  role of pragmatism in, 17–23
  sense of control afforded by, 103
  Soviet psychology, 23–25
engineering
  cognitive sciences and, 50
  computer science and, 51–52
  interdisciplinary multilevel psychology
    and, 47
  metaphors drawn from, 29, 35–39,
    40–43, 159
  reductionism and mechanistic
    explanation, 76–77
entheogens and therapy, 132–34
epistemology
  in contemporary empirical
    psychology, 36
  empirical psychology and, 6
  epistemic closure based on belief, 86
  epistemological suspicion, ix
  grounded in emotional needs and
    cognitive patterns, 103
  methodological and epistemological
    issues in empirical psychology, 158

naturalist epistemology, 41–42
use of metaphors, 31–32
ethnopsychoanalysis, 122
European Enlightenment, 9
explanation
  art as self-knowledge, 142–43
  behaviorism and, 19–22
  burden of producing a unified, 13
  descriptive versus discursive
    explanation, 44–47
  formal model of scientific
    explanation, 7–8
  immanence, desire and, 86–87
  interdisciplinary multilevel psychology
    and, 134–38
  life-affirming drive contained in, 88
  mechanistic in contemporary empirical
    psychology, 76–79
  need for, 102–3
  offering predictive
    consequences, 123–24
  reflexive process between belief and
    explanation, 8–9, 133–34, 160
  relationship with doubt, 1–2
  relation to superstition, 158
  salience associated with, 106–7
  Soviet synthesis of descriptive
    explanation and goals, 24
  use of pharmaceutical drugs and, 125

Fanon, Frantz, ix, 116–17, 118, 122–23
Freud, Sigmund, viii, 12, 14, 20–21, 40–42,
    88, 107–8, 109–11, 112, 114–15, 116–
    18, 131, 159

German psychology, 10–17
good old-fashioned artificial intelligence
    (GOFAI), 52

Hegel, G. W. F., 142–43, 145–46
Hempelian model, 7
historical methods, 7, 26
history
  of cognitive science, 22–24
  context of knowledge production
    and, ix
  of empirical psychology, 5–10, 13, 23,
    50–54, 61

of human sciences, 48
of hysteria, 16–17
interdisciplinary multilevel psychology
and, vii, 158
link to psychology, 25
of metaphors of mind, 33–35, 41
as necessary component of psychology,
124, 160
personal history and agency, 105,
112, 138–39
philosophy of science and, 74, 75–
76, 81
popular psychology and, 97
relationship to anthropology, 73,
120, 159
human nature
biomedical model of, 126–30
codification of, 9
differing versions of, 24–25, 159–60
dominant representations of, 91
as embodiment of local knowledge
practices, 88
functionally normative models of, 72
implications for notions of, 72
mythological origin story of, 84, 88–89
objective explanations of, 106–7
philosophy of science and, 74–76
psychic unity and, 80–81
psychoanalysis and, 109–13
psychology and, 23
study of, 8, 16
understanding through
psychology, 1–3
universalist project of, 121–22
use of metaphors about, 42, 46
human sciences
broader goals of, 43–44
constraints on, 138–39
critical psychology and, 70–72
discursive methods used in, 42
discursive space of personhood
provided by psychology, 88–89
higher-level conditions spelled
out in, 66
institutionalization of, 14
interdisciplinary multilevel psychology
and, 47–48, 54, 160
legitimacy of, 7, 15

psychology's position between natural
and human sciences, 6, 54–55, 74–
76, 109
replication crisis of psychology, 58–59
as root of experimental
psychology, 10–11
hypothetico-deductive method, 28, 57

identity
addiction and, 138–39
contemplating through art, 141
in contemporary empirical
psychology, 88–89
contextualized identity, 113–14
discourse concerning, 2
ego identity, 122
elements of, 70–71
entheogen therapy and, 132–33
identity theory, 64–65
psychoanalysis and, 111
social identity, 105–6
imagination
as central to science and art, 72–73
expectations created by, 83
in Greek culture, 85
negative evolution of knowledge
practices, 13
relation to arts and analogical
thinking, 43
required to understand empirical
data, 28
role in cultural arrangements,
143, 145–46
sensible affective knowledge and,
146, 148
understanding ourselves through, 150–
51, 152–53, 154
immanence
arts of immanence, 153–56
desire, explanation and, 86–87
India, psychoanalysis in, 117–18
individualism, 105–7
interdisciplinary multilevel psychology
example including
psychopharmacology, 134–40
use of metaphor in, 47–49
using contemporary empirical
psychology, 52–54

262   INDEX

James, William, 10–11, 14, 17–23, 32, 58–59, 79–80, 102, 153–54

knowledge
    art as self-knowledge, 141–43
    emotions and direct
        perception, 147–48
    sensible affective forms of, 145–46

literature and drama, 148–51
local knowledge practices
    drug therapy embedded in, 128
    explanation and, 88
    psychology as, 25–27
long-term memory (LTM), 7, 78

magical thinking, 90–91, 100–1. *See also*
    popular psychology
mechanistic explanation, 76–79
memory
    assumptions about, 14–15
    capacity in, 19
    cognitive science and, 37
    concept of trauma through study of, 12
    effect of art on, 150–51, 152–53
    individualism and, 105
    long-term memory (LTM), 7, 78
    memory consolidation, 30
    metaphors concerning, 29–30
    muscle memory, 147
    neuroscience and, 65
    popular psychology and, 101
    public memory, 142
    shifts in portrayals of, 34–35
    social memory, 155
metaphor
    in cognitive science, 51–53
    descriptive versus discursive
        explanation, 44–47
    discursive and descriptive
        functions of, 3
    in empirical psychology, 28–29
    history of metaphors of mind, 33–35
    issues in use of, 56–57, 72–73,
        81, 133–34
    magical thought and, 110
    metaphors from biology and
        engineering, 35–39

pragmatic assessment of
    contemporary, 39–44
toward an interdisciplinary
    psychology, 47–49
as useful fictions, 31–33
use of in literature and art, 142–43
what qualifies as metaphor, 29–31
methodology
    behaviorism and, 19–21
    effect of methodologism on
        psychology, 13–15
    how metaphysical background
        informs, 26
    hypothetico-deductive, 28
    individual differences and, 15
    introspection, 23–24
    issues in contemporary empirical
        psychology, 54–57
    observation and theory relying on, 10
    statistics and questionable research
        practices, 66–70
mimesis, 47–48, 124, 126, 142–43, 148–49
mimetic arts
    art as self-knowledge, 141–43
    cinema, 151–53
    drama and literature, 148–51
Mind
    approaching from various
        perspectives, 73–74
    assessment of metaphors of, 39–44
    cognitive science metaphors for, 50–52
    concept of in modern era, vii–ix
    contemporary metaphors of, 29, 35–39
    critics of metaphors of, 52–54
    descriptive versus discursive
        explanations of, 44–47
    dualistic language describing, 31
    as fictions in search of
        corroboration, 31–33
    history of metaphors of mind, 33–35
    ideal metaphors of, 47–49
    impact of neuroscience on study
        of, 63–65
    implications for notions of human
        nature, 72
    implicit claims about the mind in
        ancient metaphor, 5–6

INDEX 263

insight offered by empirical psychology, 74–76
issues in methodology in study of, 54–57
issues in replication in study of, 58–62
limits of pragmatism and, 79–81
limits of science of the mind, 158
mechanical philosophy of, 78
study of aligned with social and cultural context, 9
using empirical psychology to conceive of, 29

modernity, xi, 10–14, 85, 90, 97, 110–14, 119–20, 125, 160
music and trance, 154–56
mysticism
inner-worldly mysticism, 95
Judeo-Christian, 25
of Plotinus and neo-Gnostics, 91
religious knowing, 101
this-worldly mysticism, 92, 95
mythology
drug use and, 125, 129
in German psychology, 11
implicit claims about the mind in ancient, 5–6
individualism and, 105
as a mimetic representation of reality, 97
modernity and, xi
presented through the arts, 149
role of in popular psychology, 90, 95
self as a core aspect of, 106
similarities with psychology, 44
treating psychology as, 82–84, 88–89, 103, 157–58

narrative
about origins of mortality, sexuality, and society, 84
appraisal of truth and knowledge through, 72–73
aspirational narratives, 133–34, 151
biblical, 121
in cinema, 152
historical causal narratives, 112
history as, 160
in literature, 150–51
metaphysical, 100–1
mythical narratives, 5–6

participatory ritual and, 153
of personal agency, 85
schizoid and narcissistic, 94–95
as self-affirmation, 102
self-narratives, 101
in traditional systems, 94
neo-Darwinian, 21, 41–42, 159
neuroscience
affective neuroscience, x–xi, 37
in contemporary empirical psychology, 63–65
Nietzsche, Friedrich, 160
nomological-deductive model, 7
nomothetic, 15, 23–24, 27, 46, 52–53, 58, 75–76, 106, 131, 133–34, 137, 146, 150–51

ontological suspicion, viii–ix
order
in Classical age, 86
communicating through metaphor, 44
creating through analogical reasoning, 29, 161
creating through popular psychology, 91, 94–95, 100
cultural order, 83
expressing explanation through, 88
fragmentation of through analogical knowledge, 161
liturgical order, 144, 149
mythical hope of, 88
as purpose of models, 43
reinforcing through psychology, 103
rendered from science, 88
social order, 144–45, 157–58
as spiritual positivism, 99
supra-individual, 16
Symbolic Order, 114–16

perception–action systems, 147
philosophy of mind, x–xi, 157
philosophy of science, 3, 74–76, 81
phrenology, 63
popular psychology. *See also* contemporary empirical psychology; empirical psychology; psychology
as attempt to cure lack of control, 90–92, 103

264 INDEX

popular psychology (*cont.*)
  belief in and practice of, 100–2
  central message of, 98–100
  criticisms of, 92–93
  subgenres of, 95–97
  versus traditional wisdom, 93–95
positivism, 10–17
post-Darwinian, 6, 22, 72, 119–20
pragmatism
  limits of in contemporary empirical
    psychology, 79–81
  role in psychology, 17–19
psychoanalysis
  in the 20th century, 123
  as discursive method, 109–13
  in Egypt, 119–20
  ethnopsychoanalysis, 122
  in India, 117–18
  other examples of, 120–24
psychodynamic approach, 126–30
psychology. *See also* contemporary
    empirical psychology; empirical
    psychology; popular psychology
  as attempt to cure lack of control, 1–
    3, 103
  good uses of, x–xi
  as a mythological system, 88–89
  summary of author's critical
    project, 157–61
  summary of author's positive
    project, 158
  suspicious uses of, viii–ix
  toward an interdisciplinary
    psychology, 47–49
  use of in contemporary society, vii–viii
psychopharmacology
  benefits and drawbacks of drug
    therapies, 125–26
  biomedical verus psychodynamic
    approaches, 126–30
  entheogen therapy, 132–34
  interdisciplinary multilevel psychology
    example, 134–40
  pathology and medication, 130–32
psychophysiology, 13, 24–25

Questionable Research Practices
  (QRPs), 66–70

reductionism, 76–79
reflexive creative practices. *See* art and
    reflexivity
reform, 72–74
reliable
replication, 57–62
representation, 34–35, 95, 97, 100, 112,
    126, 142–43, 148–49
research practices, questionable, 66–70
ritual
  art as self-knowledge, 144–41
  in cinema, 151–53
  developing, 97–99
  emotive ritual, 148–49
  habits as basis for, 98–99
  individualism and, 105
  as occluding real limits of science of
    mind, 158
  participation through attention and
    belief, 153
  in pleasure-inducing activities, 138
  in popular psychology, 90–91
  psychological need for, 100–2, 103
  purpose of, 96–97
  shared experience of
    performance, 147–48
  Vedic ritual in India, 118

science
  attraction of, 54–55
  distinctions from superstition, 82,
    85, 103
  early cognitive, 22–23
  hopes of unity in, 76–77
  hyothetico-deductive, 10
  imagination as central to, 72–73
  limits of science of the mind, 158
  obscuring efficacy of, 46–47
  order rendered from, 88
  philosophy of in contemporary
    empirical psychology, 74–76
  positivist science promoting
    autonomy, 159
  psychology as, x, 6–10, 19–22
  psychology as a moral science, 127–28
  reductionism and mechanistic
    explanation, 76–79
  replication crisis of psychology, 58–62

role in popular psychology, 90, 94,
    100, 102
sociology of, 70–71
use of statistics in, 69–70
secularism
    Auguste Comte's codification of, 13
    Cartesianism and, 9, 35
    discourse and, 112
    effect of the Enlightenment on, 94
    effect of the Reformation on, 85
    individualism and, 102, 105–6
    psychoanalysis and, 110–11
    science as language of
        explanation, 54–55
    secular modernity, 160–61
self-help literature, 90. *See also* popular
    psychology
self-knowledge, art as, 141–43
sensible affective knowledge, 145–48
social identity, 105–6
social interactionism, 113–14
sociological issues
    communication and social
        position, 141
    with role and function of empirical
        psychology, 70–72
Soviet psychology, 23–25
statistics, 66–70

therapy
    behavioral therapy, 6, 40
    discursive methods, 159

embedded in local knowledge
    practices, 128
entheogen therapy, 132–34
mechanistic descriptive biomedical
    models and, 111–12
mythology and, 82
narrativization of the mind through, xi
primal scream therapy, 98
psychoanalysis, 109–10
psychodynamic therapy, 126–27
psychology as, 112–13
psychotherapy, 122–23
purpose of discursive therapy, 107
talk therapy, 6, 125, 131–32
traditional wisdom, versus popular
    psychology, 93–95
trance and music, 154–56

the unconscious, 107–9

validity
    in contemporary empirical
        psychology, 57–62
    individual differences and, 15–17
Vienna, 10
Vygotsky, Lev, 23–24, 123

WEIRD (Western, educated,
    industrialized, rich, and democratic)
    societies, 61–62, 70–71, 80–81
Wundt, Wilhelm, vii–viii, 11–15, 19–20,
    23, 58–59, 107